UNDERSTANDING GEOGRAPHICAL AND ENVIRONMENTAL EDUCATION

Also available from Cassell:

P. Wiegand: *Children and Primary Geography*
K. Carlton and E. Parkinson: *Physical Sciences*

Understanding Geographical and Environmental Education

The Role of Research

Edited by
Michael Williams

CASSELL

Cassell
Wellington House   215 Park Avenue South
125 Strand   New York
London WC2R 0BB   NY 10003

© Michael Williams and the contributors 1996

First published 1996

British Library Cataloguing-in-Publication Data
A catalogue record for this book is available from the British Library.

ISBN   0-304-33271-2 (hardback)
       0-304-33273-9 (paperback)

Typeset by Action Typesetting Ltd, Gloucester
Printed and bound in Great Britain by Redwood Books, Trowbridge, Wiltshire

Contents

The Contributors

John Bale is Reader in Geographical Education at Keele University, England. He has written widely on various areas of geography, ranging from the teaching of the subject in the primary school to the teaching of economic and industrial geography at advanced and undergraduate levels. His current research interests lie in the links between geography in higher education and secondary schools. In addition he has pioneered the geographical study of sports.

Sharon Bennett is a Research Fellow in the Centre for Innovation and Research in Environmental Education in the Faculty of Environmental Sciences, Griffith University, Australia. A former secondary-school teacher of geography, she is now the co-ordinator of an action research project on global perspectives in the Australian school curriculum.

Graham Butt is a Lecturer in Geography Education at the School of Education, University of Birmingham, England. He is a member of the Geographical Association, has chaired its Assessment and Examinations Working Group and currently edits the 'Assessment Matters' section of *Teaching Geography*, one of the journals of the Association. His research interests include both the use of language in geographical education and pupil assessment.

Simon Catling is a Senior Lecturer in the School of Education at Oxford Brookes University, Oxford, England. He has been President of the Geographical Association. He has special interests in initial teacher education and in aspects of the development of graphicacy in children. He has written geography textbooks for young children.

Graham Corney is Lecturer in Educational Studies (Geography) at the Department of Educational Studies, University of Oxford, England, and Fellow of St Anne's College. His research interests combine geographical education and teacher thinking and he teaches and supervises Postgraduate Certificate in Education (PGCE), Masters and Doctoral students in geographical education.

Richard Daugherty is Professor of Education and Head of the Department of Education at the University of Wales, Aberystwyth. He is Past President of the Geographical Association and, from 1991 to 1993, chaired the Curriculum Council for Wales. Among his research interests are national assessment policy, moderation of assessment and assessment procedures in public examinations.

John Fien is Deputy Dean of the Faculty of Environmental Sciences, Griffith University, Australia. He is the Director of the Master of Environmental Education programme at Griffith University. He has extensive involvement in professional associations, having been President of the Australian Association for Environmental Education (1990–92), a member of the National Council of the Australian Geography Teachers' Association since 1980 and the editor of its journal *Geographical Education* since 1985. He is also Founder and First Chair of the Australian Federation of Societies for Studies of Society and Environment.

Nicholas H. Foskett is a Lecturer in Education at the University of Southampton, England. He lectures in initial teacher training and Masters programmes in the fields of geographical and environmental education and educational management. His current research includes a study of environmental education in the post-compulsory and training sectors of education with particular reference to policy development and implementation.

Rod Gerber is Associate Professor and Head of the School of Social, Business and Environmental Education at the Queensland University of Technology, Brisbane, Australia. His recent research interests have focused on learning in graphics, the nature of self-directed learning in the workplace and remembering curriculum changes. He has concentrated on the use of qualitative approaches to research in geographical education.

John Hillcoat was formerly a Research Fellow in the Centre for Innovation and Research in Environmental Education in the Faculty of Environmental Sciences, Griffith University, Australia. A former statistical consultant and lecturer in statistics, he is now involved in action research approaches to improving teaching and learning in environmental studies.

Ashley Kent is Senior Lecturer in Geographical Education and Co-ordinator for Geography at the University of London Institute of Education, England. He has long-standing professional interests in curriculum development; post-16 geography; fieldwork strategies; the new technology; and the professional development of geography teachers. He has co-authored a number of textbooks, the most recent being *Understanding Human Geography: People and their Changing Environments*. He has been engaged in a number of geography education research exercises, several for the International Geographical Union. He is Junior Vice-President of the Geographical Association.

David Lambert is a Senior Lecturer at the University of London Institute of Education, England. He is a member of the Management Team for the Postgraduate Certificate in Education (PGCE) course and he has particular responsibility for 170 beginning teachers in east London. He is also a PGCE Course Tutor for geography and has published articles on the National Curriculum and its assessment, and on initial teacher education, as well as a series of geography textbooks for Key Stage 3 (11-14-year-olds) in England.

David Leat, following a PhD in human geography at the University of Exeter, taught for eleven years in the state sector, including a four-year spell at a field study centre. In 1989 he was appointed as the Postgraduate Certificate in Education (PGCE) geography tutor at the University of Newcastle-upon-Tyne, England. His research interests are in student teachers' learning about teaching and in teaching thinking through geography.

William E. Marsden is a Professor of Education in the University of Liverpool, England. His research interests are in geographical education, the history of the curriculum, and the history of urban education. Publications include *Evaluating the Geography Curriculum*, *Unequal Education Provision in England and Wales: The Nineteenth Century Roots*, *Educating the Respectable*, and *Geography 11-16*.

Janice Monk is Executive Director of the Southwest Institute for Research on Women and Adjunct Professor of Geography at the University of Arizona, USA. She earned her BA (Hons) at the University of Sydney and her PhD at the University of Illinois at Urbana-Champaign. She is interested in social and cultural geography, especially feminist work, the history of women in geography, and curriculum and staff development in geographic education. She has co-authored or co-edited five books, most recently *Teaching Geography in Higher Education* and *Full Circles: Geographies of Women over the Life Course*, as well as many articles and book chapters. Dr Monk received honours from the Association of American Geographers in 1992 for her contributions to gender research.

Margaret Roberts is Lecturer in Education at the University of Sheffield Division of Education, England, where she has responsibility for the initial teacher education of secondary school geography specialists. She has been carrying out longitudinal research into the implementation of the geography National Curriculum in secondary schools in England since 1989.

Miriam Moscovitch Steiner has been Director of the World Studies Project, based in the School of Education, Manchester Metropolitan University, England, since 1990. She is a Canadian who has worked in Manchester for over twenty years as a classroom teacher, member of the staff of a Development Education Centre and local education authority adviser.

Philip Stimpson is a Senior Lecturer in Curriculum Studies at the University of Hong Kong. His research interests combine geographical education and environmental education and are particularly concerned with the cultural context of curricula and curriculum development. He has acted as an environmental and geographical consultant for the Hong Kong Government and the World Wide Fund for Nature (Hong Kong), where he has been involved in curriculum development and implementation research.

Joseph P. Stoltman is Professor of Geography at Western Michigan University, Kalamazoo, USA. His professional experience in the classroom has spanned elementary to college levels, and he has completed research on geographical education and geography curriculum development at several levels of schooling. He was Chair of the Commission on Geographical Education of the International Geographical Union from 1980 to 1988, and has recently served as Secretary of the Committee on the Teaching of Science of the International Council of Scientific Unions. He is active in the definition and preparation of geography standards as part of the educational reform movement in the USA.

Daniella Tilbury is a Lecturer in Education in the Department of Education at the University of Wales, Swansea. Her doctoral thesis, which focused on teacher education, provoked questions about the quality and direction of environmental education in the 1990s. She has acted as an environmental education consultant in a number of European countries including Denmark, Spain and Gibraltar. Her research interests lie in initial and in-service teacher education.

Rex Walford is a University Lecturer in Geography and Education and currently Head of the Department of Education at the University of Cambridge, England. He is Past President of the Geographical Association and Founder Chairman of the Council of British Geography. His recent books include *Horizons in Human Geography* (edited with Derek Gregory), *Viewpoints on Geography Teaching* and *Challenging Times* (edited with Pat Machon). He was a member of the Geography Working Group which devised the National Curriculum for geography in England and Wales. He is a Fellow of Wolfson College, Cambridge.

Patrick Wiegand is a Senior Lecturer in the School of Education at the University of Leeds, England. He has research interests in educational cartography and young children's understanding of distant places. He has written several books on geographical education and edited a number of school atlases, including the award-winning *New Oxford School Atlas*.

Michael Williams is a Professor and Dean of the Faculty of Educational Studies at the University of Wales, Swansea. His research interests are in the fields of geographical education, curriculum studies and the continuing professional development of teachers. His books include *Geography and the Integrated Curriculum*, *Teaching European Studies*, *Language Teaching and Learning: Geography*, *Designing and Teaching Integrated Courses*, and *In-Service Education and Training*.

David R. Wright is an Honorary Fellow of the University of East Anglia, Norwich, England, and an Office for Standards in Education (OFSTED) school inspector. He is co-author of Philips *Children's Atlas* and of Philips/WWF *Environmental Atlas* and *Kingfisher Pocket Atlas*. He is the author of more than seventy articles on geographical and environmental education, including four articles in *Internationale Schulbuchforschung*.

Foreword

Professor Hartwig Haubrich

Chairman of the Education Commission of the International Geographical Union

It is a great pleasure and a privilege for me to write the foreword to this important collection of research papers. Over the last twenty years research in geographical education and environmental education has increased in quality and quantity. Substantial progress has been made in many directions. Not only have researchers developed small-scale and larger-scale projects which have addressed a wider range of topics, they have also employed increasingly sophisticated research methods.

From the perspective of the Education Commission of the International Geographical Union, we have been heartened to welcome researchers from an increasing number of countries to our regional and global symposia. A feature of these symposia has been the successful attempts made by researchers to engage in international collaborative projects, bilateral and multilateral. More experienced researchers have worked closely with the less experienced. We have witnessed in a short period of time the blossoming of the research careers of many colleagues drawn not only from the universities and other institutions of higher education but also from schools and colleges. There is still a great deal of scope for research in geographical education and environmental education, which draws its inspiration from the action research tradition and from the 'teacher as researcher' tradition. There is also much scope in such traditions as comparative education and cross-cultural studies as well as in the more well-trodden fields of educational psychology and sociology of education.

Environmental educationists have often been more successful in attracting the interest of international agencies, governments and non-governmental organizations. The result has been a higher level of research funding and a variety of research approaches which have built as much upon the traditions of the natural sciences as upon the social sciences. Geographical educators and teachers have made considerable contributions to this field and, conversely, have learned much from environmental educators. There remains much to be gained from close co-operation between researchers in geographical education and environmental education. One of the strengths of this collection of papers is that it has brought together in a single volume contributors from both of these inter-related fields, though the role of geographical educators occupies a more prominent position.

The book has an international flavour, though it should be emphasized that the contributors represent the English-speaking communities. This is partly an acknowledgement that much research in geographical and environmental education has been conducted in countries where English is the medium of communication. But these countries do not hold the monopoly, and it is to be hoped that the success of this book will serve to stimulate editors and writers from different linguistic cultures to produce similar collections.

This book is a useful 'state-of-the-art' publication. It should be read widely by teachers as part of their continuing professional development, by student teachers who are interested in up-to-date reviews of research in topics which concern them as developing professionals, and by researchers seeking expert introductions to research methodologies written in the precise contexts of geographical and environmental education. It should also find its way to policy-makers who may be seeking justification for strengthening geographical and environmental education in the curricula of educational institutions at various levels. It would be very encouraging if it were read by the purse-holders of research funds, who might be persuaded to release more funding for topics in geographical and environmental education.

The Education Commission of the International Geographical Union is committed to promoting research and to providing the arenas in which research findings from various parts of the world can be disseminated. Represented in these pages are many individuals who are well known in the Education Commission and play leading roles in the success of its work. This book serves to draw attention to the importance of the Education Commission, while at the same time alerting us to newcomers to research in our field of interest who are making significant contributions to the knowledge, understanding and skills without which progress cannot be made in the promotion of our subject in schools, colleges, institutions of higher education and in adult education.

Introduction

Michael Williams

The immediate stimulus for this book was a seminar held in 1993 at the University of Southampton. It was part of the programme of the annual conference of geography tutors in British university departments of education, concerned with the current state of research in geographical education. The tutors addressed the recurring questions of all educational researchers, including: What is research? Why do people engage in it? Who benefits from it? What are the differences between private research undertaken by individuals and funded projects? What methods are available for conducting research? How can we be sure that our findings are valid and reliable? What are the most effective ways of disseminating them? In a conversation with John Huckle immediately after the seminar, we talked about the need for active researchers to contribute to a book which would draw together current writing and experience in the broad field of research with a direct bearing on geographical and environmental education. Our concern was to produce a reader-friendly and easily accessible guide for new and more experienced researchers, addressing some of the questions above.

Our starting point was this statement from our proposal submitted to the publisher:

> Overall, we wish to demonstrate that research in geographical education and environmental education is a very broad field. It draws on a range of social theory and employs a wide variety of methodologies. The chapters and case studies will illustrate how research is conducted at a variety of scales (classroom, school, regional, national, international) and focused on documentation (historical records, legislation, policies, plans, tests, curriculum materials), persons (pupils, students, teachers, student teachers), ideologies (classical, vocational, reconstructionist, postmodernist) and curriculum (policies, plans, implementation, evaluation). We wish to show that research may be conducted successfully by teachers in their own classrooms, by academics working as individuals and by research teams working on funded projects. We also want to assert the links between theory, research and practice.

Having agreed a structure for the planned contents, we mailed a general invitation letter to colleagues on several networks of researchers in the UK and overseas, seeking their comments on the publishing project as a whole and offering them the opportunity to contribute chapters. The responses were generally positive and encouraging, though some drew attention to omissions and a perceived lack of balance between national contributions, ideological positions, substantive issues and methodological considerations.

Some of these simply reflect the current state of development of the field, while others are a function of the small number of active researchers in particular research areas who were precluded from contributing to this publication because of research, personal and other pressures. Indeed it was a combination of such pressures which, sadly, resulted in John having to withdraw from the project at the completion of the planning stage.

In seeking to achieve an authoritative and reasonably comprehensive coverage we were guided by others who had provided over-arching frameworks. Borg, in his much-used introductory textbook on educational research (1963), applied criteria of control versus reality for his three broad classifications of basic, applied and action research.

In basic research, control and precision are dominant criteria and, as Kerlinger (1993, p. 98) states:

> basic research is research done to test theory, to study relations among phenomena in order to understand the phenomena with little or no thought of the applications of the results of the research to practical problems.

For Borg (1963, p. 19), applied research is 'concerned primarily with establishing relationships and testing theories in the field setting', and Kerlinger (1993, p. 98) extends this by emphasizing that applied research is 'directed towards the solution of specified practical problems in delineated areas and from which amelioration or improvement of some process or activity, or achievement of practical goals is expected'. For Borg, action research 'involves the application of the steps of the scientific method to classroom problems. Action research usually employs the highest level of reality and the least amount of control and precision of the three types' (p. 20). More than thirty years after Borg wrote his descriptions of these three classifications, the tensions between them remain, and each has been substantially refined and disaggregated into sub-sets which have attracted communities of researchers who assert their specialisms, appearing often to be engaged in competition.

Fien (1992), drawing on the work of Habermas (1972), presents a different though related trilogy. Starting from three ideological positions, he distinguishes three forms of research: process–product, interpretive and critical. Like Borg's classifications, these run as threads through the ensuing chapters:

> Process–product research represents a *technical* interest in achieving mastery and control over the world, which involves empirical-analytical modes of research. Interpretive research is founded upon the human *practical* interest in understanding the social dynamics of the lifeworld and participating in social life with understanding. The third human interest, emancipation, represents the *critical* need to act rationally, free from the constraints of authority, tradition, ignorance.
>
> (Fien, 1992, p. 266)

Whereas process–product research is typified by the use of experimental and survey methods, ethnographic and case study research are typical of the interpretive form, and critical research includes action research and critical ethnography.

These classifications not only help in locating particular studies in research domains and therefore permitting one to assume certain ideological positions which direct research action, but also guide us to the motives of researchers in geographical and environmental education. In this book, attention is drawn to the research behaviour of students, student teachers, teachers, academics and policy-makers.

There can be no doubting the policy imperative which has stimulated the great majority of research studies in geographical and environmental education. Researchers have focused on issues and problems in curriculum development at various scales: classroom, whole-school, local community, national and international, from the novice teacher to the European Union and the United Nations. Relatively few researchers in geographical and environmental education have addressed the theoretical issues which underpin the policy-related studies. However, even within the broad policy field there are variations in motives.

Finch (1986, pp. 2–3) has proposed four reasons for adopting a policy orientation in research. The first, which she describes as cynical, is that this is where funds are available to support research. Secondly, a policy orientation 'brings positive benefits in the development of the knowledge created through research and the disciplines within which it is rooted'. Thirdly, 'a social scientist has an obligation to use her or his skills, usually acquired at public expense, to contribute to public debate about issues of the day.' Fourthly, it is impossible to avoid it.

Taylor (1985, p. 45), writing as an educational researcher, offers a different perspective:

> One of the chief functions of research in the social sciences in general, and in education in particular, is to make us aware of the existence and the dimensions of the problems, to reveal their interconnections, to rule out some of the more obvious 'solutions', to add to and refine the concepts we employ to describe and to evaluate phenomena, to indicate what aspects are foreground and which background – in other words to sensitize us to what otherwise might be ignored, misunderstood or acted upon in blind faith.

This notion of sensitization goes some way towards the emancipatory role of research. This has grown partly from the work of critical action researchers and partly from the writings of sociologists such as Giroux, who, in an essay on schooling as cultural politics (1989, p. 138), refers to teachers as 'transformative intellectuals' who are:

> bearers of critical knowledge, rules and values through which they consciously articulate and problematize their relationship to each other, to students, to subject matter, and to the wider community ... The category of emancipatory authority dignifies teacher work by viewing it as a form of intellectual practice.

These views have been articulated in the teacher-as-researcher movement, in which the concepts of 'teacher emancipation' and the role of the teacher as a 'reflective practitioner' are fundamental. The external researcher is identified as a facilitator who contributes to the work of the teacher rather than someone who sees the teacher as a provider of data to be worked on in some distant place in the interests of other audiences – a servant rather than a robber.

It is common in supervising research students or working alongside classroom teachers on research projects to find them shying away from research methods which yield statistical data. Research in geographical education, though less so in environmental education, reflects this nervousness. This is a function partly of the research training of many educational researchers, and partly of inadequate research support facilities in academic institutions. At a time when the technology for handling sophisticated data has passed from massive computers to desktop PCs (personal computers), one might have expected a flood of research publications in geographical and environmental education employing increasingly complex statistical tools. Instead there has been a growth in naturalistic inquiry with a focus on research which emphasizes meaning, insight and understanding.

It is in discussions about objectivity, reliability, validity and generalizability that the tensions between researchers are most evident. Advocates of quantitative research criticize the more qualitative for not paying sufficient attention to these concepts. Rarely in geographical education research publications is there reference to concurrent, predictive, convergent, criterion-related, internal and external validity, all terms associated with an objectivist view of research. However, just as rare are references to concepts of validity which have emerged from the qualitative side. In a comprehensive review, Maxwell (1992) draws on a number of philosophical concepts and arguments to support his classification of five types of validity that concern qualitative researchers: descriptive, interpretive, theoretical and evaluative validity and generalizability (pp. 284–5). These are important for researchers attracted to qualitative research, and are highlighted in recent approaches such as narrative analysis (e.g. Cortazzi, 1993). The general issue has been well stated by Schratz (1993, p. 1):

> By paying more attention to the original *voices* of the actors in everyday life they tried to make room for a broader view of the social reality of their research. This has led researchers to break with some of the established conventions of objectivity, reliability and validity. In order to get beneath the surface of everyday activities and institutional structures new approaches in educational research developed ranging from ethnographic studies, naturalistic inquiry or case studies to more recent enterprises such as action research, biographical analyses and profile studies.

The opening chapters of this book address the three broad research approaches which characterize geographical and environmental education, giving a contextual background against which the following chapters can be read. Williams (Chapter 1), Gerber (Chapter 2) and Fien and Hillcoat (Chapter 3) review the distinctive characteristics of the technical and quantitative, the interpretivist and the critical, emancipatory approaches. Subsequent chapters indicate how active researchers have pursued particular investigations and how they reflect on the theoretical and practical implications of their work. They are in some cases retrospective, in others portrayals of work in progress, and in others again futuristic and speculative.

The chapters by Stimpson (Chapter 4), Tilbury and Walford (Chapter 5) and Stoltman (Chapter 6) highlight internationalism in both geographical and environmental education. Corney's review (Chapter 7) reflects the concerns of some of the contributors who felt that they were being cornered by their chapter titles into particular, narrowly conceived research methods when their own work was heavily eclectic in character.

Many of the following chapters focus on specific techniques. Catling (Chapter 8) addresses the crucial issue for geographical and environmental education of mapwork skills and, in a wide-ranging review, demonstrates the scope of studies in this field. Wiegand (Chapter 9), Stimpson (Chapter 10) and Roberts (Chapter 11) discuss and illustrate three of the commonest research techniques: interviews, questionnaires and case studies. Hillcoat (Chapter 12) and Bennett (Chapter 13) write on research methods with a more recent currency, whose popularity reflects a shift from a more quantitative to a more qualitative orientation.

The next two chapters start from a focus on important pedagogical issues: textbooks (Chapter 14) and children's writing (Chapter 15). Chapters 16–20, by contrast, are in the broad field of policy research. Steiner (Chapter 16) focuses on global education, a broad field in which both geographical and environmental education have important roles. In research terms, she addresses the importance of evaluation studies, demonstrating eclectic approaches which she has applied in her work. Foskett (Chapter 17), Lambert (Chapter 18) and Daugherty (Chapter 19) are strongly British in their emphasis. The transformation of the school curriculum in England and Wales, with its radical changes in the content and modes of student assessment in school geography, is of special interest to scholars and researchers in policy-making and comparative studies at classroom, whole-school and national levels. Lessons from it, with a broader relevance for nations experiencing rapid political change, relate to the strengths and weaknesses of strong curriculum centralization and the role of professionals in determining the nature of geographical and environmental education. The British emphasis continues in Leat's chapter (20), which is concerned with improving students' learning through processes of cognitive acceleration.

Marsden (Chapter 21), Monk (Chapter 22) and Bale (Chapter 23) survey fields relatively undeveloped in geographical and environmental education. Marsden's retrospective, historical methodology contrasts with Bale's more futuristic emphasis on postmodernism. Monk alerts us to the importance of gender in research studies in geographical and environmental education. Her chapter opens up a wide variety of directions for researchers interested in classrooms, students, teachers and curriculum materials.

In the final chapter, Kent (Chapter 24) describes the experience of one large university institute in promoting research in geographical and environmental education. The emphasis is on the work of part-time and full-time students on Masters courses. This chapter reminds us of the research work undertaken for dissertations and theses by teachers and other professionals who may be seconded from their jobs or who may undertake studies part-time over extended periods. Not all of their work finds its way into widely read publications. It is to these pioneers, the teachers-as-researchers, who contribute substantially through research to the improvement of teaching and curriculum design in geographical and environmental education, that this book is dedicated.

REFERENCES

Borg, W.R. (1963) *Educational Research: An Introduction*. London: Longmans, Green.

Cortazzi, M. (1993) *Narrative Analysis*. Lewes: Falmer.

Fien, J. (1992) 'What kind of research for what kind of teaching? Towards research in geographical education as a critical social science.' In A.D. Hill, (ed.) *International Perspectives on Geographical Education*. Skokie, IL: Rand McNally.

Finch, J. (1986) *Research and Policy: The Uses of Qualitative Methods in Social and Educational Research*. London: Falmer.

Giroux, H.A. (1989) 'Schooling as a form of cultural politics: towards a pedagogy of and for difference.' In H.A. Giroux and P. McLaren (eds) *Critical Pedagogy, the State and Cultural Struggle*. Albany, NY: State University of New York Press.

Habermas, J. (1972) *Knowledge and Human Interests*. London: Heinemann.

Kerlinger, F.N. (1993) 'Science and behavioural research.' In D.S. Anderson and B.J. Biddle (eds) *Knowledge for Policy: Improving Education through Research*. London: Falmer.

Maxwell, J.A. (1992) 'Understanding and validity in qualitative research,' *Harvard Educational Review*, **62**, (3), 279–300.

Schratz, M. (ed.) (1993) *Qualitative Voices in Educational Research*. London: Falmer.

Taylor, W. (1985) 'The organization and funding of educational research in England and Wales.' In J. Nisbet, J. Megarry and S. Nisbet (eds) *World Yearbook of Education 1985: Research, Policy and Practice*. London: Kogan Page.

Chapter 1

Positivism and the Quantitative Tradition in Geographical and Environmental Education Research

Michael Williams

Questions are often raised about the respectability of geographical and environmental educational research which does not acknowledge the canons of a particular research paradigm. I use the term 'research paradigm' loosely to cover a range of methods described by different researchers, advocates and critics as classical, traditional, scientific, quantitative and positivist. In this chapter I shall seek to clarify the roots of this paradigm and indicate its importance in research in geographical and environmental education.

The concern with respectable research was lucidly addressed in the context of sociology by Clinard (1970, p. 68), who argued:

> If sociology is to achieve full respectability in the academic and larger world, sociologists need (1) more firsthand acquaintance with the data of the real world, (2) the raising of more significant questions and significant research problems about the social world around them, (3) a clearer recognition of the cultural variability of human behavior and its importance for scientific generalization, and (4) wider recognition of the necessity to test more of the research findings by application to the social control of the world around them.

Clinard emphasizes that sociologists had failed to 'delineate a distinctive scientific view of social phenomena' (p. 64). The roots of this search for a scientific sociology which could ape research in the natural sciences, echoed in geography and the environmental sciences as well as in geographical and environmental education, are to be found in the history of positivism.

For the positivist, a distinction has to be made between phenomena which can be carefully observed, accurately recorded and classified and those interpretations of human phenomena which focus on feelings, understandings and meanings. Doubt and ambiguity are to be removed and objectivity asserted. Thus, in research terms, there is an emphasis on continually improving those methods which enable social phenomena to be directly observed, described and measured. The researcher collects the data and takes them away to be collated, analysed and interpreted. The social facts so established provide the basis for formulating patterns of behaviour which Durkheim (1938, p. lvi) describes as 'collective ways of acting or thinking having a reality outside the individuals'. The product of these research endeavours is positive science, which achieves respectability in so far as the data are valid and reliable.

In positivism, there is a premium on following the scientific method familiar in the natural sciences in order to design research studies. This method follows an orderly sequence of steps (Borg, 1963, p. 6):

1. Recognition of the problem.
2. Definition of the problem in clear, specific terms.
3. Development of hypotheses.
4. Development of the techniques and measuring instruments that will provide objective data pertinent to the hypotheses.
5. Collection of data.
6. Analysis of data.
7. Drawing conclusions relative to the hypotheses based upon the data.

Studies which follow this have a number of distinguishing characteristics. New research problems emerge from previous investigations in the same field, yielding a continuing, cumulative record of data and interpretations. The testing of carefully and precisely defined hypotheses is conducted through a process of scientific sampling and instrument design. Data are in numerical form and are subjected to statistical testing and manipulation using a variety of statistical strategies and techniques. Determination of dependent and independent variables is important, so that correlations between social phenomena can be detected. Tests of significance and of error are applied and care is taken to demonstrate the reliability and validity of the data. There is a search not only for significant correlations but also for causal connections, since their meticulous exploration may yield general laws of universal applicability, enabling events to be predicted and controlled. By accumulating a body of such laws, it is possible to build a theory of human behaviour.

These positivist characteristics have been strongly advocated as the basis for educational research. Thus Borg (1963, p. 6) argues:

> The scientific method offers the best approach that man has thus far developed for the solution of problems. The steps of the scientific method may be applied not only to the problems of the scientific laboratory but are equally applicable to the problems faced by the school teacher in his classroom.

Echoing this firm commitment is this strong assertion by Campbell and Stanley (1963, p. 2) in the introduction to their influential text on experimental and quasi-experimental research designs:

> This chapter is committed to the experiment: as the only means for settling disputes regarding educational practice, as the only way of verifying educational improvements, and as the only way of establishing a cumulative tradition in which improvements can be introduced without the faddish discard of old wisdom in favor of inferior novelties.

Campbell and Stanley focus on control and experimental groups, on pre-tests and post-tests and, most importantly, on measures of internal and external validity. While their work can be read strictly in the context of experimental and quasi-experimental design, it has importance in a broader context which includes studies as diverse as surveys and studies of pupil assessment.

In the fields of geographical and environmental education, many studies are associated with positivism, and several of these are discussed in subsequent chapters. In the experimental context, the works of Jahoda and Piaget are much quoted. Quantitative studies are reviewed by Stoltman (Chapter 6) in the context of the large-scale, international projects of the International Association for the Evaluation of Educational Achievement and the International Assessment of Educational Progress. These are designed to yield broad patterns; the research task is to devise reliable and valid cross-cultural research instruments.

At a more modest level, though still in the field of international survey research, is a study reported by Knight and Rice (1984) – a thorough and detailed inquiry in the quant-itative tradition:

> The study was a non-experimental, *ex post facto* survey to ascertain the relationship of certain independent variables to dependent variables, especially the relationship of knowl-edge of geography to attitude towards six nationalities of the Americas. *Ex post facto* research is one in which the independent or dependent variables exist as a result of such influences as maturation, culture, schooling, sex, age and the like. Observation thus starts with the existing variables, and the independent variables are studied in retrospect for their possible effects on the dependent variable (Kerlinger, 1966, p. 360). Although *ex post facto* research is often regarded as less desirable than experimental research, there are many problems which cannot be explored by experimentation. *Ex post facto* research includes such notable studies as Piaget's studies of children's thinking (1970) and the authoritarian studies of Adorno *et al.* (1950). In geography and other social sciences causal-chain or temporal explanations, which involve the relationship of variables over a long period of time, it is an accepted mode of explanation (Harvey, 1969, p. 80).

To achieve their goals, the researchers used a design which follows a rigorous pattern characteristic of the cross-national quantitative survey using a small number of instru-ments.

We can now turn to some of the critiques made of this research tradition. Thus Blumer (1969, pp. 26–7) writes:

> The overwhelming bulk of what passes today as methodology is made up of such preoccu-pations as the following: The devising and use of sophisticated research techniques, usually of an advanced statistical character, the construction of logical and mathematical models, all too frequently guided by the criterion of elegance, the elaboration of formal schemes of imported schemes such as input–output analysis, system analysis and stochatic analysis, studious conformity to the canons of research design; and the promotion of particular pro-cedures such as survey research, as the method of scientific study.

In similar vein, Walford (1991, p. 1), taking his cue from the writings of Medawar, asserts:

> In practice, however, it is now widely recognized that the careful, objective, step-by-step model of the research process is actually a fraud and that, within natural science as well as within social science, the standard way in which research methods are taught and real research is often written up for publication perpetuates what is in fact a myth of objectivity (Medawar, 1963) ... natural science research is frequently not carefully planned in advance and conducted according to set procedures, but often centres around compromises, short-cuts, hunches, and serendipitous occurrences.

Despite these criticisms, it is important to emphasize the place of experimental and quasi-experimental designs in geographical and environmental education research. Quantitative studies have a role in eclectic investigations (Chapters 7, 11 and 14). The collection of quantitative data is often a significant preliminary stage, which helps to shape an inquiry, opening up avenues for exploration, indicating hypotheses worth testing and closing off areas not worth investigating further. In the gathering of factual data, as, for example, in the study of aspects of graphicacy in classrooms, the use of carefully designed tests is important (Chapter 8). So is the use of objective questions in studies which employ interviews (Chapter 9) and questionnaires (Chapter 10) to gather data in order to construct patterns of behaviour. There is no doubt that valuable cognitive, affective and behavioural data can be gathered using these techniques. There is also no doubt that in some circumstances such data can be validated and made more reliable through the use of supplementary qualitative studies.

The positivist tradition is relatively undeveloped in research in geographical education, and the debate about its strengths and weaknesses is rarely encountered in the literature. By contrast, in research in environmental education it is a very live contemporary issue (see Chapters 3 and 5). Fien, Tilbury and Walford's reviews stand alongside the work of such other environmentalist educationists as Hart, Huckle, Robottom and Posch. They reflect a drive in educational research and the social sciences, on the one hand, and science education, on the other, to develop alternative research paradigms. Robottom and Hart (1993, p. 592) argue for a '*meta-research agenda in science educational research* – that is, an agenda for research *about* research in science education and environmental education' asserting that, 'Until recently, a combination of naturalism, empiricism and positivism has dominated the methodological framework for the behavioural and social sciences.' They go on to emphasize that:

> Within the last decade, the discussion about issues surrounding different approaches to educational research has progressed beyond consideration of quantitative versus qualitative methods of data collection to consideration of paradigms as distinct genres of educational research – genres whose distinctiveness lies not in the main forms of data collection (i.e. different tools in the researcher's toolbox) but in the assumptions which prefigure what is to count as appropriate research topics, appropriate research questions and even appropriate research outcomes, in addition to appropriate research methods. In short, what is distinctive about research paradigms is not their forms of data collection but their ideology or political theory.
>
> (Robottom and Hart, 1993, 593–4)

They explore these issues in depth before proposing a meta-research agenda which starts from two important questions (p. 598):

> does environmental education research of the positivist/applied science/quantitative kind tend to begin by taking for granted a set of external goals for curriculum development in the field (see Hungerford 1983, Robottom 1990)?

> Does environmental education research of the positivist/applied science/quantitative kind tend to adopt a behaviourist perspective in the way it conceives the relationship of subject-matters and learners?

The implications of this analysis for practice can be seen in the Environment and School Initiatives (ENSI) Project, co-ordinated by the Centre for Educational Research and Innovation of the Organization for Economic Co-operation and Development. This project, which has been thoroughly described by Posch (1993, 1994a, 1994b), used an action research model to explore three dimensions of environmental education:

1.   the environment as a sphere of personal experience and emotional commitment;
2.   the environment as an object of interdisciplinary learning and research;
3.   the environment as a sphere of socially important action.

These demonstrate the shift away from the cognitive domain towards the affective domain in student learning, and towards more humanistic, interpretive and radical directions for research in environmental education. A similar trend can be detected in the field of science education which Davis *et al.* (1993), writing in the context of the United States, perceive to be in crisis. Their focus is on the transition in science education from objectivism to constructivism, and they argue that 'Stark differences in world view (ontology, epistemology and axiology) exist between objectivism and constructivism' (p. 628). They agree with Johnson's (1987, p. xiii) assertion that 'The objectivist paradigm is reaching the limits of its usefulness' and assert (Davis *et al.*, 1993, p. 628):

> In contrast to the objectivist view of learning is an epistemological paradigm based on constructivism (von Glasersfeld 1987, 1989) and a belief that individuals construct personal realities which make sense to them. Constructivists believe that knowledge is constructed based on what 'works' and what is 'good' in the particular context in which the cognizing individual is operating (von Glasersfeld 1989). This does not mean that individuals exist in isolation but they must negotiate with others in order to develop a mutually shared meaning (Bauersfeld 1988, Ernest 1990). This negotiation involves communication which is the process through which individuals come to develop some understanding of others' realities (Sless 1986).

What is evident in these writings is a disenchantment with an objectivist paradigm which has failed to address some of the educational issues deemed to be important for some researchers. That the choice of issues is itself subject to the world views of the researchers is recognized by the scholars quoted above. Nevertheless, there are undoubted pressures from many influential sources which serve to reinforce the view of positivist researchers that there is still much life in their preferred paradigm. These pressures are most obvious in the accountability movement in education, which seeks measures of effectiveness, efficiency and economy in curriculum improvement. The demands for evidence of a quantitative kind to demonstrate prevailing patterns, to provide evaluative data and to show the effects of reforms on educational standards, cannot be denied. It is important that the techniques used to satisfy the demands of external, often fund-awarding, agencies are located in the broader perspective of the nature of educational research. It is clear that techniques must be selected to meet clearly identified research needs. Being an expert research 'technician' in particular methods, while commendable in itself, must be balanced by a clear understanding of the social, political and philosophical contexts in which the techniques are located. In both geographical and environmental education research, these contexts are being unravelled, leading to a greater awareness of the strengths and weaknesses of various research paradigms and opening up potentially fruitful avenues for future investigations.

REFERENCES

Adorno, T.W., Frenkel-Brunswick, E., Levinson, D. and Sanford, R. (1950) *The Authoritarian Personality*. New York: Harper and Row.
Bauersfeld, H. (1988) 'Interaction, construction and knowledge: alternative perspectives for mathematics education.' In D.A. Grouws, T.J. Cooney and D. Jones (eds) *Effective Mathematics Teaching*. Hillsdale, NJ: Lawrence Erlbaum.
Blumer, H. (1969) *Symbolic Interactionism*. Englewood Cliffs, NJ: Prentice-Hall.
Borg, W.R. (1963) *Educational Research: An Introduction*. London: Longmans Green.
Campbell, D.T. and Stanley, J.C. (1963) *Experimental and Quasi-experimental Designs for Research*. Chicago: Rand McNally.

Clinard, M.B. (1970) 'The sociologist's quest for respectability.' In W.J. Filstead (ed.) *Qualitative Methodology: Firsthand Involvement with the Social World*. Chicago: Markham.

Davis, N.T., McCarthy, B.J., Shaw, K.L. and Sidani-Tabbaa. A. (1993) Transitions from objectivism to constructivism in science education.' *International Journal of Science Education*, **15** (6), 627–36.

Durkheim, E. (1938) *The Rules of Sociological Method*. Trans S.A. Solovay and J.H. Mueller, ed. G.E.G. Catlin, New York: Free Press.

Ernest, P. (1990) *The Philosophy of Mathematics Education*. Philadelphia, PA: Falmer.

Harvey, D. (1969) *Explanation in Geography*. London: Edward Arnold.

Hungerford, H. (1983) 'The challenges of K-12 environmental education.' Paper presented at the First National Congress for Environmental Education Futures: Policies and Practices, University of Vermont.

Johnson, M. (1987) *The Body in the Mind: The Bodily Basis of Meaning*. Chicago, IL: University of Chicago Press.

Kerlinger, F.N. (1966) *Foundations of Behavioral Research*. New York: Holt, Rinehart and Winston.

Knight, C. and Rice, M.J. (1984) 'Geographic knowledge and attitude.' In H. Haubrich (ed.) *Perception of People and Places through Media*. Freiburg: Education Commission of the International Geographical Union.

Medawar, P. (1963) 'Is the scientific paper a fraud?' *Listener*, **12**, September.

Piaget, J. (1929) *The Child's Conception of the World*. London: Routledge and Kegan Paul.

Piaget, J. (1970) *The Science of Education and the Psychology of the Child*. New York: Orion Press.

Posch, P. (1993) 'Research issues in environmental education.' *Studies in Science Education*, **21**, 21–48.

Posch, P. (1994a) 'Changes in the culture of teaching and learning and implications for action research.' *Educational Action Research*, **2** (2), 153–61.

Posch, P. (1994b) 'Networking in environmental education.' In M. Pettigrew and B. Somekh (eds) *Evaluation and Innovation in Environmental Education*. Paris: OECD/CERI.

Robottom, I. (1990) 'Environmental education: reconstructing the curriculum for social responsibility?' *New Education*, **VII**, 61–77.

Robottom, I. and Hart, P. (1993) 'Towards a meta-research agenda in science and environmental education.' *International Journal of Science Education*, **15** (5), 591–605.

Sless, D. (1986) *In Search of Semiotics*. London: Croom Helm.

von Glasersfeld, E. (1987) *The Construction of Knowledge: Contributions to Conceptual Semantics*. Seaside, CA: Intersystems Publications.

von Glasersfeld, E. (1989) 'Cognition, construction of knowledge, and teaching.' *Synthese*, **80**, 121–40.

Walford, G. (ed.) (1991) *Doing Educational Research*. London: Routledge.

Chapter 2

Interpretive Approaches to Geographical and Environmental Education Research

Rod Gerber

A RATIONALE FOR INTERPRETIVE APPROACHES

As the debate about 'What is human science?' unfolds around them, most geographical and environmental educators just want to get on with their research studies into issues or problems which they believe are important for their areas of knowledge. In many ways these educators have been indoctrinated by the approaches characterized by the quantitative revolution, in which logical empiricism and the positivist thinking associated with the scientific method prevailed. Instead of entering into conversations about the nature of knowledge, as described by Polkinghorne (1989), or adopting a 'house of research method' approach as described by Gerber (1993a, p. 40), or considering whether research questions are ontological (referring to what is being researched) or methodological (referring to how something is being researched) (Marton, 1993, p. 1), it has been much easier to assume these things and get on with the research!

Hermeneutics, the science of interpretation, has been advocated by geographical theorists since the 1970s as a useful means for understanding human actions and consequences as they relate to people-environment relationships (Bauman, 1978; Bleicher, 1980; Buttimer, 1974; Gregory, 1978; Tuan, 1971). In the area of geographical education the use of interpretive approaches to research has been rather limited and slower to develop than for the discipline of geography. Initially, they emerged out of studies of critical pedagogy (e.g. Bartlett, 1983, 1989). Later, studies with a stronger phenomenological basis (Gerber, 1991, 1992, 1994) began to capture the spirit of the interpretive process and to use the principles of phenomenology in the area of geographical and environmental education.

The focus on interpretation as the basis for providing meaning to research studies in geographical and environmental education is a prime reason for the increasing popularity of qualitative research in this area. Taylor (1993, p. 173), paraphrasing Chinn (1985), states that the strengths of qualitative research are:

> that it provides methods to challenge the myths of the ultimate truth, objectivity, the perfect method, scientific supremacy, empirical evidence, higher authority and significance. Qualitative methods allow exploration of humans by humans in ways which acknowledge the value

of all evidence, the inevitability and worth of subjectivity, the value of a holistic view, the integration of all patterns of knowing, the limitations of empirical evidence in relation to studying humans, the value of ethical justification, aesthetic criticism, and personal intro-spection and the limitations of the meaning of statistical significance.

Lancy (1993, p. 9) states that 'those who subscribe to the qualitative paradigm conduct their work within a phenomenological framework.' As described in the *Encyclopedia of Philosophy* (Collier Macmillan, 1972, pp. 135–51), phenomenology emphasizes the meanings that people ascribe to their own existence and experience. Phenomenological statements are non-empirical and descriptive and they describe phenomena that are experienced. The principal task in phenomenological research is to discover, explore and describe 'uncensored phenomena' (Spiegelberg, 1970, p. 21). In so doing, the researcher seeks intuitively the essences of particular phenomena, brackets his or her own beliefs about the phenomena, encourages participants to reflect on their experience of the phenomena, and aims to detect the intentionality in people's experience of them. Lancy (1993, p. 9) summarizes this research enterprise as follows:

> Thus a researcher taking a phenomenological approach avoids, as much as possible, the use of assumptions about the phenomenon under study; avoids reducing complex reality to a few 'variables' and minimises the use of instruments that are reactive and that greatly influence the reality she or he is trying to study. Such a researcher tries to go into the field with an open mind, to carry out investigations in which the conclusions are post hoc rather than a priori. Operating like a natural historian, the researcher observes, records, classifies, and concludes, seeking wherever possible, to capture the reality of the subjects and not only her or his own reality.

A critical aspect of this approach to research is that it is non-dualistic by nature. The traditional Cartesian view is that it is possible to separate theoretical aspects from practical ones (Markova, 1982). In the area of learning, writers in the publication edited by Marton *et al.* (1984) concluded that the act and outcome of learning were two intertwined aspects, illuminating, in conjunction with each other, the meaning of the variation between students. Therefore, the object of the research (the problem) and the subject (the learner) are not separate: the subject's experience of the object is a relation between the two (Marton, 1993, p. 3) In his study of teachers' remembering a curricular change to a humanities course, the author (Gerber, 1993b) demonstrated that the act of remembering is a joint process in which the researchers work with the teachers to reconstruct their experience of the actual change. This process resides in the interactions that these people have had with other people in a particular social context and the discursive practices that have occurred (Middleton, 1987). Marton (1993, p. 4) concludes that 'an experience is a relationship between object and subject and encompasses both. The experience is as much an aspect of the object as it is of the subject.'

Therefore, the quality of the different approaches to phenomenological research resides in working with people in their own life-worlds of experience from either a first-order or a second-order perspective. What is crucial is that the context in which the experience occurs is recognized as essential to its meaning, for it is the context that mediates the meaning that emerges from the discourses that provide much of the data in these studies. This is true for all types of phenomenological research method, including empirical phenomenology, phenomenography, reflective phenomenology and socio-cultural research.

WHICH RESEARCH QUESTIONS?

Tesch (1990, pp. 21–72), in her overview of the field of qualitative research, concludes that four types of qualitative research may be discerned:

1.   research that studies the characteristics of language, such as content analysis or discourse analysis;
2.   research that aims at the discovery of regularities, grounded theory or naturalistic inquiry;
3.   research that seeks to discern meaning, such as phenomenology or case study;
4.   research that is based on reflection, heuristic research or educational connoisseurship.

Interpretation is an essential element of these research studies. Critics of qualitative research believe that the element of subjectivity is the one that weakens any of the above-mentioned types of research. However, as will be demonstrated later in this chapter, this perceived 'weakness' can be made quite powerful if the appropriate phenomenological principles are adhered to during the research process.

The challenge for interpretive researchers is to conduct research studies in the knowledge that the reality that is perceived by participants in the research process is constantly changing because of the dynamic nature of our experience of phenomena. People may experience a particular phenomenon in a different set of contexts, such as finding one's way in familiar territory, in a foreign country, at night or after the staff Christmas party. The way-finding experience is likely to be different in some of these contexts. It is the challenge for interpretive researchers to accept these variations in experience and to place them in their relative contexts. Therefore, it may be concluded that reality is context-based.

What is important for researchers is the search for alternative constructions of reality that are open to many possible explanations for observed phenomena, few of which can be ruled out in advance of the study. Therefore, interpretive researchers are opportunistic as they investigate complex issues or problems about which little is known with certainty.

It is the growing lack of certainty in people's knowledge of specific phenomena that has encouraged interpretive researchers to expand their investigations. For example, it has been assumed that everyone in the fields of geographical and environmental education were meaning similar things when they used either of these two fundamental terms. Studies by the author in the area of geographical education (Gerber, 1991, 1994) indicate that this is not the case and that four or five qualitatively different variations are held by trainee geography teachers. It is suspected from anecdotal evidence gained in the compilation of the *International Charter on Geographical Education*, the policy document of the International Geographical Union on the development and implementation of geographical education in countries around the world, that these variations are widely held among geographical educators around the world. Similar studies need to be completed in the area of environmental education, since it is likely that similar variations exist there.

It follows, then, that the research questions that should be asked by interpretive researchers are open-ended ones that capture either the essence or the variation of the experience of relevant phenomena in geographical and environmental education. As will be shown later, the focus on the essence of, or the variation in, the experience will depend on the research method used; for example, the essence of an experience may be derived from a strictly phenomenological study whereas the qualitatively different variations will be derived from a phenomenographic study.

The open-ended nature of a good research question can be demonstrated by considering a phenomenon as apparently straightforward as *geography*. The choice of the research question depends on the purpose of the research study. If it is to determine teachers' understandings of the phenomenon of geography, then a research question should be framed to capture that intent. If the question aims to capture the teachers' experience of geography as the basis for their understanding of the concept, then it is necessary for the researchers to frame a non-technical question that may be used to elicit the teachers' experiences of geography. Some suggestions for an appropriate research question on this topic include the following:

1.   What are teachers' experiences of geography?
2.   How do teachers understand geography?
3.   How do teachers use geography in their teaching?

In a broader context, it is possible to illustrate some different types of research study that may be designed, implemented and analysed by interpretive researchers in the areas of geographical and environmental education. They include:

1.   studies of students' and teachers' conceptions of different geographical and environmental concepts;
2.   studies of the essence of people's experience of geographical and environmental phenomena;
3.   investigations of learning in geography;
4.   studies of people's reflections and rememberings of specific phenomena;
5.   studies of how learners develop meaning of geographical and environmental concepts in different educational contexts;
6.   the use of discourse in the learning process in geography and environmental studies.

Geography and environmental studies have their own sets of technical terms, that is, their distinctive *concepts* such as spatial distribution and environmental competence. Dictionaries and textbooks inform both educators and students what these concepts mean. However, since their meaning actually resides in the minds of the learners or the educators, it is highly likely that people's understandings of both of these concepts will vary from the textbook definitions, and they may vary according to the learning context. Investigations into the nature of the discipline of geography (Gerber, 1991) and geographical information systems (Gerber, *et al.*, 1992) are indicative of such research. Variations in experienced meaning of the same concept are likely to occur across the different learning contexts that are evident in different countries where there are varying cultural aspects and linguistic variations, and within a specific educational context.

If researchers want to develop an *experience*-based interpretation of selected phenomena, it is desirable for them to investigate people's experience of each phenomenon and to deduce the essential general attributes of each one. One phenomenon common to geographical and environmental education is fieldwork. What is the essence of the fieldwork experience? Despite the apparently numerous studies that have been conducted about the phenomenon of fieldwork, it is unlikely that any experientially based studies have been conducted to establish what these essential general attributes are. Similarly, they have not been determined in distinctive contexts such as schools, universities, field-study centres or homes.

What do people *learn* about some aspect of geographical or environmental education, or how do they learn this information? It is quite possible to obtain a set of categories of description of people's experience for each learning context. Knowing what a junior high-school geography class understands by the use of common terms such as 'weather' and 'climate' is likely to provide a number of insights into the nature of the learners that may offer guidance for the selection of content, the range of resources and the sequence of learning to be undertaken in a study of these areas. While these outcomes will be interesting in their own right, they are likely to offer greater richness if they are placed in a specific educational context.

In phenomenographic studies of learning, close attention is given to searching for the qualitatively different conceptions held by students as they undergo learning experiences. In addition, there is a consideration of the learners' knowing that they are making these different statements. For example, if a geography teacher wants to know whether his or her students have learned the concept of weather, it is quite feasible for the teacher to present his or her students with a writing task, before studying weather, in which a well-designed, non-technical question is framed and the students are required to complete the task, preferably in a written form. They are then required to complete a similar or the same task upon completion of the curricular unit. An analysis of the two sets of conceptions will reveal the extent to which any qualitative changes have occurred in the students' understanding of the concept of weather. Such an outcome may be confirmed by discussing with the students the extent to which they appreciate the different conceptions of weather that they have exhibited.

Instead of engaging in protracted longitudinal studies of learning or curricular change in geographical and environmental education, interpretive researchers may implement investigations that require people to *reflect* on their practices and to *remember* their intentional actions during these events. Remembering their roles in the implementing of a humanities curriculum (Gerber, 1993b), considering the development of the concept of planning (Rogoff, Baker-Sennett and Matusov, 1993) and exploring responses to local composting activities in waste management (Shanahan and Saljo, 1993) offer some suggestions for interpretive researchers to follow. The quality of such studies will depend on the extent to which the researchers are faithful to the philosophies that underpin their selected research methods.

Following Svensson's (1985) lead, *contextual analyses* with regard to selected aspects of geography or environmental studies could provide a basis for powerful research investigations. These may lead to generalizations about understanding selected phenomena, ranging from domain aspects, such as drainage basins, climatic change, urban areas or desertification, to pedagogic aspects, such as hazard-risk reduction education, fieldwork learning through simulation or virtual worlds. These are likely to offer fruitful ways for investigating how students develop their conceptions of the above-mentioned phenomena and for unravelling how the particular learning context assists or hinders the learning process. It would be interesting to find out how students learning their geography by open access methods may develop different understandings of specific geographical concepts to those developed by students learning via face-to-face methods.

Studies into the use of *discourse* in the learning process in geography and environmental studies may also be illuminating. Instead of seeking to define and describe learning in geography and environmental studies in a 'neutral' sense, this type of study focuses on the exploration of the intertextuality between discourses in learning geography and environmental studies to show how the learning is construed by the students and the teachers. Conceptions of learning are culturally based, but their dominant investigation from traditional scientific discourse tends to hide these differences. Learning can therefore be considered in terms of human activity and shared experiences in a complex world rather than being described in terms of cognitive processes. This is a very different way of considering, for example, how students learn about industrialization in various developing and developed countries. Such studies offer the chance to incorporate aspects of language and culture into learning specific concepts in differently defined contexts in geography and environmental studies.

GATHERING DATA FOR INTERPRETIVE RESEARCH

Since interpretive researchers collect data of people's experience of certain phenomena, they normally engage in some form of discourse with a range of people in a designated social context. Since the social context in which the experience occurs is the basis for the mediation of the meaning of the participants' memory of the experience of the phenomenon, the data gathered in a remembering process cannot be 'single-minded' (Middleton and Edwards, 1990); that is, it does not emanate only from the minds of the participants to the experience. Rather, it is a 'dialogical' experience (Markova and Foppa, 1990) in which the discourse is established among the researchers and the participants to develop shared meanings of the latter's experience of the phenomenon. For example, if the object of the research was to understand how community members appreciated landscapes, the data derived from such a study would consist of the shared meanings of the participants' experience of a range of views of different landscapes as they emerged in different types of discourse with the researchers.

Therefore, the act of remembering is a joint process in which the researchers work with the participants to reconstruct their experience of the specific phenomenon; that is, their appreciation of landscape. The researchers seek to elicit from each participant his or her fullest recollection of his or her experience of landscape. They will usually do so in interviews by asking leading questions, making suggestions, structuring responses, asking for descriptions of particularly striking landscapes, probing for fullest understanding, seeking themes, seeking clarifications and placing comments in perspective (Kvale, 1983). In addition, data may be acquired by asking the participants to express their views about landscapes in graphic forms such as drawings, diagrams and maps. Alternatively, their behaviour during the actual experience of appreciating landscape may be recorded; for instance, by videotaping or by completing a behaviour matrix. This will enable the researchers to capture the range of responses by the participants to their actual and remembered experience of the landscapes.

Phenomenological principles such as reduction, internal and external horizon, essence and intentionality are used to gather relevant data. It is the task of the researcher to bracket his or her views about the phenomenon under investigation in order to obtain the fullest account of the participants' experience of landscape. Jonsson *et al.* (1991, p. 5) state, therefore, that this process reflects a dialogical one in which several voices are entered and where an institutionalized social practice organizes discourse and remembering.

Marton (1992) further emphasizes that the prime form of data-gathering consists of the interview, which aims to make that which is unthematized into the object of focal awareness. Therefore, the researcher should not make up too many questions in advance, nor should she or he determine too many details before the actual interview. This is to ensure that the interview is the joint exploration of the actual experience of the phenomenon. Its starting point is usually a non-technical question that introduces the phenomenon. This question is normally introduced after the participants have been exposed to an experience of the phenomenon; for example, when they have viewed a range of views of different landscapes or just visited a couple of distinctive landscapes. The non-technical nature of the question is intended as the catalyst for commencing the dialogue. In the case of the current example of the appreciation of landscape, this question may take the form of: 'What aspects of landscapes enable you to appreciate them?' after a preliminary introductory discussion between the researcher and the participant. Alternatively, the researcher may commence with the question: 'Can you tell me something interesting about landscapes that you have seen? if there has not been time for a preliminary discussion about the phenomenon.

Researchers such as Miles and Huberman (1984) have argued that the preliminary analysis of data should proceed concurrently with the collection of the data. Sowden and Keeves (1990, p. 654) propose the following reasons for doing this:

1. There is a danger in the collection of a huge amount of qualitative data that the analysis will become such a daunting task that it will jeopardize the completion of the study.
2. Concurrent analyses will identify gaps in the data and new hypotheses and relationships emerge while it is still possible to collect relevant data.
3. Ongoing analyses permit the preparation of an interim report that is reassuring for the client and facilitates the flow of funding for the study.

Consequently, they urge all qualitative researchers to maintain detailed documentary records of the data collected.

INTERPRETIVE ANALYSIS IN GEOGRAPHICAL AND ENVIRONMENTAL EDUCATION RESEARCH

Once the data are organized in a digestible form, they can be analysed. Sowden and Keeves (1990, pp. 654–5) declare that the analysis of qualitative data passes through three interrelated stages:

1. data reduction where the primary task is to code the data;
2. data display in the form of a matrix so that patterns are evident in a form that can be used in the presentation of results; and
3. conclusion drawing and verification to establish whether the conclusion is soundly drawn from the evidence available.

They detail a variety of tactics for deriving meaning in interpretive analyses. These include:

1. counting the number of instances that an event or a relationship occurs, such as the number of times that students refer to a catchment in a study of water quality;
2. noting patterns and themes, such as the regularities in students' perceptions of deserts as hot, dry places or the essential attributes of learning to use maps;
3. imputing plausibility; for example, checking back on the data to confirm that the general attributes of environmental interpretation as expressed by a selected group of visitors to an environmental theme park are acceptable;
4. clustering events, actions, beliefs or values into groups; for example, in a study of urban land use, grouping all of the responses that relate to business activities as opposed to those that are related to residential activities;
5. using metaphors to detect new and different perspectives of a phenomenon, such as seeing the actions of tactile mappers as those of lateral thinkers who maximize the environment through sound and touch;
6. developing categories to organize the data into like cases; for example, the development of conceptions and sub-conceptions of learning the concept of region;
7. the compositing of factors and categories to form more generalized and meaningful relationships; for example, the essential attributes of the experience of landscape or the general attributes of an ecosystem;
8. noting relationships among the data to systematize the search process; for example, noting the relationship between the adoption of waste recycling methods and media advertising in a waste management study;
9. detecting mediating factors in the social context of the research experience, such as a community's attitude to public transport in a study of transportation in an urban area;
10. building a logical chain of evidence to explain people's behaviour; for example, linking people's attitudes to parklands to current government policy on the use of parkland area and the patterns of usage of local parklands;
11. constructing a causal chain to involve a temporal sequence of events; for example, establishing that students' inability to orienteer through a forest occurred because they were unable to use a compass and an orienteering map, as well as their continuous display of a poor sense of direction.

While this list is useful, it does not indicate the intensive iterations that occur during the interpretive analytical process. The process of reading and re-reading the verbatim transcripts and other forms of discourse involves the researchers participating in a process of clarification of data in which the meaning of the experiences emerge from the data. Essentially what the researchers are seeking are similarities or differences in the experience of the particular phenomenon.

Studies which are seeking similarities or essences are phenomenological studies that use differing forms of analyses, all of which adhere to either transcendental principles as proposed by Husserl or existential principles as proposed by Heidigger. Phenomenological analytical methods such as those of Giorgi (1986), Ihde (1986) and van Manen (1990) are indicative of the more widely used Husserlian approach to the study of phenomena. Each of these theorists offers techniques for the thematizing of data to extract the essence of people's experience of a phenomenon. For example, Giorgi (1985) details the five steps of his phenomenological psychological method as extending from the reading of the entire description of one subject to obtain a sense of the whole through to the expression of a typology of concepts of the phenomenon. This typology represents the essence of the experience of the phenomenon. For example, the data from a study on learning geography through simulated experiences may be analysed in this way to thematize the nature of this experience.

Those studies that seek to detect the variations in people's experience of selected phenomena usually involve phenomenographic analysis, which Marton and Saljo (1984) describe as a non-algorithmic, interpretive 'discovery procedure'. Whereas phenomeno-logical studies normally deal with individual responses for analysis, phenomenographic studies deal with collective data. Marton (1992, p. 9) says that this is because the same participant may express more than one way of understanding the phenomenon. Since the data are dealt with *en masse*, they usually consist of a large body of transcripts. Marton goes on to describe the method for reducing this mass of data and introducing meaning into the variations in the participants' experience of the phenomenon. The following steps are involved:

1. selection of the relevant from the irrelevant data in relation to the selected phenomenon;
2. identification and grouping of the distinct ways of understanding the phenomenon by commencing to thematize the reported experiences;
3. establishment of the relations between the groups of conceptions; that is, the features of the categories of description that characterize the variations in how the phenomenon is experienced, conceptualized or understood;
4. determination of the logical relations that exist between the categories of description, expressed as an outcome space – a graphic that explains the extent of linkages among the categories of description.

As Marton (1992, p. 10) stresses, the different steps in phenomenographic analysis should occur interactively because each step has implications for succeeding as well as preceding steps. He emphasizes that once categories of description and the outcome space have been found, 'they can be reapplied to the data from which they originate.' Since each set of conceptions is contextually bound, it is only possible to make conceptual, rather than statistical, generalizations about the data.

When the phenomenographic type of analysis was applied to people's conceptions of a geographical information system or GIS (Gerber, *et al.*, 1992), after three or four iterations of reading the data and discussing the different experiences the researchers discovered that the group of GIS professionals and academics agreed that five variations were evident. GIS was experienced as:

1. a graphics interface;
2. a geographical data organizer;
3. a data collection representation;
4. the process of interaction between an expert in geographical information and extensive data sets to solve geographical problems;
5. an evolving spatial technology.

The resulting outcome space revealed that conceptions 1 and 2 focus on independent aspects of the GIS – the graphics interface in conception 1 and the database in conception 2. Conception 3 focuses on both aspects. Conceptions 4 and 5 represent interest in GIS that goes beyond conception 3 to emphasize expert users of GIS and the possibilities that they see in using GIS technology for solving geographical problems.

Some recent interpretive approaches to research have placed greater emphasis on the context that mediates the meaning of the data gathered and on the nature of the discourse used to gather the data. These approaches, typified by the sociocultural approach, do not focus only on similarities or differences that are grounded in phenomenological principles. Rather they are underpinned by activity theorists such as Leontiev (1981) and Vygotsky (1978), and their studies focus on cognition in everyday learning. Examples of this type of research include problem solving and situated reasoning (Saljo and Wyndhamn, 1990), the concept of planning (Rogoff, Baker-Sennett and Matusov, 1993) and the analysis of development processes (Rogoff, Radziszewska and Masiello, 1993). Analyses, here, take the form of incisive interpretations that use quantitative and qualitative data to illuminate the way the context of the experience mediates the meaning of the actual experience and the discourses that are used to reflect on the everyday experience. Any of these topics could be used in the interpretation of the use of geography and environmental studies in everyday living.

Whichever interpretive approach is used, even if it involves the use of some of the more recently developed computer software, it will be a rather time-consuming one compared with doing quantitative research. This is the price that qualitative researchers pay for making detailed analyses of rich contextual data.

ASPECTS OF QUALITY IN INTERPRETIVE RESEARCH

Inevitably the different types of qualitative research are questioned on the grounds of their validity and reliability. As Giorgi (1988, pp. 168–9) points out, the concepts of validity (a correspondence between a proposition and the ability of a referent to match the proposition) and reliability (the consistency of the match) belong to mainstream psychology and are tied to logical-empirical philosophy. By focusing on the use of phenomenological reduction and the concern for essences, Giorgi (1988, pp. 172–5) concludes that the reduction prevents a researcher from making empirical claims, and that the search for essences prevents the researcher from drawing conclusions about particulars and so directs his or her attention toward the essentials of a phenomenon. He states (p. 174) that:

> If the essential description truly captures the intuited essence, one has validity in a phenomenological sense. This means that one adequately describes the general essence that is given to the consciousness of the researcher. If one can use this essential description consistently, one has reliability.

Tschudi (1989) presents a very clear argument as to why people who use qualitative and/or quantitative approaches to research should adopt similar approaches to the question of validity in their studies. He argues that whatever 'tribal banners' researchers use to describe their type of research, interpretations and conclusions must be justified. Such a concern for validity should be viewed as a means for guarding against human error.

Interpretive researchers are as passionate about their approaches to the research enterprise as are quantitative researchers. Therefore, while most interpretive researchers would ultimately agree with the argument expressed by Tschudi, many are uneasy about the use of the terms 'validity' and 'reliability', because these two terms use the language of logical empiricism. Therefore, theorists such as Ihde (1986), Spinelli (1989) and Kvale (1989) prefer to refer to the search for truthfulness rather than the search for validity in their studies.

The telling point to be made here is that the search to justify the conclusions of one's research normally occurs in the form of some measurement or formula for the quantitative researchers, whereas it is a pervasive process for interpretive researchers. The author (Gerber, 1993a, p. 45) has suggested that four fundamental aspects enable this pervasive process to be pursued consistently throughout the research endeavour. These are as follows:

1. In the conceptualisation of the research question which becomes the aim of the study, the researcher should ensure that the overall research question is organised in such a way that it reflects the qualitative research approach to be employed. For example, in a phenomenological study to investigate the social effects of a natural hazard such as a tropical cyclone the research question could be 'What is the nature of the human experience of a tropical cyclone?' whereas in a phenomenographic study on developing thinking skills in geography the research question could be 'How do high school students learn to think about people-environment relationships?'

2. A pilot study should be used as a constructive device to refine the actual data-gathering questions. The real purpose of the pilot study is, therefore, to refine the non-technical questions so that they elicit from the participants in the study the fullest account of their experience of a particular phenomenon. The best non-technical question should be derived from a selection of questions that have been tried out with participants of the type and context that will be involved in the actual study. For example, in a study to ascertain how high school students viewed satellite images of parts of the world the following questions were tried out with a small number of high school students:

    (a) What do you understand about these pictures?
    (b) What makes these pictures special?
    (c) How are these pictures useful for studying geography?
    (d) What do these pictures tell you about the world?

The final question proved to be the one that offered the most access to the students' experience of remotely-sensed satellite images. It was, therefore, used to commence the series of interviews that were conducted to understand high school students' experience of satellite imagery.

3. The collection of the data in interpretive research is a process that should be followed using the appropriate set of methodological principles. Often, interviews are used for this purpose. A sense of truthfulness to the research method is achieved when the researcher who undertakes phenomenological interviews: brackets his/her own lived experiences of the particular phenomenon; probes for fullest understanding of the participants' experience by revisiting their responses again and again until the external horizon of their experience is reached; and focuses on the intentional aspects of the participants' experience, i.e. the defining characteristic of human consciousness.

In an example of an interpretive researcher collecting data on teachers' experience of action for the environment, truthfulness of this process was achieved by the following actions:

    (a) Commence the interview by posing the relevant non-technical question, e.g. how do you act as an environmentally responsible citizen?
    (b) Take significant aspects of the participant's response and ask the person to reflect on his or her response until the fullest account of their experience is attained, e.g. select aspects of the participant's response and have him or her develop some examples of what they mean by acting responsibly for the environment.

    (c) Refrain from injecting any of the researcher's beliefs about environmental responsibility into the conversation.

    (d) Gradually reduce the participant's experience of action for the environment until the essential aspects of this experience emerge. This involves a continuous process of reflection and reiteration of the participant's experience until its key elements are clear to the researcher.

Once the data have been obtained, they are prepared in a form ready for analysis, e.g. as a transcription of an interview. The method of checking here involves the checking of the data with the audiotape or videotape of the interview for accuracy. The researcher can then feel comfortable in the knowledge that s/he has acted consistently throughout the data-gathering phase.

4. The analysis of the data will maintain this sense of truthfulness if it employs the following set of hermeneutic rules:

    (a) Orienting the analysis toward the phenomenon, e.g. how is recycling practised in a community?

    (b) Describing the phenomenon, e.g. recycling, as it appears to the participants rather than how it is observed by the reseacher.

    (c) Treating all aspects of the responses as being of equal importance, i.e. horizontalisation of the data.

    (d) Checking the data for structural features that demonstrate the linkages amongst the different variations or the general similarities. This results in the development of essences of experience in the case of phenomenological studies and categories of description in the case of phenomenographic studies.

    (e) Using intentional variation as a basis for testing the clarity of the conceptions or meanings of the experience of a phenomenon.

The element of truthfulness, therefore, necessitates that the researchers understand the philosophy that underpins each of the interpretive methods that they seek to use. Once the relevant philosophical principles have been grasped, then it offers the challenge for the researchers to apply them methodically to the research context at each step. As a result, interpretive researchers are able to make conceptual generalizations from their studies concerning experiences in specific contexts.

CONCLUSION

Peshkin (1993, p. 28) has declared that 'no research paradigm has a monopoly on quality. None can deliver promised outcomes with certainty. None have the grounds for saying "this is it" about their designs, procedures, and anticipated outcomes.' This claim should form a continuous echo for researchers in geographical and environmental education. Those who use interpretive research methods should appreciate the potential that these approaches offer for geographical and environmental education and maximize these types of study.

To maximize the potential of interpretive research, geographical and environmental educators need to read more widely in the areas of qualitative research methods, philosophy, epistemology and ontology. It is much more than a case of finding a research method and using it in a study with people in geographical and/or environmental education. It is a thorough research experience that is based on a known set of procedures and rules that have to be applied consistently and truthfully to a designated research question. It is certainly not a 'soft' approach to research in geographical and environmental education. In some ways, therefore, it is more demanding than doing quantitative research, because the rules and procedures for conducting quantitative research are more widely known and accepted than those that fit under the umbrella of interpretive approaches. This will change, as more researchers disseminate more outcomes from their interpretive research studies and educators can see the additional benefit of context-rich studies based on the experiences of the participants and not those of the researchers.

REFERENCES

Bartlett, V.L. (1983) 'Questions and viewpoints: the art of interpretation in geography.' *New Zealand Journal of Geography*, April, 7–13.

Bartlett, V.L. (1989) 'Critical inquiry: the emerging perspective in geography teaching.' In J. Fien, R. Gerber and P. Wilson (eds) *The Geography Teachers' Guide to the Classroom*. Melbourne: Macmillan.

Bauman, Z. (1978) *Hermeneutics and Social Science*. New York: Hutchinson.

Bleicher, J. (1980) *Contemporary Hermeneutics: Hermeneutics as Method, Philosophy and Critique*. London: Routledge and Kegan Paul.

Buttimer, A. (1974) *Values in Geography*. Resource paper no. 24. Washington, DC: Association of American Geographers.

Chinn, P. (1985) 'Debunking myths in nursing theory and research.' *IMAGE: Journal of Nursing Scholarship*, **xvii** (2), 45–9.

Collier Macmillan (1972) *The Encyclopedia of Philosophy*. London: Collier Macmillan.

Gerber, R. (1991) 'Students' conceptions of the nature of geography – a phenomenographic invest-igation.' Paper presented to the conference of the Human Sciences Research Association, Gothenburg, Sweden.

Gerber, R. (1992) 'Phenomenography as an important qualitative approach to research in geo-graphy.' Paper presented to the International Geographical Union Symposium on Geographical Education, Boulder, Colorado.

Gerber, R. (1993a) 'A sense of quality – qualitative research approaches for geographical educa-tion.' In H. Jager (ed.) *Liber Amicorum Gunter Niemz*. Frankfurt: Goethe University Press.

Gerber, R. (1993b) 'A socio-cultural approach to curriculum change.' Paper presented to the National Conference of the Australian Curriculum Studies Association, Brisbane.

Gerber, R. (1994), Variations in the experience of geography by pre-service geographical educa-tors', *Geographical Education*, **7** (2).

Gerber, R., Buzer, S., Worth, C. and Bruce, C. (1992) 'Is a GIS a GIS? Or coming to an experi-ential understanding of GIS.' Paper presented to the National Conference of the Australasian Urban and Regional Information Systems Association, Gold Coast.

Giorgi, A. (ed.) (1985) *Phenomenology and Psychological Research*. Pittsburgh: Duquesne University Press.

Giorgi, A. (1986) 'A phenomenological analysis of descriptions of concepts of learning obtained from a phenomenographic perspective.' *Fenomenografiska Notiser*, **4**, 18–77.

Giorgi, A. (1988) 'Validity and reliability from a phenomenological perspective.' In W. Baker, M. Rappard and H. Stam (eds) *Recent Trends in Theoretical Psychology*. New York: Springer-Verlag.

Gregory, D. (1978) 'The discourse of the past: phenomenology, structuralism and historical geo-graphy.' *Journal of Historical Geography*, **4**, 161–73.

Ihde, D. (1986) *Experimental Phenomenology: An Introduction*. New York: G.P. Putnam's Sons.

Jonsson, L., Linell, P. and Saljo, R. (1991) 'Formulating the past: remembering in the police interrogation.' *Activity Theory 9/10*, 5–11.

Kvale, S. (1983) 'The qualitative research interview – a phenomenological and a hermeneutic mode of understanding.' *Journal of Phenomenological Psychology*, **14**, 171–96.

Kvale, S. (1989) *Issues of Validity in Qualitative Research*. Lund: Studentlitteratur.

Lancy, D. (1993) *Qualitative Research in Education*. New York: Longman.

Leontiev, A. (1981) 'The problem of activity in psychology.' In J. Wertsch (ed.) *The Concept of Activity in Soviet Psychology*. Armonk, NY: Sharpe.

Markova, I. (1982) *Paradigms, Thought and Language*. Chichester and New York: Wiley.

Markova, I and Foppa, K. (eds) (1990) *Dynamics of Dialogue*. New York: Harvester Wheatsheaf.

Marton, F. (1992) 'Phenomenography,' In *International Encyclopedia of Education*. Oxford: Pergamon Press.

Marton, F. (1993) 'Towards a pedagogy of awareness.' Paper presented at the 5th EARLI conference, Aix-en-Provence, France.

Marton, F. and Saljo, R. (1984) 'Approaches to learning.' In F. Marton, D. Hounsell and N. Entwistle (eds) *The Experience of Learning*. Edinburgh: Scottish Academic Press.

Marton, F., Hounsell, D. and Entwistle, N. (eds) (1984) *The Experience of Learning*. Edinburgh: Scottish Academic Press.

Middleton, D. (1987) 'Collective memory and remembering: some issues and approaches.' *Quarterly Newsletter of the Laboratory of Comparative Human Cognition*, **9**, 2–5.

Middleton, D. and Edwards, D. (eds) (1990) *Collective Remembering*. London: Sage.

Miles, M. and Huberman, A. (1984) *Qualitative Data Analysis: A Sourcebook of New Methods*. Beverly Hills, CA: Sage.

Peshkin, A. (1993) 'The goodness of qualitative research.' *Educational Researcher*, March, **22** (2), 23–9.

Polkinghorne, D. (1989) 'Changing conversations about human science.' In S. Kvale (ed.) *Issues of Validity in Qualitative Research*. Lund: Studentlitteratur.

Rogoff, B., Baker-Sennett, J. and Matusov, E. (1993) 'Considering the concept of planning.' In M. Haith, J. Benson, B. Pennington and R. Roberts (eds) *Future-oriented Processes*. Chicago, IL: University of Chicago Press.

Rogoff, B., Radziszewska, B. and Masiello, T. (1993) 'Analysis of developmental processes in sociocultural activity.' In L. Martin, K. Nelson and E. Tobach (eds) *Cultural Psychology and Activity Theory*. Cambridge: Cambridge University Press.

Saljo, R. and Wyndhamn, J. (1990) 'Problem-solving, academic performance and situated reasoning: a study of joint cognitive activity in the formal setting.' *British Journal of Educational Psychology*, **60**, 245–54.

Shanahan, H. and Saljo, R. (1993) 'Purchases, food habits and waste management in households: exploring responses to local composting.' *Journal of Consumer Studies and Home Economics*, **17**, 197–205.

Sowden, S. and Keeves, J. (1990) 'Analysis of evidence in humanistic studies.' In *International Encyclopedia of Educational Evaluation*. Oxford: Pergamon Press.

Spielgelberg, H. (1970) 'On some human uses of phenomenology.' In F. Smith (ed.) *Phenomenology in Perspective*. The Hague: Martinus Nijhoff.

Spinelli, E. (1989) *The Interpreted World: An Introduction to Phenomenological Psychology*. Newbury Park, CA: Sage.

Svensson, L. (1985) 'Contextual analysis – the development of a research approach.' Paper presented to the Second Conference on Qualitative Research in Psychology, Leusden, The Netherlands.

Taylor, B. (1993) 'Phenomenology: one way to understand nursing practice.' *International Journal of Nursing Studies*, **30** (2), 171–9.

Tesch, R. (1990) *Qualitative Research: Analysis Types and Software Tools*. Lewes: Falmer.

Tschudi, F. (1989) 'Do qualitative and quantitative methods require different approaches to validity?' In S. Kvale (ed.) *Issues of Validity in Qualitative Research*. Lund: Studentlitteratur.

Tuan, Y. (1971) 'Geography, phenomenology and the study of human nature.' *Canadian Geographer*, **15**, 181–92.

van Manen, M. (1990) *Researching Lived Experience*. London, Ontario: The Althouse Press.

Vygotsky, L. (1978) *Mind in Society: The Development of Higher Psychological Processes*. Cambridge, MA: Harvard University Press.

Chapter 3

The Critical Tradition in Research in Geographical and Environmental Education Research

John Fien and John Hillcoat

> A paradigm is a worldview, a general perspective, a way of breaking down the complexity of the real world. As such, paradigms are deeply embedded in the socialization of adherents and practitioners. Paradigms tell them what is important, legitimate, and reasonable. Paradigms are also normative, telling the practitioner what to do without the necessity of long existential or epistemological consideration. But it is this aspect of paradigms that constitutes both their strength and their weakness – their strength in that it makes action possible, and their weakness in that the very reason for action is hidden in the unquestioned assumption of the paradigm.
>
> (Patton, 1990, p. 37)

The paradigm upon which a research methodology is based is often not seen as important because the logic and precision of the scientific method allow research to be independent of ideology. However, research methodologies are very much a puppet of their underlying assumptions. Lather (1989, p. 12) suggests that ideology and methodology share characteristics:

> each is concerned with the creation of consensus, of shared meaning within a particular community; each focuses on how to go about constructing and supporting explanations; each is prescriptive in terms of establishing a reliable foundation for our understanding of social reality; each is concerned with validation; each is enforced.

The outcome of these underlying assumptions is significant as they 'prefigure what is to count as appropriate research topics, appropriate research questions, and even appropriate research outcomes' (Robottom and Hart, 1993, p. 18). Therefore, the precision and rigour of research methods do not allow them to escape the influence of the paradigm which legitimates them. As LeCourt declares, 'the role of ideology does not diminish as rigour increases and error is dissipated' (quoted by Lather, 1989, p. 13).

Research paradigms determine whether research assists in the maintenance of the *status quo* in society or helps to transform the dominant social paradigm. As a result, it is important to examine the politics of the different research paradigms which were introduced in Chapter 1 – the positivist, interpretivist and critical paradigms. This is done in the first section of this chapter. The second section examines the 'logics in use' of critical research, with an emphasis upon three principles of procedure necessary for quality educational research. Before the conclusion, this chapter briefly explores three critical research methods that may be used by geographical and environmental education researchers: discourse analysis, critical ethnography and action research.

THE POLITICS OF RESEARCH PARADIGMS

Electing to use one or the other of the three major research paradigms introduced in Chapter 1 represents a political choice on the part of the researcher. However, only the critical research paradigm has an explicit political emphasis. The political agendas of positivist and interpretive research are generally implicit and thus remain hidden from view as unacknowledged assumptions of the researcher, the research process and the research outcomes.

The positivist research paradigm views reality as existing outside the human being. Acquiring knowledge is seen as a process of gathering information that is independent of the researcher. This leads to the notion that knowledge is objective, generalizable and predictable. As a result, it is claimed that the use of appropriate methods can minimize or eliminate researcher bias and allow the undertaking of value-free research. In this tradition, educational research is conducted mainly using quantitative methods based on statistical techniques. These methods involve formulating and testing hypotheses and using probability to gauge the generalizability of the results obtained from a sample to the population being studied.

Instrumental rationality is a key underlying assumption of positivist research. This technicist approach to social life is reflected in a number of features of contemporary western society, the pervasiveness of which is testimony to the influence of positivism in preserving the established order. Characteristics of instrumental rationality embedded in the positivist research paradigm include reductionism, a preoccupation with means over ends, the separation of facts and values, prioritizing pragmatism over ethics, and a desire to measure, manipulate, predict and control.

The interpretivist research paradigm has a very different set of underlying assumptions to the positivist paradigm. Schwandt (1994: 18) proposes that the goal of interpretive research is:

> ... an abiding concern for the life world, for the emic point of view, for understanding meaning, for grasping an actor's definition of a situation ... The world of lived reality and situation-specific meanings that constitute the general object of investigation is thought to be constructed by social actors. That is, particular actors, at particular times, fashion meaning out of events and phenomena through prolonged, complex processes of social interaction involving history, language, and action.

Therefore, the view of reality for the positivist is radically different from that of the interpretivist. The former views reality as external to the individual whereas the latter maintains that reality is internally constructed. The interpretivist challenges the positivist on a number of points. First, it is claimed that positivist research is not value-free as its proponents maintain. Secondly, the notion that research can establish theories of human behaviour to be used for general prediction purposes is false. Researchers in the interpretive tradition argue that human behaviour is too diverse and complex to be described through generalizations and theories. Interpretivists maintain that human behaviour is situation-specific and that any attempt to systematize human behaviour will give rise to incomplete and unreliable knowledge.

Probability, hypotheses and statistical techniques have little relevance for interpretive research. Consequently, its results cannot be generalized and replicated. Research methods in the interpretivist paradigm place value on the thorough exploration of meaning in a specific context. Thus, they can assist the researcher in understanding 'reality' within a particular context. Additionally, although interpretive data are not replicable, there is still scope for general principles and themes to be transferred to other settings.

Advocates of the critical paradigm agree with the interpretivist critique of the positivist paradigm. However, critical researchers maintain that the interpretive paradigm does not take into account the fact that our subjective views are not only internally constructed but also influenced by persuasive social forces. In other words, individuals or groups cannot be considered separately from their societal context. The critical perspective entails a commitment to socially transformative research for the common good of individuals within society. Robottom and Hart (1993, pp. 15–16) state:

> Critical theory has been described as ideologically orientated inquiry ... becoming critical means exposing one's ideological bases, penetrating one's ideological assumptions through critique. Whereas 'critical' can mean internal criticism from the perspective of analytical questioning of argument and method, it can also mean developing a conception of reality that ties ideas, thought, and language to social and historical conditions; that is, social criticism based on notions of power and control.... these meanings [are combined] so that becoming critical means developing an analytic posture toward arguments, procedures and language using a lens related to issues of power and control in relationships and developing an action-orientated commitment to common welfare.

Researchers advocating the critical paradigm use critical reflection or reflexivity to be openly ideological in their approach. This provides the means by which they can ask searching questions about the *status quo*. As a result, the critical perspective is the only research methodology which seeks to transform the dominant social paradigm.

Critical theory and critical research

The adjective 'critical' has a negative connotation for many people. However, in social theory, 'critical' relates to the work of the Frankfurt School of critical theorists, who sought to develop roles for researchers as critics of oppressive social structures and as advocates of egalitarian social change. This emancipatory sense is the meaning intended when people speak of critical education and critical research. Three key questions to be answered in this chapter are: 'What is a critical approach to educational research?'; 'Why is one important for researchers in geographical education and environmental education?'; and 'What forms does such research take?'

Gibson (1986) asked a similar set of questions when he inquired, 'Why should teachers be interested in critical theory?' He answered his question by arguing that critical theory 'addresses itself to questions which are of vital concern to all teachers' such as:

> Why do some children persistently fail in school? Why are some pupils so unmotivated and so difficult in the classroom? Why do we teach what we do? Why are schools organised as they are? These are urgent and familiar questions.

(Gibson, 1986, p. 2)

Critical theory not only provides a framework for answering important questions such as these; even more importantly, it directs teachers towards an analysis of the causes and consequences of the problems encompassed in the questions and towards a range of possible solutions. Gibson continues his case for a critical theory of education by arguing that:

> Critical theory attempts to explain the origins of everyday practices and problems, but it goes further. It claims to offer replies to those awkward questions which ask what should be done. What should be the relationship between teacher and pupil, teacher and teacher? What should be taught? How should schools or classrooms be organised? Critical theory is not simply explanatory, but is committed to enabling change towards better relationships, towards a more just and rational society. In identifying the biases and distortions which prevent healthy personal and social growth, it helps teachers to free themselves and their pupils from those malforming constraints. In asserting that individuals and groups should be in control of their own lives, it has as its goal that people should be able to determine their own destinies.
>
> (Gibson, 1986, p. 2)

Thus, critical curriculum theorizing is based on a view of education as a *critical social science*. Fay (1987) defines critical social science as an attempt to understand the oppressive features of a society in a rationally responsible and scientifically respectable manner, and in such a way that this understanding stimulates people to want to transform society and emancipate themselves and others. Fay outlines three related objectives for critical social science: scientific understanding, social critique and social transformation. Thus, he argues that critical social science:

> seeks a theory which will simultaneously *explain* the social world, *criticize* it, and *empower* its audience to overthrow it. Thus, such a theory needs not only to be able to reveal how a particular social order functions, but also to show the ways it is fundamentally unsatisfactory to those who live in it, and to do both of these things in such a manner that it itself becomes the moving force helping to transform this order into something radically different.
>
> (Fay, 1987, p. 23, italics in original)

A critical social science approach to an area of social life such as educational research would be *scientific, critical* and *practical*, as a result of these three goals. It would be scientific because it would seek to provide comprehensive explanations subject to public, empirical evidence; it would be critical in its unmasking and analysis of the structures of oppression which hinder educational reform; and it would be practical in the sense of providing teachers and other educational stakeholders, such as students and parents, with the sorts of understanding, skill and motivation they need to bring about desired changes.

Thus, critical educational research is not value-free. Indeed, as Lather (1986a, 1986b) argues, it is openly ideological and exposes as false the claims to neutrality and objectivity in positivist and interpretive approaches to research. Critical educational research is grounded in a vision of social change and democratic values, in that it seeks to empower teachers and students to participate in programmes of research – and also of curriculum development and professional development – that claim to have them as beneficiaries. Thus, critical approaches to research recognize that educational research is 'a value-constituted and value-constituting enterprise, no more outside the power/knowledge nexus than any other human creation' (Lather, 1991, p. 27). Consequently, 'just as there is no neutral education ..., there can be no neutral research' (Lather, 1986a, p. 257). Acknowledging this situation, Carew and Lightfoot (1979,

p. 23) argue that educational researchers are 'not merely the lens of a camera' but 'selective interpreters of the classroom scene':

> No matter how quantitative and objective the research strategy appears, there is a point when researchers offer their interpretations, use their intuitions, and apply their values. Research, therefore, is a selective process that combines empirical data, rational thinking, judgment, and intuition. Each of these modes of understanding and analysing phenomena are valid and valuable and can be made conscious parts of the research process.

The supposed objectivity of positivist and interpretive research has been critiqued by many other writers besides Lather and Carew and Lightfoot (e.g. Bredo and Feinberg, 1982; Feinberg, 1983; Atkinson and Delamont, 1985; Carr and Kemmis, 1986). Fien (1992) has traced the dominance of positivism within the international geographical education research community, and has been critical of the 'external expert' role adopted by researchers, the disempowerment of teacher-participants, the lack of a self-reflective stance on research, the political conservatism and the apparent blindness to ideology that pervade so much research in geographical education. In its place, he has recommended that research and curriculum development in geographical education be integrated through programmes of professional development, in which university researchers act as research assistants and facilitators for teacher-researchers. There had been no response to these arguments from geographical education researchers at the time of writing (February 1995). However, debates over research philosophy are a vibrant aspect of the international environmental education research community and have led to the publication of a 400-page edited collection from a research symposium (Mrazek, 1993) and a book on *Research in Environmental Education: Engaging the Debate* (Robottom and Hart, 1993).

The debate within environmental education between established positivist interests (which controlled the editorship of the flagship *Journal of Environmental Education* for many years) and their critics has led to the demand that researchers in environmental education – and geographical education for that matter – should be explicit about the values which guide the research process. Hesse (1980, p. 247) summarized this position by arguing that 'The attempt to produce value-neutral social science is increasingly being abandoned as at best unrealizable, and at worst self-deceptive, and is being replaced by social sciences based upon explicit ideologies.'

The values or interests that guide critical educational research are located in the traditions of critical social science outlined above (Carr and Kemmis, 1986; Carr, 1989). They are also within a range of poststructural philosophies and approaches, including feminism and critical semiotics. However, an indication of the vibrancy within this alternative or 'new paradigm' research community is the critique of critical theory, especially by feminist researchers, that has been sustained throughout the 1990s. Indeed, Lather (1992) and others such as Denzin and Lincoln (1994) have sought to establish post-structural approaches to research as a distinct research paradigm.

THE 'LOGICS IN USE' OF CRITICAL RESEARCH

Whatever philosophical position is taken, acknowledging that the research process and the interests that guide a particular study are value-laden does not negate the need for rigorous standards in the selection, justification and use of particular research procedures or in the validity and reliability of data, interpretations and conclusions.

The nature of the standards and criteria for validity and reliability may be different for different research methodologies and methods. Nevertheless, each has its own 'logics in use' which must be followed. Howe and Eisenhart (1990, pp. 6–8) list three principles of procedure that may be followed to help ensure that appropriate standards in educational research are maintained. These include:

1. an understanding of the values and background assumptions that underlie the research methodology;
2. congruity between research philosophy and method; that is, between the research objectives and questions and the research design;
3. the effective application of specific data collection and analysis techniques.

These three criteria for research standards are used as a framework to structure the ideas presented in this chapter and recurring in Chapters 12 and 13. The first and third criteria are discussed first, as a basis for outlining the variety of research methods used by critical researchers to link their research philosophy or methodology with their research designs (the second criterion). This sequence of ideas provides an immediate link between the introduction to critical research methods in the final sections of this chapter and Chapters 4, 5, 10 and 11, which focus on related research methods.

Understanding the assumptions underlying critical methodology

Research methodology is described by van Manen (1990) as the philosophical framework which guides any research activity; it is the paradigm or tradition within which the research problem is framed and which guides the selection of research objectives, and consequent data-gathering and analysis techniques. It thus comprises 'the fundamental assumptions' about 'the general orientation to life, the view of knowledge, and the sense of what it means to be human' that direct the particular mode or method of inquiry in a study (van Manen, 1990, p. 27). Carr and Kemmis (1986) describe critical educational research as 'critical' in the sense in which Marx wrote of 'criticism':

> we do not anticipate the world dogmatically, but rather wish to find the new world through criticism of the old; ... even though the construction of the future and its completion for all times is not our task, what we have to accomplish at this time is all the more clear: *relentless criticism of all existing conditions*, relentless in the sense that the criticism is not afraid of its findings and just as little afraid of conflict with the powers that be.
>
> (italics in original; quoted in Carr and Kemmis, 1986, p. 137–8)

The link between criticism of existing social conditions and empowerment for social change implied in this definition is reflected in Fay's case for a critical social science. In contrast with positivist and interpretive research, which uncritically endorses existing social conditions, Fay (1987, p. 23) argues that there is a need for an approach to research:

> which will not only be scientific, but which will also be critical of current practices and institutions in the sense of showing them to be ... based on a false understanding of human need and possibility. It will also be one which has practical power to lead to social revolution on the basis of enlightening people as to their true nature ..., and thereby ... provide the means by which the salvation of the human race can be effected.

In an earlier work, Fay (1977) outlined some of the practical characteristics of a critical approach to research. These include being 'clearly rooted in concrete social experience' and arising from, and seeking to address, the life problems of individuals and groups; identifying with the subjects of research by 'naming' those for whom it is directed and seeking their enlightenment from false consciousness; uncovering the social processes that create and maintain their problems; and providing strategies by which such processes may be challenged. Fay (1977, p. 109) summarized these features of critical research when he wrote that it 'arises out of the problems of everyday life and is constructed with an eye towards solving them'.

The concept of critical social science has several implications when applied to educational research. These have been explored in depth by a number of writers (e.g. Comstock, 1982; Carr and Kemmis, 1986; Grundy, 1987). Carr and Kemmis (1986, pp. 129–30, 179–80) have identified five implications of relevance to research in geographical education and environmental education. They argue that critical education research should:

1. eschew positivist notions of rationality, objectivity and truth in favour of a dialectical view of rationality;
2. be grounded in the experiences and interpretations of teachers and other participants in the educational process;
3. distinguish ideologically distorted interpretations in teachers' understandings of their experiences (instances of false consciousness) from those that are not;
4. identify aspects of the existing social order that frustrate the attainment of critical educational goals;
5. integrate theory and practice by providing a language and strategies for action to address false consciousness and obstructions to critical pedagogy, and also by providing support for teachers who wish to engage in further critical reflection and action.

These characteristics establish three tasks for the critical educational researcher: understanding, ideology critique and educative action (Deetz and Kersten, 1983). *Understanding* provides descriptions of the social experience being researched from the perspective of insiders, that is, those with whom the research is being conducted. Thus, critical inquiry has a base in the naturalistic inquiry of interpretive ethnography and case study research. However, *ideology critique* questions the legitimacy of naturalistic descriptions of experience and seeks to uncover the ideological processes of hegemony that may distort participants' understandings of their experience. As Sharp (1982, pp. 63–4) notes of interpretive ethnography:

> Such a perspective overlooks the fact that social beings are born into and are socially constituted by a world already made, that structured patterns of social relations already preexist the individual and generate specific forms of social consciousness, generate linguistic and hence cognitive possibilities, and socially structure available life chances, technical means, and facilities. In other words, there is a level of social reality, *sui generis*, which is existentially independent of consciousness and which must form part of the object of any science wishing to understand human behavior.

However, critical research does not accept the crude Marxist determinism that might be concluded from this position (as in Reynolds, 1980–1). Rather, it seeks to make problematic those aspects of experience that are often taken for granted, as normal or natural, in order to uncover layers of meaning that are not normally part of human consciousness. Thus, Cornbleth (1990, p. 55) argues that educational research should adopt a critical perspective on experience:

> our inquiries ought to probe beneath the veneer of supposedly self-evident and self-justifying assumptions and practices and enable us to expose contradictions and possibilities inherent in historically- and culturally-formed school circumstances. Such inquiry is necessarily inter-pretive as well as material, incorporating participant conceptions and acknowledging our own values. What is called for, then, is inquiry that is sensitive to context and contradiction, including meanings to participants, and critical of prevailing school practices and illusions that impede realization of human potential and social justice.

Thus, ideology critique is undertaken for the two related goals of ideological enlighten-ment and empowerment for emancipation. *Educational action* develops from these goals to foster the capacity of all participants in the research process to engage in self-renewal through participating in educational practices that are free and unrestrained.

Putting these three features of critical research together, Fay (1987, p. 74) has described the purpose of critical research as fostering 'the emergence of people who know who they are and are conscious of themselves as active and deciding beings, who bear responsibility for their choices and who are able to explain them in terms of their own freely adopted purposes and ideals'. Thus, critical educational researchers recognize that their work is 'politically charged' as they seek to 'define, control, evaluate, manipu-late and report' (Lather, 1991, p. 12).

Research techniques and their application

The third of Howe and Eisenhart's (1990) principles for maintaining standards in educa-tional research involves the effective application of specific data collection and analysis techniques. However, as well as being effectively applied, research techniques need to be congruent with research methodology and method. This is because research tech-niques 'emerge from a theoretical position and therefore reflect values, beliefs and dispositions towards the social world' (Popkewitz, 1978, p. 29).

The dialectical relationship between data collection and analysis in critical research makes describing research techniques a complex undertaking. This situation is made more complex by the 'openly ideological' nature of critical research processes. Angus (1986, p. 72) argues that 'no sensible distinction between theory and data' is possible in critical ethnography because the 'generation of data through observation and partic-ipation involves selection and interpretation that must reflect judgements that are theoretically based'. 'Text' is a term that may be used to describe data generated and interpreted within a particular theoretical framework or discourse. This section provides a brief introduction to the techniques used in the generation and interpretation of text in critical research. They are derived primarily from other qualitative research methods.

The generation of text

There are three primary techniques for collecting data in critical research: observing behaviour, listening to informants and studying documents. These techniques generate 'text' which can be 'read' in order to produce explanatory understanding. This is a postmodernist interpretation of speech and action as a 'text-analogue' (Hoy, 1990, p. 52). Thus, speech and action provide 'social signs which can be read, [or] signs which indicate ... a number of things are happening in any social situation' (Gore, 1990, p. 103).

An important element of the generation of text is the role of the researcher. As Kirk (1989, p. 48) notes, 'the curriculum inquirer is an active agent in both the production and reproduction of the curriculum process.' This means that critical researchers must adopt a reflexive approach to the effects of their actions on the experiences of others during research. The researcher cannot enter a teacher's world purely as an observer, a 'lens of a camera' (Carew and Lightfoot, 1979, p. 23). Clandinin (1985, p. 365) argues for an interactive research process in which, 'Inevitably, the data collected reflects my own participation in the classroom and my own personal practical knowledge colors the interpretations offered. The research process is, accordingly, an interactive, dialectical one.' Thus, the text that emerges from the process of working with a teacher is a shared one in which '[n]either the teacher nor the researcher emerges unchanged' (Clandinin, 1985, p. 365). Accordingly, Bartlett (1989, p. 24) describes the role of the researcher in the generation of text as that of a co-equal co-respondent participant in the research, responsible for action as much as any other participant in the research'.

The interpretation of text

Critical research differs from research in the interpretive tradition in that it does not make a hard distinction between data, interpretation and theory. In interpretive ethnography, theory is seen as being derived from data whereas, in critical ethnography, theory and data are seen as a duality, in 'an essential dialectical interplay' (Angus, 1986, p. 72). Concepts and theories from critical theory are used to organize both the collection and the interpretation of data in the generation of text. The text is then analysed within a critical theoretical framework which (1) provides insights which guide the further collection of data, and (2) allows for comparison and contrast and for the reflexive development and redevelopment of theory. This process has two implications for research design.

First, the interplay of theory and data necessitates researchers being conscious that research is a reflexive act. It must incorporate sensitivity to the influence of the research process upon oneself and participants and, above all, integrity in the generation of text and its interpretation to arrive at the conclusions of the study.

Secondly, it means that critical research designs do not follow a predetermined sequence of data collection followed by analysis. The theory-driven nature of critical research means that the initial analysis, classification and organization of data often takes place during the fieldwork itself. Indeed, there is a cyclical relationship (often with numerous feedback loops) between the initial theorizing, data collection and the preliminary analysis of data, which guides the refinement of the research questions, the possible determination of research directions, and decisions about when to extend or end data collection. As a result, critical researchers need to be open to issues in the development of the study, with the research design evolving as the participants and the researcher gain experience and insights into the processes being investigated.

LINKING RESEARCH METHODOLOGY AND METHOD

'Research method' is the term used to describe the portfolio of data collection and analysis techniques that is used to operationalize a particular research methodology. Three major research methods employed by critical educational researchers are:

1. discourse analysis;
2. critical ethnography;
3. action research.

The differences between them may be identified by the relative emphasis given to the three tasks of understanding, critique and action outlined above as the three tasks of the critical educational researcher. The focus of discourse analysis is critique and involves the sustained deconstruction of ideas, educational materials and pedagogical actions. The focus of critical ethnography is both understanding and critique. Action research is characterized by a focus on all three tasks: understanding, critique and action.

Two of these research methods, action research and discourse analysis, are defined further in Chapters 12 and 13. These chapters also provide case examples of the respective research methods and outline particular issues which researchers seeking to use them in geographical education and environmental education research might note.

Discourse analysis

Discourse analysis is a form of deconstruction. The methods grouped under this broad title are based on the assumption that an individual's world view is socially constructed. Thus the chief goal of discourse analysis is to reveal the ways in which a world view, or ideology, is constructed through text. Succesful discourse analysis offers opportunities to highlight the processes by which meanings are generated and value-laden. The process of 'critical reading' may serve as an emancipatory activity for researchers, and for those who use the research.

Critical ethnography

An emphasis on understanding and critique in research is characteristic of the research method of critical ethnography (e.g. Angus, 1986; Anderson, 1989; Carspecken, 1991; Quantz, 1992; Kinchloe and McLaren, 1994). Critical ethnography is a form of 'theoretically sensitive ethnography' (Kirk, 1989, p. 8). In education, it extends the purpose of naturalistic inquiry – that of providing interpretive accounts of human experience – through 'a closer examination of how the historically shaped human subject creates not only the social world, but also the theories, conceptions and understandings of it' (Thomas, 1982, p. 132). Thus, critical ethnography is theory-driven and takes the basically phenomenological approaches of interpretive ethnography, usually within the theoretical frameworks of critical social science (Maseman, 1982, p. 1). As Kickbusch (1984, pp. 100–1) argues, it is a research approach:

> which combines social phenomenology with a critical perspective, a theory of social totality, an approach which identifies the context within which school meanings are negotiated

and which permits analysis of meanings beyond the level of consciousness. Although descriptive studies of the phenomenology of schooling are illuminating, by merely dwelling at the level of [teachers'] consciousness we ignore the inner mechanisms of reproduction and transformation.

Such an approach is sensitive to the structuring of action and, according to Sharp and Green (1975, p. 25), has the potential to transcend false consciousness and help researchers to develop a 'sociology of situations, their underlying structure and interconnections, and the constraints and contingencies they impose'.

Nevertheless, critical ethnographers in education do respect the experiences and interpretations of those with whom they are working. They recognize the power of teachers' 'language of practice', which is often embodied in thought and action rather than speech but which, nevertheless, provides 'clues to the way they organise their world' (Yinger, 1987, p. 314).

Critical ethnography in education seeks to provide research accounts that are sensitive not only to the experiences of teachers and students but also to 'the dialectical relationship between the social structural constraints on human actors and the relative autonomy of human agency' (Anderson, 1989, p. 249). According to Angus (1986, p. 66), critical ethnography is based on:

> an ongoing awareness of the fundamental human agency of social actors while simultaneously remaining aware that the subjective consciousness of individuals may conceal underlying structural relationships which are capable of distorting and limiting, or of enhancing and enabling, negotiated systems of meanings.

Action research

'Action research' is a name for a group of research techniques which seek to bring about change as a direct result of the research process. This is the third, the educative action element, of critical research, which seeks both research outcomes and action outcomes. While the research outcome is often in the form of enriched understanding by those involved, the action outcome is not pragmatic action for its own sake, but purposeful action that follows from a deep, critical and empathetic understanding of a given situation.

Tripp (1990) argues that the two key elements of action research, 'reflection' and 'action', need to be carefully explained if the distinctiveness of critical action research is to be maintained. First, he argues that the conscious analysis or reflection stage of action research distinguishes it from the casual 'plan, act, sense and re-plan' cycle by which we operate in everyday life. The difference lies in the 'strategic action' that flows from critical reflection:

> The difference is that action research is conscious and deliberate, a characteristic that leads to strategic action. Strategic action involves action based on understanding that results from *rational analysis of research quality information*, in contrast to action that is a result of habit, instinct, opinion, or mere whim on the one level, and irrelevant, subjective, or incomplete knowledge on the other.
>
> (emphasis added; Tripp, 1990, p. 159)

Secondly, he argues that critical action research becomes 'critical' when it focuses on the social context and social effects of teaching, and engages the teacher in acting to change the material or ideological contexts of his or her work to produce 'forms of consciousness and practice that would not have been available within the initial situation or practice' (p. 164). A quotation from Tripp (1990, p. 163), but changing his English teaching example to a geography teaching one,[1] illustrates this important dimension of critical action research:

> Teachers' projects become socially critical when they become aware of the social implications of their practice and begin to work on those ... For instance, a teacher found that, although she wanted her students to display the results of their research into overpackaging in the local supermarket foyer, she shied away from public involvement. Her immediate response was to ask, 'How can I change what I'm doing to better achieve my theoretical aims in my practice?' That was a practical response with no social elements or dimensions: it was simply about how to do something better.

Tripp (1990, p. 162) would argue that a critical range of action research questions in this example would include some of the following:

- Why is there such a gap between my aims in teaching and their implementation?
- Why has my teaching come to take its present form? Is the neglect of student social action characteristic of other aspects of my approach to teaching? If it is, how did this form of teaching become a habit?
- How long has it taken me to realize this concern? Why? How did I come to recognize the problem now?
- Why did the students not insist on a public display of their work?

Smyth (1987, p. 158) adds the following questions as examples of issues for critical action research:

- Where do my ideas about teaching/learning come from historically?
- How did I come to appropriate these ideas?
- What social and cultural conditions cause me to continue to endorse the ideas I hold about teaching/learning?
- Whose interests do my ideas actually serve?
- What power interests between myself and students are expressed in my teaching practices?
- Do my practices accommodate to the dominant ideology?
- How do I encourage resistance by those who are oppressed?
- In view of this, are there grounds for radically changing the way I teach?

Such questions involve problematizing taken-for-granted assumptions and practices within a critical framework. Addressing the constraints on good teaching practice through action research involves not only 'collecting good research data, and planning and implementing a change in practice [or context]' but also 'evaluating the possibilities according to some idea of what is "good" in terms of increasing social justice' (Tripp, 1990, p. 162).

CONCLUSION

The chief attraction of critical research approaches for those wishing to understand geographical and environmental education is that they represent research methods to apply oneself. Protagonists of positivist research identify its value in their power to generalize across educational situations, while supporters of interpretivist research claim validity for it in its potential to serve as a mirror for other practitioners. In so doing, both positivist and interpretivist groups of researchers define a boundary between those who do research and those who consume it. Critical research tolerates no such boundary and, in its focus on identifying and overcoming the barriers to progressive educational change, provides a range of methods for practitioners in geographical and environmental education to take control of research processes for themselves.

Wideen and Andrews (1987, p. 77) describe teachers as critical researchers when they become:

> interested in systematic, concrete and particular examination of their own practices, under-standings and situations, which become the subject and the object of their critical reflection; and systematically changing their practice is one of the primary means by which they act to change the situations in which they work.

Carr (1989, p. 33) describes research of this type as 'liberatory', as it empowers particip-ant researchers to resist manipulation by 'enlightening' them, through personal inquiry, reflection and action, as to the ideological roots of their existing purposes, beliefs, actions and contexts of work. Such enlightenment, he argues, can 'empower' them to think and act in more rational and autonomous ways.

In their book *Reclaiming the Classroom: Teacher Research as an Agency for Change*, Goswami and Stillman (1987) list the following five benefits for educational practi-tioners of adopting the overt role of critical researcher:

1. Their teaching can be transformed in important ways: they can become theorists, articulating their intentions, testing their assumptions, and finding connections with practice.
2. Their perceptions of themselves as writers and teachers can be transformed. They can step up their use of resources, form networks, and become more active profes-sionally.
3. They can become rich resources who can provide the profession with information it simply does not have. After all, teachers know their classrooms and students in ways that outsiders cannot – and they can observe closely, over long periods of time, with special insights and knowledge.
4. They can become critical, responsive readers and users of current research, less apt to accept uncritically others' theories, less vulnerable to fads, and more authoritative in their assessment of curricula, methods and materials.
5. They collaborate with their students to answer questions important to both, drawing on community resources in new and unexpected ways.

These are five benefits which positivist and interpretivist research cannot provide.

NOTES

1. Tripp's original example was of a teacher who wanted her students to write the class diary in their own words.

REFERENCES

Anderson, G.L. (1989) 'Critical ethnography in education: origins, current status, and new directions.' *Review of Educational Research*, **59** (3), 249–70.

Angus, L.B. (1986) 'Research traditions, ideology and critical ethnography.' *Discourse*, **7** (1), 61–77.

Atkinson, P. and Delamont, S. (1985) 'Bread and dreams or bread and circuses? A critique of "case study" research in education.' In M. Shipman (ed.) *Educational Research: Principles, Policies and Practices*. Lewes: Falmer.

Bartlett, V.L. (1989) 'In the beginning: text, context and pupil-attention in initial classroom encounters.' Unpublished PhD thesis, University of Queensland.

Bredo, E. and Feinberg, W. (1982) 'The critical approach to social and educational research.' In E. Bredo and W. Feinberg (eds) *Knowledge and Values in Social and Educational Research*. Philadelphia, PA: Temple University Press.

Carew, J.V. and Lightfoot, S.L. (1979) *Beyond Bias: Perspectives on Classrooms*. Cambridge, MA: Harvard University Press.

Carr, W. (1989) 'The idea of an educational science.' *Journal of Philosophy of Education*, **23** (1), 29–37.

Carr, W. and Kemmis, S. (1986) *Becoming Critical: Education, Knowledge and Action Research*. Lewes: Falmer.

Carspecken, P. (1991) 'Critical ethnography in educational research.' *Critical Pedagogy Networker*, **4** (3), 1–4.

Clandinin, D.J. (1985) 'Personal practical knowledge: a study of teachers' classroom images.' *Curriculum Inquiry*, **15** (4), 361–85.

Comstock, D.E. (1982) 'A method for critical research.' In E. Bredo and W. Feinberg (eds) *Knowledge and Values in Social and Educational Research*. Philadelphia, PA: Temple University Press.

Cornbleth, C. (1990) *Curriculum in Context*. Lewes: Falmer.

Deetz, S.A. and Kersten, A. (1983) 'Critical models of interpretive research.' In L.L. Patnam and M.E. Pacanowsky (eds) *Communication and Organizations: An Interpretive Approach*. Beverley Hills, CA: Sage.

Denzin, N.K. and Lincoln, Y.S. (1994) *Handbook of Qualitative Research*. Beverley Hills: Sage.

Fay, B. (1977) *Social Theory and Political Practice*. London: George Allen and Unwin.

Fay, B. (1987) *Critical Social Science*. London: Polity.

Feinberg, W. (1983) *Understanding Education: Toward a Reconstruction of Educational Inquiry*. Cambridge: Cambridge University Press.

Fien, J. (1992) 'What kind of research for what kind of teaching? Towards research in geographical education as a critical social science.' In D. Hill (ed) *International Perspectives on Geographic Education*. Boulder, CO: Centre for Geographic Education. University of Colorado at Boulder.

Gibson, R. (1986) *Critical Theory and Education*. London: Hodder and Stoughton.

Gore, J (1990) 'Pedagogy as text in physical education teacher education: beyond the preferred reading.' In D. Colquhoun and D. Kirk (eds) *Physical Education, Curriculum and Culture*. Lewes: Falmer.

Goswami, D. and Stillman, P.R. (eds) (1987) *Reclaiming the Classroom: Teacher Research as Agency for Change*. Upper Montclair, NJ: Boynton/Cook.

Grundy, S. (1987) *Curriculum: Product or Praxis?* Lewes: Falmer.

Hesse, M. (1980) *Revolution and Reconstruction in the Philosophy of Science*. Bloomington, IN: Indiana University Press.

Howe, K. and Eisenhart, M. (1990) 'Standards for qualitative and quantitative research: a prolegomenon.' *Educational Researcher*, **19** (4), 2–9.

Hoy, D. (1990) 'Jacques Derrida. In Q. Skinner (ed.) *The Return of Grand Theory in the Human Sciences*. Cambridge: Cambridge University Press.

Kickbusch, K.W. (1984) 'Curriculum-in-use and the emergence of practical ideology: a comparative study of secondary classrooms.' *Journal of Curriculum Theorizing*, **6** (4), 98–143.

Kinchloe, J. and McLaren, P. (1994) 'Rethinking critical theory and qualitative research.' In N. Denzin and Y. Lincoln (eds) *Handbook of Qualitative Research*. Thousand Oaks, CA: Sage.

Kirk, D. (1989) 'Curriculum research and educational praxis.' *Curriculum Perspectives*, **9** (4), 41–50.

Lather, P. (1986a) 'Research as praxis.' *Harvard Educational Review*, **56** (3), 257–77.

Lather, P. (1986b) 'Issues of validity in openly ideological research: between a rock and a soft place.' *Interchange*, **17** (4), 63–84.

Lather, P. (1989) 'Ideology and methodological attitude.' *Journal of Critical Theorising*, **9** (2), 7–26.

Lather, P. (1991) *Feminist Research in Education: Within/Against*. Geelong: Deakin University Press.

Lather, P. (1992) 'Critical frames in educational research: feminist and post-structural perspectives.' *Theory into Practice*, **XXXI** (2), 87–99.

Maseman, V.L. (1982) 'Critical ethnography in the study of comparative education.' *Comparative Education Review*, **26** (1), 1–15.

Mrazek, R. (ed.) (1993) *Alternative Paradigms in Environmental Education Research*. Troy, OH: NAAEE.

Patton, M.Q. (1990) *Qualitative Evaluation and Research Methods. 2nd edn*. Beverley Hills, CA: Sage.

Popkewitz, T.S. (1978) 'Educational research: values and vision of social order.' *Theory and Research in Social Education*, **6**, 20–39.

Quantz, R. (1992) 'On critical ethnography (with some postmodern considerations).' In M. LeCompte, W. Millroy and J. Preissle (eds) *The Handbook of Qualitative Research in Education*. San Diego: Academic Press.

Reynolds, D. (1980–1) 'The naturalistic method and educational and social research: a Marxist critique.' *Interchange*, **11** (4), 77–89.

Robottom, I. and Hart, P. (1993) *Research in Environmental Education: Engaging the Debate*. Geelong: Deakin University.

Schwandt, T.A. (1994) 'Constructivist, interpretivist approaches to human inquiry'. In N.K. Denzin and Y.S. Lincoln (eds) *Handbook of Qualitative Research*. Thousand Oaks: Sage Publications.

Sharp, R. (1982) 'Self-contained ethnography or a science of phenomenal forms and inner relations.' *Journal of Education*, **164**, (1), 48–63.

Sharp, R. and Green, A. (1975) *Education and Social Control*. London: Routledge and Kegan Paul.

Smyth, J. (1987) 'Transforming teaching through intellectualizing the work of teachers.' In J. Smyth (ed.) *Educating Teachers: Changing the Nature of Pedagogical Knowledge*. Lewes: Falmer.

Tripp, D. (1990) 'Socially critical action research,' *Theory into Practice*, **29** (3), 158–66.

Thomas, J. (1982) 'Review of praxis and method: A sociological dialogue with Lukacs, Gramsci and the early Frankfurt School by Richard Kilminster', *Urban Life*, **11** (1), 129–32.

van Manen, M. (1990) *Researching Lived Experience: Human Science for an Action Sensitive Pedagogy*. Albany, NY: State University of New York Press.

Wideen, F. and Andrews, I (1987) *Staff Development for School Improvement: A Focus on the Teacher*. Lewes: Falmer.

Yinger, R. (1987) 'Learning the language of practice.' *Curriculum Inquiry*, **17** (3), 293–318.

Chapter 4

Cross-cultural Approaches in Geographical and Environmental Education

Philip Stimpson

> Now Somers was English by blood and education, and though he had no antecedents what-
> soever, yet he felt himself to be one of the responsible members of society as contrasted
> with the innumerable irresponsible members. In old, cultured, ethical England that distinc-
> tion is radical between the responsible members of society and the irresponsible ... It is a
> caste distinction ... between the proletariat and the ruling classes.
>   But in Australia nobody is supposed to rule and nobody does rule, so the distinction falls
> to the ground ... The proletariat is all the time responsible, the only source of authority.
>
> (Lawrence, 1950, p. 27)

Somers, a recent immigrant in the 1920s to Australia, is trying to come to grips with his
new surroundings. He is attempting to understand the way that his new neighbours think
and perceive the world. At the heart of it is Somers' view of what is 'right' and what is
'wrong', what is valuable and what is not, what is important and what is irrelevant.
These perspectives on life reflect the patterns of thinking, feeling and potential actions
that are learned throughout a persons' lifetime. It is what Geertz (1973) has called 'the
webs of significance'. Hofstede (1991) described this as a form of mental programming
or software of the mind, to use a contemporary computer analogy. The common term
for such mental software is 'culture'.

In research in geographical and environmental education, we are largely concerned
with explaining learning and teaching behaviour. Why, for example, do some students in
Asia-Pacific countries, as Saarinen (1988) found, draw Eurocentric world maps rather
than using Pacific orientations? Why are geography teachers in South East Asia seemingly more reluctant to adopt more socially relevant curricula than their counterparts in
Australia? Causes and interpretations are often multiple and multifarious. One important
factor, however, is often to be found in the values, beliefs and norms which the actors in
these educational scenes hold. It is these values, etc., which determine the webs of
significance referred to earlier.

Returning to D.H. Lawrence's semi-autobiographical novel, Somers was focusing on
differences between the collective programmings of the mind that distinguish one group
of people from another. Lawrence was attempting to illuminate two contrasting sets of
feelings, thoughts and manners of behaving as a basis for understanding contrasts in the

ways of life in the two countries. This is at the heart of cross-cultural inquiry. In such studies, within the more limited confines of geographical and environmental education, researchers seek to understand differences in what is taught, how teaching and learning takes place and the ways curriculum reform is carried out. These and other topics for research are examined with reference to variations in the perceptions of education within particular sociocultural contexts.

In recent years, there have been an increasing number of such studies in geographical and environmental education (e.g. Gerber, 1990; Saarinen, 1988; Lee, 1993; besides these are the many reports at International Geographical Union (IGU) Education Commission symposia such as Fung and Lee, 1990; Gourley *et al.*, 1992; Mitchell, 1992; Niemz and Stoltman, 1992; Wong, 1992; Rikkinen, 1994). Despite these papers, there has in general been little discussion in geographical and environmental education circles as to how to carry out cross-cultural curricular studies. On the other hand, much work has been done for a considerable time in the fields of psychology, sociology, anthropology and management. Indeed, Whiting (1961) attributes the first discussion of cross-cultural methodology to Tylor in a paper in 1889. A number of useful reviews are to be found in the literature of these other fields (e.g. Ford, 1967; Lonner and Berry, 1986).

This chapter is concerned with methodological issues in cross-cultural research. The aim is not to set out detailed procedures but rather to highlight some key issues and to suggest some directions practice might take. The chapter attempts to review and bring into the literature of geographical and environmental education some of the understanding reached elsewhere. Three important interrelated issues come out of this and form the focus for discussion, namely the nature of how research in cross-cultural studies is conceptualized, the dilemma of data collection and finally the problem of inference. However, before looking at these I examine in a little more depth the nature of cross-cultural analysis.

CROSS-CULTURAL ANALYSIS IN GEOGRAPHICAL AND ENVIRON-MENTAL EDUCATION

As I have suggested earlier, cross-cultural analysis in geographical and environmental education uses the understanding of a populace's feelings and thoughts – Geertz's webs of significance – as viewpoints from which to interpret and explain educational differences between regions of the world or between sub-groups in society within countries. Analyses are usually comparative in structure and cultural in interpretive strategy. Some studies adopting cultural analysis are not strictly comparative; they emphasize how the unique cultural context of an education system has given rise to a particular sort of geographical and environmental education. Examples of this type include Ballantyne (1992), Dean (1992) and Keidel (1992). One might argue that they are really only cross-cultural by implication. None the less, many examples of this type are to be found in the comparative literature. Whether these are better termed 'cultural' rather than 'cross-cultural' is open to debate, and I suspect that the answer lies in the interpretation intended by the writer and the perspective adopted by the reader.

An example at this point may help to clarify what is meant by cultural interpretation and cross-cultural analysis. In a study in Hong Kong, the distinctivness of Chinese culture provided meaning to an analysis of the relationship between attitude and behaviour among grade 12 geography students aged about 17 years, when researchers were faced with what at first seemed an unexpected set of results in comparison with those derived from Euro-American studies.

A questionnaire survey was used to assess the level of pro-environmental attitude, the level of stated environmentally sensitive behaviour and the degree of personal locus of control; that is, how far individuals feel personally empowered to act. As expected, environmentally positive attitudes and an internal locus of control (a feeling of empowerment) were indicated by students who said that they were likely to behave in an environmentally sensitive way. Conversely, environmental negative attitudes and external control linked with a propensity to act in a less sensitive manner. Similar studies are mainly from North America and Europe and suggest that we might also find students exhibiting insensitive behaviour but pro-environmental attitudes because they have not internalized a personal locus of control. This interpretation views learners as independently minded and self-motivated individuals. The data recorded, details of which can be found in Stimpson (1994), actually showed a propensity to act environmentally alongside environmentally negative attitudes and external locus of control. Some young people in Hong Kong act environmentally despite not really believing that their actions count or are worthwhile.

The Eurocentric–North American view expressed an individualistic set of societal values. However, Asia-Pacific and China are frequently characterized, in contrast, by more collective, less individualistic perspectives (Hofstede, 1991). Young Chinese people in Hong Kong are expected to be obedient and conform to the wishes of their parents and elders. Filial compliance is the expected norm and desired. Hong Kong students understand that approbation comes from accepting superordinate directions as to how to act. Their culture is marked by large power distance. This is not to say that all young people in the territory blindly do what they are told, but there is a tendency to accept and respond positively to instructions from institutions such as the environmental protection agency. Traditional Chinese values, and the peer pressure associated with them, place collective demand above individual desire. In fact collective demand and individuality are largely seen as separate. They do not conflict. They are a part of the complementary yin and yang of traditional Chinese life. The survey results, seen in this cultural context, are not difficult to understand; students may not necessarily feel that environmental quality is personally important to them but they will act appropriately because it is expected of them in their culture.

In some writings, the terms 'cross-cultural' and 'cross-national' seem to be used interchangeably. The distinction between them takes us into muddy waters that need clarification. They are related, but have distinct implications. The term 'cross-cultural' is often used in a very loose way, rather like the terms 'environment' and 'climate'. The latter are used both in their conventional but limited physical sense and in wider analogous ways to reflect social context, as is the adjective 'cultural'. Cross-national studies in geographical and environmental education are largely concerned with differences in teaching and learning, etc. between countries. They are also used with reference to distinct national identities within countries, such as that of Scotland within the United Kingdom. The description 'cross-national' reflects a measurement unit which comprises a specific sociopolitical spatial entity. Beliefs and social norms are not intended at the centre of interpretation. It is only when curricular and learning differences or similarities are attributed to the varying values, beliefs and norms which different groups of people hold as important that one starts to move into the realm of cross-cultural study. Some studies, of course, lie on the boundary. The well-known studies of the International Association for the Evaluation of Educational Achievement (IEA) are in essence of this type, being cross-national but occasionally adopting cross-cultural perspectives.

Cultural interpretation occurs at varying levels of specificity. Some research explicitly sets out to interpret differences in terms of the cultural values of the actors involved. In others, culture is expressed only as a background variable and plays little or no part in providing meaning to the findings. In some, while the title 'cross-cultural' may be used, values, etc., are not alluded to at all. These distinctions seem rarely to be addressed in many so-called 'cross-cultural' studies within geographical and environmental education, and researchers need to make it clear where they stand.

CONCEPTUALIZATION OF THE CROSS-CULTURAL PROBLEM

The way a particular cross-cultural question is conceptualized is a major determinant of the sorts of inference that can be drawn in the end. The presence of a theoretical construct to underpin cross-cultural study is vital. Eckensberger (1979), illuminating the issue, set out a number of methodological models researchers have either explicitly or implicitly adopted. (He was working in the field of cross-cultural psychology, but there are many similarities with the situation in educational research.) A first model, which incidentally is frequently used in research in geographical and environmental education, focuses on topics such as descriptive relationships between the actions of teachers and learners and the situations in which they work. The approach is often associated with the application of tests of difference to educational data derived from two or more cultural contexts. It is, however, generally devoid of substantive behavioural theory, which would allow the researcher to address the impact of culture directly. Without explicit theory, it is difficult to fit the relationships which are found into any systematic body of knowledge. Research is piecemeal, idiographic and difficult to take forward. Poortinga and Malpass (quoted in Lonner and Berry, 1986, p. 19) were more critical and commented on the risk of 'naive empirical realism' and of the interpretation of 'differences between cultural groups in terms of variables which are hardly more than impressionistic labels'.

In a second model, Eckensberger (1979) described attempts to solve the problems inherent in the use of the first model through examining causal relationships between teacher or learner behaviour and sociocultural context variables. A researcher might, for example, frame a study within the Dunkin and Biddle 3P (presage/context, process and product) model. The teacher or learner outcomes are expressed in terms of either process or product and sociocultural context as a presage or conditioning variable. Constructs such as Hofstede's power distance, collectivism, masculinity–feminity, etc., might be used to define cultural context. By contrast with the previous model, this permits direct analysis of cultural impact.

The drawback with the second model is that correlations have tended to be weak. Other models adopt a more holistic ecological approach and accept that causes and effects are difficult to separate. The focus, instead of being strictly correlational, is on identifying associations and juxtapositions of cultural and learning elements. These analyses potentially suffer from problems of lack of clarity and precision or from often near-incomprehensible complexity as multiple interrelationships are presented. It is clear that there are no easy answers to the search for appropriate theoretical frameworks. However, for researchers in the field of cross-cultural analysis it is important to address the problem and for researchers to make their own standpoints clear.

Research paradigm and design

Questions about conceptual framework are part and parcel of wider issues of method-ological strategy. Matters concerning the choice of conceptual framework and research paradigm are intertwined. Central to much educational research is the belief that the correctness of claims can be evaluated against evidence and that generalizations and theories are formulated with reference to objective data. Cross-cultural studies, because of the intangibility of culture, however, present researchers with particular problems. As I have noted earlier, in cross-cultural studies in geographical and environmental educa-tion, researchers attempt to describe similarities and differences in behaviour of teachers and learners with reference to socio-economic factors. The manner in which the problem is conceived, as reflected in the theoretical framework and the sorts of outcome seen as desirable and acceptable, directs research towards particular paradigms and research designs.

This brings into focus questions about the appropriateness of positivist as opposed to illuminative approaches in cross-cultural study. While a full discussion of the general quantitative-qualitative debate is outside the scope of this chapter and is indeed well dealt with elsewhere (e.g. Cohen and Manion, 1994, for brief introduction; Gerber, in this volume), some of the main issues as they effect cross-cultural research are briefly outlined below. Nevertheless, it is perhaps worth pointing out that it is easier to say what is wrong with a particular perspective than it is to offer categorical advice as to which line to take.

On the one hand, Poortinga and Malpass (1986, p. 18) contended that 'the most essential characteristic of scientific investigation and the one which makes it differ from non-scientific inquiry is that scientific statements should lend themselves to empirical investigation. This implies that the correctness of a contended situation can be evaluated against some alternative statement which explains and predicts a different state of affairs.' Such a paradigm has clear positivistic leanings. On the other hand, a traditional hypothesis-testing approach against a null is not generally realistic or tenable. Ideas of null hypotheses are feasibly operationalized only when observed geographical and envir-onmental curricular and learning differences can be attributed to some specific factor. These have to be put forward at the outset, and the researcher has to look to some form of randomized assessment in which the effects of other attributes are controlled. These, and in particular the latter, are usually not reasonable presumptions in cross-cultural research. Subjects are defined by their membership of defined cultural groups, over which the researcher has no control in respect of intra-group diversity. In cross-cultural studies, the non-equivalence of subjects has to be recognized at the outset. Con-sequently, the most that can be hoped for is a quasi-experimental post-test-only design within what Campbell and Stanley (1966) have called 'static group comparison'.

Questions about the credibility of experiment and quasi-experiment in cross-cultural studies (Verba, 1971) have moved some researchers, on the other hand, towards the view that studies should be embedded in more humanistic and ecological interpretations. Hypothesis-testing is replaced by a focus on theory which emerges from and is grounded in the particular situations examined. Attention is centred on understanding teachers' and learners' experiences within their different cultural settings. As Gerber notes, in Chapter 2 the qualitative researcher seeks to capture what people say and do within their social context, in which the researcher operates. Yet these paradigms, with their emphasis on personal interpretation, may not be able to divorce inferences from the circumstances in which the researcher is placed, with consequent claims of bias. Strauss and Corbin (1990) note that a major challenge of qualitative research is to break through the inevitable biases, prejudices and stereotyped perspectives that researchers bring to any analytical situation. As complexities increase, as they do in cross-curricular study, so does the risk. Those using a qualitative focus argue that in complex, multifaceted research situations, positivism is unlikely to yield useful results. None the less, it has to be recognized that many of the outcomes in cross-cultural interpretive research are highly speculative. Description, which often forms the hub of the research, must be rigorous in action and convincing, trustworthy, sound and truthful in outcome. Only then, argue Powney and Watts (1987), can implications be drawn which permit valid generalization and enhance the body of knowledge.

DATA COLLECTION

Whether the approach is essentially interpretive, illuminative and largely qualitative, or normative, quasi-positivistic and generally quantitative, data collection presents numerous hazards for the unwary. The methodological weaknesses associated with the diffuse, multi-attribute world of cross-cultural study seem almost inevitable. If they are to be minimized, the adoption of strictly parallel inquiry and the standardization of collection procedures and instruments across cultures are essential requirements as far as they are possible.

Cultural transferability is at the heart of the problems in data collection. Whether we are dealing with test questions in a quantitative study or an interview/observation schedule in a qualitative study, an assumption of common validity has to be accepted. Identical test or interview items, however, do not guarantee equal percepts or behaviour among those being studied. For example, questions about governmental control over the curriculum may be perceived from completely different starting points by workers in liberal western democracies and others from socialist autocracies. If questions are interpreted differently, as a consequence of different past experiences, then only qualified credence can be given to any similarities or differences which are proposed. A similar problem was found at the classroom level in the evaluation of earth and environmental science understanding in the present IEA Third International Science and Maths Study (TIMSS). This is seeking to examine teaching and learning across more than fifty countries, and one focus is on the varying nature of the implemented curriculum and the different sorts of value and learning behaviour which are being adopted. The largely North-American-initiated project treats earth and environmental science in a physics-chemistry-biology context. Consequently, the sorts of classroom activity that it was initially proposed to assess were typical of laboratory-based subjects. In some countries, and in particular those with a British curricular tradition, earth science teaching normally takes place in geography classes. These have a rather different set of classroom styles and strategies from those originally envisaged. The requirement for parallel inquiry consequently necessitated adaptation of the original design to accommodate the variations in learning environment which became apparent during piloting.

Equivalence also assumes past experiences are similar, and generally this is not the case. Thus, for example, comparison of the problem-solving ability of two cultural groups, when teaching in one espouses pupil inquiry while the other argues for teacher-centred approaches, is likely to be doomed to failure. Who is to say what pupils who are taught didactically would be able to do if they were encouraged to work in a more independent, heuristic fashion? Researchers need to be clinically satisfied about the confidence of all subjects to perform the tasks prior to embarking on them. Again, this is only something which becomes apparent through careful piloting and by providing those being assessed with the opportunity to practise expected routines. In general, the chances of subjects successfully responding to particular research foci are widened if multiple measures related to a single dimension are used, rather than single measures. Verba (1971) also argues for a combination of general items and culture-specific items in respect of each dimension.

In both conventional paper-and-pencil testing and interviewing, it is common to provide stimulus material. This often takes the form of a problem or situation. Contextualizing questions enables researchers to be a little more certain that they are targeting what they intend. However, what may have relevance and significance to one group of people may not to another. Somehow stimuli must cross – or have equivalence across, if parallel forms are used – at least urban–rural, male–female and old–young divides, let alone national cultural differences. Partly because of this and partly in a search for greater depth, researchers frequently substitute interviews for written tests. It is hoped that by talking through a problem, difficulties associated with the nature of appropriate stimuli can be circumvented. However, in some societies children do not expect that it is appropriate for them to voice their views. Moreover, as Irvine (1983) noted, social conventions may prescribe set answers to spoken questions. Consequently the hoped-for improvement in the depth and richness of responses is not always forthcoming.

Language presents numerous difficulties and cannot be ignored. There is the obvious problem of loss of information during translation. Back-translation and the use of geographical and environmental researchers from the cultures under investigation, who are cognizant of teachers' and pupils' language conventions, will help to minimize this. Powney and Watts (1987), for example, offer a useful extended discussion of this issue. More serious, however, is the way that some languages are better vehicles for putting over certain sorts of ideas than other languages.

Where cross-cultural study is being carried out with English as the base language, Brislin (1986) offers the following suggestions for writing readily translatable English. These will not solve all problems but will help to minimize many:

- Use short, simple sentences of fewer than 16 words, with one idea per sentence.
- Use the active rather than the passive voice (although in some languages, such as Tagalog from the Philippines, the passive is commonly used and therefore readily accepted).

- Repeat nouns rather than substituting them with pronouns.
- Avoid metaphors and colloquialisms.
- Avoid the subjunctive, as often languages outside Europe do not have an equivalent form to 'could', 'would' and 'should'.
- Add sentences to provide necessary context.
- Use specific rather than general terms, for example, write 'cows' rather than 'live-stock'.
- Avoid vagueness through the use of terms such as 'probably' or 'usually'.
- Use words which are familiar to the translators.

To this list, Verba (1971) added a plea for open questions. These permit a richness of reply which can help to illuminate the true meaning intended by the respondent. All these suggestions are common sense. Indeed, many reflect good general advice for the setting of items in questionnaires and interview schedules whether for a cross-cultural study or not.

Equal problems in data collection are found in humanistic studies, where 'softer', more interactive and more sensitive methods are employed. For example, observation and case studies are often thought appropriate when seeking to examine the actions of individuals within their own social settings. The small numbers of subjects that can be studied on practical grounds inevitably draws researchers towards case study. It is often used for understandable reasons of limited resources and the potential depth and rich-ness of the data it can offer. Use is also encouraged by the seeming impossibility of controlling for individual differences. Even if one could take account of variables such as age, sex or socioeconomic status, there are still vast differences in the way people respond to the same situation, depending on personality and, not least, on how they feel over the period of observation. But case studies are not without risk. How far is one able to generalize? If all we are left with is a few culturally contrasting vignettes of teacher or pupil behaviour or beliefs concerning geographical or environmental educa-tion, cultural attribution as a basis for interpretation becomes highly speculative. Accounts need to be placed side by side, key information coded and highlighted, as a basis for drawing out similarities and differences (Ford, 1967). Triangulation and rep-lication are essential. The aim must be rigorous systematic analysis if credible generalizations are to be produced.

Watching, listening and learning, it is argued, provide for holistic interpretations of pupil and teacher actions which can rarely be achieved by other means. Observation allows access to the subtleties of behaviour. However, it is unlikely that the observer has no effect on those observed, and vice versa. To a greater or lesser degree, the behaviour observed generally changes simply as a result of being studied and with the situational context in which it is studied. Pure naturalistic settings as a means to avoid the artificial-ity associated with much formal testing are in reality hard to achieve. The difficulties associated both with becoming an 'invisible' observer and of 'invisibility' itself are well reviewed in Berg (1989). All that can be hoped for if we are going to attempt compar-isons is that sufficient relationship and trust have been built up so that Hawthorne effects, whereby subjects alter their behaviour because they know they are subjects in research study (Berg, 1989), are minimized and so that all involved – observer and observed – react in a similar manner across cultures.

CONCLUSION: A QUESTION OF INFERENCE

In cross-cultural geographical and environmental education, we attempt to describe and explain differences and similarities in terms of educational concepts with reference to sociocultural factors. More important than debates about whether positivistic or interpretive strategies are used is the realization that *a priori* conceptions about the nature of cross-cultural differences (or similarities) within geographical and environmental education have a profound effect on the nature of the research topic. This in turn determines the sorts of inference which can be drawn, or at least how reliable they are. The important consideration is inference. This means realizing, whichever strategy is used, what can safely be inferred and what cannot and, when we can infer, with what reliability. Inference is at the heart of methodological issues in cross-cultural analysis. The central problem is constructing studies so that the desired inferences can reasonably be attempted. This means, as far as it is humanly possible, protecting inferences by excluding or evaluating alternatives (Poortinga and Malpass, 1986).

This chapter has attempted to run a broad brush over some of the problems and point to some possible solutions that have been suggested in kindred areas. In geographical and environmental education, cross-cultural research questions lie somewhere between the occasionally narrow, quasi-experimental studies in psychology and the broad, holistic framework of classic anthropology. None the less, if researchers in geographical and environmental education ignore many of the lessons offered by these fields of study, they do so at their peril.

REFERENCES

Ballantyne, R. (1992) 'South African images of the world: the effect of apartheid education.' *Proceedings of the International Geographical Union's Commission on Geographical Education Symposium, Colorado, August 2–7.* Boulder CO: Centre for Geographic Education, University of Colorado at Boulder.

Berg, B. (1989) *Qualitative Research Methods.* Boston, MA: Allyn and Bacon.

Brislin, R.W. (1986) 'The wording and translation of research instruments.' In W.J. Lonner and J.W. Berry (eds) *Field Methods in Cross-cultural Research.* Beverly Hills, CA: Sage.

Campbell, D.T. and Stanley, J. (1966) *Experimental and Quasi-experimental Designs for Research.* Chicago, IL: Rand McNally.

Cohen, L. and Manion, L. (1994) *Research Methods in Education.* 4th edn. London: Routledge.

Dean, B.D. (1992) 'The Chinese image of themselves and the world.' *Proceedings of the International Geographical Union's Commission on Geographical Education Symposium, Colorado, August 2–7.* Boulder, CO: Centre for Geographic Education, University of Colorado at Boulder.

Eckensberger, L.H. (1979) 'A metamethodological evaluation of psychological theories from a cross-cultural perspective.' In L. Eckensberger, W. Lonner and Y.H. Poortinga (eds) *Cross-cultural Contributions to Psychology.* Lisse: Swets and Zeitlinger.

Ford, C.S. (1967) *Cross-cultural Approaches.* New Haven: HRAF Press.

Fung, Y.W. and Lee, J.C.K. (1990) 'A comparative study of geographical curricula in Hong Kong and China with reference to their contribution to environmental education.' *Abstracts and Papers of the International Geographical Union Commission on Geographical Education Symposium, Hong Kong.* Hong Kong: Department of Curriculum Studies, University of Hong Kong.

Geertz, C. (1973) *The Interpretations of Cultures.* New York: Basic Books.

Gerber, R. (1990) 'Asian geographical educator's perceptions and practices.' *Abstracts and Papers of the International Geographical Union Commission on Geographical Educational Symposium, Hong Kong*. Hong Kong: Department of Curriculum Studies, University of Hong Kong.

Gourley, J., Saarinen, T.F. and MacCabe, C.L. (1992) 'Map images of the world from British Commonwealth students.' *Proceedings of the International Geographical Union's Commission on Geographical Education Symposium, Colorado, August 2–7.* Boulder, CO: Centre for Geographic Education, University of Colorado at Boulder.

Hofstede, G. (1991) *Cultures and Organizations: Software of the Mind*. London: McGraw-Hill.

Irvine, S.H. (1983) 'Testing in Africa and America: 'the search for routes.' In S.H. Irvine and J.W. Berry (eds) *Human Assessment and Cultural Factors*. New York: Plenum.

Keidel, G.S. (1992) 'A comparison of world sketch maps.' *Proceedings of the International Geographical Union's Commission on Geographical Education Symposium, Colorado, August 2–7.* Boulder, CO: Centre for Geographic Education, University of Colorado at Boulder.

Lawrence, D.H. (1950) *The Kangaroo*. London: Penguin.

Lee, J.C.C. (1993) 'Geography teaching in England and Hong Kong: contributions towards environmental education.' *International Research in Geographical and Environmental Education*, **2** (1), 25–40.

Lonner, W.J. and Berry, J.W. (1986) *Field Methods in Cross-cultural Research*. Beverly Hills, CA: Sage.

Mitchell, D. (1992) 'How children think about others.' *Proceedings of the International Geographical Union's Commission on Geographical Education Symposium, Colorado, August 2–7.* Boulder, CO: Centre for Geographic Education, University of Colorado at Boulder.

Niemz, G. and Stoltman, J. (1992) 'The field trials on InterGeo II.' *Proceedings of the International Geographical Union Commission on Geographical Education Symposium, Colorado, August 2–7.* Boulder, CO: Centre for Geographic Education, University of Colorado at Boulder.

Poortinga, Y.P. and Malpass, R.S. (1986) 'Making inferences from cross-cultural data.' In W.J. Lonner and J.W. Berry (eds) *Field Methods in Cross-cultural Research*. Beverly Hills, CA: Sage.

Powney, J. and Watts, J. (1987) *Interviewing in Educational Research*. London: Routledge and Kegan Paul.

Rikkinen, H. (1994) 'Finnish self-image and sterotypes of its neighbours.' In H. Haubrich (ed.) *Europe and the World in Geography Education. Geographiedidaktische Forschungen, Vol. 22.* Nuremberg: Selbstverlag des Hochschulverbandes für Geographie und ihre Didaktik.

Saarinen, T.F. (1988) 'Centering of mental maps of the world.' *National Geographic Research*, **4**, 112–27.

Stimpson, P.G. (1994) 'Environmental attitudes and behaviour: locus of control and cultural context.' *Proceedings of the Regional Conference of the International Geographical Union, Prague, August 22–6.* Prague: International Geographical Union.

Strauss, A. and Corbin, J. (1990) *Basics of Qualitative Research*. Newbury Park, CA: Sage.

Verba, S. (1971) 'Cross-cultural survey research: the problem of credibility.' In I. Vallier (ed.) *Comparative Methods in Sociology*. Berkeley, CA: University of California Press.

Whiting, F. (1961) 'The cross-cultural method.' In F.W. Moore (ed.) *Readings in Cross-cultural Methodology*. New Haven: HRAF Press.

Wong, K.Y. (1992) 'Hong Kong's image of the world and the world's image of Hong Kong.' *Proceedings of the International Geographical Union's Commission on Geographical Education Symposium, Colorado, August 2–7.* Boulder, CO: Centre for Geographic Education, University of Colorado at Boulder.

Chapter 5

Grounded Theory: Defying the Dominant Paradigm in Environmental Education Research

Daniella Tilbury and Rex Walford

> The field of research in environmental education needs to address the important task of adequately sustaining environmental education – of revitalising personal, professional and curriculum development in the field. However, it is our observation that environmental education research is somewhat moribund ... Worse, the research paradigm adopted in much environmental education research, however well intentioned, may actually counter the achievement of some of those purposes.
>
> (Robottom and Hart, 1993a, p. 3)

ENVIRONMENTAL EDUCATION RESEARCH: FAILING TO RESOLVE THE CRITICAL CURRICULUM QUESTION

Environmental education, despite being a young area of learning, has evolved at an explosive pace. No other single educational area has developed as fast and with as much acceptance (Lahiry *et al.* 1988). Only thirty years ago the term 'environmental education' was relatively unknown and frequently misinterpreted (Fensham, 1978). Now it has gained world-wide recognition, forming the basis of major national and international environmental strategies (e.g. Council of Europe, 1988; Department of Environment, 1990; International Union for the Conservation of Nature and Natural Resources, 1991; UNESCO, 1992).

It was as a result of growing concern over changes in environmental conditions that the UN spearheaded a number of international conferences in the 1970s which gave formal recognition and validity to this area of learning. Even so, it was not until the 1980s that significant developments occurred.

Today, nearly three decades after its first appearance and despite the rising status of environmental education, schools and teacher education institutions are still failing to prepare students adequately in this field (Tilbury, 1993). A historical review of the development of environmental education research provides insight into why it has failed to resolve the critical curriculum question – how to achieve the goals of environmental education.[1]

PUTTING ENVIRONMENTAL EDUCATION RESEARCH INTO PERSPECTIVE

Boosted by a national Environmental Education Act, the United States initiated and led the thrust of environmental education research in the 1980s. Specifically, researchers at the University of Southern Illinois, including Volk and Hungerford, played a very influential role in identifying research priorities in the field and in determining the course of environmental education developments throughout the decade.

Robottom and Hart (1993b) point out how these researchers – the 'Carbondale Group'; – dominated the studies reported in the *American Journal of Environmental Education*. The group's work on curriculum development and evaluation, reproduced and supported by UNESCO-UNEP's International Environmental Education Programme (IEEP), had significant impact on European, Asian and Australian research too. As a result, the Carbondale team set the agenda for world-wide developments in the field.

These researchers, together with a number of other individuals such as Fensham, Linke, Lucas and Stapp –'influential founders' of environmental education (Greenall Gough, 1993) – were all trained scientists. Their background undeniably tinged their interpretation of environmental education and shaped their research inquiry. Quantitative approaches, perceived by them as the only truly scientific and therefore valid form of investigation, dictated the line of developments.[2] Despite the holistic nature and interdisciplinary approach of environmental education,[3] an understanding of its practices was primarily evolved from correlational and experimental research during the 1980s. The publications show that, during this time, research was essentially non-social and apolitical. The language, methods and approach of studies reflect the role played by, and the value attached to, scientific research. Iozzi (1981) reported that 90–92 per cent of studies were primarily quantitative.

Over a decade later, environmental education research is still essentially scientific in nature: 'Much of the research in ee [environmental education] takes the form of ascertaining the congruence between outcomes and assumed goals and seeking empirically (objectively) to derive generalisations (theory) and hence legitimate scientific knowledge' (Robottom and Hart, 1993a, p. 31). Approaches such as psychometrics, behaviour analysis, natural resource management, human ecology and statistics figure significantly. The bibliographies of most studies can mislead any reader into interpreting environmental education as essentially a branch of science education.

The environmental crisis has been attributed to the pervasiveness of the Cartesian world view and its scientific, reductionist and fragmented outlook on the environment (Ferguson, 1980; Capra, 1982; Houston, 1982; Greig *et al.* 1989). In the same way, the dominant scientific paradigm and its narrow, fragmented research focus can be blamed for the failure of researchers to ascertain why environmental education has not yet achieved its goals.

THE SCIENTIFIC PARADIGM: IS IT INCOMPATIBLE WITH ENVIRONMENTAL EDUCATION?

No research paradigm has a monopoly on quality. None can deliver promising outcomes with certainty. None can have the grounds for saying 'this is it' about their designs, procedures and anticipated outcomes.

(Peshkin, 1993, p. 28)

Some educationists argue that the behaviourist, positivist, instrumental and deterministic stance on research favoured by the applied science paradigm is incompatible with environmental education (Robottom and Hart, 1993a). They are critical of this paradigm for imposing the social values of the researcher on to education in a way which disempowers the teachers and learners. Robottom's (1990. p. 3) concern is that such research contradicts the objectives of environmental education, since it lends itself to 'a social control which is guided by unexamined goals usually set by the researchers'. Essentially, Robottom and Hart (1993a) object to the application to the social and political world of environmental education of what they see as an inadequate form of inquiry: 'this approach, although pervasive in most dimensions of environmental education and supported by its own forms of renewal, is flawed as a theory for environmental education' (Robottom and Hart, 1993a, p. 4). This argument that some forms of inquiry conflict with the nature of environmental education can be dangerous. Certainly, researchers must defy the dominant scientific paradigm, but only in an effort to attain methodological balance, rather than on the grounds that this perspective is incompatible with the nature of environmental education. Although the dominance of the scientific model has damaged the progress of environmental education, it would be inconsistent with the holistic nature of this area to exclude this research dimension.

Only by developing a complete understanding of environmental education problems can its goals realistically be addressed in the 1990s. A range of disciplinary perspectives and conceptually diverse frameworks of investigation is required. Essentially, research needs to consider the methodological contributions of research from other disciplines, such as anthropology, sociology, philosophy, psychology and geography, and especially their more qualitative methods.

No single paradigm can incorporate the complexity and interdisciplinary nature of a field which covers such areas as ecology, environmental ethics, and global and outdoor education. Environmental education is not only diverse but also dynamic, interdisciplinary and interactive. It now needs to consider alternative paradigms of research. Some recent work on action research (Muhlebach and Robottom, 1990; Elliott, 1991) and critical theory (Fien, 1992) challenges the scientific paradigm and its 'objectivist' approach to understanding environmental education practices. However, environmental education is still to discover the unique and valuable perspective which the 'grounded theory' method discussed below, can offer on its crucial curriculum questions in the 1990s.

WHAT DOES GROUNDED THEORY HAVE TO OFFER ENVIRONMENTAL EDUCATION?

The concept of grounded theory was initially developed by Glaser and Strauss (1967) in the early 1960s, during an observational study of hospital staff's handling of dying patients. This methodology differs from other traditions in that theories are grounded in data generated through the research act and not developed before or after data analysis. It can complement other approaches, such as action research and critical theory, in attempting to build a more complete picture of environmental education practices.

Its value lies in its defiance of the dominant scientific paradigm in environmental education research and its objectivist approach. This is due to:

1. its narrative and rich descriptive data about the contexts, beliefs and activities of participants, capturing the complexity of environmental education processes and the multifaceted nature of curriculum change. These processes are often inaccessible to objectivist, numerical and statistical studies.
2. its naturalistic stance. Unlike many other approaches, grounded theory attempts to represent educational processes as they occur naturally, rather than as they may be manipulated by the investigator.
3. its phenomenological view, which assumes that the social process may create multiple realities. This contrasts with the dominant positivist view about the world which assumes that there are social objective facts. Grounded theory examines the subjective elements and meanings which participants attribute to environmental education or its processes.
4. valuing both the etic (investigators') and emic (subjects') accounts of research. It opposes the empiricist tradition underlying the scientific paradigm, which assumes that the investigator's version is the only reliable one.
5. challenging the traditional role of the researcher. In most scientific work, the researcher is detached from the setting to avoid bias. In grounded theory the researcher becomes immersed in the context and relies on his or her personal interpretations in order to collect and analyse data.
6. its multiple data-gathering method. This not only allows the researcher to probe into the complex and dynamic processes which have been overlooked by previous research but also permits internal verification of data.
7. its generative, constructive approach. This contrasts with the testing and building of theory which has been the essence of previous work.

The next section considers more specifically the contributions of this methodology to environmental education at the teacher education level.

RESEARCH AT THE TEACHER EDUCATION LEVEL: FROM DESCRIPTION TO EXPLANATION

> Most of environmental education literature is descriptive ... limited attention [is] given to theory or model building in the field.'
>
> (Marcinkowski, 1993, p. 39)

Previously, curriculum research into environmental education in teacher education has been limited to describing and quantifying curriculum provision at this level (Coon, 1980; Stapp *et al.*, 1980; Gayford, 1987; Oulton, 1991; Williams, 1992). Research is now required which will explain existing patterns of provision and identify reasons why schools and teacher education institutions are still failing to prepare students adequately in this field.

The dearth of previous work in this area means that there are no existing theories from which hypotheses can be drawn and tested. The generative approach of the grounded theory method can thus add a new dimension to research. It can help advance curriculum development by highlighting the processes and conditions operating in and on educational institutions to influence the nature of environmental education provision.

Furthermore, there is a need for research which will not only address the problems of environmental education but also capture the complexities and realities of the education system. Previous studies have failed to do this. Yet only by locating environmental education issues in a wider context can the constraints on curriculum development be considered realistically. The grounded theory method can address such issues.

In the next section we outline the key premises of the grounded theory approach and describe the model of fieldwork practice associated with it. We define the constant comparative method of data collection and interpretation and the significance of an eclectic approach to theory construction. The section exemplifies the methodology by describing a research design developed for the discovery of a grounded theory of curriculum provision and change in environmental education at the teacher education level.

EXPLORING GROUNDED THEORY

Grounded theory uses an open research design, where the variables or categories emerge in the process of the research (Conrad, 1978; Anderson, 1990). Once identified, the variables are checked and rechecked, and either 'saturated' or reformulated with the help of an eclectic approach. The primary goal is to identify the core variable which forms the basis of the theory.

Grounded theory has no fixed rules but includes a number of distinct features, such as theoretical sampling, constant comparison and coding methods, that ensure conceptual development and density. These techniques provide a framework for research which does not tie the researcher down to specific kinds of data or theory, but permits him or her to develop a variety of investigatory styles and aims in diverse social settings. Furthermore, these methods are modified and developed in response to the researcher's requirements and/or changing contexts within studies.

Always underlying any grounded theory study is the question of how to capture and make sense of the complex phenomena under study. This is achieved by extensive data collection, which enables the researcher to map conceptually dense data and overcome simplistic conceptions of the phenomena under study.

EVOLVING GROUNDED THEORY

This section outlines the grounded theory method by referring to the research design of a study into the discovery of a grounded theory of curriculum provision and change in environmental education at the teacher education level. The theory identified the primary variables, which explain current provision and influence curriculum development in environmental education. Figure 5.1 shows the grounded theory's principal components. It is the influence of, and the interaction amongst, these four main categories of variables that determine the existing and evolving provision of environmental education in the teacher education institutions studied.[4]

The grounded theory method requires researchers to devise their own combination of procedures and research instruments in response to particular structures and contexts.

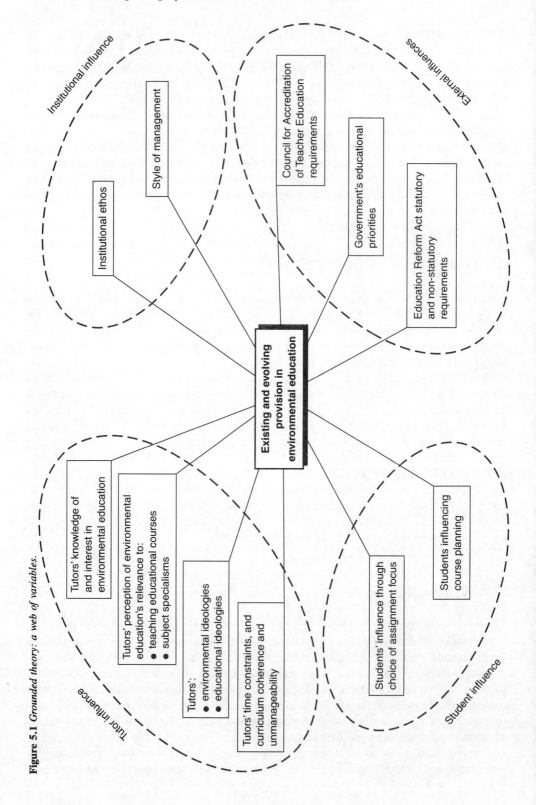

Figure 5.1 *Grounded theory: a web of variables.*

Thus, this is not an attempt to propose a model of fieldwork practice which could be translated directly into a structure of data collection and interpretation for other investigations. Instead, the study is used to exemplify certain components of this methodological framework.

Data collection and analysis

In this method, categories and variables emerge from the field so that theory is not superimposed on the data. This inevitably means that data collection and analysis occur simultaneously (Burgess, 1985; Sherman and Webb, 1988). Thus, the researcher must collect, code and analyse the data, from the first day in the field.

Data collection begins with widely focused descriptive observations. After analysing initial data, the researcher can narrow down the investigation. As the observations become further focused, selective ones are made.

The goal is to discover a 'core variable' which becomes the basis for the generation of theory. This variable has three essential characteristics: it recurs frequently in the data; it links data together; and it explains much of their variation. Continuous collection and analysis of the data combined with rigorous analytic thinking will eventually yield such a variable, which 'illuminates' the main theme of the subjects' behaviour and explicates 'what is going on in the data' (Glaser, 1978, p. 94).

The *tutor influence* was identified as the core variable in the discovery of a grounded theory of curriculum provision and change in environmental education (see Figure 6.1). The researcher first recorded each observation and interview onto a data sheet. These data were then coded broadly; the codes were later categorized into groups and further refined. Initially, there was a whole variety of codes, each accomplishing a different purpose. Some originated in the process of the data analysis, others were prompted by members of staff; some raised questions, and others pointed to examples of data which reinforced particular categories. Once codes were categorized and refined, explicit links between the data were sought. Major groups of influence were then identified and the relationships between them explored. The researcher then sought for instances which would stretch the diversity of the data, in order to capture the widest possible range on a category. When confident that no additional data could develop the properties of the categories or variables (that is, that theoretical saturation had occurred), the researcher plotted a web of variables which captured the essence of the grounded theory (see Figure 5.2).

Constant comparison

The constant comparative method of data analysis forms the basis for the generation of a grounded theory. This approach has been explored in depth by Glaser and Strauss (1964), Newcombe and Conrad (1981) and Blase (1982). It aims through comparison to form a theory that encompasses as much behavioural variation as possible.

The researchers look for patterns when collecting and analysing data. They compare incident with incident, incident with subject's accounts and the latter with other subjects' accounts. They can thus distinguish between similarities and differences among incidents and attempt to clarify these by establishing core variables.

Stage 1: Coded data with broadly defined codes
e.g.

If environmental education is about change, if it is about attempting to get children   NAEE
involved with the environment, then I am afraid of the consequences it can have for   OBST
education. Its ideology would change education dramatically.

These codes are there to raise questions like: 'Is the *nature* (NAEE) of environmental
education an *obstacle* (OBST) to its development?'

Stage 2: Grouped codes which dealt with similar areas of investigation
e.g.
   Obstacles?
       PERS (personal elements influencing curriculum change)
       PROB (problematic nature of environmental education)
       TCON (time constraints)
       CATE (the Council for Accreditation of Teacher Education)

Stage 3: Categorized codes and the refined data collection process
     (a) Refined some codes and dropped others
         Dropped – REAL
         Refined – RECG to CONT; CDEV to PIDE;

     (b) Established relationships between existing codes
         Links – PROB → CCRT

Stage 4: Identified major groups of influence

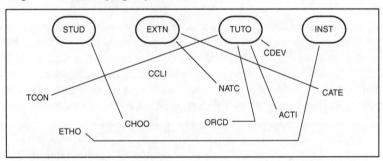

Stage 5: Saturation occurred and a web of variables emerged

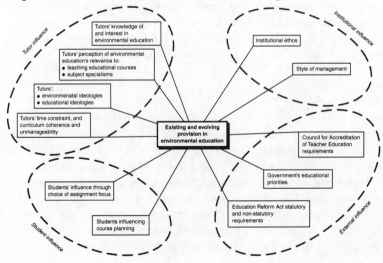

Figure 5.2 *The coding process.*

In this study, data were coded between and within different groups, at a variety of levels. This increased the validity of the data and strengthened the categories emerging from the findings (see Figure 5.3). In addition to the comparison of data within an institution and between the two initial case studies in phase 1, further comparisons were made in phase 2 with data from three other institutions.

The eclectic approach

Grounded theory is based on the multimodal or eclectic approach (Goetz and LeCompte, 1984) of data collection involving a variety of research techniques and instruments. It enables data collected in one way to be used to cross-check the accuracy of data gathered in another, a procedure often referred to as 'triangulation' (Denzin, 1970; Adelman, 1981; Cohen and Manion, 1989). Triangulation prevents the investigator from accepting too readily the validity of initial impressions; it enhances the scope, diversity and clarity of constructs developed during the course of the investigation; and it assists in correcting biases (Glaser and Strauss, 1967).

The study used here as an example, employed research instruments traditionally associated with ethnographic qualitative research, such as participant observations, interviews, questionnaires, key informants and analysis of course documents.

The sampling procedure

The grounded theory method depends not on probabilistic sampling but on theoretically informed selection. Groups may be chosen in an attempt to *minimize* comparability and attain maximum similarity in data generated by the group of samples. This strategy increases the verification of categories and facilitates the generation of basic properties. Glaser and Strauss (1967) contend that these conditions aid the researcher in spotting fundamental differences between the categories and in establishing a set of conditions useful for prediction.

The researcher may instead choose to *maximize* comparison between the groups in an attempt to spot fundamental uniformities or variations within categories. Maximum diversity yields a denser theory which helps delimit its scope (Glaser and Strauss, 1967).

In this study, institutions in England were chosen on the basis of theoretical relevance. Only institutions which offered both Bachelor of Education (BEd) and Postgraduate Certificate in Education (PGCE) courses for the upper primary years were considered. Accessibility, openness and willingness to be studied were also important criteria. As Ball (1984, p. 78) explains, 'This openness, I would argue, provides one of the important bases of the value and power of participant observation ... and brings it nearer than any other social science methods of capturing patterns of collective actions as they occur in real life.'

Twelve teacher education institutions were visited during the case study selection process. From these, two initial case studies, on which most of this research is based, were chosen, not only because of their willingness to participate in the study but also because they were about to revise the entire initial training primary courses. Course

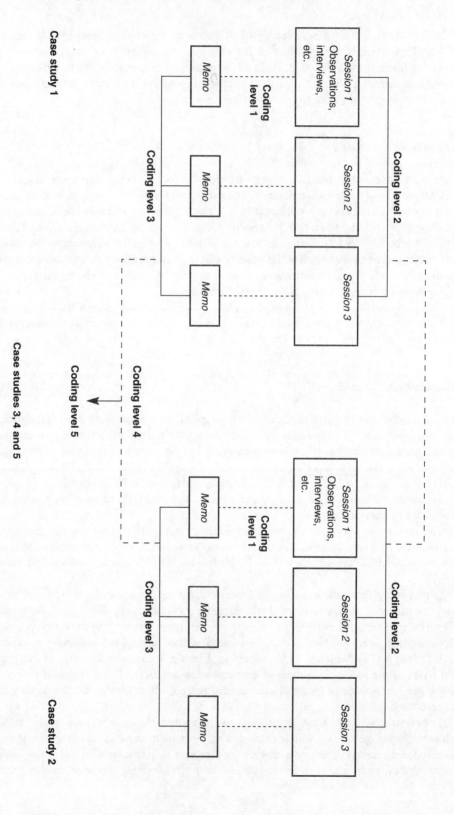

Figure 5.3 *Coding data: the constant comparison method.*

review was an important criterion for selection since it allowed the study of environ-mental education and its place in the curriculum development process, rather than just its introduction into the existing curriculum.

The sampling method chosen for phase 1 of the study called for the minimization of differences between comparative groups. In phase 2, three other institutions were visited in order to refine the categories further and verify the variables which constitute the theory. Although these three institutions also offered BEd and PGCE courses in the middle years of schooling, no other variables were controlled. It was intended that this more random sampling would provide simultaneous maximization and minimization of both the differences and similarities of data and cover a wider range of variables.

Validity and reliability

> Rather than test-retest reliability or research replication qualitative research calls for some-thing akin to an internal consistency measure of reliability.
>
> (Fielding and Fielding, 1986, p. 43)

In grounded theory, the data collection process is subjective, as the researcher is select-ing as well as interpreting and recording data (Ball, 1984). As a result there is a need to verify the internal validity or reliability of these data.

Various techniques were used to measure the internal validity of the study used here as an example. The accuracy and consistency of the data were checked primarily through 'respondent validation' (Fielding and Fielding, 1986), where the subjects judge the validity of the accounts. Facts, interpretations and analysis were checked with 'informants' who worked closely with the researcher (see Ball, 1981). On occasions, discussions with other staff members also gave opportunities for informal validation. Key informant validation was a significant aspect of this work, as field notes and researchers' impressions were discussed with the informant at the end of the day (see Smith and Geoffrey, 1968). Also, as in Wolcott's (1978) study, the validation pro-cedure was enhanced by the responses of other selected members of staff to the transcribed and coded material. In addition, the researcher compared the research notes or memos with entries in key informants' diaries. Internal validity was also achieved through triangulation.

The term 'external validity' refers to how widely the findings of the present study can be generalized to the greater population. The research aimed for what Goetz and LeCompte (1984, p. 9) term 'translatability' of generated findings, rather than outright transfer to institutions not investigated. Translatability requires research methods and analytic categories to be identified so explicitly that comparisons can be conducted in further studies. This study outlined the research procedure in a systematic and detailed manner and included examples of the transcribed and coded data to facilitate the trans-latability of its findings.[4]

CONCLUSION: DEFYING THE DOMINANT PARADIGM

> To date, there appear to be too few efforts which are grounded in research in the field [of environmental education], in part due to the absence of syntheses and critical reviews of

research. Moreover, the resulting dearth of models leaves many researchers either to synthesise the relevant research on their own, to adapt existing models from other fields or, more simply, to rely upon either limited or uninspected popular models.

(Marcinkowski, 1993, p. 39)

Research in the 1990s must reorient itself towards methodologies which defy the dominant 'applied science' paradigm and its 'objectivist' and quantitative approach to understanding environmental education practices. The grounded theory approach outlined can make a vital contribution to environmental education by addressing such research needs. This qualitative, naturalistic, flexible, interpretive, eclectic and generative research method can add a new dimension to the research (specificially, in investigations of attitudinal changes to the environment and of the impact of teaching and learning styles in environmental education). It may provide fresh insight into why the goals of environmental education are still not effectively developed some twenty-five years after its first appearance in the school curriculum.

NOTES

1. Environmental education is an area of learning which seeks to interest and involve students in issues of environmental quality. It not only considers immediate environmental improvement as an actual goal, but also addresses educating for sustainability in the long term.
2. This follows Kuhn's (1970) argument that it is the differing epistemologies and their corresponding assumptions that distinguish the various research methodologies. These assumptions shape the nature of the research by determining what are appropriate topics, questions, methods and even outcomes.
3. Environmental education uses holism as its philosophical basis. It is concerned with how people interact with the total environment and with addressing environmental problems holistically through an interdisciplinary approach within the curriculum (Tilbury, 1993).
4. For a detailed description of the processes and results of this study, see Tilbury (1993).

REFERENCES

Adelman, C. (1981) *Uttering, Muttering: Collecting, Using and Reporting Talk for Social and Educational Research*. London: Grant McIntyre.

Anderson, G. (1990) *Fundamentals of Educational Research*. Lewes; Falmer.

Ball, S. (1981) *Beachside Comprehensive: A Case Study of Secondary Schooling*. Cambridge: Cambridge University Press.

Ball, S. (1984) 'Beachside reconsidered: reflections on a methodological apprenticeship.' In R. Burgess (ed.) *The Research Process in Educational Settings: Ten Case Studies*. Lewes: Falmer.

Blase, J. (1982) 'A socio-psychological theory of teacher stress and burnout.' *Educational Administration Quarterly*, **18** (4) 93–113.]

Burgess, R. (1985) *Field Methods in the Study of Education*. Lewes: Falmer.

Capra, F. (1982) *The Turning Point*. London: Wildwood House.

Cohen, L. and Manion, L. (1989) *Research Methods in Education*. London: Holt, Reinhart and Winston.

Conrad, C. (1978) 'A grounded theory of academic change.' *Sociology of Education*, **51**, 101–12.

Coon, H. (1980) 'Prologue: environmental education in teacher education.' In M. Bowman and J. Disinger (eds) *Environmental Education in Action IV: Case Studies of Teacher Education*. Ohio: ERIC/SMEAC.

Council of Europe (1988) *Resolution of the Council and Ministers of Education Meeting with the Council of Environmental Education.* No 88/C177/03). Strasbourg: Council of Europe.

Denzin, N. (1970) *The Research Act in Sociology.* London: Butterworth.

Department of Environment (1990) *This Common Inheritance: Britain's Environmental Strategy.* London: HMSO.

Elliott, J. (1991) *Developing Community-focussed Environmental Education Through Action-research.* Monograph. Norwich: Centre for Applied Research in Education, University of East Anglia.

Fensham,. P. (1978) 'Stockholm to Tbilisi – the evolution of environmental education.' *Prospects* **VIII** (4), 446–55.

Ferguson, M. (1980) *The Aquarian Conspiracy.* London: Granada.

Fielding, N. and Fielding, J. (1986) *Linking Data.* Beverly Hills, CA: Sage.

Fien, J. (1992) *Education for the Environment: A Critical Ethnography.* Brisbane: University of Queensland.

Gayford, C. (1987) 'Training and education in relation to environmental problems.' *Annual Review of Environmental Education,* 1, 10–11.

Glaser, B (1978) *Theoretical Sensitivity.* Berkeley, CA: Sociological Press.

Glaser, B. and Strauss, A. (1964) 'The social loss of dying patients.' *American Journal of Nursing,* **64**, 112–21.

Glaser, B. and Strauss, A. (1967) *The Discovery of Grounded Theory.* Chicago, IL: Aldine.

Goetz, J. and LeCompte, M. (1984) *Ethnography and Qualitative Design in Educational Research.* Miami: Academic Press.

Greenall Gough, A. (1993) *Founders in Environmental Education.* Geelong: Deakin University Press.

Greig, S., Pike, G. and Selby, D. (1989) *Greenprints for Changing Schools.* London: World Wide Fund for Nature/Kogan Paul.

Houston, J. (1982) *The Possible Human.* London: J.P. Tarcher.

International Union for the Conservation of Nature and Natural Resources (1991) *Caring for the Earth: A Strategy for Sustainable Living.* London: Earthscan Publications.

Iozzi, L. (1981) *Research in Environmental Education 1971–1980.* Columbus, OH:ERIC/SMEAC.

Kuhn, T. (1970) *The Structure of Scientific Revolutions.* Chicago, IL: University of Chicago Press.

Lahiry, D., Sinha, S., Gill, P., Mallik, U. and Mishra, A. (1988) *Environmental Education: A Process for Pre-Service Teacher Training Curriculum Development.* IEEP Series No. 26. Paris: UNESCO.

Marcinkowski, T. (1993) 'A contextual review of the qualitative paradigm in EE research.' In R. Mrazek (ed.) *Alternative Paradigms in Environmental Education Research.* Troy, OH: North American Association for Environmental Education.

Muhlebach, R. and Robottom, I (1990) *Supporting Community-based Environmental Education: Report of the Environmental Education and Computer Conference Project,* Deakin Institute for Studies in Education. Geelong: Deakin University.

Newcombe, J. and Conrad, C. (1981) 'A theory of mandated change.' *Journal of Higher Education,* **52** (6), 555–77.

Oulton, C. (1991) 'Environmental education and initial teacher education.' *Annual Review of Environmental Education,* 4, 12–18.

Peshkin, A. (1993) 'The goodness of qualitative research.' *Educational Researcher,* **22** (2), 23–9.

Robottom, I. (1990) 'Beyond behavourism: making environmental education research educational symposium.' *Contesting Paradigms in Environmental Education Research.* Annual Conference of the North American Association for Environmental Education, San Antonio, TX.

Robottom, I. and Hart, P. (1993a) *Research in Environmental Education: Engaging the Debate.* Geelong: Deakin University.

Robottom, I and Hart, P. (1993b) *Research in Environmental Education: Study Guide and Reader.* Geelong: Deakin University.

Sherman, R. and Webb, R. (1988) *Qualitative Research in Education: Focus and Methods.* Lewes: Falmer.

Smith, L. and Geoffrey, W. (1968) *The Complexities of an Urban Classroom: An Analysis Towards a Grounded Theory of Teaching.* New York: Holt, Rinehart and Winston.

Stapp, W., Caduto, M., Mann, L. and Nowail, P. (1980) 'Analysis of pre-service environmental education of teachers in Europe and an instructional model for furthering this education.' *Journal of Environmental Education*, **12** (2), 3–10.

Tilbury, D. (1993) '*Environmental education: developing a model for initial teacher education.*' Doctoral research thesis, Cambridge University.

UNESCO (1992) *UN Conference on Environment and Development: Agenda 21*. Switzerland: UN.

Williams, R. (1992) 'Report of a survey of provision for environmental education in initial teacher training.' In R. Williams (ed.) *Environmental Education and Teacher Education – Preparing for Change and Participation*. Brighton: ENED.

Wolcott, H. (1978) 'The man in the principal's office: An ethnographer'. In H. Wolcott (ed.) *Writing Up Qualitative Research*. New York: Holt.

Chapter 6

An International Perspective on Research in Geographical Education

Joseph P. Stoltman

International research in geographical education is a domain rich in potential for both theoretical and applied studies. The feasibility of conducting research that includes scholars co-ordinating studies in several countries is enhanced, even encouraged, by the availability of modern telecommunications. The sharing of data and the instant collaboration via facsimile, telephone or electronic mail has reduced many of the burdens and time constraints. However, the technical capability to work together has raced ahead of the state of the art for most international research in fields related to education, including geographical education (McClellan, 1994). Often the paradigms used to structure international research studies are not consistent with the most recent developments, or with traditional requirements for scientific studies. International research in education requires special consideration for and attention to the many differences, both cultural and historical, that form the basis for learning, such as the curriculum, the structure of the schools, the ages of students, the financing of schools, and the value placed on educational achievement. However, the difficulties of designing and conducting international studies should not preclude the benefits to knowledge that may be reaped as a result of well-designed research.

This chapter looks at and discusses four aspects of international research that have implications for geographical education, and of which researchers should be aware. The first part discusses the importance of bibliographic sources that should be consulted when considering international research. A significant amount of information about international research in geographical education has been compiled, and familiarity with prior studies is important. The second part discusses several different kinds of international research study that either focus on or have implications for geographical education. These studies are in science, mathematics, and political science as well as geography, and they are significant in the paradigms they represent. The third part of the chapter looks at how international research is designed, and the fourth section discusses the reasons why it is important to undertake international research.

The different parts of the chapter do not exhaust the international research issues which relate to geographical education. However, they are, in my judgement, important influences in the way research in the field either is or should be undertaken and applied.

RESEARCH IN GEOGRAPHICAL EDUCATION: BIBLIOGRAPHIC STUDIES

There is no single source for international studies in geographical education, and the richness of the field is in the many bibliographies prepared by researchers and organizations in different countries. The international studies are often a minor section of a larger treatment of the research literature, but none the less, such bibliographies are important sources for both theoretical and applied studies and for ideas on possible studies with international dimensions. For example, a bibliography of research in Britain (Graves, 1972) reviewed a century of progress in the teaching of the subject. While it is not devoted specifically to research on geography teaching, there are numerous citations of research studies among the 1402 entries. This research was addressed in a second bibliography, which dealt with the implications for international research studies (Naish, 1972). Comprehensive bibliographies and reviews devoted to research in geography teaching have also been published in other countries, including Germany (Sperling, 1978). In the United States, for example, bibliographies and status reports of research on geographical education include numerous citations of international research. In some there is only general concern with research (Anderzohn, 1963), while several others include research as a major topic (Ball, 1969; Stoltman, 1985) and still others feature discussions of the current status of research (Rice and Cobb, 1978; Saveland and Pannell, 1978).

An essential resource for information on international research in geographic education is doctoral dissertations. Dissertations are classified by topic in *Dissertation Abstracts International*. However, the classification of some doctoral dissertations is further refined in a series of publications. The National Council for the Social Studies in the United States has published a series of listings of dissertations completed in social studies education, including geography (Chapin, 1974; Gross and de la Cruz, 1971; Hepburn and Dahler, 1983; McPhie, 1964; Wrubel and Ratliff, 1978). The listings reflect both the topics and the extent to which geographical education has been included in doctoral-level research.

International research in geographical education has also been treated in special comparative studies and papers that contain important reference sections. These include the international study of research and research methodology in geographical education completed by the Commission on Geographical Education of the International Geographical Union (Graves, 1984). The volume includes articles from researchers in eleven countries describing the state of research on the teaching of geography. A monograph on German research in geographical education from the Commission on Geographical Education (Birkenhauer and Marsden, 1988) presents articles on didactics with a review of research in geographical education in the Federal Republic of Germany from 1975 to 1984. A similar review for the United States presents a similar broad perspective (Stoltman, 1991), as do the British and German publications on the developments in the field, which include extensive bibliographies.

One final important source for information on research in geographical education, including international research, is the information database made available by the ERIC Clearinghouse for Social Science/Social Studies Education. Since its inception, the Clearinghouse has catalogued and microfiched many hundreds of thousands of documents that would probably not have been published in the literature represented by journals and books (Educational Resources Information Centre, 1994).

In summary, the bibliographies, listings of graduate research dissertations, ERIC Clearinghouse documents, current literature from educational geography and the social studies, and reviews of research represent the major sources for researching international studies on geographical education.

INTERNATIONAL RESEARCH: IMPLICATIONS FOR GEOGRAPHICAL EDUCATION

There are several different types of international research pertinent to, though not exclusively focused on, geographical education, three of which are discussed below. The first includes the broadly based, large-scale studies making international comparisons of education that may inform the process of research in geographical education. The second includes those studies that use geography as the medium to investigate broader topics, such as attitudes and perspectives that cut across society. The third includes those studies from geographical education that are international in their intent, including researching the international perspectives of a national group without actually comparing those perspectives among international groups.

This section then looks at international studies that focus directly on geographical education.

Large-scale international studies

Perhaps the best large-scale, international studies are those by the International Association for the Evaluation of Educational Achievement (IEA) (Postlethwaite and Wiley, 1992; Rosier and Keeves, 1991; Travers and Westbury, 1989) and the International Assessment of Educational Progress (IAEP) (IAEP, 1989). The IEA studies collect similar data from a number of countries co-operating in the study, following a standard format. The data are processed following a model that permits cross-national analysis and reporting. The best examples of international research by the IEA are in the areas of science and mathematics education, although reading, literature, French and English as foreign languages, and civics education have been surveyed. Geography is included as earth science in the IEA studies, since that is its role in the curriculum in many countries, rather than as a social science. The IEA studies are large and the reports on education internationally are comprehensive.

The significance of the IEA studies for geographical education is that they provide an important view of how a large international project is organized, carried out and reported. Like science and mathematics, geography is included in the curriculum of most countries and could be a topic for large, international research on a periodic basis. These studies demonstrate how that might be accomplished.

Research with implications for geographical education

The way that children view people in other countries and belonging to other cultures has been of interest to researchers in sociology, psychology and anthropology as well as geography. *Children's Views of Foreign Peoples* was designed to study the mental images and stereotypes that children from ages 6 to 14 years have of people in other parts of the world (Lambert and Klineberg, 1967). It examined the views of eleven groups of children in ten countries (both English and French samples were used in Canada). It included 3300 children. The protocol for the research used an interview technique of open-ended questions in the child's language.

The implications for geographical education of this study are twofold. First, the content of the research was geography. It dealt with the views that a group (in this case children in various countries) holds of other peoples and cultures in the world. This is a major component of the geography curriculum that children study in most countries of the world. Second, once those views of other peoples are known, it looked at what can be done in geography instruction internationally to avoid stereotyping of groups or bias towards certain cultures. Both are critical questions for international research in geographical education.

RESEARCH ON INTERNATIONAL PERSPECTIVES OF A NATIONAL SAMPLE

Research that is international in its focus but does not entail collecting data from samples of students in different countries makes up this model. Researchers examine the perspectives and knowledge that students in one country have of people in another, with no direct involvement of the other countries. This research has been in the literature for a considerable time (Johoda, 1963; Piaget and Weil, 1951; Pike and Barrows, 1979). One study from this group has been selected for discussion.

Pike and Barrows (1979) investigated the knowledge of and attitudes toward other countries of fourth-, eighth- and twelfth-grade students in the United States. The sample of 1728 students was chosen using a three-tier procedure, selecting:

1. a stratified random sample of fifty counties in the United States;
2. a random sample of two schools for each of the three grade levels in each county;
3. a random sample of students at the specified grade level within schools.

Four student survey instruments were developed and administered for each grade level by the researchers; (1) background and interest; (2) knowledge test; (3) measure of attitudes towards other nations and peoples; and (4) perceptions of other nations and peoples.

While this study was complex and the report extensive, there are several conclusions notably relevant to teaching geography. First, outside regular course work, television was perceived as the most important influence upon students' thinking about, attitudes to and opinions of other countries and peoples. Secondly, the study revealed serious misconceptions among students at each grade level regarding the location of major nations, suggesting a large deficit of basic knowledge about the world. Thirdly, a disturbing lack of geographical knowledge was apparent from the study (for example, 77 per cent of eighth-graders and 61 per cent of twelfth-graders selected non-European countries as members of the European Union). Fourthly, the study provided some evidence of the extent to which ethnocentrism diminishes with age and schooling.

The practical and international significance of this is that it provides an important baseline of information, data and instruments for replication studies. It looks at the larger question of international perspectives by virtue of its overall focus, but the sub-sets of the study and the data-collection techniques present important data on their own. It emphasizes the importance of international research as the outward look from a country, or the international dimension of an educational and larger social system. The topics researched, including the interests, knowledge, attitudes and perceptions of schoolchildren towards other nations and cultures, seem to be important to the teaching of geography in any country.

International studies in geographical education

International studies that focus directly on geographical education have addressed several types of issue and research question. Four types of international research in geographical education will be discussed: curriculum, textbooks, international surveys, and student achievement. Each brings a particular dimension to the question of how research should be conducted.

International curriculum research

Curriculum design and development in geographical education are a national concern. However, at times there are major reform or educational change movements in different countries at the same time. These are sometimes linked together through international networks of scholars and curriculum developers, who exchange ideas on the emerging trends in the discipline of geography and implement programmes for the latest ideas to be incorporated in the curricula of the schools. In some instances, international research has included the cross-currents of curriculum development in a general way, such as looking at the influences in other countries of the High School Geography Project (Gunn, 1972). Other researchers have studied the relationships and interactions of specific curriculum developments within countries (Marsden, 1980). Marsden was interested primarily in the development of the German Geography Curriculum Project, but found that comparisons with the High School Geography Project in the United States and the Geography for the Young School Leaver Project in England and Wales were signficant research questions. The image of geography, the social contexts for the discipline, and the role of national funding for the projects were each considered, along with other factors, in the analysis.

The significance of this research in curriculum development lies in the cross-fertilization of ideas in geography teaching. The scope and structure of a curriculum are based on theory and research that are generally based in one country or culture. Cross-cultural curriculum development and design are becoming a more prominent element of educational research in many countries. The international comparative studies of curriculum and their implications within and between countries are important considerations for geographical education.

International textbook comparisons

The analysis of textbooks published in specific countries or in regions of the world, such as Western Europe, and how they treat the other countries of the region or world, have been a topic of concern in geography teaching since the early part of the twentieth century. Studies have been carried out of domestic textbooks that examine accuracy of information about other countries or nationalities as well as that about the country's own geography and peoples (Boden, 1977; Matley, 1987; Mehlinger, 1989). In addition, textbooks are checked for accuracy of information, including that on maps and in graphic materials.

The importance of textbook analysis research to geographical education is that it examines the accuracy with which young people are informed about their own country and the rest of the world through the information provided by scholars in those countries. Textbooks have a role in nationalizing a population and building patriotism for a country. Accuracy and scholarly objectivity in the preparation of geography textbooks are verified and validated through international textbook analysis research.

International survey research

International surveys of students to make comparisons on a number of topics, ranging from geographic literacy to environmental concerns, are found in the literature. Perhaps the most publicized was the survey of international knowledge of geography conducted by the Gallup Poll (National Geographic Society, 1988). This used the same survey in eight countries in addition to the United States (Gallup Organization, 1989b). It was administered in the former Soviet Union within a few months of its completion in the other countries (Gallup Organization, 1989a). The survey sampled people 18 years of age and older in order to collect data on knowledge of and attitude towards geography as a content area.

The main intent of the study was to collect data that could be used as a measure of American adults' knowledge of geography against the knowledge of similar groups in other countries. It was undertaken at a time when educational reform was in the formative stages, and it was important for educational policy decisions in the United States to document the fact that American students were not as well versed in geography as their counterparts in other parts of the world.

The survey has educational and practical significance for international studies in geographical education. The educational significance lies in the baseline data that it provided for each of the participating countries. The survey incorporated scientific sampling and data collection, a weakness of many other international comparison studies. While there was considerable disagreement on the types of question that were asked and the effects of curriculum structure on student knowledge, there was general agreement that the survey was conducted in a scientific manner. Baseline data will enable future researchers to make comparisons to the 1988 data in order to estimate whether change has taken place in the geographical understanding of similar groups of students.

Another significant educational aspect of the study was the response pattern for each country. The data provide an opportunity for each country to analyse the validity of the survey items and appraise the educational importance of the results. The data may be useful in evaluating curriculum and in addressing larger issues of educational reform, both within and among collaborating countries.

The practical significance of the survey and its subsequent reports was twofold. First, it verified earlier observations of geographical understanding among the youth in several different countries, using similar data collection techniques (Barrows, 1981). In the United States, for example, the wide attention to geographical illiteracy in the popular media was tempered somewhat. The United States sample did not do well in the ranking of geographical knowledge for the national samples, but it was not last in all categories. The study provided data on the basis of which scholars and policy-makers could evaluate the importance of geography, and ask whether the geographical knowledge included in the survey was important for the citizens of the country to know. The overwhelming response was 'Yes', and the survey results helped justify the inclusion of geography in national educational goals and priorities.

International studies of student achievement

One of the most widely used approaches to international research in geographical education entails the administration of the same measure of achievement or knowledge in geography to students in several different countries. The mean scores on the instrument are then compared, and the relative achievement of each group may be determined. An example was the InterGeo Project of the Commission on Geographical Education of the International Geographical Union (Niemz, 1984, 1988; Niemz and Stoltman, 1992; Stoltman and Niemz, 1992b). InterGeo I was developed by an international team of test designers and reviewers. Questions relative to the curriculum in geography for secondary students were collected from twenty countries, reviewed for overlap and organized in a sample achievement test. The test was then circulated for international review to corresponding members of the Commission on Geographical Education. The comments and ratings for the items on the prototype instrument were used to develop a final test (Stoltman and Niemz, 1992a).

This final version was distributed to corresponding members of the Commission for administration to secondary students in their countries. Data were sent to a central data-processing centre, processed, and returned to the individual for interpretation and analysis. Each researcher prepared a country interpretation of the results. The data for all the countries were analysed and interpreted (recognizing the lack of scientific controls during the data-collection stage), and used to prepare a comparative report on the achievement for the international samples on the InterGeo II instrument.

The educational significance of studies centring on geographical achievement internationally is very restricted. Due to the absence of sampling and administration controls, the cross-comparisons made are limited in their validity. There is, however, educational significance for such studies within countries where the curriculum is being reviewed, and the test provides a sampling of what students in other countries are expected to know and be able to do with geographical content and skills. Perhaps the practical significance of the achievement studies lies in the collaboration it encourages among a group of international geographical educators. The work on such a project provides an opportunity for discourse and study on what is important internationally in geographical education.

DESIGNING AN INTERNATIONAL PROJECT IN GEOGRAPHICAL EDUCATION

There are several important considerations for an international research project in geographical education. They include traditional concerns, such as selecting a research topic, the research team, the research design, communications, analysis of data, funding, and the presentation or publication of results. There are also five broad categories that international research needs to take into account:

1. data collection instruments;
2. sample selection;
3. curriculum;
4. parental influences;
5. teachers.

There is no set international research design that takes care of those categories, since the range of issues and the interactions between the research and extraneous aspects of any study are complex. However, international research projects in geographical education should examine how the following categories will influence the study.

Data collection instruments

International research in geographical education needs measurement instruments that are culturally fair, interesting for the respondents, and sound in the scientific attributes of data collection. Tests and surveys must be formulated by international committees of specialists in geography, curriculum and testing, on the basis of the curricula of the countries that will participate in the research. When the research entails classroom components there should be teachers involved in the development and review process. Critiques of prior measurement instruments and surveys must feed into the process of design and development of cross-national instruments. Similar caution is needed in using interviews, written survey techniques and participant observation. Data collection must be objective and bias-free in its conformity to the research design.

Sample selection

National probability samples of schools and students are the requirement for larger studies. Participants in research studies that are to be generalized to the entire population must be carefully drawn from that population using scientific sampling procedures. The reality of international research in geographical education is that researchers often rely upon samples that are convenient, say in existing classrooms in schools where colleagues on a research project have easy access to students. Using a sample of respondents that does not meet strict sampling procedures is acceptable as long as the procedure is clearly explained and the sample carefully described. There are examples of international research studies that have used various types of sampling techniques with considerable success (Stevenson *et al.*, 1986). The sampling procedures of other recognized international studies should be reviewed for their appropriateness to any geographical education research being planned.

Curriculum considerations

International studies generally face the question of what constitutes the curriculum, and that determines the content validity of the measurement instruments. The formal curriculum is a major consideration and careful analysis must be made to factor it within a comparative study. Curriculum considerations must also extend to the way the geography materials are rendered in the classroom and other settings. The amount of time practising or working with geographical content may make a considerable difference, despite the appearance of similar materials in each of several countries' curricula. There is also the question of external or exit examinations and proficiencies. A period of years studying geography to pass an examination in one country may produce different outcomes in another country where there is no formal assessment.

The informal curriculum also influences geographical learning. While much more difficult to deal with in designing a research study, it is important to recognize its influence and account for it when feasible. The role of homework and how much is assigned, and the influence of media in presenting information that may enhance or supplement the formal curriculum, should be taken into consideration. Often there is no way the researchers can control for such variables. In some instances, however, the collection of data on them may be sensible and helpful in the analysis and interpretation.

Parental influences

The fact that education extends beyond the school is widely recognized, and the home and parents have a significant role to play in learning. Some cultures make high demands on children for educational attainment, while others give more attention to the child's social development. Many of the cultural factors that affect learning are rooted in the context of the parents' attitudes towards or values in education. Cultural differences and the factors that affect the relative importance of education are significant elements of cross-national and cross-cultural research, which geographical education studies should consider.

Classroom teachers

The role of the teacher in the formal learning environment is especially important, and the degree to which that role extends outside of school is a significant factor for learning. The characteristics of teachers, their backgrounds, formal studies, experiences and a myriad other considerations compound investigations of the teacher's role. The investigation of these and other variables in the role of the teacher in geographical education needs to be researched.

THE IMPORTANCE OF INTERNATIONAL RESEARCH

It seems likely that international studies in education will take on greater importance in years to come. They provide opportunities to evaluate the patterns of strengths and weaknesses within a country, on the basis of an international set of criteria. As countries continue to co-operate more and more closely as entities, or as major regional groupings, the performance of a national population on international standards becomes of greater relevance. In that context, international research in geographical education is important for three compelling reasons.

First, international research provides an opportunity to learn from other countries' successful educational programmes. This international exchange is essential in order to build understanding of the processes that lead to high-quality geography instruction and learning in the curriculum. There is a need to search for and develop better ways to teach and learn geography. The careful comparison of models for geographical education can result in the beneficial transplants of ideas.

Secondly, the intellectual and scholarly pursuit of international research is interesting and rewarding. Geographical educators in different parts of the world ask many of the same questions; for example, 'How do teachers elsewhere approach basic conceptual development among their students?' or 'What kinds of instruction results in students doing very well in one aspect of geography, but poorly in another?' There is and should be the intellectual curiosity to seek answers to those and other questions.

Thirdly, international research in geographical education can have an important impact upon policy-makers. It is a source of information on the successes or failures of one's own or another country's educational system, and on how it can be improved. Preliminary assessments of options for educational reform may be obtained by examining educational programmes in other countries.

SUMMARY

International research in geographical education is the result of key questions asked by scholars and teachers in the field, and of dissatisfaction with the present way of teaching geography or with performance on comparative measures of geography achievement. Whatever the scale or area of focus for international research, each study undertaken contributes to collective knowledge about the topic. Studies are important in their own right, but, in order to be fully useful to the geographical education community internationally, certain standards of research must be attained. These are reflected in bibliographies and reports in the broader research literature, which is the essential starting place in designing and carrying out an international research project.

REFERENCES

Anderzohn, M.L. (1963) *A Selected Bibliography of Geography Education for Curriculum Committees*. Normal, IL: National Council for Geographic Education.
Ball, J.M. (1969) *A Bibliography for Geographic Education*. Geography Curriculum Project. Athens, GA: University of Georgia.
Barrows, T.S. (1981) *College Students' Knowledge and Beliefs: A Survey of Global Understanding*. New Rochelle, NY: Change Magazine Press.
Birkenhauer, J. and Marsden, W. (eds) (1988) *German Didactics of Geography in the Seventies and Eighties: A Review of Trends and Endeavours*. Munich: Didaktik der Geographie.

Boden, P. (1977) *Promoting International Understanding through School Textbooks*. Braun-schweig: Georg Eckert Institute for International Textbook Research.

Chapin, J.R. (1974) *Social Studies Dissertations: 1969-1973*. Boulder, CO: Social Science Education Consortium.

Educational Resources Information Center (1994) *ERIC: Index*. Washington, DC: US Department of Education.

Gallup Organization (1989a) *A Gallup Survey of Geographic Knowledge in the Soviet Union*. Princeton, NJ: Gallup Organization.

Gallup Organization (1989b) *Geography: An International Gallup Survey*. Princeton, NJ: Gallup Organization.

Graves, N.J. (1972) *Geography in Education: A Bibliography of British Sources, 1870-1970*. Sheffield: Geographical Association.

Graves, N.J. (ed.) (1984) *Research and Research Methods in Geographical Education*. London: University of London Institute of Education.

Gross, R. and de la Cruz, L. (1971) *Social Studies Dissertations, 1963-1969*. ERIC Clearing-house for Social Studies/Social Science Education.

Gunn, A.M. (ed.) (1972) *High School Geography Project: Legacy for the Seventies*. Vancouver, BC: International Geographical Union, Commission on Geographical Education.

Hepburn, M.A. and Dahler, A. (1983) *Social Studies Dissertations, 1977-1982*. ERIC Clear-inghouse for Social Studies/Social Science Education and Social Science Education Consortium.

IAEP (1989) *A World of Differences: An International Assessment of Mathematics and Science*. Princeton, NJ: Educational Testing Services.

Jahoda, G. (1963) 'The development of children's ideas about country and nationality.' *British Journal of Educational Psychology*, **33** 47-60.

Lambert, W.E. and Klineberg, O. (1967) *Children's Views of Foreign Peoples*. New York: Apple-ton-Century-Crofts.

Marsden, W.E. (1980) 'The West German Geography Curriculum Project: a comparative view.' *Journal of Curriculum Studies*, **12** (1), 13-27.

Matley, I (1987) 'In search of mutual understanding: the Netherlands-United States Textbook Study.' *Professional Geographer*, **39** (1), 80-3.

McClellan, M. (1994) 'Why blame schools?' *Research Bulletin*, **12** 4.

McPhie, W.E. (1964) *Dissertations in Social Studies Education: A Comprehensive Guide*. Wash-ington, DC: National Council for the Social Studies.

Mehlinger, H.D. (1989) 'American textbook reform: what can we learn from the Soviet experi-ence?' *Kappan*. **70** (1), 29-33.

Naish, M.C. (1972) *Some Aspects of the Study and Teaching of Geography in Britain: A Review of Recent British Research*. Sheffield: Geographical Association.

National Geographic Society (1988) *Geography: An International Gallup Survey*. Princeton, NJ: Gallup Organization.

Niemz, G. (1984) 'Improving geographic curricula by analyzing student achievement in geo-graphy.' In 25th International Geographical Congress Committee (ed.) *International Geographical Congress: Abstracts of Papers*. Paris: 1984.

Niemz, G. (1988) 'International project on geographical achievement of students.' In R. Gerber and J. Lidstone (eds) *Skills in Geographical Education Symposium '88*. Brisbane: International Geographical Union Commission on Geographical Education.

Niemz, G. and Stoltman, J.P. (1992) 'Cross-national testing in geography: a report.' In A.D. Hill (ed) *Interdependence in Geographic Education*. Boulder, CO: Center for Geographic Education.

Piaget, J. and Weil, A. (1951) 'The development in children of the idea of the homeland and of relations with other countries.' *International Social Science Bulletin*, **3** 561-78.

Pike, L.W. and Barrows, T.S. (1979) *Other Nations, Other Peoples*. Washington, DC: US Gov-erment Printing Office.

Postlethwaite, T.N. and Wiley, D.E. (eds) (1992) *The IEA Study of Science II: Science Achieve-ment in Twenty-Three Countries*. Oxford: Pergamon.

Rice, M.J. and Cobb, R.L. (1978) *What Can Children Learn in Geography?: A Review of Research*. Boulder, CO: Social Science Education Consortium.

Rosier, M.J. and Keeves, J.P. (eds) (1991) *The IEA Study of Science I: Science Education and Curricula in Twenty-Three Countries*. Oxford: Pergamon.

Saveland, R.N. and Pannell, C.W. (1978) *Some Aspects of the Study and Teaching of Geography in the United States: A Review of Research, 1965–1975*. Sheffield: Geographical Association.

Sperling, W. (1978) *Geographiedidaktische Quellenkunde: Internationale Basisbibliographie und Einführung in die wissenschaftlichen Hilfsmittel*. Duisburg: Verlag fur Padagogische Dokumentation.

Stevenson, H.W., Lee, S.-Y and Stigler, J.W. (1986) 'Mathematics achievement of Chinese, Japanese, and American children.' *Science*, **231**, 693–9.

Stoltman, J.P. (1985) 'Geography in education.' In C.D. Harris (ed.) *Geographical Bibliography for American Libraries*. Washington, DC: National Geographic Society.

Stoltman, J.P. (1991) 'Research on geography teaching.' In J. Shaver (ed.) *Handbook of Research on Social Studies Teaching and Learning*. New York: Macmillan.

Stoltman, J.P. and Niemz, W.G. (1992a) 'The field trials report on InterGeo II.' In A.D. Hill (ed.) *Interdependence in Geographic Education*. Boulder, CO: University of Colorado.

Stoltman, J.P. and Niemz, W.G. (1992b) 'InterGeo II: the development and field trials of an international geography test.' In A.D. Hill (ed.) *International Perspectives on Geographic Education*. Boulder, CO: University of Colorado.

Travers, K.J. and Westbury, I. (eds) (1989) *The IEA Study of Mathematics I: Analysis of Mathematics Curricula*. New York: Pergamon.

Wrubel, P.R. and Ratliff, R. (1978) *Social Studies Dissertations: 1973–1976*. Boulder, CO: Social Studies Education Consortium.

Chapter 7

An Eclectic Approach to Qualitative Research Design in Geographical Education

Graham Corney

This chapter is concerned with some of the issues relating to the planning and design of a qualitative research study. Books on research methods are widely available; however, they often discuss design issues in general terms, and where they do refer to specific studies, these rarely include examples from the field of geographical education. Yet it is much easier for a researcher to understand the issues that need to be taken into account in planning a study, and to appreciate the advantages and limitations of the options available, when these are related to the field in which he or she is working, and, particularly, when their significance can be seen in the context of a specific study.

This chapter, therefore, aims to provide a checklist which summarizes important issues relating to design, and to discuss some of them in more detail in relation to a research study which brings together geographical and environmental education – how beginning secondary school geography teachers think and teach about environmental topics, and what seem to be the influences on them. It needs stressing here that space precludes more than a brief comment on many issues, and careful selection has been made to provide a fuller comment on some of the issues specifically related to this study.

RESEARCH TRADITIONS AND ECLECTICISM

The emphasis in this chapter is on the qualitative research tradition, some of the recurring features of which are described by Miles and Huberman (1994, pp. 5–7):

- there is close contact with the everyday life of individuals and groups;
- the aim is to obtain an overall understanding of the context under study;
- researchers try to collect data about and understand the meanings underlying the actions of the people involved from their perspective;
- researchers make interpretations of the material in various ways, remaining close to the original data;
- relatively little standardized instrumentation is used at the outset;
- most analysis is carried out with words.

However, the qualitative research tradition is probably best viewed as a number of related approaches, each with its own methodology and underlying philosophy. In some respects, these approaches are similar to the concept of paradigms in geography and in geographical education; different groups of researchers draw up different classifications and explain the characteristics of each approach in differing terms, and the emphasis given to different approaches or paradigms itself varies over time.

For example, Atkinson *et al.* (1993, pp. 16–31) describe seven approaches that have been used in British qualitative research: symbolic interactionism, anthropology, socio-linguistics, ethnomethodology, evaluation, neo-Marxist ethnography, and feminist research. Anderson and Burns (1989, pp. 69–72) and Miles and Huberman (1994, p. 5) draw on Jacob's (1987) taxonomy, which describes five approaches: ecological psychology, holistic ethnography, ethnography of communication, cognitive anthropology and symbolic interactionism. There is, however, recognition in all three texts that much research combines elements of different approaches.

This last point is important not only within the qualitative tradition, but also between that traditional and others (such as confirmatory or correlational, experimental, action research, historical). Some researchers choose, for a particular study, a methodology which follows closely the characteristics of one research tradition or even one approach within that tradition. Other researchers, while working mainly within one tradition or approach, are more eclectic.

This recognition serves to highlight an important principle: the choice of research tradition or approach, as well as that of specific methods of data collection and analysis, should be made in relation to the particular aims of the study and in order to answer its specific research questions. The suitability of choosing approaches and instruments for the purpose, and the resulting eclectic approach to research, is commonly asserted.

Bell (1993, pp. 5–6), states that:

> different styles, traditions or approaches use different methods for collecting data, but no approach prescribes or automatically rejects any particular method ... Classifying an approach ... does not mean that once an approach has been selected, the researcher may not move from the methods normally associated with that style. The approach adopted and the methods of data collection selected will depend on the nature of the inquiry and the type of information required.

Miles and Huberman (1994), in their essential text *Qualitative Data Analysis*, note that 'we tend to be pragmatic ... any method that works – that will produce clear, verifiable, credible meanings from a set of qualitative data – is grist for our mill, regardless of antecedents' (p. 3); and emphasize that, 'the analytical issues that arise as a study is bounded, focussed, and organised ... must be dealt with uniquely in any particular study' (p. 16).

Davies *et al.* (1985), also concerned with qualitative methods, write, 'our case is that mono-methodic cases in social studies are only contingently justifiable ... because they are easier to handle or because they provide purity' (p. 289) and:

> in principle, we do not believe in integrating methodologies insofar as this would involve integrating theoretical perspectives ... But we think it wilfully damaging not to juxtapose methods and their datafruits within perspectives and then to ask the more difficult question of how far it is possible ... to listen with profit to the stories yielded by differing perspect-ival tongues, forbidding anyone, for the moment, to drown out the others. The orientation towards research we will call eclectic'.

(Davies *et al.*, 1985, p. 291)

This chapter adopts a similarly eclectic approach to design: it advocates an understanding by the researcher of both the main qualitative research approaches and the overall research traditions; and it advocates careful and reasoned decisions in the planning phase so that the design of a study is best fitted to answer the particular questions posed.

ISSUES OF RESEARCH DESIGN WITHIN A QUALITATIVE RESEARCH APPROACH

The following list summarizes some of the main considerations which need to be taken into account in setting up the design for a qualitative research study. These are drawn from my own experience in carrying out research and supervising teachers studying for a higher degree in geographical education, and are adapted from some established texts (Anderson, 1990; Anderson and Burns, 1989; Bell, 1993; Miles and Huberman, 1994). The considerations are intended to provide an appropriate checklist for designing any qualitative research study.

1. What are the preliminary considerations?
   1.1 Selecting a topic:
   - Why is it important?
   - What is the problem being investigated?
   - What tentative research questions can be developed at this stage?
   1.2 Deciding on an overall methodology:
   - What qualitative research approaches might be appropriate?
   - How much shape is wanted in the design at the outset?
   1.3 Practical issues:
   - How will research decisions and their rationale be recorded?
   - How might the different phases of the research be timed?
2. What is the conceptual framework?
   - What areas of literature can you draw on?
3. What are the refined research questions?
   - What might be expected to happen, and why?
4. What is the plan of study?
   - What will be the sources of evidence?
   - How will the evidence be sampled?
   - How will the evidence be collected?
   - What meaning will the evidence have?
   - What sorts of analysis will be carried out?
   - How will the findings be written up?
5. What is the shape and timing of the research design overall?

However, the reasons underlying a research study – as well as its purpose – influence the design, especially the depth of treatment of particular considerations. Thus, in a postgraduate diploma-level study, it is helpful to be aware of all the considerations above, but the level at which they are addressed will depend on course requirements and expectations, while in a doctoral study or for a major research project, these issues will need to be considered in greater depth.

In addition, although the checklist has been written in linear form and can be followed in that way, in practice each of the steps is likely to be revisited more than once, and decisions about one aspect continually inform others, so that there is a gradual process of focusing and clarifying the design. In the commentary which follows, the headings refer to those in the checklist.

Preliminary considerations

About the topic

A first step in the process of designing a study is choosing a topic for investigation. This probably involves thinking about several topics, reviewing their advantages and limitations, and narrowing down the list through reading, discussion and reflection. Several factors can be considered in this process, but, as with many decisions about research, there is likely to be a trade-off between competing demands, and the eventual decisions are likely to represent a compromise. Factors to be considered at this stage include personal interest – for many people, this arises from their work; academic considerations, such as reading about any existing research in the topic area, and being aware of course requirements or supervisor's specialisms if the research is for an advanced award-bearing qualification; and practical considerations, such as the time available, and ease of access to libraries and to the people or 'cases' who are the focus of the research.

The process of choosing a topic and clarifying ideas about the research should also include two essential features; noting possible research questions for each topic, and identifying a problem which can be investigated in each. Both of these lead to the development of a clear focus and purpose for the study. Helpful advice about defining a research problem is given in Anderson (1990, Ch. 3, including a useful summary of ten characteristics of a good thesis research problem), and framing questions is given in Bell (1993, Ch. 2).

About methodology

While clarifying the topic, a problem and preliminary questions to be investigated, it is a good idea to consider overall research traditions and various approaches within them. This allows evaluation of some of the advantages and limitations of different approaches and the methods usually associated with them, in relation to the topic, problem and questions which seem to be emerging. The sections and chapters in this book present one way of categorizing research traditions; Gerber's chapter (Chapter 2) on qualitative research reviews some of the main approaches within that tradition. Other useful references include Cohen and Manion (1989), which is an essential basic text, Bell (1993, Ch. 1) and Anderson (1990, Pt III).

Probably one of the most important early decisions about methodology is whether the study will be more quantitative or qualitative in emphasis. Anderson and Burns (1989, Ch. 3) highlight helpfully the distinction between these traditions when they refer to 'modes of inquiry' as confirmatory and interpretive. After contrasting them under several heads, they conclude that 'confirmatory inquiry seeks verification of theory and is nomethetic and experimental. In contrast, interpretive inquiry seeks to generate theory and is idiographic and naturalistic ... however, studies of classrooms do not fall neatly into these two extremes' (p. 81).

Similarly, an important decision related to qualitative research is the degree to which the design is shaped at the outset. Some qualitative researchers prefer to make the main decisions about design before beginning data collection so they have a prestructured design; others prefer to have a more open, flexible design in which increasing familiarity and understanding of the people and situations being studied lead to continual evolution and dynamism. Useful discussions about the degree of shape can be found in Measor and Woods (1991, pp. 60–2) and Miles and Huberman (1994, pp. 16–18).

In thinking about all aspects of methodology, however, it is worth remembering the points made at the start of this chapter – that one need not draw only on one tradition or approach, but should be in a position to select what seem to be the appropriate methods for the purpose.

Practical issues

This section is included to emphasize the importance of systematically recording all decisions made, not only in the design stage but throughout the research. Advice about record-keeping is given in many texts, often related to specific issues, such as the literature review or data storage and retrieval. It is essential, however, to note, record and be able easily to retrieve details of any decisions made affecting the research. The format is less important than the fact that recording is carried out rigorously and systematically, so that it is possible to review and learn from these decisions, as well as having a ready source of evidence to help in writing the methodology section in a thesis or report.

This area of preliminary considerations is illustrated in relation to the 'Teaching about Environment Topics' example discussed below.

Defining a conceptual framework

Having decided on a topic, identified a problem and a set of tentative questions, and begun to consider the general shape of the methodology, the next step is to define a conceptual framework.

Miles and Huberman (1994, pp. 18–22) provide useful guidance. They describe a conceptual framework as explaining 'either graphically or in narrative form the main things to be studied – the key factors, constructs, or variables – and the presumed relationships among them'. Their preference is for a graphical form, allowing the researcher 'to specify the "bins" that hold discrete phenomena, to map likely relationships, to divide variables that are conceptually or functionally distinct, and to work with all of the information at once'.

An initial framework might summarize the researcher's preliminary ideas, and this can be successively developed by adding variables and relationships from the literature and perhaps from evidence collected in the study.

The advantages of developing a conceptual framework are that it helps the researcher to:

- think about and conceptualize the phenomena;
- carry out an effective literature search;
- redefine the research questions;
- guide the collection and interpretation of evidence.

The purpose of reviewing the literature is to obtain an overall understanding of the state of knowledge and the major problems in the topic area, and to be able to draw on this in interpreting evidence in the study. In writing this up, it is usually helpful to use similar headings to the conceptual framework and group under these the writing of different authors; to discuss in more detail any work which seems to be particularly important for the study being undertaken; and to evaluate research methods developed in other studies which might be useful. Practical advice about reviewing the literature can be found in Anderson (1990, Ch. 8) and Bell (1993, Ch. 3).

Refining research questions

The research questions can now be refined on the basis of the conceptual framework and preliminary review of the literature. In many studies, questions are sequenced into two main parts: first, descriptive questions, through which the researcher intends to summarize or categorize the evidence, and to identify variations among phenomena; secondly, associational questions, through which the researcher will attempt to relate certain features to others (see Anderson and Burns, 1989, pp. 86–8).

The plan of study

> A research plan is a blueprint for organising evidence. The plan outlines how the evidence will be sampled, gathered, and analysed. The plan will determine, in part, how well the questions under study will be addressed. The evidence gathered during a study is given meaning by the conceptual framework, but an existing conceptual framework can only do so much. The research plan must be such that the evidence gathered allows the researcher to modify existing frameworks and develop new ones.
>
> (Anderson and Burns, 1989, p. 94)

In considering elements of the research plan, it is worth remembering that, essentially, qualitative research emphasizes description, understanding, and interpretation of events and of the behaviour of persons and groups in their context, and attempts to explain the meanings underlying these events and behaviours.

Sources of evidence

In qualitative research, sources of evidence can include people – for example, geography teachers, students or policy-makers; settings – for example, classrooms, field visits, staffrooms or offices; and situations – for example, teaching situations like student group work, teacher questioning class, or planning or review meetings.

Decisions about sampling

These will reflect the qualitative research concern with in-depth studies of people and events in context. Some decisions may be made at the outset while others may be taken as the study proceeds. Qualitative sampling tends to be purposive and theory-driven, relating to the people or behaviours forming the focus of study. Miles and Huberman (1994, pp. 27–34) note that sampling involves setting boundaries to define the case(s) being studied both practically (time and means) and in relation to the research questions, and creating a frame to define the processes or constructs on which the study is based. They provide a useful discussion of the issues involved, a typology of sampling strategies, and guidance for establishing criteria for sampling (see also Anderson and Burns, 1989, pp. 98–102; Cohen and Manion, 1989).

An aspect of research which relates to both the sources and sampling of evidence is the process of negotiating access to people, settings and situations, and the necessity of agreeing about shared expectations with people involved in the study. Bell (1993, Ch. 5) provides useful practical advice on these points, and Miles and Huberman (1994, pp. 47–8) supplement their discussion with a set of 'questions for agreement with study participants'.

Methods for collecting evidence

In qualitative research, the methods can be summarized as follows:

- *asking*, either orally through interviews (which may be taped), or in written form, including questionnaires, all with varied degrees of structure;
- *collecting*; for example, student handouts or photographs taken in lessons, or policy documents;
- *observation* (which may be audio- or videotaped); for example, making field notes or using a systematic observation schedule in a lesson or meeting.

Many texts review the purposes, advantages and limitations of data collection instruments (e.g. Walker, 1985, Chs. 3, 4; Cohen and Manion, 1989; Anderson, 1990, Pt IV; Bell, 1993 Pt II).

Ascribing meaning to the evidence

This is particularly important in qualitative research because it is one of the main research purposes, and because statistical procedures for validity and reliability are inappropriate. It is an issue addressed more particularly in analysing evidence; however, several principles need to be considered at the design stage because they affect other aspects of the plan of study.

Anderson and Burns (1989, p. 162, Ch. 6) note the importance of matching 'the strengths of particular sources of evidence with the demands of the research study' and of recognizing that 'multiple sources of evidence are more likely to provide ... understanding ... to solve the problems [researchers] pose or answer the questions they raise'. They also suggest consideration of two questions: 'First, is the evidence meaningful to researchers and other people with whom they come into contact (e.g. colleagues, clients, practitioners)? Secondly, is the evidence of sufficient quality to ensure its credibility and accuracy?' Their ensuing discussion points out some implications and includes five recommendations for 'Enhancing the meaning of evidence' (see also Miles and Huberman, 1994, Ch. 10).

Analysing the data and writing up the findings

These are two aspects of qualitative research which can be tentatively considered at the design stage, but are most likely to be considered fully as the researcher becomes familiar with the nature of evidence being collected. To continue the practice of referring to useful readings, however, the following provide helpful advice for these processes: Anderson and Burns, 1989, Ch. 7; Bell, 1993, Chs. 11, 12; Miles and Huberman, 1994, Chs. 4–12.

The overall shape and timing of the design

Finally, within this sequence of design activities, it is advisable to produce an overall summary of the research design, including timings. The progress of research rarely follows the initial timings envisaged, but the exercise of drawing up a schedule which can be referred to from time to time helps the researcher to meet self-imposed or externally imposed deadlines.

TEACHING ABOUT ENVIRONMENTAL TOPICS

This section refers to an example of a research study in progress to illustrate some of the considerations noted above which seem to be especially important in this research. It focuses on how beginning secondary-school geography teachers think and teach about environmental topics, and what seem to be the influences on them. The evidence on which this section is based is drawn from notes and records made as decisions were taken on the basis of reading, discussion with colleagues and reflection – though in retrospect, these are not always as detailed as they might have been! (see my section on 'practical issues' above.)

Preliminary considerations

The initial thoughts for this research study arose from previous experience and interest. The area of interest developed through the experience of teaching geography graduates on an initial teacher education course. The topic was originally stated as 'beginning geography teachers and their learning about teaching environmental topics in secondary schools'. The problem identified was that teaching environmental topics seemed to present beginning teachers with decisions about teaching strategies, including the teacher's role and approach to student values education, and selecting appropriate subject matter.

This seemed to me to be an important area for several reasons:

- Preliminary reading suggested that there were research frameworks that could be both drawn on and contributed to, including the areas of geographical and environmental education, teacher thinking and teacher education.
- The study was expected to provide useful feedback about the geography component of the Postgraduade Certificate in Education (PGCE) course taught in an English university department of educational studies.
- It was thought the study would provide evidence to contribute to the debate about the nature of initial teacher education, especially the value of school and higher-education experiences (see Ruddock, 1991).

Tentative research questions were initially drawn up:

1. How and what do beginning teachers teach about the environment?
2. What account do they take of subject matter and pedagogical considerations in making their choices?
3. Do their beliefs about teaching and their pedagogical practices change during the course of the PGCE year and first year of teaching?

First thoughts about methodology developed from the increasing realization that learning to teach was a very individual process, as were the sorts of thing that seemed to be influential in that process. A qualitative approach, therefore, seemed most appropriate, and, taking into account the nature of the PGCE course and the need to collect data about individuals in context, five methods of data collection were identified:

1. an autobiographical interview at the start of the year with a small sample of student teachers (to ascertain their thinking at the start of the year);
2. a sequence of lesson observations and related pre-lesson and post-lesson interviews with these students (to observe their practice, which might not be the same as what they said in interviews about it);
3. an end-of-course interview with each of them (to discover their thinking at the end of the year);
4. a questionnaire given to the whole geography group on three occasions during the year (to provide a contextual background in which to set the sample);
5. two interviews with the sample students on two occasions during their first year of teaching (to follow up some students into their first teaching post, to gain additional data).

The conceptual framework

The initial thoughts and research questions were revised after developing a conceptual framework along the lines suggested above, and through further reading, discussion and reflection (see Figure 7.1).

The topic became more focused and conceptualized, being stated as 'how beginning secondary school geography teachers think and teach about environmental topics, and what seem to be the influences on them'. It was seen to relate to three main areas of theory:

Figure 7.2 *The conceptual framework.*

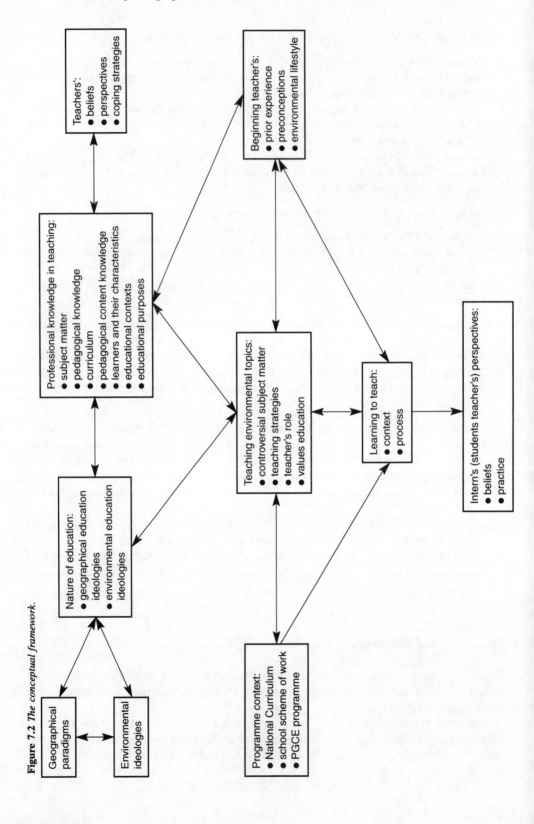

1. *Contemporary thinking and research in geographical and environmental education.*
   Drawing on the literature, it was possible to identify several conceptual areas:
   (a) Teaching about environmental topics can be regarded as a controversial issue
       and, therefore, involves making decisions about:
       (i) teaching strategies including the role of the teacher (Stenhouse, 1975)
           and the approach to values education for students (Fien and Slater,
           1985; Huckle, 1985; Slater, 1992);
       (ii) the selection of subject matter and case studies (Posch, 1993);
       (iii) underlying ideologies of environmentalism (O'Riordan, 1992), educa-
           tion (Slater, 1992) and environmental education (Fien, 1993; Huckle,
           1992).
   (b) These decisions are likely to be made in the context of the National Curricu-
       lum and a school's scheme of work. At the time of data collection,
       environmental geography was specified as one of the five Attainment Targets
       in the English Statutory Orders for Geography in the National Curriculum
       (DES, 1991); environmental topics could be identified in the other four; and
       environmental education was specified as one of the cross-curriculum themes
       (National Curriculum Council, 1990).
   (c) Beginning teachers themselves are likely to have their own environmental
       interests and lifestyles, and these may reflect the current interest and public
       concern about environmental issues.
2. *Research in teacher thinking.* This suggested that:
   (a) teachers draw on a variety of professional knowledge in teaching, including
       pedagogical content knowledge, which consists of subject matter knowledge
       plus knowledge of the learner, the curriculum, the context, and pedagogy
       (Shulman, 1986, 1987; NCRTE, 1989; Calderhead, 1993);
   (b) teachers' beliefs and ideologies influence the way in which they view and
       draw on these sources of knowledge (Connelly and Clandinin, 1990;
       Gudmunsdottir, 1990); particularly useful concepts include teacher's 'coping
       strategies', selected to negotiate institutional constraints in their teaching in a
       particular context (Lacey, 1977; Hargreaves, 1984), and teacher's 'perspect-
       ives', seen as a co-ordinated set of ideas and actions used in dealing with
       some problematic situation, which reflect the effects of personal beliefs and
       contextual influences (Zeichner *et al.*, 1987).
3. *Research on teacher education.* This highlighted:
   (a) the influence of prior experience and preconceptions on the process of learn-
       ing to teach (Kennedy, 1990; NCRTE, 1989; Calderhead, 1988, 1991);
   (b) the influence of beginning teacher's conceptions about learning to teach
       (Calderhead 1988 and 1991);
   (c) the nature and philosophy of initial teacher education programmes (Benton,
       1990; Feiman-Nemser, 1990; McIntyre, 1990; Cochrane-Smith, 1991).

The refined questions

The refined research questions are given below. Comparison with the initial questions
shows the greater detail and precision which had been reached at this stage.

1. At the start of the PGCE year:
    (a) what knowledge, understanding and beliefs do student teachers have about:
        (i) environmental topics in geography;
        (ii) teacher's professional knowledge;
        (iii) how they will learn to teach?
    (b) what interaction of personal and contextual factors seems to influence their knowledge, understanding and beliefs (their images?) in these areas?
2. During their PGCE year and their first year of teaching:
    (a) do their knowledge, understanding and beliefs in these areas change, and if so how?
    (b) how does their practice develop?
    (c) what interaction of personal and contextual factors seems to influence their perspectives in these areas?

The plan of study

The plan of study (similar to that described above) is summarized in Table 7.1. Further detail, explanation and justification is given for certain aspects in the sections which follow.

Table 7.1 *Plan of study: Year 1.*

Timing	Phase	Sources of evidence	Collection of evidence	Product
Autumn	1. Interns at the beginning	Whole group of geography interns Case interns PGCE Programme	Structured writing Taped interview Documents	Numerical summary Vignettes Written analysis
	2. Joint school-university experience	Sample university experiences Sample school experiences Case interns	Observation; interviews – field notes, tapes Written assignments; profile	Written descriptions and analyses
Spring		Whole group Case interns	Structured writing Taped interview	Numerical summary Vignettes – emerging themes
	3. School experience – Phase 1	Case interns	Lesson observations – field notes; intern documents Pre- and post-lesson taped interviews Written assignments; profile	Written descriptions and analyses – ongoing themes
Summer	4. School experience – Phase 2	Case interns	Lesson observations – field notes; intern documents Pre- and post-lesson taped interviews Written assignments; profile	Written descriptions and analyses – ongoing themes
	5. Interns at the end of the year	Whole group Case interns	Structured writing Taped interview	Numerical summary Vignettes – themes Synthesizing the stories

Sources of evidence

These consisted of the whole group of geography interns (student teachers) at certain times providing an overview and helping to situate the sample who were to be the focus of the research. These interns were learning to teach through a combination of university-based and school-based activities where they worked with university tutors, school mentors and other teachers.

Decisions about sampling

These reflected the overall purpose of the research, its specific setting and its methodological approach. Several important decisions were made:

1. Schools rather than interns were first selected because school context was thought to be an important influence on learning to teach. The criteria adopted for selection of schools was their choice of public examination syllabuses (for example, though not solely, General Certificate of Secondary Education Avery Hill and General Certificate of Education Advanced Level Geography 16–19 syllabuses) and the school's own scheme of work. Together, these suggested where possibilities for teaching about environmental topics were most favourable.

    Individual mentors from among the possible range of schools were then an important criterion. Consideration was given to those who would allow interns to teach environmental topics during the times of school experience in the PGCE course, those I knew to be professionally willing to encourage interns to reflect and practise in a guided but individual way, and those who were themselves interested in educational research.

2. The interns were placed in schools mainly following normal practice. This took into account their own preferences and previous experience, and the knowledge of the university tutors, who tried to match interns with mentors and types of school.

3. Initially, four schools and their complement of eight geography interns formed the sample. The normal practice of pairing interns as far as possible was followed. It was thought that a pair working in the same context might provide insight into the ways in which individual interns taught and the factors that influenced them. It was also thought that four schools and eight interns would cover unanticipated problems with either schools or interns, and allow progressive focusing on a smaller sample if that seemed to become desirable as the research progressed.

4. The time schedule for data collection and analysis was largely conditioned by the organization of the PGCE programme. This reflected the study's naturalistic approach to research.

5. Sampling of lessons was considered in principle, but the exact nature of this part of the plan was left open in the initial design stage so that a more informed decision could be taken nearer the events and with a fuller understanding of the topic area.

Earlier in this chapter, reference was made to the importance of negotiating access to people involved in the study. This was important in this case because of the dual role of the reseacher as both researcher and tutor (see below). A set of ethical principles was designed at an early stage and these guided the researcher's behaviour (see Clandinin and Connelly, 1988).

Methods for collecting evidence

The choice of instruments was conditioned by the research questions and the method-ological approach adopted. This demonstrates the eclectic approach to research adopted in the study, illustrating the points made about suitability of methods for purpose noted at the start of the chapter. They are summarized in Table 7.1.

Ascribing meaning to the evidence

In order to help with this process, it was important in the design stage to be clear about the research philosophy. The philosophy adopted was that of research as interpretive inquiry (Anderson and Burns, 1989, pp. 67–70, 72–80). The purpose was seen as an attempt to understand the teaching of beginning geography teachers on environmental topics, and in particular to discover and analyse their perspectives and to attempt to generate theory in this area. The research plan was seen as naturalistic.

It could also be related to Cohen and Manion's (1989, Ch. 5) typology of 'observa-tion studies', reflecting the degree of structure in the setting (natural to artificial) and imposed by the observer (unstructured to structured). The study setting was seen to be towards the natural end of the continuum, with a slightly more structured than unstruc-tured observer stance. This latter factor was largely conditioned by time constraints.

Consequent on this philosophy, the role of the researcher was considered. The researcher was conceptualized as an involved interpreter (Anderson and Burns, 1989, p. 78). I was involved in the culture and through my involvement was attempting to construct meaning out of events to provide understanding to other people who were not present.

This role seemed to match my position as university tutor working with the geography interns and as researcher. It was recognized that further conceptualization of this role was needed, but at the outset, the following points were highlighted:

1. the existence of this dual role, so that it would be important to monitor carefully the stance of any actions taken in both roles;
2. recognition that evidence about how interns viewed the research should be obtained at various times and in different ways, including opportunities for getting at their views in the absence of the tutor;
3. the need for the researcher to make a virtue out of this dual role, because it allowed access to data that other people might not be able to obtain but which could help with understanding the perspectives of the interns; for example:
    (a) programme-wide data, and philosophy (because the researcher helped to establish the programme);
    (b) intern opportunities for learning through university activities, especially unanticipated events which could be important;
    (c) interns' work in school, both their teaching and discussions with mentor;

(d)   interns' profiling and written assignments as part of the course;
(e)   mentors' teaching and views about interns' learning (to provide insight into the context);
(f)   the researcher's own views as tutor about interns' learning.

CONCLUSION

This chapter has provided a checklist of considerations relating to qualitative research design, and an example of a qualitative research study on teaching environmental topics in geography. Some of the issues of design have been illustrated in greater detail through this example.

Selective emphasis is inevitable, given the scale of the task of designing qualitative research and the number of important issues that need to be considered, especially when related to constraints of space.

However, in addition to providing more detailed discussion about certain design considerations, the chapter has attempted to illustrate the philosophy that in any qualitative research study, the most important feature is to choose from among research traditions, approaches and methods what seems to be most appropriate to the purposes of a particular study. In this way, the chapter represents a view in favour of eclecticism in approach to qualitative research design.

REFERENCES

Anderson, G. (1990) *Fundamentals of Educational Research*. Basingstoke: Falmer.

Anderson, L.G. and Burns, R.B. (1989) *Research in Classrooms – The Study of Teachers, Teaching, and Instruction*. Oxford: Pergamon.

Atkinson, P., Delamont, S. and Hammersley, M. (1993) 'Qualitative research traditions'. In M. Hammersley, (ed.) *Educational Research – Current Issues. Vol. 1*. London: Paul Chapman.

Bell, J. (1993) *Doing Your Research Project*. Buckingham: Open University Press.

Benton, P. (ed.) (1990) *The Oxford Internship Scheme: Integration and Partnership in Initial Teacher Education*. London: Calouste Gulbenkian Foundation.

Calderhead, J. (1988) 'The development of knowledge structures in learning to teach'. In J. Calderhead, (ed.) *Teachers' Professional Learning*. Lewes: Falmer.

Calderhead, J. (1991) 'The nature and growth of knowledge in student teaching'. *Teaching and Teacher Education*, **7** (5/6), 531–5.

Calderhead, J. (1993) 'The contribution of research on teachers' thinking to the professional development of teachers.' In C. Day, J. Calderhead, and P. Denicolo, (eds) *Research on Teacher Thinking – Understanding Professional Development*. London: Falmer.

Clandinin, D.J. and Connelly, F.M. (1988) 'Studying teachers' knowledge of classrooms: collaborative research, ethics, and the negotiation of narrative'. *Journal of Educational Thought*, **22** (2A), 269–82.

Cochrane-Smith, M. (1991) 'Re-inventing student teaching.' *Journal of Teacher Education*, **42**, (2) 104–18.

Cohen, L. and Manion, L. (1989) *Research Methods in Education*. Beckenham: Croom Helm.

Connelly, F.M. and Clandinin, D.J. (1990) 'Stories of experience and narrative enquiry.' *Educational Researcher*, **19** (4), 2–14.

Davies, B., Corbishley, P., Evans, J. and Kenwick, C. (1985) 'Integrating methodologies: if the intellectual relations don't get you, the social will'. In R.G. Burgess, (ed.) *Strategies of Educational Research – Qualitative Methods*. Lewes: Falmer.

DES (1991) *Orders for Geography in the National Curriculum*. London: HMSO.

Feiman-Nemser, S. (1990) *Conceptions in Teacher Education*. Issue Paper 90–2. East Lansing, MI: National Center for Research in Teacher Learning, Michigan State University.

Fien, J. (1993) *Education for the Environment: Critical Curriculum Theorizing and Environmental Education*. Melbourne: Deakin University.

Fien, J. and Slater, F. (1985) 'Four strategies for values education in geography.' In D. Boardman, (ed.) *New Directions in Geographical Education*. Lewes: Falmer.

Gudmunsdottir, S. (1990) 'Values in pedagogical content knowledge.' *Journal of Teacher Education*. **41** (3) 44–52.

Hargreaves, D.H. (1984) 'Teacher's questions: open, closed and half-open.' *Educational Research*, **26**, (1) 46–52.

Huckle, J. (1985) 'Values education through geography: a radical critique.' In D. Boardman, (ed.) *New Directions in Geographical Education*, Lewes: Falmer.

Huckle, J. (1992) 'Environmental education: teaching for a sustainable future.' In B. Dufour, (ed.) *The New Social Curriculum*. Cambridge: Cambridge University Press.

Kennedy, M.M. (1990) *A Survey of Recent Literature on Teachers' Subject Matter Knowledge*. Issue Paper 90–3. East Lansing, MI: National Center for Research on Teacher Learning, Michigan State University.

Lacey, C. (1977) *The Socialisation of Teachers*. London: Methuen.

McIntyre D. (1990) 'Ideas and principles guiding the internship scheme'. In P. Benton (ed.) *The Oxford Internship Scheme: Integration and Partnership in Initial Teacher Education*. London: Calouste Gulbenkian Foundation.

Measor, L. and Woods, P. (1991) 'Breakthroughs and blockages in ethnographic research: contrasting experiences during the Changing Schools Project'. In G. Walford, (ed.) *Doing Educational Research*. London: Routledge.

Miles, M.L. and Huberman, A.M. (1994) *Qualitative Data Analysis*. Thousand Oaks, CA: Sage.

National Center for Research on Teacher Education (NCRTE) (1989) *Teacher Education and Learning to Teach Study*. East Lansing, MI: Michigan State University.

National Curriculum Council (1990) *Environmental Education: Curriculum Guidance 7*. York: NCC.

O'Riordan, T. (1992) 'The environment'. In P. Cloke (ed.) *Policy and Change in Thatcher's Britain*. Oxford: Pergamon

Posch, P. (1993) 'Research issues in environmental education.' *Studies in Science Education*, **21**, 21–48.

Ruddock, J. (1991) 'The language of consciousness and the landscape of action: tensions in teacher education.' *British Educational Research Journal*, **17** (4), 319–31.

Shulman, L.S. (1986) 'Those who understand: knowledge growth in teaching.' *Educational Researcher*, **15** (2), 4–14.

Shulman, L.S. (1987) 'Knowledge and teaching: foundations of the new reform.' *Harvard Educational Review*, **57**, (1), 1–22.

Slater, F. (1992) '... to travel with a different view.' In M. Naish (ed.) *Geography and Education*. London: University of London Institute of Education.

Stenhouse, L. (1975) *An Introduction to Curriculum Research and Development*. London: Heineman.

Walker, R.W. (1985) *Doing Research – A Handbook for Teachers*. London: Methuen.

Zeichner, K.M., Tabachnick, B.R. and Densmore, K. (1987) 'Individual, institutional and cultural influences on the development of teachers' craft knowledge.' In J. Calderhead, (ed.) *Exploring Teachers' Thinking*. London: Cassell.

Chapter 8

Technical Interest in Curriculum Development: A Programme of Map Skills

Simon Catling

Research into children's understanding of maps and mapping has followed two avenues. One has been concerned with appreciating the ways in which children's map skills and concepts develop. The second has been to understand how children develop their awareness and understanding of the environments in which they live. In research approaches in both areas, children have been involved in reading, using and making maps. While the purpose of the research into mapping skills has been to provide a more informed basis for the preparation of educational map skills programmes, the research into children's environmental cognition has been multifaceted and included examination of the ways children 'map' familiar and unfamiliar environments. Yet, if anything, it is the research into children's environmental understanding which has raised awareness that children's mapping capabilities may well be underestimated.

The application of research to the development of map skills programmes has a lengthy history. Rushdoony (1968) proposed a 'gradation of map-reading skills' for 4–14-year-olds. Boardman (1983) proposed a programme of map skill development between the ages of 5 and 19. Winston (1984) and Stoltman (1992) have set out similar programmes for 5–14-year-olds and 5–12-year-olds.

This chapter considers some of the methodologies employed in researching children's understanding of maps and the use made of research findings in the development of educational map skills programmes. In the first section, several examples of research approaches are given and some conclusions are drawn and questions raised. In the second section, the development of two types of map skills programme are discussed, one being the advice given to teachers about developing map skills with primary-age children (5–11 years) and the other the preparation of a textbook series for primary-age children.

RESEARCHING MAP SKILLS

Spencer, *et al.* (1989) highlight the limitations of research into children's understanding of maps. One is the dependency on a Piagetian model of developmental stages, which they argue has often been taken too literally and has resulted in the notion, for example, that children cannot really understand maps until the age of 7. Another relates to the variety of methodologies that have been used in researching children's understanding and use of maps. These have been drawn from different disciplines and with different purposes in mind. Spencer *et al.* conclude that, despite the range of research studies, still relatively little is known about children's map-reading skills. Liben and Downs (1989) agree. Matthews (1992) and Gerber (1992) take a more positive view, though they agree that there are limitations in and to the research. They suggest that what is currently known provides a helpful basis for developing educational map skills programmes to improve children's understanding.

As Spencer *et al.* (1989) and Liben and Downs (1989) indicate, a variety of research approaches have provided insight into children's map use and understanding. In particular, these have been drawn from the disciplines of geography, education and psychology. They share an attempt, through the use of sample groups (at times across ages and sometimes within a narrow age band), to identify the characteristics of children's competence or limitations to it. This is generally set in a normative context by reference either to related research or to their research with older or younger children. There are usually claims of statistical validity for the findings even when the numbers involved are small – sometimes as low as ten to twenty children selected from a single school or kindergarten.

The purpose of this chapter is to illustrate some of the research approaches that have been used, not to provide details about the methods or findings of particular studies. These can be pursued elsewhere (e.g., Boardman, 1983; Spencer *et al.*, 1989; Matthews, 1992; Gerber, 1992; Wiegand, 1993; van Dijk *et al.*, 1994). The examples referred to below are largely focused on younger children, some on very young children. In the area of cognitive mapping and related studies of the genesis and development of map competence in children, the bulk of studies have focused on children between 3 and 12 years of age (Liben and Downs, 1989; Spencer *et al.*, 1989).

Research into children's map understanding has frequently investigated specific aspects of map capability, including their:

- representations of the environment through map drawings and what these show of children's development and style of mapping (Hart, 1979; Matthews, 1992);
- use of maps in the environment, particularly in the context of problem solving (Bluestein and Acredolo, 1979; Spencer *et al.*, 1989);
- use of toys and models to replicate or create environments, as alternatives to mapping activities (Blaut and Stea, 1974; Hart, 1979; Siegal *et al.* 1978);
- understanding of aerial photographs as map surrogates (Stea and Blaut, 1973; Spencer *et al.*, 1989);
- competence in map skills (Carswell, 1971) including the use of co-ordinates (Spencer *et al.*, 1989), symbols (Gerber, 1984) and scale (Towler and Nelson, 1968; Gerber, 1981).

RESEARCH APPROACHES

Map drawing

Inviting children to draw maps of familiar environments is an established research approach (Matthews, 1992). Its purposes have included: discovering which features in an area are known to individuals and groups of children (Bishop and Foulsham, 1973; Hart, 1979); the styles of spatial organization children use in drawing their maps – whether they use linear or aerial styles and how accurate the maps are as spatial repres- entations (Matthews, 1992; Hart, 1979); and the types of representation which children use on their maps, such as pictograms, plan views and abstract symbols (Matthews, 1992). Linked to the research into children's drawing of features on maps are studies of the way specific features are drawn, such as, buildings or hills (Gerber, 1992; Wood, 1992).

This research approach has taken two forms. One has been to take children on a walk around an area and then ask them to draw a map of the route they have taken. They may be taken individually (Piche, 1981) or in a group (Bishop and Foulsham, 1973). The other approach has been to ask children to draw their route to school or their home area (Matthews, 1992). Depending on the purpose of the research, children's maps are analysed in a variety of ways. In studies of children's perceptions of the features of the environment, the frequency with which types of feature and particular features occur is noted, illustrating the nature of the landmarks, nodes and routes that are important to children (Bishop and Foulsham, 1973; Hart, 1979; Matthews, 1992). With studies of map style, in which the interest is in the schema the child applies to representing the environment, consideration will be given to the overall arrangement of the map, perhaps taking into account the sequence of its drawing (Spencer and Lloyd, 1974; Hart, 1979). Examination of map accuracy involves considering how closely children's maps relate to a surveyed map of the same area. Children's maps may be scored for 'configuration' accuracy – the extent to which features and layout are in roughly the correct places – rather than 'metric' accuracy, which focuses on how far features are away from their correct location (Hart, 1981). The analysis of what Matthews (1992) calls 'cartographic competence', which focuses on the nature of the symbols children use in their maps to represent features, tends to judge the symbols in a continuum from pictorial to plan to representational, in which a colour or a shape may stand for a feature (Gerber, 1992; Matthews, 1992; Wood, 1992).

Setting aside the detailed findings, the key outcomes of research using these approaches indicate that children:

- identify features in the early years which are relevant to their own interests, later moving towards 'adult' notions of features, routes, etc.;
- can draw their own maps of real areas with increasing detail and accuracy with age and with experience of environments;
- tend to draw pictorial signs initially to represent features, developing an appreciation of plan-view through drawing vertical views, and then drawing plan shapes and symbols, though they often use a variety of these map signs together.

Using maps

Experimental approaches have largely focused on problem-solving' approaches (Bluestein and Acredolo, 1979; Spencer *et al.*, 1989). The purpose has been to encour- age children to use a map of a layout to find a particular item or route, or to use maps in the 'real world' to find their way around (Ottosson, 1987). The value of this research is that it has involved children in using maps. The limitation is that little work has been done with children outside laboratory conditions and in older age groups. These methods are also intensive, involving one-to-one, researcher-child working.

Two types of laboratory research have been undertaken, both involving children carrying out instructions using a map in a large-scale space. One experimental approach provides children with a large-scale map of a room in which they have to find an item shown on the map (Bluestein and Acredolo, 1979; Presson, 1982). In this case, the children look at the map and then go to find the item. The other approach provides children with a map of a maze-like route layout, which shows that, though there are alternative paths, there is only one route through (Spencer *et al*, 1989). Here the children are allowed to carry the map with them. In both cases, the way the children carry out the task is observed and their successes and errors noted.

Using their own classroom environment offers a third approach as a familiar area to children. This is not strictly a laboratory context for research, since it is full of the ordinary 'noise' of the spatial layout and features of a classroom (Downs *et al.*, 1988). It is much nearer to the everyday context of mapping and map reading than the simplified environment of laboratory conditions will allow.

Naturalistic studies of map skills are limited. One approach (Ottosson, 1987) has involved setting children the task of finding their way from one location to another in a real environment using a standard map. They are assessed on their ability to orient the map, to follow the route they have planned and to overcome errors they make. Observation of the children's actions are supplemented by interviews with them as they undertake the task, in order to appreciate the reasons for their decisions. An earlier study by Walker (1980) involved children following a route using a map in a more limited environment, in which various features had to be passed to find a 'treasure', and the accuracy of route following using the map was scored.

Three key outcomes from research using these approaches indicate that children:

- can interpret plans of familiar features and small areas from an early age;
- can relate maps to the environment in which they are from an early age, given a very clear context in which to do so, and can achieve this in more complex environments with increasing age and experience;
- are able to use a map to find features, follow a pre-planned route or work out their own route around an area and then follow it, with increasing accuracy and complexity with increasing age and experience.

Using models

A third research approach, more directly linked to research into environmental understanding, has been the use of models. The interest has lain in giving children the opportunity to use 'environmental' toys or model features in an enactive approach to research rather than requiring them to draw or talk about what they can see, are doing, or understand. This attempts to overcome the limitations of the iconic or verbal approaches (Towler and Nelson, 1968; Towler, 1970; Blaut and Stea, 1974; Stea and Taphanel, 1974; Siegal *et al.*, 1978; Hart, 1979, 1981; Weatherford, 1985). The focus is on using models as representations of places, and, in that sense, as surrogates for maps.

Three research approaches have been used. Toy play has provided the opportunity for children to make model environments using a variety of 'environmental' toys, such as road pieces, buildings, vehicles and animals (Blaut and Stea, 1974). The child is then asked to move through the environment by driving a vehicle or walking a person along the road or path from one feature to another. Judgements are made about how far the child has produced an imitation environment and can model a 'real-life' activity in it. Encouraging the child to make up a story based on the model environment can also be judged in terms of the sense the child has of the landscape.

The second approach has been to ask children to model, rather than draw, a familiar area (Hart, 1979, 1981). The model is then analysed in relation to the real area for the types of feature included and its spatial layout. Interest in the process of modelling the landscape means that a child is observed while undertaking the task, encouraged not to forget vital features, helped to realize that he or she can enlarge the model and change it, encouraged to talk about what he or she is doing, and asked to take the observer for a 'walk' or 'drive' around the model when the child is satisfied with it. A modified version of this approach has been to create a large-scale, walk-through model environment, which children are asked to model with small-scale replica or toy features, against which judgements of accuracy are made (Herman and Siegal, 1978; Siegal *et al.*, 1978).

Thirdly, models have been used in experimental contexts, children being asked to replicate layouts or features from one model on to another. This is usually linked to a map skill, such as the use of reference systems or scale (Towler and Nelson, 1968; Towler, 1970); and again, it is accuracy in the task which is measured.

From these research approaches emerge findings which indicate that children:

- from an early age are able to create model environments which are 'like' real environments;
- can relate models to the environment and to each other increasingly with age and experience;
- can make models of familiar areas with increasing accuracy with age and experience.

Using surrogate maps

A fourth approach to understanding children's map skills has been to use vertical aerial photographs (Blaut *et al.*, 1970; Dale, 1971; Stea and Blaut, 1973; Spencer *et al.*, 1989). These are seen to be more accessible to young children than maps, since they have the same vertical perspective but are photographs rather than selective and symbolic representations. The purpose is to judge the extent to which children can recognize and identify information from this unfamiliar view of the world.

Two research approaches are worth noting. One has involved children being shown the vertical aerial photograph and then encouraged to point out, name and talk about what they can see (Dale, 1971; Spencer *et al.*, 1989). This has proved successful using photographs of areas both familiar and unfamiliar to the children. In the second approach, children make tracings from the photograph, thus creating their own 'map' of the area which, when the photograph is removed, they are encouraged to talk about, recalling the features they have drawn (Blaut *et al.*, 1970).

Key outcomes from these research approaches indicate that children:

- can identify features on vertical aerial photographs from an early age and do so in increasing detail with age and experience, whether they are looking at a familiar or an unfamiliar area;
- can recall features shown in a photograph from their 'map tracing' of part of the photograph.

Identifying discrete map skills

The fifth approach to researching children's understanding of maps has focused on the study of discrete map skills, covering such elements as symbols, co-ordinates and scale. The purpose has been to identify the way in which children understand and use particular map skills. There has been a variety of analyses of the elements of the map (Catling, 1978), from which Gerber and Wilson (1984) derive four key properties: plan-view, map language, arrangement and proportion. Studies of children's understanding of *plan-view* have focused on how they appreciate the perspective of maps, and this has linked into the use of map drawing, map use and aerial photographs already discussed (Catling, 1979; Gerber, 1981, 1992). Research into the *language* of maps has examined a variety of features, including the use of colour, point, line and area symbols, and words on maps (Gerber, 1992). Research into *arrangement* has examined children's ideas about relative locational relationships (Gerber, 1992), the understanding of co-ordinates (Spencer *et al.*, 1989) and relative and compass directions (Gerber, 1992). Consideration of children's ideas of *proportion* has led to studies of relative size, the use of scale and estimation of distance (Gerber, 1992).

Research into particular map properties has taken several forms. Studies of children's ideas of map perspective have applied some of the techniques noted above, such as, examining the way children draw individual features or maps of their school or an area (Gerber, 1992; Matthews, 1992), what children can identify about a place from a vertical aerial photograph (Dale, 1971; Blaut and Stea, 1974) and the extent to which children can use a plan of a layout of a room or route (Walker, 1980; Spencer *et al.*, 1989). The extent to which children indicate spatial layout and structure, show the plan-shape of features and identify them is taken to provide evidence of appreciating a bird's-eye-view, though these three approaches provide rather different types of information and insight. Research into map language has focused more on providing map-based exercises for children, in which they are asked questions and undertake activities aimed at elucidating such aspects as the way they identify and interpret symbols (Dale, 1971; Spencer *et al.* 1989), have preferences for colour symbols (Gerber, 1992), find ease or difficulty in reading different alignments of type (Gerber, 1992) and can identify patterns on the map (Heamon, 1973).

These approaches have tended to be based on paper-and-pencil exercises, though in some cases interview techniques have been used (Spencer *et al.*, 1989), usually where the children are regarded as too young to write responses. Observational techniques have been applied in studies of children's use of reference systems in relation to maps, including the use of models (Towler, 1970) and boards having axes and colour codes, as well as boards with letter/number grids (Spencer *et al.*, 1989). Map-based activities have also been used in studies of co-ordinates and compass directions (Charlton, 1975). In all cases, the emphasis has been on the accuracy of children's use of these skills. This has also been the case in studies of the use of scales on maps, whether these have used models and appropriate-sized shapes to replicate the arrangement and relative proportions shown in the model (Towler and Nelson, 1968), or maps and measuring activities (Salt, 1971). Similar approaches have been used in research on children's understanding of relief on maps (Boardman, 1983).

Research into teaching approaches has also been undertaken, including the use of different resources, such as aerial photographs versus maps (Muir and Blaut, 1969; Ellis, 1974), and the administration of pre- and post-tests to children on particular map skills, between which the children are given a course in those skills aimed at improving their competence (Carswell, 1971; Ellis, 1974; Atkins, 1981). The use of control groups in some of the studies (Ellis, 1974; Atkins, 1981) has provided a basis for evidence of the impact of teaching – in one case, evidence of long-term impact in a follow-up test conducted a year later (Atkins, 1981).

Noting just some of the findings from these research approaches, it would appear that children:

- from an early age can identify what a symbol stands for on a map, though it is rather later that understanding of the meaning and function of the symbol emerges;
- from an early age can appreciate the perspective of maps;
- from an early age can begin to use co-ordinate systems, and use them with increasing sophistication with age and experience;
- from an early age can follow directions on maps;
- find it difficult to relate distances on the map to real distances on the ground, even with large-scale maps, until later than the period when other mapping skills are competently used, though from quite early in childhood they can indicate relative sizes and proportions;
- can have their competence in map skills improved with teaching at all ages.

Emerging features

Spencer *et al.* (1989) and Liben and Downs (1989) raised concerns that there are limitations to the focus, quality and findings of much of the research into map understanding and skills because there are problems with drawing comparable conclusions from the disparate variety of research approaches. This would lead, alarmingly, to discounting much of value in the multifarious research into map understanding and skills that has been undertaken. It may not be perfect, but it is helpful to consider what guidance it can offer, an approach which has been adopted by Boardman (1983), Catling (1988), Matthews (1992) and Wiegand (1993). So what tentative indicators, rather than firm outcomes, about the characteristics of map understanding and skill can be identified? Are there any pointers that help in the development of educational map skills programmes? Even severe critics (Liben and Downs, 1989) are willing to subscribe to the characteristics which Stoltman (1992) has noted, namely that:

- map skills develop gradually but nevertheless from very early in childhood;
- the development of skills depends on the nature and variety of children's experience and on their cognitive level and maturity, and the skills become increasingly sophisticated with use;

- the development of map skills depends on the quality of the maps provided and, for children, the context in which they are used;
- children need to be provided with appropriate encouragement and support in developing their understanding.

From these very broad conclusions, three emerging features of the research can be detailed.

First, there is support for the view that children as young as 4 years have what Blaut (1991) has termed 'protomapping' skills, shown by their ability to move about the familiar environment with some sureness (Spencer *et al.*, 1989), to model imitative and real environments (Blaut and Stea, 1974; Hart, 1979), and to identify features on aerial photographs and large, strongly coloured maps (Spencer *et al.* 1989). This indicates that children entering school have a potential which can and should be harnessed.

Secondly, there is evidence that the skills which children use in mapping the environment – learning about its features and spatial structure – and in map reading and use are built up by accretion, depend on experience and may be enhanced best through focused and structured support (Boardman, 1983; Matthews, 1992; Gerber, 1992). It seems that key map properties such as plan-view or perspective are not particularly problematic for children (Boardman, 1983; Spencer *et al.*, 1989), though the identification of map symbols should not be taken to mean that young children have a clear sense of their representational meaning in relation to the real world (Liben and Downs, 1989; Gerber, 1992). Maps for commercial use and for school teaching should be designed with thought for such things as colour, the number of features on the map and the spacing, type and layout of words (Gerber, 1992). Though it may be inappropriate to focus on the metric scale of maps with young children, ideas of proportional and configurational relationships and distances – such as near to, next to and far from – can be used, while co-ordinates can be introduced certainly in the early stages of schooling (Boardman, 1983; Spencer *et al.* 1989; Gerber, 1992).

Thirdly, there is some support for the view that children can use prepared maps of small, familiar areas before they are able to draw or make their own with usable accuracy. They respond readily to challenges using maps that have a problem-solving approach in an active, field-based context (Spencer *et al.* 1989; Matthews, 1992), even if that area is only within the school building, though the school grounds and local streets can also be used.

However, the research is not without its limitations. Spencer *et al.*, (1989) and Liben and Downs (1989) have indicated some of these, but there are others which need to be addressed. I have chosen four of these.

First, researchers rarely seem to take into account the need to apply findings from one area of research to their test or experimental design in another. For example, while noting that in drawing maps young children tend to draw pictographic signs, such as the side of a house, and pictorial views from above, such as the detail of the roof, researchers do not exploit the potential value of using iconic symbols on maps in research with young children. The emphasis seems, invariably, to be on modified architect-style maps or on versions of conventional maps such as the British Ordnance Survey type, rather than on using picture maps, many of which children and adults see and use regularly.

Secondly, while there is an increasing trend with children in the 3–6 age group to use practical, field-based activities, these are underused, or indeed just not followed through, with older children, especially in the upper school grades. The active use of maps in research by Bluestein and Acredolo (1979), Walker (1980), Ottosson (1987) and Spencer *et al.*, (1989) has yet to be extended to studies of map properties such as those of scale and the use of co-ordinates.

Thirdly, much of the research is focused on the study of discrete groups of children, sometimes of two, three or more ages, whose achievements are compared. While this is informative, the dearth of longitudinal studies in map understanding and skills in children leaves it unclear how such aspects as environmental experience and learning, map teaching and changes in the types of map being used affect the development of map understanding and skills.

Fourthly, there has been little attempt to study the sorts of map activity and resource which children are more likely to use in book-based, educational map skills programmes. Some inferences can be drawn from the use of colour on maps, type size and direction, and aerial photographs of model and real environments alongside maps of the same environments. This does not, however, take account of the reading skills children need to use to read names and instructions, the use of places and model environments which are unfamiliar, or working alone or with support on the tasks such books contain, whether after or without experience of activities using maps in environments.

DEVELOPING A MAP SKILLS PROGRAMME

Structuring map skills

As research has developed, researchers and educators have tried to draw together sequences and structures in map understanding and skills to provide a framework for planning map programmes (Rushdoony, 1968; Boardman, 1983; Catling, 1983, 1988; Winston, 1984; Blaut, 1991; Stoltman, 1992). To some extent, these frameworks are conjectures, because the limitations of research mean that either one or two studies form the basis for a judgement about the age at which a child can learn a skill, or inferences are drawn from research which does not really substantiate them. The focus has been on sequencing the aspects of mapwork which children are considered to need and on providing teaching suggestions that support development (Boardman, 1983; Winston, 1984; Catling, 1988; Stoltman, 1992).

Boardman's analysis of research in terms of symbols, location, direction and scale has provided a useful guide, though some more recent research findings indicate that it needs modification. A modified version of the sequence developed by Boardman (1983; see below) attempts to take into account recent research, though it focuses only on 3–11-year-olds. It indicates that there is much in terms of *active learning* that can be undertaken in pre-school nursery and playgroup settings, as well as in kindergarten or infant classes for 5–7-year-olds and during the remaining primary years of schooling. It provides a guide for a wide range of practical activities.

Children should normally learn to be able to do the following:

From 3 to 5 years:

• move toy vehicles, people and animals around large-scale playmat picture maps of different types of local environment, using roads and paths, and talk about what they are doing;

- create layouts of environments using toys, which are imaginary but increasingly imitative of 'real-world' layouts, and use toys such as model furniture to make generalized layouts of familiar small-scale areas, such as rooms;
- draw routes between objects placed on large sheets of paper, such as a road between buildings, and navigate a vehicle along them;
- identify a variety of features on large-scale vertical aerial photographs of a familiar area and of places they do not know;
- talk about features and activities on, and trace journeys around, an area shown in a picture map;
- recognize a few features on a large-scale, full-colour abstract map of a small area about which they are talking with older children or adults;
- make journeys within their familiar environments and take others on these routes, talking about the features or landmarks they are passing;
- retrace routes along which they have walked and been able to observe landmarks and directions;
- use a large-scale map, drawn as a vertical view of the features, of a room or open space with a limited number of features in it, to find features they are shown on the map in that environment, especially when they have been helped to orient the map to the area;
- use colour-based co-ordinates to find items on a grid layout.

From 5 to 7 years:

- follow and give directions using terms such as 'left', 'right', 'forward', 'back';
- describe the relative location of features of environments they are in, using terms like 'in front of', 'nearby', 'behind';
- sort objects by their shapes and relative sizes;
- draw round the base of toy and life-size objects, remove the object and recognize that the shape left is its plan-view;
- make a model layout showing some of the features in an area they are familiar with and navigate a vehicle around the area;
- draw picture maps and maps using symbols of routes or small areas with which they are familiar;
- make a tracing of features on a large-scale vertical aerial photograph and identify those features when the photograph is no longer present;
- use a large-scale map of their own familiar environment to identify features and routes;
- use a large-scale map of a small, familiar environment to find their way around and identify named features;
- give locations on a grid system using alpha-numeric co-ordinates;
- estimate relative distances, using terms such as 'nearer than', further away', and relative sizes, using terms like 'larger' and 'smaller'.

From 7 to 9 years:

- draw a moderately accurate free-hand map of such features as a table, a room and an outside area they can see;

- draw a free-hand map of a familiar area or a route that cannot be seen from one site;
- relate a large-scale map of a room, building or grounds to a familiar environment to find where features are and the way around;
- use a large-scale map and a street map of a familiar area that cannot be viewed at once to identify features and routes in the environment;
- use a large-scale vertical aerial photograph with a map of the same familiar area to identify features and routes;
- add features using pictures or symbols to a large-scale map of a room or the school grounds;
- begin to use some conventional symbols in making their own maps of real or imaginary places, and provide a key;
- measure distances in a room and in an open area using metre rules, tape measures and trundle wheels with reasonable accuracy;
- measure straight-line distances on a large-scale map using a scale bar;
- make a model to show part of a familiar or imaginary environment, such as a row of shops or an island;
- give locations on a grid system using four-figure co-ordinates;
- use a compass to find and give the four cardinal compass directions and the four intermediate directions;
- use the points of the compass when giving directions on a map when there is a compass rose present.

From 9 to 11 years:

- use plan shapes and symbols to show specific features on maps they draw, and include a key;
- draw a reasonably accurate free-hand map of a familiar area or a route that cannot be seen from one site;
- use the sixteen points of the compass to give and follow directions;
- indicate compass directions in the neighbourhood;
- align a large-scale map of the school and neighbourhood, using landmarks and compass points;
- use a conventional large-scale map to find the way around an area and relate position on the ground to location on the map;
- understand the purpose of the information that surrounds a map, including the title, key, scale bar, grid co-ordinates and compass;
- begin to use six-figure grid references to locate points on maps;
- begin to have some sense of the real distance meaning of measurements made on large-scale maps of familiar areas;
- begin to draw reasonably accurate scaled maps of familiar areas, such as the classroom and school grounds, using measurements they have made;
- begin to make a moderately accurate scaled model of part of the local area showing features of the area;
- measure the straight-line distance between two points on maps of progressively smaller scales and begin to measure the winding distances along roads on maps;
- compare symbols for the same features on maps of progressively smaller scales;
- begin to recognize that the generalization on maps increases with the decrease in scale;

- begin to appreciate that some symbols on small-scale maps are in disproportionate size to the real features they represent;
- begin to describe a route on a map from statements of direction and distance;
- recognize from the layer tinting and contour lines on maps that the landscape shown is not flat;
- annotate a sketch map of an area shown in a vertical aerial photograph to show the variety of features;
- begin to search for locations on atlas maps using longitude and latitude.

Such an outline is not without its limitations. The use of a two-year 'stage' structure is arbitrary and can mislead, though it serves to link with many national pre-school and schooling periods. Children's rate of development and maturation between 3 and 5 years is considerable, as it is between 5 and 7 years; for individuals it can vary enormously, sudden at some periods of time and slow during others. What is outlined on a sequential guide such as that above should be taken simply as a guide, not as a rigid framework. Flexibility of opportunity should be encouraged and, where possible, the individual child, not the guide, should be the focus of planned activities. However, in defence of such educational map skills guides, it should be noted that teachers are not working in research or individualized teaching contexts with just a couple or very small groups of children, but are moving constantly between individuals and groups in large classes, where they have to be attentive to the needs of all the children the whole of the time. Programmes of map skills, like any other programme, have to take account of what may be manageable by the teacher as opposed to the ideal teaching situation.

Applying research to teaching materials for children

Boardman's sequence provides less help in indicating how book-based programmes for developing map understanding and skills should be structured. The same caveats as above apply here too, because the author of the book programme recognizes it will be mediated, and probably modified, by the teacher. None the less, there have been thoughtful attempts to apply the findings of research to materials designed for children in schools. The development of the Australian *Jacaranda Atlas Programme* (Butler *et al.* 1983) was planned to take into account the evidence from research into children's understanding of maps at a range of scales (Gerber, 1992). The introductions in its *resource books* outline the sequence of the development of the map skills around which the series is constructed. Similarly, a skill-based structure underpins the *US Maps, Charts and Graphs* series (Foreman and Allen, 1989), though this is further structured by a concentric approach moving from 'The Places Around Me' to 'The World' over seven books. Both series assume the discrete teaching of map skills and understandings, as Table 8.1 illustrates (Boardman, 1983; Gerber, 1992). They draw on a range of types and scales of maps (see Table 8.2)

In the UK, research into children's understanding of maps and into their map skills was used in constructing the *Mapstart* series of three books aimed at children from 6 to 11 years old (Catling, 1992). The series set out to introduce children to a range of map skills, map types and map scales. These are also indicated in Tables 8.1 and 8.2. Mapstart has been through two editions (Catling, 1985, 1992). Essentially the second

Table 8.1 *Map skills and understanding in three educational map book programmes for children*

Map understanding and skills	Map Book series		
	Jacaranda Atlas Programme (Australia)	Maps, Charts, Graphs (USA)	Mapstart (UK)
Plan view and map perspective	*	*	*
Symbols and key, including map language	*	*	*
Location and reference	*	*	*
Arrangement of features	*	*	*
Directions, both relative and compass	*	*	*
Distance and scale, including relative proportion and measurement	*	*	*
Selection of features	*	*	*
Purpose of the map	*	*	*

Table 8.2 *Map types introduced in three educational map book programmes for children.*

Map types	Map books series		
	Jacaranda Atlas Programme (Australia)	Maps, Charts, Graphs (USA)	Mapstart (UK)
Oblique aerial views and photos:			
model environments	*		*
real environments	*		*
Vertical aerial views and photos:			
model environments	*		*
real environments	*		*
Picture maps	*	*	*
Plans of individual features	*		*
Large-scale plans of environments	*		*
Large-scale maps of environments	*	*	*
Route maps, such as street maps	*	*	*
Maps of:			
imaginary places	*	*	*
real places	*	*	*
National conventional maps:			
large-scale			*
medium-scale			*
small-scale	*	*	*
Satellite and landsat photos, images and composites	*		*
Atlas maps	*	*	*

Source: Catling, 1992, published by Collins-Longman. Reprinted by permission of the publisher.

edition was prepared with the same intentions as the first, but three key modifications were made, linked to tentative research indications and English and Welsh National Curriculum requirements (DES, 1991). First, the use of picture maps was included alongside the continuing use of model and large-scale real environments in the first book. Secondly, activities on measuring on maps were introduced in the second book and extended in the third. Thirdly, cognitive map drawing and using maps in surveys were extended from the first into the second and third books.

The series has been built around the development of discrete map understanding and skills, kept in the context of maps and environments. Thus, the title on each page or page-spread highlights the focus for the child, as does the accompanying text. This is further reinforced by the activities, using the maps, photographs and pictures. This was one of the key principles in developing the series; another was the use of vertical aerial photographs throughout as the link between the maps and the 'real' world. Drawing on the research literature, and in line with the arguments made by Blaut (1991), the use of both familiar objects and 'environments' (namely toys and models), and of photographs showing the relatively unfamiliar plan-view of these and real environments, aimed to build on evidence of what it was thought children can recognize and identify information from. For the second edition, it was decided (though without direct support from research findings) that the use of picture maps, which have highly iconic symbols enabling children to recognize features readily, would help support children's early understanding of the purposes and uses of maps. The following list summarizes the principles that underpinned the development of the Mapstart series.

The principles governing the Mapstart series are:

- a structured scheme for the development of map skills, which introduces children to the elements of maps, specifically plan-view, location and direction, map language, scale, selection of information and map purposes, and revisits these in each book with increasingly complex demands;
- the use of oblique and vertical photographs of toys and models, with maps of these, because they are familiar and link to children's experience and viewpoints;
- the use of oblique and vertical aerial photographs of real environments at large scales, as well as maps at the same scale, which are of the area immediately around a school, so that children can readily identify features and relate to the context of the area;
- through the use of aerial and satellite photos, drawings, plans and maps, to stimulate and foster children's interest in the world around them, both their local area and other places;
- the provision of practical activities which involve children finding information from the map and finding out about how the map works through focusing discretely on key elements of it;
- the provision of opportunities aimed at developing children's knowledge and use of language related to spatial movement and representation;
- to cover the range of map scales, from plans of individual objects to small-scale atlas maps, and use a variety of types of map including plans of objects and areas, picture maps and conventional maps;
- through the use of the series, to encourage:
  - children to use maps effectively, both in the real environment and for study, with the purpose of enabling them to learn to obtain information about places readily from maps of many types;
  - the use of children's own experience and environments, and of additional resources to extend their awareness and understanding beyond the ideas and activities introduced in each book;
  - the teacher to develop ideas and resources for children in their own situation.

The series structure moves from the large to the small-scale both within each book and across the three books, again reflecting the view that gradually more complex understandings and skills can be introduced. The following list (Catling, 1992) presents the focus of each book and indicates the changes in level of cognitive demand, the introduction of additional contexts and map types, and the spiral nature of the structure of the series. The objectives of *Mapstart 1* are:

- to build spatial awareness through the use of familiar objects, toys, the locality of the school, picture maps of places and space photos of Earth;
- to extend understanding and use of vocabulary associated with spatial location, organization and movement;
- to provide continuity throughout the book by the use of vertical aerial photos;
- to introduce the perspective of plans and maps and the representational characteristics of maps;
- to encourage observation of features and relationships in oblique and vertical photos and maps;
- to foster appreciation of the Earth as a globe.

The objectives of *Mapstart 2* are:

- to develop awareness of spatial form through the use of familiar features and localities;
- to extend understanding and use of geographical vocabulary associated with spatial location, organization and movement, and to reinforce the use of vocabulary associated with maps;
- to extend use of the specific skills involved in map reading, including the use of symbols and the map key, compass directions, alpha-numeric co-ordinates for giving grid references, the purpose and function of an index, and scale bars for measuring straight-line distances;
- to extend skills in identifying features and places on maps and in giving and following route directions;
- to foster awareness of the wider world, particularly the British Isles;
- to encounter the location of many of the places specified in the English and Welsh National Curriculum geography requirements;
- to show the relationship between the large-scale plan, the small-scale atlas map and the globe;
- to provide continuity throughout the book through the use of vertical aerial and space photos;
- to help initiate the appreciation that any map is a selective representation of a part of the Earth's surface, not a replica of it.

The objectives of *Mapstart 3* are:

- to extend understanding and use of the specific skills involved in map reading, including the use of symbols and the map key, compass directions, four- and six-figure grid references, scale bars for measuring distances, and the purpose and function of a contents page and index;
- to extend understanding and use of vocabulary associated with map reading;
- to provide continuity in the use and reading of vertical aerial and space photographs;
- to extend understanding that maps can be used in surveys of localities, as records of areas and for planning future developments;
- to extend skills in identifying features and places on maps and in following and planning routes;

- to reinforce understanding of the nature of maps as selective representations of the Earth's surface;
- to introduce Ordnance Survey maps at a range of scales, including the 1:10,000, 1:25000 and 1:50,000 scales, and their symbols and keys;
- to develop understanding that the globe can be represented as a flat surface and to introduce some of the projections that are used;
- to introduce the use of latitude and longtitude;
- to introduce the use of thematic maps;
- to provide information about the British Isles and United Kingdom;
- to introduce physical and political world maps;
- to encounter the location of the features and places specified in the English and Welsh National Curriculum geography requirements;
- to extend understanding of the relationship between large-scale plans, small-scale atlas maps and globes.

In terms of the development of children's understanding of key map properties through the three books, Table 8.3 outlines the continuity and changing emphasis between the books, focused on the large-scale maps and vertical aerial photographs used in all three.

Thus the Mapstart series reflects, as do the *Jacaranda Atlas Programme* and *Maps, Charts, Graphs*, the underlying characteristics of map understanding identified by Stoltman (1992), though such series cannot provide the very active and supportive 'classroom' learning environments which Blaut (1991) would wish for pre-school and school-age children.

CONCLUSION

Research into map understanding and map skills has provided some important pointers for the development of educational map skills programmes, in both guidance for teachers and materials for children. Though there are still many unanswered and unresearched questions, what is known of children's understanding can be built upon, even if later modified. For example, the research has shown the importance of using models and vertical aerial photographs in appreciating views and knowledge of environments. It has also shown that pictorial styles of mapping are used by children in their own map-making. This has been noted in the arguments put forward for the early development of map teaching with children (Spencer *et al.* 1989; Blaut, 1991) and taken up in developing teaching programmes (Stoltman, 1992) and creating materials for children in map book programmes (Catling, 1992). The research in these areas is not by any means conclusive, but it is a starting point. Further research will help to refine our understanding and enable the improvements of such guidance and materials.

There is much else that needs to be researched. One area which is developing rapidly, but of which little is known in terms of its value in helping children to understand maps, is computer-based mapping. The development of CD-ROM software, giving access not just to global atlases but also to a wide variety of mapping detail, scale and type, enabling interplay and manipulation of maps of particular places (Airphoto

Table 8.3 *The focus of content related to large- and medium-scale maps in each of the three* Mapstart *series books.*

Map element	Book 1	Book 2	Book 3
Perspective or plan view:			
model environments	*		
real objects	*	*	
real environments	*	*	*
Plans:			
model environments	*		
real objects	*	*	
real environments	*	*	*
Maps of areas:			
imaginary environments	*	*	
real environments	*	*	*
Picture maps	*	*	*
'Conventional' maps	*	*	*
Relating maps and aerial photos to each other	*	*	*
Symbols:			
shape	*	*	*
colour	*	*	*
point, line, area		*	*
key	*	*	*
Direction:			
relative	*	*	
compass		*	*
Routes	*	*	*
Location:			
relative	*	*	
co-ordinates		*	*
Maps as proportional reductions	*	*	*
Size and measurement:			
relative	*	*	
metric measures		*	*
scale bar		*	*
Map-making and surveys	*	*	*

Source: Catling, 1992, published by Collins-Longman. Reprinted by permission of the publisher.

Group, 1994), indicates that this is an area which will be important in teaching map understanding and skills and is in need of empirical research. Much more research is needed into exploring the environment using maps, as well as into classroom-based learning and 'disc-world' mapping. It may well be the link between the last and the first areas which provides exciting and challenging ways forward in developing children's map understanding and skills.

NOTE

1. Three sources are referred to throughout this chapter in relation to research into mapwork: Gerber (1992), Matthews (1992) and Spencer *et al.* (1989). These provide a rich source of information on research approaches and findings from the work of their authors, as well as extensive bibliographies to support examination of the original sources.

REFERENCES

Airphoto Group (1994). *Discover York: Interactive Geography.* Barwell: Airphoto Group/Ordnance Survey.

Atkins, C.L. (1981) 'Introducing basic map and globe concepts to young children.' *Journal of Geography,* **80,** 228–33.

Bishop, J. and Foulsham, J. (1973) 'Children's images of Harwich.' *Working Paper No. 3.* Architectural Psychology Research Unit, Kingston Polytechnic.

Blaut, J.M. (1991) 'Natural mapping.' *Transactions of the Institute of British Geographers,* NS **16,** 55–74.

Blaut, J.M. and Stea, D. (1974) 'Mapping at the age of three.' *Journal of Geography,* **73,** 5–9.

Blaut, J.M., McCleary, G.S. and Blaut, A.S. (1970) 'Environmental mapping in young children.' *Environment and Behaviour,* **2,** 335–49.

Bluestein, N. and Acredolo, L.P. (1979) 'Developmental changes in map reading skills.' *Child Development,* **50,** 691–7.

Boardman, D. (1983) *Graphicacy and Geography Teaching.* London: Croom Helm.

Butler, J.E., Clough, R.V., Gerber, R., Senior, C., Smith, S. and Wilson, W. (1983) *Jacaranda Atlas Programme: Resource Book 1* and *Resource Book 2.* Milton: Jacaranda Press.

Carswell, R.J.B. (1971) 'Children's abilities in topographic map reading.' *Cartographica,* Monograph 2, 40–5.

Catling, S. (1978) 'The elements of the map.' *Classroom Geographer,* March 2–10.

Catling, S. (1979) 'Maps and cognitive maps: the young child's perception.' *Geography,* **64,** 288–96.

Catling, S. (1983) 'The development of children's map ability.' In J. Fien, R. Gerber, K. Laws and P. Wilson (eds) *Research in Geographical Education.* Brisbane: Australian Geographical Research Association.

Catling, S. (1985) *Mapstart 1, Mapstart 2* and *Mapstart 3.* 1st edn. Harlow: Collins-Longman.

Catling, S. (1988) 'Using maps and aerial photographs.' In D. Mills (ed.) *Geographical Work in Primary and Middle Schools.* Sheffield: Geographical Association.

Catling, S. (1992) *Mapstart 1, Mapstart 2* and *Mapstart 3.* 2nd edn. Harlow: Collins-Longman.

Charlton, K. E. (1975) 'A study of pupil understanding of map symbolism, scale, direction and location in the age range 8–13 years.' Unpublished MPhil thesis, University of Leeds.

Dale, P.F. (1971) 'Children's reactions to maps and aerial photographs.' *Area,* **3,** 170–7.

DES (1991) *Geography in the National Curriculum.* London: HMSO.

Downs, R.M., Liben, L.S. and Daggs, D.G. (1988) 'On education and geographers: the role of cognitive development in geographic theory.' *Annals of the Association of American Geographers,* **78,** 680–700.

Ellis, A.K. (1974) 'Concept and skill development in a primary geography unit utilizing alternative learning progressions.' *Journal of Geography,* **73,** 20–6.

Foreman, D.I. and Allen, S.J. (1989) *Maps, Charts, Graphs.* Cleveland, OH: Modern Curriculum Press.

Gerber, R. (1981) 'Children's development of competence and performance in cartographic language.' In P. Wilson, R. Gerber and J. Fien, (eds) *Research in Geographical Education.* Brisbane: Australian Geographical Research Association.

Gerber, R. (1984) 'Factors affecting the competence and performance in map reasoning.' *Cartography,* **13,** 205–13.

Gerber, R. (1992) *Using Maps and Graphics in Geography Teaching.* Brisbane: International

Geographical Union Commission on Geographical Education.

Gerber, R. and Wilson, P. (1984) 'Maps in the geography classroom.' In J. Fien, R. Gerber and P. Wilson (eds) *The Geography Teacher's Guide to the Classroom*. South Melbourne: Macmillan.

Hart, R. (1979) *Children's Experience of Place*. New York: Irvington.

Hart, R. (1981) 'Children's spatial representation of the landscape: lessons and questions from a field study.' In L. Liben, A.H. Patterson and N. Newcombe (eds) *Spatial Representation and Behaviour Across the Life Span*. New York: Academic Press.

Heamon, A.J. (1973) 'The maturation of spatial ability in geography.' *Educational Research*, **16**, 63–6.

Herman, J.F. and Siegal, A.W. (1978) 'The development of cognitive mapping of the large scale environment.' *Journal of Experimental Child Psychology*, **26**, 389–406.

Liben, L.S. and Downs, R.M. (1989) 'Understanding maps as symbols: the development of map concepts in children.' In H.W. Reese, (ed.) *Advances in Child Development and Behaviour*. New York: Academic Press.

Matthews, M.H. (1992) *Making Sense of Place*. Hemel Hempstead: Harvester Wheatsheaf.

Muir, M.E. and Blaut, J.M. (1969) 'The use of aerial photographs in teaching mapping to children in the first grade: an experimental study.' *Minnesota Geographer*, **22**, 4–19.

Ottosson, T. (1987) 'Map reading and wayfinding.' *Goteborg Studies in Educational Sciences*, **65**.

Piche, D. (1981) 'The spontaneous geography of the urban child.' In D.T. Herbert, and R.J. Johnston (eds) *Geography and the Urban Environment. Vol. 1*. Chichester: Wiley.

Presson, C.C. (1982) 'The development of map reading skills', *Child Development*, **53**, 196–9.

Rushdoony, H.A. (1968) 'A child's ability to read maps: summary of research.' *Journal of Geography*, **67**, 213–22.

Salt, C.D. (1971) 'An investigation into the ability of 11–12-year-old pupils to read and understand maps.' Unpublished MA thesis, University of Sheffield.

Siegal, A.W., Herman, J.F., Allen, G.L. and Kirasic, K.C. (1978) 'The development of cognitive maps of large- and small-scale spaces.' *Child Development*, **50**, 582–5.

Spencer, D. and Lloyd, J. (1974) 'A child's eye view of Small Heath, Birmingham.' *Research Monograph No. 34*. University of Birmingham.

Spencer, C., Blades, M. and Morsley, K. (1989) *The Child in the Physical Environment*. Chichester: Wiley.

Stea, D. and Blaut, J. (1973) 'Some preliminary observations on spatial learning in school children.' In R.M. Downs and D. Stea, (eds) *Image and Environment*. Chicago, IL: Aldine.

Stea, D. and Taphanel, S. (1974) 'Theory and experiment on the relation between environmental modelling ('toy play') and environmental cognition.' In D. Canter and T. Lee (eds) *Psychology and the Built Environment*. New York: Wiley.

Stoltman, J. (1992) *Teaching Map and Globe Skills, K-6*. Skokie: Rand McNally.

Towler, J.O. (1970) 'The elementary school child's concept of reference systems.' *Journal of Geography*, **69**, 89–93.

Towler, J.O. and Nelson, L.D. (1968) 'The elementary school child's concept of scale.' *Journal of Geography*, **67**, 24–8.

van Dijk, H., van der Schee, J., Trimp, H. and van de Zijpp, T. (1994) 'Map skills and geographical knowledge.' *International Research in Geographical and Environmental Education*, **3**, (1), 68–80.

Walker, R.J. (1980) 'Map using abilities of 5 to 9 year old children.' *Geographical Education*, **3**, 545–54.

Weatherford, D.L. (1985) 'Representing and manipulating spatial information from different environments: models to neighbourhoods.' In R. Cohen, (ed.) *The Development of Spatial Cognition*. Hillsdale, NJ: Lawrence Erlbaum.

Wiegand, P. (1993) *Children and Primary Geography*. London: Cassell.

Winston, B.J. (1984) *Map and Globe Skills: K-8 Teaching Guide*. Macomb: National Council for Geographic Education.

Wood, D. (1992) *The Power of Maps*. London: Routledge.

Chapter 9

Interviews

Patrick Wiegand

The process of interviewing has been described as a means of 'collecting talk' (Powney and Watts, 1987). Like conversation, the methodology is flexible, interactive and adaptable. However, because talk is dynamic, something is lost as soon as it is collected and recorded. It has been compared in this respect to recording rainfall: what you have left in the rain gauge is water, which is only a little like rain (Whitehurst, 1979).

The purpose of an interview is to obtain information. Three conditions are necessary for success (Cannell and Kahn, 1968):

1. The information required must be *accessible* to the interviewer. The interviewee may, for example, have forgotten the information wanted or may not construe events in the way the questions are framed.
2. The respondent must *understand* what is required. This involves the interviewer helping the respondent to make an appropriate selection from his or her store of information or experiences.
3. The respondent must *want to co-operate* with the interviewer and to answer accurately and truthfully.

Provided these conditions are met, data can be obtained from the respondent. However, an interview is more than just transfer of information, and the information that results is not neutral. The interplay between the interviewer and the respondent inevitably involves bias, the sources of which include possible misconception of the questions by the respondent and misunderstanding of the answers by the interviewer. The attitudes and opinions of the interviewer and a possible tendency to project those views onto the respondent may also distort the information gained. Colour, religion, class and gender may all play a part in the social interaction between interviewer and interviewee. In Ladd's (1972) study of how black adolescent boys from low-income families viewed their housing and environment, the interviews were conducted by black males. It seems from the evidence that the respondents would have been less likely to share their feelings of what their environment meant to them and what aspirations they had for the future with white females. Lidstone, however (1981), raises the question of possible incompatibility between the dual role of teacher and researcher interviewer, in his study of his own pupils' perception of their geography teachers' objectives and the textbooks and activities involved in their geography course.

There are at least two ways of dealing with bias (Kitwood, 1977). One is to build controls into the procedure so that bias is counteracted (for example, by having a number of interviewers with different biases). Another is to accept that it is probably impossible to bring every aspect of an interpersonal encounter under control, and that this is simply a limitation of the methodology.

Bias may be especially problematic when children and young people are interviewed, as the methodology often presupposes that respondents have insight into their own behaviour. Young respondents may be far less able to decentre and reflect on their thinking and actions. They may also be more inclined to provide the interviewer with what they think the interviewer wants to hear and be keen to get the answers 'right'. The detail of conversational exchanges may be crucial in examining interview results. For example, children come to expect from their school experiences that a follow-up question implies their first response was incorrect. Inferences from interview data are often made simply on the basis that the questions that are asked look as though they will measure what they claim to measure. This apparent 'face validity' has been challenged, and some commentators hold the view that interview data really need to be matched with some independently obtained measure that has previously been shown to be valid (Cannel and Kahn, 1968). There appears, however, to be general agreement that while the *validity* of interviews may be suspect, the methodology of interviewing usually exhibits a fair degree of *reliability*.

INTERVIEWS IN GEOGRAPHICAL EDUCATION

There are a number of different classifications of interview types (Cohen and Manion, 1989; Good, 1963; Moser and Kalton, 1971), none of them entirely suited to reviewing research in geographical education, not least because many researchers are coy about revealing details of their interviewing methodology. Powney and Watts (1987) distinguish between the *respondent interview* and the *informant interview*. In the former the interviewer retains control of the whole process. It may be tightly or loosely structured, but the essential feature is that there is a set of questions to be answered and it is the interviewer's agenda that is dominant. In the informant interview, the opposite is the case. These interviews can also be either tightly or loosely structured, but here the interviewee imposes the agenda. The interviewer is inviting the interviewee to express his or her interests and concerns in a freer way.

Another dimension is the extent to which the content and procedures of the interview are structured in advance. At one end of the scale is a *closed* situation, in which interviewers have a schedule of the sequence and the wording of questions, from which they do not deviate. At the other end of the scale is the more *open* situation, which has greater flexibility and freedom. The content, sequence and wording of questions are in the hands of the interviewer and, although the procedure is still planned in advance, opportunities of exploring potentially fruitful avenues are taken on the way.

Structured interviews are usually thought necessary where, for purposes of comparability, the research is taking place in a number of different settings. This is fairly common in geographical education, where comparative data are gathered from a number of locations around the world. Perhaps the best example is the massive cross-cultural study by Lambert and Klineberg (1967) of children's conceptions of their own national group and other nationalities. Twelve countries were involved and a total of 3300 children aged 6, 10 and 14 were questioned. A highly standardized and structured series of questions was asked, starting with 'What are you?' This first question was devised to see whether children referred to themselves first as (for example) 'a boy' or 'a German', 'a Turk', etc. Perhaps unsurprisingly, the investigators found that children did not refer to themselves primarily by nationality, although there were significant differences between countries. Indeed, Jahoda later (1963) found that nationality featured very low indeed in children's self-images, and few children understood the word when probed. One of the difficulties with highly structured interviews is that the apparent simplicity of questions can render them opaque to respondents. After all, it is difficult to see how you might respond to the question 'What are you?', particularly given translation into other languages and contexts. As a further example of cross-cultural work, see the large-scale, UNESCO-sponsored project which looked at the way adolescents use and value their spatial environment in Argentine, Australia, Mexico and Poland (Lynch, 1977). In this, a structured interview schedule was provided for participants as well as a set of common instructions for the respondents to draw maps.

Hart (1979) provides a further example of a structured interview in his study of the spacial activity, place knowledge, place use and place values of the children in 'Inavale', a typical New England town:

1. Tell me the 10 places you like the most in and around Inavale.
2. Tell me all of those places you dislike in and around Inavale.
3. Tell me all of those places you think are dangerous in and around Inavale.
4. Tell me all of those places you think are frightening in and around Inavale.

(Hart, 1979, p. 156)

Hart reports that these structured interviews failed to offer a richly detailed picture of children's place feelings. His respondents displayed a tendency to 'identify places that were part of the common stock of valued places rather than unique, personally important places and to describe those places as they were socially known rather than personally felt'.

Three kinds of item are commonly used in the construction of structured interview schedules: fixed alternative items, open-ended items and scale items.

Fixed alternative items (where the respondent must choose between yes/no, agree/disagree, etc.) have maximum reliability, as measurement is uniform and results are easily coded, but they are by nature superficial and many respondents fail to find either of the alternatives provided satisfactory. Newson and Newson (1976), for example, asked 700 mothers, 'Would you call your child an indoor child or an outdoor child?', in order to investigate the transition of children from the home milieu to that of the wider world. Many readers will find more than the simple bipolar choice unsatisfactory in Grace and Neuhaus' (1952) attempt to access their subjects 'like' and 'dislike' of nations by asking them to complete sentences such as, 'I would rather go to war against country X than country Y'.

Open-ended items (where a question is asked and respondent has the minimum of restraint in answering) are flexible and allow the interviewer to probe to clear up misunderstanding or ask for clarity. These items allow the interviewer to make a fuller assessment of the respondents' views and can also elicit unexpected or unanticipated answers, which suggest hitherto unthought-of relationships or hypotheses. Examples in geography education include questions such as:

Has your home area changed in your memory? Do you think it has become better or worse? Why? Have you been able to do anything to change it? What do you think will really happen to this place in the next 10 years? Will you still be here? If not, where will you be?

(Lynch, 1977, p. 88)

Scale items (where the respondent indicates degrees of agreement or disagreement) can be used to measure attitudes or rank order preferences. They have been much used in perceived-distance studies, in which subjects are asked to estimate distance between points (Lee, 1970). Haubrich (1988) used such a scale in an attempt to identify the perception of the Upper Rhine border region by 15-year-olds from the three countries (France, Germany and Switzerland) that share the region. Students from each country were asked to rate nationality attributes (such as industrious, peaceful, clean, talkative, friendly, slow, rich, etc.) on a five-point scale according to how well they thought the adjective applied to each national group.

Specific mention should be made of *clinical interviews*, because of their importance in geographical education. The use of these was developed by Piaget, who interviewed children in order to ascertain their beliefs and explanations about everyday phenomena. These are small-scale, in-depth interviews in which the child determines the content and direction of the conversation. Much work in geographical education has developed from this model. Of particular relevance to geographers are those investigations by Piaget dealing with the child's conception of space (Piaget and Inhelder, 1956) and of children's understanding of nationality, homeland and foreigners (Piaget and Weil, 1951). Typically, Piaget and his associates set up 'thought experiments' in which children were challenged to examine the world from viewpoints different to their own. This included being asked to consider questions from the point of view of children from other countries and attempting to envisage scenes (such as a model of three mountains) from another perspective. Although doubts have been and continued to be cast on the contextual features of Piaget's interviews and the way in which they appear to have influenced children's responses (McGarrigle and Donaldson, 1974; Eames *et al.*, 1990), the Piagetian approach has been paramount in geographical education. Jahoda (1962), for example, extended Piaget's work by questioning children's understanding of the relationships between cities and countries, and, at a global scale, Nussbaum (1985) looked at children's understanding of the Earth as a cosmic body.

To illustrate further developments of the approach, reference may be made to a series of interviews about children's understanding of economic concepts. Schug (1990) provides a comprehensive review and notes that the methodology of such studies usually involves posing situations which illustrate economic ideas and interviewing children about their understanding or explanation of the situation. Danziger (1958), for example, interviewed forty-one Australian children between 5 and 8 years of age to investigate ownership of means of production by asking children about 'the boss'. Berti *et al.* (1982) interviewed 120 Italian children from 4–5 years old to 12–14 years, asking children who owned their own home, the bus, local factories and farms and how such ownership was acquired. Strauss (1952) interviewed sixty-six children from 4 to 11 years old. He used transactions in a store to investigate their understanding of ideas such as value, transaction and profit. Danziger (1958) came to similar conclusions but with modifications to the form of questioning and the number of resultant levels of understanding. Burris (1976) posed questions about children's understanding of the price of objects, and Schug and Birkley (1985) explored how children (aged 6–9) understand scarcity, choice, opportunity, cost, monetary value and price. In this study, seventy children from an urban pre-school and two nearby elementary schools were interviewed.

Jahoda (1979) investigated the notion of profit in the context of shop transactions and banking. Jahoda stresses a point common to much of this work: that children were trying, during the progress of the interview, to 'construct' their understanding of social events not just by repeating something they had learnt but by trying actively to reconcile their experience and what they 'knew'.

A further type of interview is the *non-directional*. In this, the respondent is responsible for initiating and directing the encounter and the attitudes expressed in it. The idea is to get at deeper perceptions and attitudes in a way as free as possible from interviewer bias. This type of interview has its roots in the Freudian approach, designed to enhance self-awareness and self-analysis. Some use of this type of interview has been made in geographical education in the exploration of free recall of childhood or other memories of place and space (see, for example, Lukashok and Lynch, 1956). These are attempts to get at the richness of childhood experience and the developmental significance of the immediate physical environment. For a non-academic attempt at a similar objective, the reader is referred to the BBC television series *All Our Children*, which documented the lives of fifty children in twelve programmes. Little is known about the methodology, but some of the results are presented in the book of the series (Woodhead and Woodhead, 1990) as continuous prose from the children as though in their own words.

Merton and Kendall (1946) outline the notion of the *focused interview*. In this, the persons involved have been through a particular situation in common (for example, they may have watched a film). The researcher analyses elements in the situation which seem significant and derives a set of hypotheses. From this an interview guide is constructed, which identifies the main areas of inquiry. The actual interview is focused on the subjective experiences of the respondent. This allows the researcher to test the validity of the hypotheses and to ascertain any unanticipated responses to the situation, giving rise to new hypotheses. What is distinctive in this approach is the prior analysis of the situation in which the subjects have been involved by the researcher. Some have looked at the introspective reports of environmental experiences as a focus (Ryan and Ryan, 1940), whereas Stillwell and Spencer (1974) interviewed children before and after exposure to a display of information in the form of posters and wall charts in order to compare the effect of visual information on attitudes towards other countries. James and Tenen (1951) explored attitudes towards ethnicity by carrying out a structured interview with thirty 13-year-old boys and girls before and after the visit of two black African women teachers. They concluded that satisfactory first-hand experiences with a target ethnic group generated a positive attitudinal change.

In geographical education research, it is often the case that interviews complement some other form of data collection. Free-recall sketch maps, for example, have been widely used to investigate children's spatial knowledge and understanding. Maurer and Baxter (1972) attempt to impose some order on such data by incorporating oral identification into the task ('Please tell what each thing is that you draw'). Butterworth (1977), in discussing children's drawings in general, says that the drawn product should not be analysed without regard for the child's intentions in drawing. Spencer and Darziveh

(1981), therefore, in their study of young children's descriptions of their local environment, encouraged children to 'talk them through' free-recall maps of their journeys.

Interviews have also been used in conjunction with aerial photographs. Dale (1971) interviewed forty primary schoolchildren to explore whether vertical aerial photographs were a satisfactory way of communicating place information to uninitiated children. He interviewed children in pairs; they also had to identify features and give preferences between maps and photographs. Anderson and Tindall (1972) used photographic stimuli too when interviewing children about their home range.

Sometimes apparatus and games have formed the focus of the interview. Middleton *et al.* (1970) devised an ingenious experiment to examine children's ability to understand that people in other countries also have systems of attitudes and preferences that may be different to their own. Their experiment was based on a rescue situation in which toy boats captained by a person from the countries under investigation had to choose different nationalities to rescue from a desert island.

Moore (1986) and Hart (1979), in describing interviews with young children in the field, provide rare detail of methodology. In separate studies, they each interviewed children during field trips in order to find out more about the interrelationship between each individual and his or her immediate environment. The selection of children to be interviewed was based on prior drawings and preliminary indoor interviews. A formal letter from the headteacher of schools concerned indicated to parents that the researcher would make direct contact with them in order to seek permission to accompany their child into the local area. Each 'interview trip' took from twenty minutes to two and a half hours. The trip itself was followed up with parent interviews (more often mothers, as 'Fathers were simply not at home enough'). Data were written up from field notes, in the form of detailed narrative, as soon afterwards as possible.

Analysis of interview data presents a number of difficulties. The ingredient is talk, and talk is not easy to unravel. The most usual form of analysis is a summary description with illustrative quotations, but statistical summaries may also be used. For example (from Lynch, 1977, p. 145):

> The following were mentioned as being the best places to live in (with reasons for the choice):
>   countryside (30 responses)
>   because of:
>   fresh air (11)
>   greenery (4)
>   quiet (3)
>   contact with people (3)
>   lack of vehicular traffic (3)
>   etc.

and (from Moore, 1986) a categorization of where children like to go after school or at weekends – for instance, 37 per cent of children like to go to 'formal' or 'official' open space (such as parks, playgrounds, sports fields) after school.

For an example of coding of interview responses, see the approach of Towler and Price (1976, p. 36). This follows Piaget's approach to investigating nationality and spatial relationship concepts:

> The child was first asked if he lived in Elmira; he was then asked if he lived in Ontario. If the child responded yes to both of these questions, he was then asked if he could live in

both places at the same time. If the child answered questions one or two incorrectly, he was classified as N1. If the child answered one and two correctly, but regressed on question three, he was classified as N2. If the child answered all three questions correctly, he was classified as N3.

Many reports on studies in geographical education research appear to have paid scant attention to how interviews were prepared and conducted. In most cases, too little information has been provided to enable the reader to evaluate the data presented. It is rare to find accounts of the interview schedule or details of how the interviews were recorded or transcribed, how selections from the data were made or how several workers in a collaborative exercise moderated their procedures. Most research, apart from a few very large funded projects, have involved small-scale investigations on a limited budget. The work appears characterized by small samples and untrained or rapidly trained research assistants (often teachers undertaking work in addition to a busy teaching programme, or students).

The overwhelming majority of interview research in geographical education appears to have been in connection with young children and their understanding of geographical ideas. There are, however, notable exceptions. In a series of careful studies of how school subjects come into being, Goodson (1987) examined how subjects compete for status, resources and territory. He deals specifically with the interplay between geography and environmental education and describes, through interviews with some of the key players in critical events, the ways in which geographers successfully fended off an attack on their entrenched position in the school curriculum by environmental education.

The evaluation of curriculum developments has also made use of interviews, most often as a follow-up to questionnaires. In Morrissey's (1987) evaluation of the Sixth Form Geography Project: Jamaica, interviewees confirmed their lack of experience and confidence in preparing curriculum materials and their lack of time. More fundamental, though, was found to be the value of the interview as a tool for probing teachers' lack of commitment to the project.

Greasley (1979) was able through interviews to ascertain that many teachers, although using Geography for the Young School Leaver materials, did not appear to have adopted the project's underlying philosophy. Further work in curriculum development may be found in Corney's evaluation of the Geography, School and Industry Project (GSIP) (Corney, 1988). Similarly, teacher response to curriculum innovation has been explored by Freeman (1981) in the context of computer-assisted learning and Yeomans and Wiegand (1993) in the context of the use of satellites in geography teaching.

A particularly interesting application in an underresearched area is Wright's (1977) interview of the textbook author E.W. Young.

YOUNG CHILDREN'S PLACE KNOWLEDGE

A number of interrelated studies were carried out in order to explore the place knowledge of young children. Much of this work involved interviewing and took place in a variety of Yorkshire schools, with children from nursery age to upper primary (see Lambert and Wiegand, 1990; Wiegand, 1991a, 1991b, 1992). Most of the interviews were conducted by me, but with the very youngest children (3–6 years of age) the interviews were conducted in groups with the nursery or reception class teacher present and contributing to the interaction. Some teachers and schools were well known to me, others not at all. In almost all cases an initial approach was made by letter to the head-teacher explaining the background to the study and outlining the proposed procedure. Some form of questionnaire, survey or class-based data collection usually preceded the interviews proper. For example, interviews about children's travel experiences were preceded by a data-collection exercise in which children had to identify countries they had heard of and indicate which ones they themselves had travelled to (Wiegand, 1991b). These were large-group or whole-class activities, which gave the children the opportunity to get to know me a little in a normal class setting before the individual interviews took place. I did not want to be seen as a teacher and so arranged for myself to be introduced as 'writing a book about what children in Yorkshire know about differ-ent places'. I wanted to try to create an atmosphere whereby the children knew that what I was doing was important and therefore they should do the best they could to help, but that, as I was not a teacher, there was no question of them 'getting it wrong'.

One of the aims with the youngest children was to identify what countries they had heard of and what place knowledge they possessed about the wider world, including any perspective that could be gained about images, stereotypes and prejudice. Work in several nursery schools over a period of approximately one week attempted to record the names of countries the children knew and other information provided by them in response to questions and stimulus material. A large chart was kept recording the in-formation offered by each child. This was compiled at the end of each day using taperecording transcripts and notes made at the time by both the interviewer and the class teacher. In order to elicit the information, children were presented with a number of pictures of varied environments and activities as well as models and dolls from other parts of the world. Games were also played, such as a 'magic carpet' one in which chil-dren, sitting on a rug, had to shout out the names of places they would like to travel to and what they thought they would find there when they went. In talking about the stimu-lus materials, children spontaneously mentioned the names of countries or places (for example, 'It's Africa' when looking at pictures of hot sandy places with black children playing, or 'She comes from Spain' when presented with a flamenco doll). These were recorded next to each child's name on the chart and later in the week the child was asked what he or she knew about that place. Any further information provided was added to the chart. At the end of the study period all the information was examined, and an attempt was made to look for patterns and to group information in order to give some idea of the early developing place awareness of young children. The earliest 'known world' of these Yorkshire children appeared to consist of France, Spain, Australia, America and Africa. In addition, a number of 'environmental assemblages' had already begun to crystallize in the minds of many of them. They were aware that some features were commonly found in association with each other, and this produced a limited number of mental environments, of which desert islands, jungles, Spanish holiday resorts, the Sahel and the North Pole were found to be prominent.

The advantages of group interviews in such circumstances are substantial. The chil-dren appear to be far less inhibited in the presence of a stranger (white male, early forties, non-Yorkshire accent) and a wider range of responses was received as children sparked ideas of each other. Doise *et al.* (1975) established that children perform at a higher level if they are interviewed in groups, appearing to decentre more readily by taking into account the responses of their peers. However, the resulting group interaction often leads to discussion off the point. Very young children, without developed social skills such as conversational turn-taking, may easily be distracted by others. The more articulate often take the lead and block the contributions of the more reticent. Seating arrangements (parts of the carpet always appear more prized than others) and the attractions of other children's clothing and possessions can lead to minor distractions, which interrupt continuity so that a topic is not adequately probed. Interviews with young children are especially sensitive to bias as the opportunities for misunderstanding questions and misinterpreting answers would appear to be greater than for older children or adults. Nevertheless, verbal interaction forms the basis of much classroom teaching. Teachers develop skills of explaining what they mean to their pupils, understanding responses and anticipating misconceptions. Such skills can be enhanced by training in observation, either directly or through the use of videotape. It is likely that the possibilities of experienced teachers acting as interviewers in educational research contexts have not yet been fully exploited.

REFERENCES

Anderson, J. and Tindall, M. (1972) 'The concept of home range: new data for the study of territorial behaviour'. In W.J. Mitchell (ed.) *Environmental Design: Research and Practice*, Vol. 1. Los Angeles: School of Architecture and Urban Planning. University of California.

Berti, A., Bombi, A. and Lis, N. (1982) 'The child's conceptions about means of production and their owners'. *European Journal of Social Psychology*, **12**, 221–39.

Burris, V. (1976) 'The child's conception of economic relations: a genetic approach to the sociology of knowledge'. Unpublished doctoral thesis, Princeton University.

Butterworth, G. (ed.) (1977) *The Child's Representation of the World*. New York: Plenum.

Cannell, C.F. and Kahn, R.L. (1968) 'Interviewing'. In G. Lindzey and E. Aronson (eds) *The Handbook of Social Psychology. Vol. 2. Research Methods*. Reading, MA: Addison-Wesley.

Cohen, L. and Manion, L. (1989) *Research Methods in Education*. London: Routledge.

Corney, G. (1988) 'What influences school centred curriculum development?' In R. Gerber and J. Lidstone (eds) *Skills in Geographical Education Symposium '88 Proceedings. Vol. 1*. Brisbane: International Geographical Union Geographical Education Commission.

Dale, P.F. (1971) 'Children's reactions to maps and aerial photographs'. *Area*, **3**, 170–7.

Danziger, K. (1958) 'Children's earliest conceptions of economic relationships'. *Journal of Social Psychology (Australia)*, **47**, 231–40.

Doise, W., Mugny, G. and Perret-Clermont, A.N. (1975) 'Social interaction and the development of cognitive operations'. *European Journal of Social Psychology*, **5**, 367–83.

Eames, D., Shorrocks, D and Tomlinson, P. (1990) 'Naughty animals or naughty experimenters? Conservation accidents revisited with video-stimulated commentary'. *British Journal of Developmental Psychology*, **8**, 25–37.

Freeman, D. (1981) 'CAL in geography. A case study of Hertfordshire secondary schools'. Unpublished MA dissertation, University of London Institute of Education.

Furth, H. (1980) *The World of Grown-ups: Children's Conceptions of Society*. New York: Elsevier.

Good, C.V. (1963) *Introduction to Educational Research*. New York: Appleton-Century-Crofts.

Goodson, I. (1987) *School Subjects and Curriculum Change*. London: Falmer.

Grace, H.A. and Neuhaus, J.O. (1952) 'Information and social distance as predictors of hostility towards nations'. *Journal of Abnormal and Social Psychology*, **47**, 540–5.

Greasley, B. (1979) 'The implementation of the Schools Council Geography for the Young School Leaver project in schools in East Anglia'. Unpublished MA dissertation, University of London Institute of Education.

Hart, R. (1979) *Children's Experience of Place*. New York: Irvington.

Haubrich, H. (1988) 'Perception of border regions'. In R. Gerber and J. Lidstone (eds) *Skills in Geographical Education Symposium '88 Proceedings. Vol. 1*. Brisbane: International Geographical Union Geographical Education Commission.

Jahoda, G. (1962) 'Development of Scottish children's ideas and attitudes about other countries'. *Journal of Social Psychology*, **58**, 91–108.

Jahoda, G. (1963) 'Development of children's ideas about country and nationality'. *British Journal of Educational Psychology*, **33**, 47–60, 143–53.

Jahoda, G. (1979) 'The construction of economic reality by some Glaswegian children'. *European Journal of Social Psychology*, **19**, 115–27.

James, H.E.O. and Tenen, C. (1951) 'Attitudes towards other peoples'. *International Social Science Bulletin*, **3**, 553–61.

Kitwood, T. M. (1977) 'Values in adolescent life: towards a critical description'. Unpublished PhD thesis, University of Bradford.

Ladd, F.C. (1972) 'Black youths view their environment: some views of housing'. *Journal of American Institute of Planners*, **38** (2), 108–17.

Lambert, S. and Wiegand, P. (1990) 'The beginnings of international understanding'. *The New Era in Education*, **71** (3), 90–3.

Lambert, W.E. and Klineberg, O. (1967) *Children's Views of Foreign Peoples: A Cross National Study*. New York: Appleton-Century-Crofts.

Lee, T.R. (1970) 'Perceived distance as a function of direction in the city'. *Environment and Behaviour*, **2**, 40–51.

Lidstone, J. (1981) 'What are we really teaching? Pupil perception on a text book based geography course'. In P. Wilson, R. Gerber and J. Fien (eds) *Research in Geographical Education. Vol. 1*. Brisbane: Australian Geographical Education Research Association.

Lukashok, A.K. and Lynch, K. (1956) 'Some childhood memories of the city'. *Journal of American Institute of Planners*, **22**, 142–52.

Lynch, K. (ed.) (1977) *Growing Up in Cities*. Cambridge, MA: MIT Press.

Maurer, R. and Baxter, J.C. (1972) 'Images of the neighbourhood and city among Black, Anglo and Mexican-American children'. *Environment and Behaviour*, **4** (4), 351–88.

McGarrigle, J. and Donaldson, M. (1974) 'Conservation accidents'. *Cognition*, **3**, 341–50.

Merton, R.K. and Kendall, P.L. (1946) 'The focused interview'. *American Journal of Sociology*, **51**, 541–57.

Middleton, M.R., Tajfel, H. and Johnson, N.B. (1970) 'Cognitive and affective aspects of children's national attitudes'. *British Journal of Social and Clinical Psychology*, **9**, 122–34.

Moore, R.C. (1986) *Childhood's Domain: Play and Place in Child Development*. London: Croom Helm.

Morrissey, M. (1987) 'Teacher participation in curriculum development in a third world country: lessons of a sixth form geography project'. In R. Gerber (ed.) *Research in Geographical Education. Vol. 3*. Brisbane: Australian Geographical Education Research Association.

Moser, C.A. and Kalton, G. (1971) *Survey Methods in Social Investigation*. London: Heinemann.

Newson, J. and Newson, E. (1976) *Seven Years Old in the Home Environment*. Harmondsworth: Penguin.

Nussbaum, J. (1985) 'The Earth as a cosmic body'. In R. Driver, E. Guesne and A. Tiberghien (eds) *Children's Ideas in Science*. Milton Keynes: Open University Press.

Piaget, J. and Inhelder, B. (1956) *The Child's Conception of Space*. London: Routledge and Kegan Paul.

Piaget, J. with Weil, A. (1951) 'The development in children of the idea of the homeland and of relations with other countries'. *International Social Science Bulletin*, **3**, 561–78.

Powney, J. and Watts, M. (1987) *Interviewing in Educational Research*. London: Routledge and Kegan Paul.

Ryan, T.A. and Ryan, M.S. (1940) 'Geographical orientation'. *American Journal of Psychology*, **53**, 204–15.

Schug, M. (1990) 'Research on children's understanding of economics: implications for teaching'. In A. Ross (ed.) *Economic and Industrial Awareness in the Primary School*. London: School Curriculum Industry Partnership/Polytechnic of North London.

Schug, M. and Birkley, C. (1985) 'The development of children's economic reasoning'. *Theory and Research in Social Education*, **13**, 31–42.

Spencer, C. and Darvizeh, Z. (1981) 'Young children's descriptions of their local environment: a comparison of information elicited by recall, recognition and performance techniques of investigation'. *Environmental Education and Information*, **1**, 275–84.

Stillwell, R. and Spencer, C. (1974) 'Children's early preferences for other nations and their subsequent acquisition of knowledge about those nations'. *European Journal of Social Psychology*, **3**, 345–9.

Strauss, A. (1952) 'The development and transformation of monetary meanings in the child'. *American Sociological Review*, **17**, 275–84.

Towler, J. and Price, D. (1976) 'The development of nationality and spatial relationship concepts in children: Canada'. In J.P. Stoltman (ed.) *International Research in Geographical Education: Spatial Stages Development in Children and Teacher Style in Geography*. Research Reports of the 23rd Congress of the International Geographical Union. Kalamazoo: Western Michigan University.

Whitehurst, G.J. (1979) 'Meaning and semantics'. In G.J. Whitehurst and B.J. Zimmerman (eds) *The Functions of Language and Cognition*. New York: Academic Press.

Wiegand, P. (1991a) 'Does travel broaden the mind?' *Education 3-13*, **19** (1), 54–8.

Wiegand, P. (1991b) 'The known world of the primary school'. *Geography*, 76 (2), 143–9.

Wiegand, P. (1992) *Places in the Primary School*. London: Falmer.

Woodhead, J. and Woodhead, M. (1990) *All Our Children*. Letchworth: Ringpress.

Wright, D. (1977) 'Authors and their books: an interview with E.W. Young'. *Teaching Geography*, **2** (4), 173–6.

Yeomans, D. and Wiegand, P. (1993) *Remote Sensing: Report on the Evaluation of the Remote Sensing Element of the Welsh Office Satellites in Schools Initiative*. Coventry: National Council for Educational Technology.

Chapter 10

Questionnaire Survey in Research in Environmental and Geographical Education

Philip Stimpson

> The world is full of well-meaning people who believe that anyone who can write plain English and has a modicum of common sense can produce a good questionnaire.
>
> (Oppenheim, 1966, p. 1)

Questionnaire survey is a frequently used method of research in geographical and environmental education. It tries to answer questions about the status of a particular situation by providing generally verifiable data. The information gathered gives snapshots at particular points in time of existing conditions. Questionnaire surveys are characterized by the nature of the planned, systematic data collection they entail. Examples include investigations of classroom practices (Robinson, 1986), emphases in geographical education (Gerber, 1990), attitudes to curricular change (Leung, 1989) and constraints on implementation (Lee, 1993). Indeed, the range of areas where questionnaires have been used is exceedingly wide (Table 10.1).

Questionnaire surveys are essentially passive in contrast with experimental studies that look for the effects of change. None the less, if suitable questions are asked, interrelationships and possible causes can be illuminated. Questionnaire surveys thus play a role in both descriptive-situational analyses and correlational studies. They are particularly useful where there are few base data available. Given the present stage of development in much of geographical and environmental education research, it is perhaps not surprising that they have been looked on favourably. However, despite the seductive appeal of their seeming simplicity in gaining copious data for relatively little effort, questionnaires are much abused. In many instances, they lead to more uncertainty than answers. Their use for collecting and organizing evidence raises many methodological issues and problems, and it is this which forms the central thrust for this chapter.

Intelligent data gathering requires a conscious effort. Tasks such as specifying objects, identifying variables, constructing an instrument and designing the survey have to be carefully thought through (Ott, 1993). There are numerous general books and chapters in books on research methods covering most of these issues (e.g. Cohen and Manion, 1994; Hoinville and Jowell, 1978; Oppenheim, 1966), and it is not my intention to replicate these. Instead, the main focus will be on a piece of questionnaire research from

Table 10.1 *Some examples of the recent use of questionnaire survey in geographical and environmental education*

Researchers	Date	Title
Ballantyne, R., Lidstone, J. and Packer, J.	1993	A critically reflexive pre-service geography teacher education course: attitudes and practice changes among graduates
Lee, J.C.C.	1993	Geography teaching in England and Hong Kong: contributions towards environmental education
Daugherty, R.	1992	The influence on classroom practice of change in public examinations: a study of GCSE geography
Karpik, M.	1992	New Zealand students' awareness of a local environmental issue
Troger, S.	1992	The perception of Africa and its people by German pupils: frameworks for development education
Weber, R.	1992	The contribution of bilingual geography teaching towards international education
Gerber, R.	1990	Asian geography educators' perceptions and practices
Tait, N.	1990	South African student perceptions of the Asian Pacific region
Corney, G.	1988	What influences school centred curriculum development: the teachers' perspective
Saarinen, T.F., MacCabe, C. and Morehouse, B.	1988	Sketch-maps of the world as surrogates for world geographical knowledge

the early 1990s in environmental and geographical education. The discussion will concentrate on methodological strategy and its influence on the final outcome of the research. (This work has now been completed and is reported in Wong and Stimpson, 1994). In order to put this in context, the chapter will start by looking at the advantages and disadvantages generally claimed for questionnaire surveys, particularly in comparison with interviews. This first section concludes by examining broad issues of optimizing design.

ADVANTAGES AND DISADVANTAGES

Advantages

The main advantage claimed for questionnaire surveys is that they are cheap and quick to administer where information from a large sample or a large population is needed. Further, they avoid the negative effects of face-to-face interviewing and provide a standardized evaluation method (Lang and Heiss, 1991).

The low cost of obtaining data is often an important consideration where researchers have a geographically dispersed target population. Many international surveys would not be practical without self-administered postal questionnaires. For example, during 1993, Ballantyne (personal communication) attempted to describe the pattern of environmental education in Asia-Pacific; the cost of such an undertaking would be prohibitive were face-to-face interviewing employed. Self-administered questionnaires avoid the high costs of hiring and training interviewers, travel and actually conducting the interviews. Interviews, which are often seen as the alternative, are particularly labour-intensive and time-consuming; in comparison, questionnaires are generally quick to administer and can rapidly sample a large population. Thus, for example, in a recent unpublished study of the way decisions were made about adopting a new environmental curriculum in

Hong Kong, interviews with 180 key personnel took nearly one year to complete with the resources available. Given an ever-changing curriculum, the comparability of early and later interviews raised questions about the internal consistency of the data set. Had this not been recognized and accommodated, this would have threatened the internal validity of the study. The use of a questionnaire would have permitted more rapid collection of data but would also have raised other difficulties, some of which are discussed in later sections.

One further advantage of questionnaires is that they are impersonal. Self-administered questionnaires avoid the problems of interviews, where choice of words or body language may unintentionally affect responses. However, this is not a simple issue. While interviewers can influence what is said, they can also help respondents understand exactly what is needed. Impersonality has gains and losses.

A major asset of questionnaire surveys is that they offer a means of collecting data in which responses are presented on a largely common basis, assuming an adequate survey design. In comparison with interview data and despite recent advances in the computer handling of qualitative transcript data, questionnaire results are easier to process.

Disadvantages

Questionnaire surveys are not without their liabilities. Payne (1951), reporting what a sample of researchers saw as the difficulties noted:

- improper wording (74 per cent)
- faulty interpretation (58 per cent)
- inadequate samples (52 per cent).

A major problem is the absence of any check on the effectiveness of the communication, even if pre-testing has taken place. If instructions as to how to complete the questionnaire, or the wording in the questions themselves, are in any way ambiguous or unclear, then the validity and reliability of the study as a whole are in doubt. Clarity of wording and simplicity of design are essential. Complicated instructions discourage response. Yet sometimes it may be difficult to achieve the necessary simplicity because the situations we seek to survey may comprise highly interrelated components.

Responses are likely to vary if those participating in the survey tackle the questionnaire in different ways. Some people read through the whole questionnaire before attempting to complete it and consequently have looked at all the questions; others, however, work directly through them. This may affect the content validity of the results. Unfortunately, there is no way of knowing in advance how people approach the answering task, or of controlling for it. Similarly, it is not always easy to check for honesty of responses without recourse to the follow-up interviews that many researchers find necessary; however, this adds time and cost.

Ensuring that the intended target in a survey is the one that actually replies can be problematic. For example, in a survey looking at the attitudes of geography departments in schools to a proposed change in the curriculum (Leung, 1989), a questionnaire was posted to the head of geography. The head was felt to be the one best able to synthesize views; yet there was no guarantee that the questionnaire would not be passed on to some one else. One way of attempting to deal with this is to check the personal details of respondents. This does not negate the problem but does help when interpreting results. Even if the intended targets reply, there is no way of knowing what their feelings were when confronted with the set of questions and how motivated they were to answer as conscientiously as desired.

Often, worries about response rate and the pattern of response are of greatest concern. Schools in many countries are inundated with requests for information both from educational authorities and from postgraduate and, increasingly, undergraduate research projects. Low response rates are to be expected but can be mitigated by personal contact and careful targeting of the sample. Cohen and Manion (1994), however, noted that response levels in postal surveys are not less than those obtained in interview surveys, and are sometimes greater. More difficult to circumvent is the tendency for those in schools who are more interested and involved in innovation to answer. This is a frequent source of bias in results from questionnaire surveys.

Burgess (1985), in seeking to promote alternative approaches, saw many questionnaire surveys as restrictive, lacking the capacity to extract the information required and exhibiting low 'informational adequacy' (Zelditch, 1962). There is clearly a maximum length of questionnaire that will be received sympathetically. As a result, some aspects of a study may have to be left out. Other research questions may not be addressed because their importance is not realized until after the data are analysed. In interviews, it is claimed that skilful interviewers can become interviewees' friends and confidants; by showing interest in the lives of those from whom they are collecting data, they are permitted to gain greater insight, and omissions can be avoided. This is particularly valuable in research on behaviour, central to much environmental research. It is not available with 'one-shot' questionnaires.

Survey design

Too often, questionnaire surveys are carried out on the basis of insufficient planning or no design. A questionnaire is not just a form to be filled out; it is an instrument to collect particular information with specific aims in mind. A plan is essential. Oppenheim (1966) suggested that it is helpful to start by deciding what sort of conclusions it is hoped to draw: are we looking, for example, for relative frequencies of different attitudes or for frequency by gender or other characteristics? This enables the researcher to identify the way results will need to be tabulated to draw conclusions. In turn, it then becomes apparent what types of question must be written and the nature of the sample population. By this careful attention to survey design, collection of irrelevant information and omission of essential questions can be avoided.

This can be illustrated by looking at a survey proposal recently brought to me by a Master's student. She was interested in teacher attitudes and responses to a set of environmental guidelines for schools which had just been published. She wanted to know to what extent teachers were aware of the recommendations, their understanding of what was implied, how far they were implementing change, and how this was being affected by factors such as teacher experience, level of training, attitude to change, teacher involvement with green groups, and resource provision. The intention was to survey biology and history teachers, as representative of science and humanities teachers taking up cross-curricular environmental responsibility. This sample was bound to be deficient, as it makes assumptions about similarities between teachers within the sciences and within the humanities, but none the less some estimate of teacher behaviour and attitudes could be made. More problematic was the hope of elucidating influences on adoption. Implicit in this was a factorial design in which the aim was to disentangle the web of influences. If there were, say, three levels of experience (new teacher, established teacher, head of department), four levels of training (non-graduate, graduate, graduate with professional training and graduate with higher degree), three attitudes (positive, negative and undecided), then the design would require $3 \times 4 \times 3 = 36$ cells. At thirty teachers per cell this would entail surveying 1080 teachers. In reality the student was proposing a long list of factors, and consequently the sample became enormous if usable data were to be produced. By not recognizing the multidimensional cell structure, no account was being taken of the interrelationship between factors, as, for example, many of the heads of department were mainly, though not exclusively, those with higher levels of training. Given the resources available, it was clearly necessary to limit the number of factors to be studied. If the issue of design had not been clarified at the outset, much time and effort might have been wasted.

A QUESTIONNAIRE SURVEY OF TEACHING STYLES IN ENVIRON-MENTAL EDUCATION

In environmental and much of geographical education, concerns have been voiced that aims and objectives frequently remain mere rhetoric (Spork, 1991). Statements of new curricular content are often not accompanied by parallel changes in classroom practice. For example, if practitioners are asked about aims, they generally indicate recognition of the importance of inquiry, attitude development and the encouragement of environmentally sensitive behaviour. Yet this is frequently not matched in the teaching strategies they adopt. However, is choice of the appropriate strategy at the heart of the matter? Researches in the US on the efficacy of particular classroom routines such as role-play and simulations have yielded contradictory results (e.g. Singletary, 1992; Fennessey *et al.*, 1974). It seems that it is not so much a matter of the strategies selected as how they are employed which is critical. Questions of classroom climate and teaching style may be of greater importance, as these mediate the outcome of particular classroom strategies. The aim of the study now described was to attempt to define the style adopted by subject teachers in Hong Kong when dealing with environmental education.

Objectives

The 16+ Certificate of Education (CE) geography curriculum in Hong Kong espouses environmental aims, but it is uncertain how far targets for experiential rather than instructional leaning are met. To evaluate the likelihood of successful adoption, an investigation was set up on the style being used by geography teachers when covering environmental topics. It also sought to see how far the style adopted was compatible with the stated aims for environmental education. The guidelines for environmental education note that learning should be open, participative and experiential (Curriculum Development Council, 1992). The research sought answers to three key questions:

- What were the perceived styles used for teaching environmental topics through the geography curriculum?
- What major types of teaching style were apparent?
- To what extent were the types compatible with styles deemed consistent with promoting environmental education?

To obtain as wide a cross-selection as possible among the geography teachers at this level in the 400 secondary schools in the territory, a self-administered postal question-naire seemed appropriate. Classroom observation or interviews with teachers were not practical alternatives, given the resources needed and teachers' reluctance to admit outsiders into their classrooms for observation.

Defining variables

Once objectives had been identified, the next step was to conceptualize the variables within the problem being studied and, in particular, to reach a common understanding of what is meant by 'style', as this constituted the key variable. The notion of 'style' needed to be both theoretically underpinned and capable of being operationalized.

It was quickly recognized that 'style' is a somewhat nebulous term with a range of asso-ciated meanings (Naish, 1988). Most definitions, nevertheless, visualize some combination of mode – the sorts of strategy and routine employed – and manner – the way we use different strategies and the atmosphere so engendered. At the centre of manner within environmental education is openness, indirectness and pupil self-direction. One way of looking at mode of teaching is to record the individual strategies a teacher uses. For example, brainstorming might be followed by a period of teacher explanation and in turn by pair work, etc. Such an approach was used by Daugherty (1992) in a questionnaire survey of teaching style in Wales. Another approach is to look at the degree of openness and pupil-centredness within a framework of general elements in an instructional event.

In the study, Gagne's (1975) eight instructional elements were used, namely:

1. activating motivation;
2. informing the learner of objectives;
3. directing attention;
4. stimulating recall;
5. providing guidance;
6. enhancing retention;
7. promoting transfer of learning;
8. providing reinforcement feedback.

While a behaviourist theory such as Gagne's has its limitations, and the more humanist perspective of, say, Rogers might be more appropriate in areas of personal and social education (Entwistle and Hownsell, 1975), it had the advantage of providing a system-atic, functional classification of teacher behaviour. This put the focus directly on the development of learning. Moreover, Gagnean precepts were felt to mirror usual practice in schools more closely. Clearly, identifying an underpinning which was theoretically appropriate and could be applied was crucial and, hence, was a central concern in setting up the study.

Writing the items

In writing the questionnaire items, the checklist of decisions by Seliltiz, Wrightsman and Cook (1976) in Cohen and Manion (1994, p. 106) provided helpful advice in directing progress (see Table 10.2). Sixteen items were constructed, each carefully matched with each element in the Gagne framework. The items comprised a classroom situation that teachers using the curriculum might have faced in dealing with environmental topics. The respondents were offered three options of varying degrees of openness and pupil-centredness in style. From these, they chose what they thought would be their most and least likely course of action. A closed or forced-choice format was used, even though an open format would have avoided the risk of insufficient options and hence the danger that items would lack validity. Further, it would have given opportunities for individuals to qualify responses. However, the aim was to define teacher behaviour rather than to explore generally their views on teaching style, and thus a forced answer seemed more appropriate. Perhaps the greatest influence on the decision was that closed-choice questions facilitated easier coding and data processing, as answers were standardized and numbers could be ascribed to predetermined categories.

The type of question used is illustrated by the item given below for 'activating motivation'. Intrinsic rather than extrinsic motivation was argued to be more appropriate for environmental education (Biggs and Telfer, 1987). The item's three options varied in type of motivation and openness. On the final questionnaire, the position of these style descriptors was randomized:

> After teaching about the citizen's role in energy conservation, you ask the students to divide into groups to discuss ways of saving energy in the school or at home. You say that:
> A. The group failing to submit a report at the end will be punished. [closed style; extrinsic motivation]
> B. The group with the most convincing argument gets a prize. [open style; extrinsic motivation]
> C. Each group must report how they would apply these ideas to their daily lives. [open style; intrinsic motivation]

Checking for validity

It was clearly of vital importance that the questions both accurately reflected the underlying constructs that the researchers sought to examine and were understandable to the teachers who would answer them. Consequently the questions were first reviewed by an 'expert panel' and secondly piloted with a small group of teachers.

In trying to get at classroom practice, it was counterproductive to talk in the abstract about actions. The aim was to get each teacher to imagine himself or herself in that position. Language had to be simple and direct but at the same time not lose the subtlety of difference between the options. This problem can be magnified if the questionnaire is in a second language or uses unusual mother-tongue phrasing. The questions were therefore given in both Chinese and English. Results from the piloting showed that, while the total length was about right, some individual items were too long or complex, with multiple component structure, or were not sufficiently clear, or contained options which were not markedly different from others in the item and were poor discriminators. As a consequence further changes were made, emphasizing the importance of pre-testing.

Table 10.2 *A guide for questionnaire construction*

A   Decisions about question content
1.   Is the question necessary? How will it be useful?
2.   How many questions will be needed to cover a particular area?
3.   Do respondents have the necessary information to answer?
4.   Does the question need to be more specific or concrete and related to the respondents' experience?
5.   Is the question sufficiently general to address the point being examined?
6.   Is the question loaded in any way?
7.   Will respondents give the information asked for?

B   Decisions about question wording
1.   Can the question be misunderstood? Is the phrasing clear? Will terms be understood?
2.   Are alternatives, where appropriate, clearly stated?
3.   Do terms make unstated assumptions? Is the wording biased in any way?
4.   Will people object to the wording? Is it sexist or racist or ageist?
5.   Would a more personalized wording encourage response?
6.   Would a more direct, or indirect, form of wording be better?

C   Decisions about form or response to the question
1.   Is a forced-choice or open-response form best?
2.   If forced choice is adopted, should a dichotomous (yes–no), multiple-choice or scale format be used?
3.   If a checklist is used, does it adequately cover the range of alternatives without overlap?
4.   Is the format for answering easy for the respondent?

D   Decisions about the place of the question in the sequence
1.   Will the answer be influenced by that for any preceding question?
2.   Do the questions develop in a natural way which will help the respondents to develop their understanding of what is being looked for?
3.   Given that a question may be sensitive, does it come too early, so that it may arouse negative feelings about the questionnaire as a whole?

Preparing the final document

With the checks made and additional items added to obtain some understanding of the respondents' educational background, the questionnaire was made ready for printing and distribution. The background items were placed in the final document before those on teaching-style. This followed the recommendation that easier questions be placed first so as to help and encourage the respondent into the document as a whole.

The final version was desktop published and printed on good quality paper. As Cohen and Manion (1994) have pointed out, the appearance of the questionnaire is vitally important. A cluttered layout is uninviting whereas plenty of space in which to answer will encourage respondents. It is often suggested that instructions should be repeated but, as it was, the sixteen items and additional background questions covered eight pages, and the aim was not to make the questionnaire overlong. For similar reasons, a note at the end asking respondents to check that no answer had been inadvertently missed out and to return the completed questionnaire was omitted, although in general this is good practice and should have been included.

A covering letter

This was written as succinctly as possible and printed on headed paper to make it clear in whose name the survey was being conducted. The one-page letter was addressed to the head of geography by name, and:

- explained the purpose of the study and its importance to both the education community as a whole and the respondents in particular;
- asked them to distribute copies of the questionnaire to other CE teachers;
- assured them of the anonymity of respondents in the final report;
- gave a contact number and a date for returning the questionnaire;
- thanked teachers for their help and offered a summary of the results should respondents like it.

Stressing the significance of the survey to the individual is important, as this can generate a sense of professional obligation which, in the absence of the incentive gifts used in many commercial surveys, can increase the rate of return. The letter, along with a stamped self-addressed envelope helped to generate a sympathetic climate for the survey.

Distribution of the questionnaire

Knowing the population to survey can sometimes be a problem. Fortunately in this case a list of all the secondary schools taking the CE exam was available from the examinations authority. This was not a complete list of all schools teaching CE geography, as a minority, particularly private schools, do not register as examination centres. Consequently this list was supplemented by ones from organizations such as the Education Department and Heads of Secondary Schools Association. It is normal practice for two teachers to take on the CE work, and from the number of schools we could be reasonably certain of the total population. There was a possibility of an overestimate in the number of teachers, as in some cases one teacher in a school may take on all the work, but this was not thought likely to have a substantial affect on the conclusions that could be drawn.

The timing of the distribution can be critical in getting a good response rate. Clearly, busy times and school holidays are best avoided. At the end of term, there is a tendency to leave questionnaires on desks and never pick them up again. It was decided, therefore, to send out the questionnaire in the period after teaching had stopped for the public examinations.

Follow-up

This is usually critical if a good response rate is to be achieved. Telephone calls were made to the heads of department to encourage returns. This had the advantage of putting the survey on a more personal footing and provided information about the actual number of staff teaching at CE level. Up to that point, it was not known for certain whether or not the original estimate of two CE teachers per school was accurate; in the event, it was proved largely correct. After two weeks, follow-up letters were sent out with replacement copies of the questionnaire.

Processing the survey data collected

The first step was to check the completeness of the data. While missing data in the background information could be accommodated, the same was not true for the style information. The few incomplete questionnaires were rejected, as it was not easy to contact the respondents again. Had the numbers of incomplete questionnaires been great or the response rate very low, this would have proved a serious problem. At the same time, a check was made to see whether respondents carried out the instructions correctly, as far as possible. Sometimes one can identify errors and correct data entries.

Once these checks were made, the data were coded on a coding frame printed on the right-hand margin of each questionnaire. In the case of the style data, the coding was of simple binary form (1 = Tick or yes and 0 = Blank or no). In the background data, answers involving aspects such as years of service were coded by category (1 = Over 1 year; 2 = 1 to 5 years; etc). A similar process would have been necessary had items on an agree–disagree scale been used. Open-ended questions would have meant classifying the responses on a sample questionnaire and allocating a code to each category.

The use of a coding frame may seem unnecessary: after all, why not just enter the data direct into the computer? In fact, it helps the researcher to concentrate when checking the data and makes data entry easier, as the eye does not have to scan the page. Any means which does this is likely to help in avoiding mistakes.

The response rate of the survey was 72.7 per cent by school and 52 per cent by estimated total number of geography teachers at that level. In Hong Kong, other questionnaire surveys in geographical education have achieved rates between 32.8 per cent and 84 per cent, so this was acceptable. However, as expected and as with other studies, the response rate from private schools was low (43 per cent).

Findings

The results of the survey data showed that geography teachers tended to adopt a more open, participative, indirect style at the beginning of lessons or when setting up topics. In dealing with the main body of a lesson they were more likely to be formal, didactic, teacher-centred and oriented to an exam which stresses factual recall. Knowledge transmission dominated experiential learning. However, there were variations, and a cluster analysis of the teachers by style revealed three main types: a progressive-inquiry-oriented type (11.9 per cent); an expositional type (26 per cent), and a teacher-directed, guided-learning type (62.1 per cent).

The picture painted cannot be considered fully adequate. For example, it has to take it on trust that all teachers interpreted the questions in the same way. What is clearly needed is triangulation and corroborative evidence from documents or, preferably, from classroom observation. None the less, the study provided a useful situational snapshot of current practice and, while the dominant style was not fully compatible with the principles set out for environmental education in the territory, it was clear that some teachers at least were following accepted practices which are conducive to effective environmental education.

CONCLUSION

Questionnaire surveys of the type described offer a valuable methodology for collecting large numbers of data. But at the heart of a decision as to whether or not to use it is a series of compromises which has to be made. Whether these are acceptable depends on the problem being studied, the research questions posed and the outcomes desired. There is often a tendency today to dismiss questionnaires in favour of interviews, diaries or something similar. This does not do justice to questionnaire surveys: all methods have assets and liabilities which must be recognized. However, if questionnaires are used, it is incumbent upon researchers to ensure that a data-collection system is created which is systematic and unbiased in its design, and that limitations are both realized and expressed.

REFERENCES

Ballantyne, R, Lidstone, J. and Packer, J. (1993) 'A critically reflexive pre-service geography teacher education course: attitudes and practice changes among graduates.' *International Research in Geographical and Environmental Education*, 2 (1), 41–50.

Biggs, J.B. and Telfer, R. (1987) *The Process of Learning*. Sydney: Prentice-Hall.

Burgess, R.G. (1985) *Strategies of Educational Research*. Lewes: Falmer.

Cohen, L. and Manion, L. (1994) *Research Methods in Education*. 2nd edn. London: Croom Helm.

Corney, G. (1988) 'What influences school centred curriculum development: the teachers' perspective'. In R. Gerber and J. Lidstone (eds) *Proceedings of the International Geographical Union's Commission on Geographical Education Symposium, Skills in Geographical Education, Brisbane, August 14–20, 1988*. Brisbane: Brisbane College of Advanced Education.

Curriculum Development Council (1992) *Guidelines on Environmental Education in Schools*. Hong Kong: Education Department, Hong Kong Government.

Daugherty, R. (1992) 'The influence on classroom practice of change in public examinations: a study of GCSE geography.' *Proceedings of the International Geographical Union Education Symposium on Interdependence in Geographical Education*. University of Colorado, Boulder, August 1992. Boulder, CO: Centre for Geographic Education. University of Colorado at Boulder.

Entwistle, N. and Hownsell, D. (1975) *How Students Learn*. Lancaster: Institute for Research and Development in Post-compulsory Education, University of Lancaster.

Fennessey, G.M., Livingston, S.A., Edwards, K.J., Kidder, S.J. and Nafziger, A.W. (1974) 'Simulation gaming and conventional instruction in the teaching of ecology.' *Journal of Environmental Education*, 5 (4), 21–4.

Gagne, R. (1975) *Essentials of Learning for Instruction*. Hinsdale: Dryden.

Gerber, R. (1990) 'Asian geography educators' perceptions and practices.' In P.G. Stimpson and L.Y. Kwan (eds) *Abstracts and Papers: International Geographical Union Education Symposium on Teaching Geography In and About Asian Pacific Countries*. Hong Kong: University of Hong Kong.

Hoinville, G. and Jowell, R. (1978) *Survey Research Practice*. London: Heineman Educational Books.

Karpik, M. (1992) 'New Zealand students' awareness of a local environmental issue'. *International Research in Geographical and Environmental Education*, 1 (1), 24–30.

Lang, G. and Heiss, G.D. (1991) *A Practical Guide to Research Methods*. 3rd edn. New York: University Press of America.

Lee, J.C.C. (1993) 'Geography teaching in England and Hong Kong: contributions toward environmental education'. *International Research in Geographical and Environmental Education*, 2 (1), 25–40.

Leung, W.K. (1989) 'Teachers' perceptions of the 1989 Certificate in Education Geography Curriculum and an analysis of possible implementation problems.' Unpublished MEd Dissertation, Faculty of Education, University of Hong Kong.

Naish, M. (1988) 'Teaching styles in geographical education.' In R. Gerber and J. Lidstone (eds) *Developing Skills in Geographical Education*. Brisbane: Jacaranda.

Oppenheim, A.N. (1966) *Questionnaire Design and Attitude Measurement*. London: Gower.

Ott, R.L. (1993) *An Introduction to Statistical Methods and Data Analysis*. 3rd edn. Belmont, CA: Duxbury.

Payne, S.L. (1951) *The Art of Asking Questions*. Princeton, NJ: Princeton University Press.

Robinson, R. (1986) 'Geography teachers' reflections on their teaching about development.' *Journal of Curriculum Studies*, **18** (4), 409–27.

Saarinen, T.F., MacCabe, C. and Morehouse, B. (1988) 'Sketch-maps of the world as surrogates for world geographical knowledge.' In R. Gerber and J. Lidstone (eds) *Proceedings of the International Geographical Union's Commission on Geographical Education Symposium, Skills in Geographical Education*, Brisbane, August 14–20, 1988. Brisbane: Brisbane College of Advanced Education.

Seliltiz, C., Wrightsman, L.S. and Cook, S.W. (1976) *Recent Methods in Social Relations*. New York: Holt Rinehart and Winston.

Singletary, T. (1992) 'Case studies of selected high school environmental education classes.' *Journal of Environmental Education*, **23** (4), 35–40.

Spork, H. (1991) 'Environmental education: a mismatch between theory and practice.' Paper presented at the 1991 Symposium of the Australian Association for Research in Education, Gold Coast, Australia.

Tait, N. (1990) 'South African student perceptions of the Asian Pacific region.' In P.G. Stimpson and L.Y. Kwan (eds) *Abstracts and Papers: International Geographical Union Education Symposium on Teaching Geography In and About Asian Pacific Countries*. Hong Kong: University of Hong Kong.

Troger, S. (1992) 'The perception of Africa and its people by German pupils: frameworks for development education.' In D. Hill (ed.) *Proceedings of the International Geographical Union's Commission on Geographical Education Symposium Interdependence in Geographic Education*, University of Colorado at Boulder, August 2–7, 1992. Boulder, CO: Center for Geographic Education, University of Colorado at Boulder.

Weber, R. (1992) 'The contribution of bilingual geography teaching towards international education.' In D. Hill (ed.) *Proceedings of the International Geographical Union's Commission on Geographical Education Symposium Interdependence in Geographic Education*, University of Colorado at Boulder, August 2–7, 1992. Boulder, CO: Center of Geographic Education, University of Colorado at Boulder.

Wong, E.M.O. and Stimpson, P.G. (1994) 'Teaching styles of Hong Kong's environmental educators in secondary schools.' *Research in Education*, **52**, 1–12.

Zelditch, M. (1962) 'Some methodological problems of field studies.' *American Journal of Sociology*, **67**, 566–76.

Chapter 11

Case Study Research

Margaret Roberts

> Case studies are inevitably always partial accounts involving selection at every stage.
> (Walker, 1980, p. 43)

GENERAL ISSUES

Case studies have been used extensively in social anthropology, sociology, psychology, medicine, law, geography and other disciplines, including educational research, for much of this century. Such wide use over a long period of time suggests that they are valuable, yet their use has not been without criticism.

In the first part of this chapter I will explore the value of case study in educational research by focusing on three questions:

1. What is case study research?
2. Why are case studies used?
3. What are the problems of using case studies?

The second part of the chapter gives an outline of part of my own case study research into the implementation of the geography National Curriculum at Key Stage 3 in three schools in England. The third part of the chapter will comment on my own research and on case study research in geographical education generally.

What is case study research?

There are some common characteristics of 'case study' as used in educational research which are worth identifying:

1. A case study focuses on one particular instance, unit or 'case'. This might be a person, a class, a school or a department. The unit is the main source of information about the case.

2.   A case study has, or develops, a focus within the unit of study. It is not exhaustive; a case study is selective in that it cannot deal with every issue related to a case and it deals with some issues in more depth than others (Walker, 1980). A case study, whatever its focus, takes into account the interrelatedness of elements within the case.

3.   The case is studied at a particular time within a particular social, economic, cultural and political context, which needs to be taken into account in interpreting the case study. Case study research has to relate the particularity of the case to the generality of the context.

4.   The case is bounded by the researchers' interests, by the theoretical assumptions they bring to the investigation and by the constraints of time and resources under which they are working.

5.   The case is studied 'within its real life context' (Yin, 1994, p. 13), rather than in some contrived experimental setting.

6.   The case is unique. It will have its own 'idiosyncratic combination of elements and events' (Mitchell, 1983, p. 188).

Although the content of a case study is determined by the boundaries suggested in the first four characteristics, these boundaries are not as clear as the list suggests. The researcher is constructing the case as the research develops by shifting the conceptual and empirical boundaries during the course of the study. The final case study is a construction rather than an object which has been studied.

To summarize, case study research in education is characterized by its focus rather than by its methodology. Case study research cannot be described as 'a research method'; it does not have its own particular techniques of investigation. It draws eclectically on the whole range of research techniques used in educational research. Generally, however, it uses a selection of *qualitative* techniques: participant and non-participant observation, interviewing, and analysis of documents and other evidence.

Why are case studies used?

The study of a 'case' has several advantages in investigating educational issues. Different researchers have highlighted particular merits.

Goode and Hatt (1952), writing about the use of case studies in the study of sociology, emphasized the preservation of 'the unitary character of the social object being studied' (p. 331). They stressed the importance of the researcher viewing the unit being studied 'as a whole' rather than falling back on 'trait analysis alone'.

The advantages of studying the whole are implicit in the writing of many educational researchers. Adelman *et al.* (1980, p. 59) saw the 'peculiar strength' of case studies being their 'attention to the subtlety and complexity of a case'. This can include conflicts between viewpoints. Anderson (1990, p. 157) stressed that case studies were 'flexible and adaptable' in that they were able to respond to change in the situation being studied. Case study could take into account the unanticipated.

Another advantage of case study research is that it can be related easily to everyday experience. Adelman *et al.* (1980, p. 59) described case study research as 'down to earth and attention holding, in harmony with the readers' own experience'. They thought it was 'strong on reality' in contrast to other research which was 'weak in reality'.

Stenhouse (1985) wrote about the accessibility of case study research to classroom teachers. He thought they would relate easily to a study of the specific because they worked in 'specific, individual situations' (p. 264). He valued the detailed archive of descriptive data collected during case study research, which provided valuable evidence. It could be used as workshop materials by practitioners. Critical study of the evidence could enable them to increase their understanding of their own particular case.

Mitchell (1983, p. 194) points out that case studies are able to explore causal links. He sees extended case studies as providing an opportunity to see how events 'chain on to one another and how therefore events are necessarily linked to one another through time'.

Kemmis (1980, p. 117) stresses the role of case study in increasing understanding and creating 'authentic knowledge' for the reader. He states that the case study worker 'attempts to transform the situation as an object of perplexity into an object of understanding'. Mitchell (1983, p. 207) sees 'the rich detail of case studies providing 'optimum conditions for the acquisition of ... illuminating insights'.

In addition to these intrinsic advantages of case study research as an approach in its own right, it can also be used to enhance quantitative research. Case studies can suggest issues to investigate which the researchers might not have anticipated. Alternatively, case studies can be used to provide rich illustrative detail to flesh out the generalizations produced by surveys.

What are the problems of using case studies?

There are two types of problem related to case study research in education. The first set of problems is related to its claim to generate knowledge. The second set is ethical.

The most common criticisms of case study research are often posed as questions: how typical is the case? How is it possible to generalize from one case? How reliable are the findings? How valid are they?

There are different views on whether a case should be typical. Borg and Gall (1989, p. 402) assume that the 'case is seen as an example of a class of events or a group of individuals'. The findings can then be used to provide insights into the class as a whole. Walker (1980, p. 34), on the other hand, states that 'one instance is likely to be as typical and as atypical as another' and suggests that it therefore does not matter which particular case is studied. He thinks that the portrayal of the particular is legitimate in itself. Mitchell (1983) suggests that typicality is not the issue. He suggests that inferences drawn from a case are based on the validity of the analysis rather than how representative the case is. Yin (1994) suggests the use of multiple case studies, so that cumulatively they can be used to produce generalizations.

This leads to the problem of generalizing from case studies. Adelman *et al.* (1980) argue that the types of generalization which can be made about case studies are different from those made from surveys or experimental research, because they are based on different views of social science. They see case study as being in the interpretative tradition rather than in the natural science tradition. The truth of case studies has to be recognized by the reader rather than guaranteed by scientific method. Stenhouse (1985,

p. 266) too emphasizes the importance of interpreting rather than generalizing from case studies, and he values 'perceptiveness and the capacity to interpret situations rapidly and to revise interpretations in the light of experience'. Stake (1980) does not see the best use of case studies being in theory building. He considers that 'a persistent attention to laws is pedantic' (p. 70). He sees the value of case studies in adding to existing experience and humanistic understanding. He sees the reader rather than the researcher recognizing 'essential similarities' and making his or her own generalizations.

Mitchell (1983) considers that case studies can be used analytically 'only if they are embedded in an appropriate theoretical framework' (p. 207). He argues that case studies can be used to explore generalizations, and to increase understanding by examining exceptions to generalizations and investigating how general principles are exhibited in practice.

The 'authentic knowledge' that the reader will gain from the case study will depend on how reliable the report is. Case study research can be as scrupulously careful in its representation of what is being studied as any other form of research. A case study usually has a large number of data from different sources, and it is up to the researcher to explain the procedures by which the data were collected, selected and presented to convince the reader of their reliability.

The validity of case study research depends on the extent to which it is accepted as true to those who are being studied and the extent to which it rings true to the outside reader. The truth cannot be proved by experiment; it has to be judged to be true in relation to the perceptions and experiences of those inside and outside the case study.

The ethical problems related to case study research are explored fully in Simons (1989). The essential issue is the conflict between the 'right to privacy' of those being studied and the 'right to know' of the public (p. 118). The rights of those being studied are particularly vulnerable in case study research because of the possibility of institutions and key individuals being identified, even when pseudonyms are used. This could be threatening. Individuals and institutions could gain or lose from the publication of the research. Simons outlines some principles of procedure designed to safeguard individual rights. These include:

● confidentiality of interview data;
● negotiated use of the data between those being studied and the researcher;
● some degree of control by participants over accounts of their case.

AN EXAMPLE OF CASE STUDY RESEARCH IN GEOGRAPHICAL EDUCATION

My own case study research is part of a longitudinal study into the impact of the English Geography National Curriculum (GNC) at Key Stage 3 (for students aged 11–14). The research began in 1989 and is reaching its final stage in 1995. Since 1991 I have focused my attention increasingly on the geography departments of three schools. These three departments have become my units of study, my 'cases'.

The focus of the study within these departments has developed during the period, but has centred on issues of curriculum, pedagogy and change. During the five-year period, I have collected documentary evidence in the form of curriculum plans and statements, schemes of work, assessment items and school brochures. I have interviewed the heads of the geography departments in each school in July every year. I have supplemented this with interviews with other geography teachers and a small amount of lesson observation in each school. As the research has progressed, several key issues have emerged and have shaped, to some extent, further investigation. One significant issue identified at an early stage of the research was the relationship between the way the head of department conceptualized the curriculum and the way the geography curriculum was planned and taught.

I will present a summary of findings[1] on this specific issue over two periods: firstly, 1989–90, before the introduction of the GNC; and secondly, 1991–94, during its implementation.

1989–90: before the introduction of the GNC

Case Study A

In School A, geography has always been taught as a separate subject. Immediately before the introduction of the GNC, the geography syllabus was structured both systematically by themes and regionally by countries. The aims in the department's curriculum document were all in the cognitive domain and were related to knowledge, understanding and skills. An extract from the syllabus for 11–12-year-olds shows the curriculum as a list of content:

> *Year One: Settlement*
> Definition of settlement; temporary and permanent homes; study of rural settlement; hierarchy of services; concept of range and threshold; urban settlement; functions of towns; the concentric urban model; urban zones – case study example of [XXX]; simple sketch map of [XXX] to show its site and situation; definition and distribution of conurbations in Great Britain.
>
> (1989)

A description of a typical lesson adds to the picture:

> We normally would have a recap on what was done in the previous lesson. I think that a lot of lessons involve blackboard work and building things up. I think we have a lot of material that reinforces the new ideas that we've taught during the lesson. And then, as far as possible, we do have exercises for the children.
>
> (1989)

Geographical education in this department was about giving students basic knowledge and skills. The teacher, the expert, had this knowledge and the role of the teacher was to transmit it to the students. Lessons in this school were formal and teacher-centred. There was widespread use of the blackboard and textbooks to convey authoritative knowledge. The students' role in lessons was to recall the previous lesson and to do 'exercises' to consolidate what had been taught then. Assessment was based on testing recall of this information, on ability to apply some principles to new data and on testing basic map skills.

The school geography curriculum had evolved from the regional and systematic descriptive geography of the 1950s and had not used or been significantly influenced by any of the syllabuses developed from the Schools Council curriculum development projects.[2]

The department's conception of 'curriculum' informed reaction to the impending introduction of the National Curriculum. Curriculum was equated with content and the GNC document was expected to define content. When the interim report was published in 1990, almost all the head of department's comments, favourable and unfavourable, were related to the content.

Case Study B

In School B too, geography was taught as a separate subject, but the thinking behind curriculum planning and practice was very different. An extract of the Year 7 syllabus is shown in Table 11.1.

Table 11.1 *'Year One: Settlement' syllabus in School B, 1989.*

Unit title	Key ideas	Skills	Examples to study
Settlement	Certain locations are more favourable for siting settlements than others	Decision-making exercise	Where to site a village
	The growth of settlements can create environmental problems	Photograph interpretation, creative writing, map analysis	Urban problem slides

The syllabus was presented as a framework of ideas and skills. The aims listed in the syllabus emphasized 'the understanding of certain concepts'. The learning of factual knowledge was not specifically listed. The skills listed in the aims and in the extract of syllabus shown in Table 11.1 included more than the basic skills of Department A. They included 'written and oral communication, graphicacy, numeracy and study skills'. The aims also extended to the study of values and attitudes. The course aimed to get students to 'challenge ideas, question issues, and to develop reasoned opinions'.

In the 1989 interview, the head of department found it difficult to describe a typical lesson:

> We try and do different things, try and show them videos, try and show them slides. There's role play and we've got a computer which we're trying. I like to think that they do something varied and they do. They don't want to listen to you all the time. They're actually involved in doing something ...
> so we try to make it a skills-based, resources-based, enquiry based type of course ... in approach it's been influenced by what we do higher up.
>
> (1989)

Geographical education was not seen as mastering authoritative knowledge which was transmitted by teacher, blackboard and textbook. Instead it was seen as the development of understanding of some general ideas through the interpretation of a wide range of resources, selected in advance by teachers. The course involved the use of a greater range of skills than in Department A, and included the discussion of different viewpoints, as different resources on the same theme gave different, conflicting viewpoints. Students were encouraged to form their own opinions.

The lower-school syllabus was influenced by what was happening higher up the school. There, GYSL[3] and the Schools Council's 16–19 Advanced Level Project[4] had shifted the upper-secondary-school geography curriculum away from one based on the knowledge and understanding of a large amount of factual information towards the understanding of what GYSL termed 'key ideas', or the essential generalizations and principles of the subject. Places were studied as exemplars of generalizations rather than in their own right. The Schools Council geography projects emphasized the interpretation of resources by students, who were expected to have a more active role, questioning data and generalizing from it rather than just learning it. So in Department B's lower-school syllabus, 'key ideas' formed the list of content, as they did in the GYSL course. Students' activities were included in the framework.

In anticipating the GNC in 1989, the head of department, instead of wondering what the content of the new National Curriculum would be, was concerned to continue operating within the curriculum framework. When the head of department was interviewed in 1990 about the interim report, there were few comments on specific content. It was as if she did not see the content. She was looking at the framework, because that is the way she conceptualized a curriculum document. She was looking for the school's own type of curriculum framework, and failed to find it.

Case Study C

In School C, school geography had always been taught as part of an integrated humanities course[5] for students aged 11–14. For over twenty years there had been a commitment to the integration of geography, history and religious education.

Some extracts from the first-year humanities syllabus for 1989 illustrate Department C's approach (Table 11.2).

Table 11.2 *The first-year humanities syllabus in School C, 1989.*

Core concept	Interpretation	Example
Patterns	What are the patterns created by phenomena and why do they exist?	Land-use survey of the village: how does it compare to other villages? Is there a similar pattern?
Change	Change in terms of time and place	Has your village changed in your lifetime? Have people's activities changed in your village?
Evaluation	What is the situation? What is your view?	Do you like your village environment? Thoughts on the advantages and disadvantages of the area
Empathy	It is important to be able to appreciate others' point of view	Different needs of people in your village, e.g. elderly, young.

The documented aims of the humanities department included both the cognitive and affective domains and put more emphasis on inquiry skills and on collaborative working than either School A or School B. The emphasis in the documentation is on the process of learning rather than the specific content, on the students' own investigations rather than on the knowledge, understanding and skills specified in a pre-planned course. Knowledge gained from the inquiry emphasized different viewpoints, including those of the students. The syllabus was shown as a list of general concepts, which were not specifically subject-related.

An extract from the 1989 interview illustrates the contrast with Departments A and B:

> They are working in groups all the time. You introduce the topic, then they brainstorm the sort of things they would like to find out about that particular topic in groups and then have to plan the data collecting ... where is the data located, what sort of data they'll want? ... and then they're into results, and then they're doing evaluation, ... and then they report back of their conclusions on each one of those particular topics.
>
> (1989)

In this school in 1989, geographical knowledge was not authoritative knowledge handed down and controlled by the teacher, or contained in authoritative textbooks, as in School A. Nor was it knowledge gained from the interpretation of resources selected by the teacher, as in School B. Instead, geographical knowledge was constructed by the students from their own inquiries, not within defined subject boundaries but related to general concepts. In this department, the students' own knowledge was valued, and the work was far more student-centred. Work which was not based on or related to students' experience was thought of as 'stultifying'. Far less of the work was done by the teacher for the students. The teacher's role had shifted away from being a source of knowledge or a provider of resources to that of a negotiator – negotiating routes through a process of inquiry with groups of students. The outcomes of learning were not predetermined. The specific facts learned, the generalizations made and the skills acquired depended on negotiated inquiry and the needs which arose during it. Resources were suggested by the teacher in relation to particular questions raised by the groups, and these resources were likely to include students and adults in the school and people in the local community.

In 1989, the GNC was expected to threaten two valued elements of the curriculum: integration, and open-ended inquiry learning. These fears were confirmed by the publication of the interim reports in 1990 and the final statutory documents in 1991.

1991–94: implementation of the GNC

As soon as the final statutory orders for geography were published in the spring of 1991 (DES, 1991), departments began to prepare their Key Stage 3 courses so that they could start implementing them in September 1991. My question was: would this mean the same thing for the three different schools?

All three schools opted to do a unit of work on settlement in Year 7, so this makes a useful point of comparison, both with the previous courses on settlement in these schools and with each other.

Case Study A

Department A's solution to the problem of planning a course within such a short period of time was to 'buy a package'. The 'package' was a set of textbooks, Key Geography, published by Stanley Thornes, supported by a teachers' guide which included a lesson-by-lesson guide and a set of assessment sheets. This series was chosen partly because the approach of its author, David Waugh, had been liked in the past and partly because of expedience. His books matched the approach of the department in many ways. Concepts and explanations tended to be presented as facts to be learned rather than arising as a result of the interpretation of data. Also, the first book in the series was the only book guaranteed to be ready for the start of the 1991 autumn term.

Almost all of Department A's lessons on settlement are based on the textbook, apart from one lesson in which students visit a nearby street of Victorian terraced housing. Students spend most lessons reading the textbook and doing the exercises. The teacher's guide to the textbook sets out a detailed syllabus, giving the content on each topic as a list of questions together with a list of key geographical terms introduced on that topic. The guide defines the curriculum in a list rather than in a framework.

The school rewrote the textbook syllabus in 1994 in the form of a framework with headings: 'Statement of Attainment', 'Key questions/Content', 'Time allowed', 'Resources', 'Activities' and 'Assessment'. This does not actually suggest a significant shift in thinking. The column on teaching resources consists mainly of page references to the textbook, and the activities column to specific exercises in the text. The curriculum is still seen as a list of content. The textbook knowledge is seen as authoritative, with students covering a certain amount each lesson. The input is from the teacher and the textbook. According to one teacher, 'you couldn't do it better.' On the visit to the Victorian houses, the main mode of teaching was in a transmission style, with the teacher telling the children about the houses and the history of the area. Students are expected to learn facts about settlement and to understand ideas. The tests, duplicated from the teachers' guide, check that they have learned this. What the department has been doing in 1991–94 is a continuation of what had happened previously.

Case Study B

Department B used the limited time in 1991 between the arrival of the final geography documents and September to set about constructing its own curriculum. What it did was to fit the new curriculum, with new content, into a framework very similar to that used previously (Table 11.3)

Table 11.3 *The 'Settlement' syllabus in School B, 1991.*

Ideas	Skills	Content	Values	Resources
Changes in layout and functions of towns and cities	Photograph analysis	Patterns of urban land use, the structure of a city	–	Slides, base map

The extract in Table 11.3, from part of the 1991 syllabus on settlement, shows the maintenance of the underpinning ideology. The Statements of Attainment in the National Curriculum document have been translated into 'key ideas'. Students are still to gain geographical knowledge and understanding from the interpretation of data selected by the teacher. The skills needed to do this are general ones which it is hoped will be transferable. There is less emphasis on the learning of terms and on factual knowledge than in School A. In this extract, there is a gap in the 'values' column, reflecting the omissions in the GNC document. In other parts of the syllabus, however, the department has included values.

A description of a typical lesson from a 1993 interview showed that not much had changed since 1989:

> Most lessons are based around some resource, it might be a book or it might be a video or it might be a map ... and the work would develop around ideas from that ... I don't think it will have changed enormously from what we had before.
>
> (1993)

Case Study C

The contrast between pre-1991 practice and the statutory requirements was greatest in School C. Could the ideology underpinning an integrated, open-ended, inquiry approach be sustained?

> They don't intend those two subjects to be integrated. We could find very little overlap ... so what we have done is set up two different departments.
>
> (1991)

Although some schools have persisted with some sort of integration, for this department it was not worth the effort. The new division of the humanities curriculum into subjects has not totally changed the way this department thinks about the curriculum, however. The broader, cross-curricular way of thinking is evident in what is included in the work on settlement; the work to be covered in geography lessons includes the historical development of settlements, going back to the Middle Ages, related to visits to York or Lincoln.

Although the statutory orders for geography specifically state that, 'an enquiry approach should be adopted for classroom activities', the rest of the document does not encourage this approach. Attainment Targets are related to content and are prescriptive rather than open-ended. Yet the activities listed in Department C's syllabus for Year 7 on settlement show how students are still encouraged to construct their own knowledge of what they are studying through a process of inquiry:

- – conduct an urban land use survey in a local village
- – design a questionnaire to find out where people work, how long they've been in the village
- – measure the distances between where students in the class live and 10 selected services
- – conduct a survey to find out why people move home
- – interview a person whose house is up for sale.

None of the knowledge students are to learn about settlement is transmitted by the teacher, and little comes from a textbook. The new framework used for setting out the syllabus in Department C includes the headings: 'Key idea', 'Assessment objectives', 'Knowledge', 'Skills', 'Attitudes and values', 'Student activities', 'Resources' and 'Method of assessment'. It appears to have drawn closer to School B's framework approach, and is much more specific about content than the previous concept-based framework was. This department is, however, maintaining the study of other people's viewpoints and the development of the students' own opinions in their curriculum.

Some of the student activities are markedly different from those in the other schools and illustrate the continuing influence of a way of thinking about curriculum. Fieldwork in School C still investigates hypotheses suggested by the students, by methods suggested by them, in an open-ended way. This contrasts with School A's didactic approach to fieldwork and with the investigative but teacher-controlled approach of School B.

Summary of findings

It would seem from these case studies that ways of thinking about subjects and pedagogies exert a continuing influence on how a common curriculum document is interpreted. Deeply held beliefs about what it is to teach and to learn are persistent. In these three schools, teachers' and students' roles have remained the same as they were before the GNC. They continue to teach in the way that they want to teach. The students, in learning about settlement, are learning very different things in the three schools. Only the outline theme is the same. The aspects of settlement and the particular settlements studied are all different.

More importantly, the mode of learning affects what they are learning. School A students probably accumulate more knowledge which can be recalled. School B students learn to investigate given data about settlement and to question it, and probably would be able to apply their investigative skills to resources presented to them on other topics. School C students learn how to set about investigating something, and would be able to use their inquiry skills to undertake further inquiries. It is difficult to say which students learn most without taking into account the different aims and the underpinning values. At present it is clear from the interviews and documentation that they are not intended by their departments to learn the same thing. How students learn to some extent defines *what* they learn. In 1994, Departments A, B and C resembled their former selves more than they did each other.

COMMENTARY

The construction of the cases

The way I have constructed my 'cases' is not the only possible way to investigate the GNC through case study. It would be possible to take a student, a class, or a local education authority as the unit of study. It would be possible to focus on other aspects of geographical education, such as the use of resources. But my cases were determined by a question which puzzled *me*. I wanted to know whether departments which were so different in 1989 could become similar. My research interest started in speculation about particular departments, rather than particular local education authorities or particular classes. So geography departments became my units of study, the sources of my information. But they were not the focus of my study as such. I was interested in the decisions they would make on how to plan and implement the GNC. The focus of my research was curriculum, pedagogy and change.

I was inevitably influenced by my own reading and my own theoretical interests. I will highlight three particular influences. The first was an interest in the implementation of the Schools Council projects of the 1970s, and in the research into the differences between their intentions and implementation (MacDonald and Walker, 1976). The second influence was the work of Douglas Barnes, and particularly his contribution to an evaluation report of TVEI[6] in which he used a theoretical framework to analyse curriculum and pedagogy (Barnes *et al.*, 1987). The third influence was qualitative research into innovation. I was impressed by the work of Dalton (1988) and Parsons (1987) investigating the impact of GYSL. Parsons' wide-ranging study includes case studies of four schools. Dalton studies two schools in considerable depth and provides a good example of detailed case study work into geographical education.

I did not try to intervene in the 'cases' in any way as I studied them. I perceived my role as attempting to find out and understand what was going on rather than to influence anything by discussion or comment. In theory, the fact that I requested particular documents and asked particular questions of key individuals could have changed events marginally, but I was not aware of any such influence.

Advantages of using a case study approach

My case studies gave me information which it would have been difficult to get in any other way. The in-depth interviews every year revealed specific outside influences on implementation, such as an impending inspection.[7] It was possible to explore issues which were important to a particular department, such as allocation of timetable time to geography, and how this was contested. It was possible to explore viewpoints on changes to the GNC and to probe the thinking behind the views expressed. It became clear that the factors influencing the implementation of the National Curriculum were complex, idiosyncratic and varied. The phrase 'delivering the Geography National Curriculum', so commonly used in the media and by many working in education during the period of my research, suggests a simple transfer of curriculum from the then Department of Education and Science to schools and from teachers to students. It was not like that. The three case studies have revealed dilemmas, decisions, compromises, successes, the disappointments and the stress of change. The process of change was not simple in any of them. The GNC was not simply 'delivered'. Certainly, according to the evidence of the case studies, the same curriculum was not received by the learners.

Problems of using a case study approach

In carrying out the research, I have had to confront the issues outlined as problems in the first section of this chapter.

First, why did I choose these particular departments? They are not a random selection, and they are not statistically representative. It did matter to me which departments I selected. I wanted to explore what happened to different approaches to geographical education when a common curriculum was imposed. So in 1989 I selected twelve schools because of their variety of approaches to geographical education. I carried out preliminary interviews and collected curriculum documents. By 1991, significant differences in the way the curriculum was conceptualized became apparent from the interview and documentary data. There were heads of departments who thought of the geography curriculum in terms of content, others who thought about it in terms of key ideas, and others as a process. It seemed worth investigating these categories further to see their effect on the implementation of the GNC. I selected one school from each category.

If these schools are not typical or representative, is it possible to generalize from the research? The cases cannot be used cumulatively, as Yin (1994) suggests, to produce generalizations, as I had selected them from different theoretical categories. Nevertheless, there are several ways in which generalizations can emerge from my research. First, as Adelman *et al.* (1980) suggest, the insights gained from analysing the data can be recognized by the reader. Secondly, the general theoretical framework which I brought to the study can be tested against the findings. Thirdly, the issues raised in the case study departments are being further investigated in questionnaire surveys to establish generalizations about the impact of the GNC.

How reliable and valid are my findings? The reliability is limited by the procedures I have used, so these have to be open to scrutiny. The research relies mainly on interviews with heads of department, even though I was aware that there was a range of views and practices within each department. In these schools, however, it was the heads of department who had key roles as interpreters of the GNC document. They translated it, with varying degrees of consultation with other members of the department, into a teaching syllabus. They had key roles in selecting resources. Another limitation is that, although supported by some opportunistic observation of classes in each school, and some interviews with students, the data I have collected are on what people said and documented, and not on what they did. There may be significant differences. The reader has to assess the reliability by judging the procedures. As with any research, the reader has to rely on the integrity of the researcher to select and present the evidence fairly. I have attempted to ensure internal validity of the data by checking both the data and the way I have categorized their departments with the heads of departments.

During the research period, I have wrestled with several ethical problems. In any detailed report of the work, the departments and individuals will be identifiable, certainly within the school, and probably within the area. Ought this to restrict what I make public? Should I include details of ongoing disputes between departments in schools, or might this affect the outcome? I have attempted, by using semi-structured interview techniques, to understand the viewpoint and actions of all the people I have interviewed and to represent them fairly. In an unequal relationship during interviews, I have sought views but not given mine. My own values will inevitably influence interpretation of the data. Should my own views be more explicit or would this stem the flow of information? If the findings could be used by decision-makers in a way that affected the interests of the departments concerned, should I publish them? It is clear that the decisions to be made by case study researchers are by no means all of a methodological kind.

Case study research in geographical education

Most detailed case study research in geographical education has been carried out by postgraduate students as part of a Masters or Doctorate degree. Often the cases studied are ones they know well – their own schools and their own departments. The work often increases understanding and provides the researcher with valuable insights, but is not widely available. The lack of published, detailed case studies of geographical education is probably accounted for by the amount of time needed to become immersed in a case and the lack of time of practitioners investigating their own 'cases' to publish. Dalton's (1988) work is the most detailed. Some other examples of case study research are listed at the end of this chapter.

CONCLUSION

Geographical education could benefit from more case study research, in spite of the problems involved in carrying it out. There is scope for case study research at a variety of scales and on a range of topics. The reality of experiences of geographical education for an individual student, for a class or within a school is often different from assumptions made about those experiences by teachers or by policy-makers. There is a need for detailed knowledge of how students learn, and of the impact of choices made by departments in constructing and implementing the geography curriculum. There is a need to study the impact of change and to question its implications. The in-depth study of particular cases offers enormous potential for increasing our understanding of geographical education.

NOTES

1. For a fuller report of this aspect of my research, including more extracts from the interviews, see Roberts (1995) under 'Case Studies in Geographical Education' below.
2. These are discussed below. See notes 3 and 4.
3. GYSL (the Geography for the Young School Leaver Project) was set up in 1970 to provide a relevant geography curriculum for those pupils who would leave school at 16. It was later developed as a public examination course for pupils of all abilities at 16. The project adopted a new approach to geography. It emphasized the understanding of concepts and generalizations through particular case studies, rather than the learning of particular facts for their own sakes.
4. The Schools Council 16–19 Project in Geography is based on a particular view of geography which emphasizes people/environment links. It encourages an inquiry approach to learning, in which students investigate issues through the interpretation of a wide range of resources.
5. Humanities courses, which developed in the twenty years preceding the National Curriculum, varied enormously, encompassing different combinations of history, geography, English, religious education, sociology, economics, etc. In School C, humanities was on the timetable in the lower school in place of history, geography and religious education.
6. TVEI (the Technical and Vocational Education Initiative) was set up by the government to encourage the development of courses for 14–16-year-olds which would be relevant to the world of work.
7. English secondary schools are currently experiencing a new system of state inspection, with whole-school inspections taking place once every four years. Reports of inspections are made public and the government has powers to take action on failing schools.

CASE STUDIES IN GEOGRAPHICAL EDUCATION

Dalton, T.H. (1988) *The Challenge of Curriculum Innovation: A Study of Ideology and Practice*. London: Falmer.

Fry, P. and Schofield, A. (1993) *Geography at Key Stage 3: Teachers' Experience of NC Geography in year 7*. Sheffield: Geographical Association.

Hamilton-Wieler, S. (1980) 'A case study of language and learning in physical geography'. In F. Slater (ed.) *Language and Learning in the Teaching of Geography*. London: Routledge.

Lewis, D. (1989) 'Writing in a humanities classroom'. In F. Slater (ed.) *Language and Learning in the Teaching of Geography*. London: Routledge.

Naish, M. (ed.) (1994) *Primary Schools, Geography and the National Curriculum: Monitoring the Implementation of Geography in the Primary Curriculum*. Sheffield: Geographical Association.

Parsons, C. (1987) *The Curriculum Change Game: A Longitudinal Study of the Schools Council 'Geography for the Young School Leaver' Project*. London: Falmer.

Roberts, M.G. (1995) 'Interpretations of the Geography National Curriculum: a common curriculum for all?' *The Journal of Curriculum Studies*, **27** (2), 187–205.

Slater, F. (1988) 'Teaching style? A case study of post graduate teaching students observed.' In R. Gerber and J. Lidstone (eds) *Developing Skills in Geographical Education*. Brisbane: Jacaranda.

REFERENCES

Adelman, C., Jenkins, D. and Kemmis, S. (1980) 'Rethinking case study: notes from the second Cambridge conference.' In H. Simons (ed.) *Towards a Science of the Singular*. CARE Occasional Publications no. 10. Norwich: Centre for Applied Research in Education.

Anderson, G. (1990) *Fundamentals of Educational Research*. London: Falmer.

Barnes, D., Johnson, G., Jordan, S., Layton, D., Medway, P. and Yeomans, D. (1987) *The TVEI Curriculum 14–16: An Interim Report Based on Case Studies in Twelve Schools*. Leeds: University of Leeds.

Borg, W.R. and Gall, M.D. (1989) *Educational Research: An Introduction*. New York: Longman.

Dalton, T.H. (1988) *The Challenge of Curriculum Innovation: A Study of Ideology and Practice*. London: Falmer.

DES (1991) *Geography in the National Curriculum*. London: HMSO.

Goode, W.J. and Hatt, P.K. (1952) *Methods in Social Research*. New York: McGraw-Hill.

Kemmis, S. (1980) 'The imagination of the case and the invention of the study.' In H. Simons (ed.) *Towards a Science of the Singular*. CARE Occasional Publications no. 10. Norwich: Centre for Applied Research in Education.

MacDonald, B. and Walker, R. (1976) *Changing the Curriculum*. London: Open Books.

Mitchell, J.C. (1983) 'Case and situation analysis'. *Sociological Review*, **31**(2), 187–211.

Parsons, C. (1987) *The Curriculum Change Game: A Longitudinal Study of the Schools Council 'Geography for the Young School Leaver' Project*. London: Falmer.

Simons, H. (1989) 'Ethics of case study in educational research and evaluation'. In R.G. Burgess (ed.) *The Ethics of Educational Research*. London: Falmer.

Stake, R. (1980) 'The case study method in social inquiry'. In H. Simons (ed.) *Towards a Science of the Singular*. CARE Occasional Publications no. 10. Norwich: Centre for Applied Research in Education.

Stenhouse, L. (1985) 'A note on case study and educational practice.' In R.G. Burgess (ed.) *Field Methods in the Study of Education*. London: Falmer.

Walker, R. (1980) 'The conduct of educational case studies: ethics, theory and procedures'. In W.B. Dockrell and D. Hamilton (eds) *Rethinking Educational Research*. London: Hodder and Stoughton.

Yin, R.K. (1994) *Case Study Research: Design and Methods*. Beverly Hills, CA: Sage.

Chapter 12

Action Research

John Hillcoat

It has been suggested in the Introduction that the different types of research methodologies – positivist, interpretive and socially critical – represent different ways of viewing what is valid knowledge and how knowledge should be generated. Cohen and Manion (1989, p. 217) and McCutcheon and Jung (1990, p. 144) suggest that there are a large number of methodological variations of action research. Regardless of the variation, however, Chesler (1991, p. 760) states that in action research, 'a commitment by the researcher to personal action-taking, and to improving the human and social condition directly, is an integral and necessary component of the knowledge generation process.' This emphasis in action research can have a number of outcomes different to those of traditional geography research approaches, including:

- advancing practical knowledge relevant to a particular situation;
- raising consciousness and empowering those involved in the research;
- taking into account the needs of all those involved in it;
- respecting and utilizing the expertise and skills of those involved;
- shared control by both researcher and participants of the questions which the research is addressing.

This chapter has two major components. The first section examines the action research method and, in particular, emancipatory action research. It discusses the types of action research, the emancipatory potential of critical reflection, the validation of data, and problematic issues in conducting emancipatory action research. The second section presents examples of action research projects.

THE ACTION RESEARCH METHOD

Definition of action research

Cohen and Manion (1989, p. 217) state that action research can be difficult to define. However, they suggest the following:

Action research is small-scale intervention in the functioning of the real world and a close examination of the effect of such intervention. By looking at a few examples of the use of the method in the research literature, we may further identify other tangible features: action research is situational – it is concerned with diagnosing a problem in a specific context and attempting to solve it in that context. It is usually collaborative – teams of researchers and practitioners work together on a project; it is participatory – team members themselves take part directly or indirectly in implementing the research, and it is self-evaluative – modifications are continuously evaluated within the ongoing situation.

Action research is often represented as a four-phase cyclical process where a *plan* is formulated, that plan is *acted* upon and the outcomes *observed*, and *reflection* is undertaken to understand the processes, strengths and weaknesses of the plan. A revised plan can then be reformulated, and the cycle begins again.

Tripp (1990, p. 159) suggests this cyclic research spiral parallels common human behaviour: we plan some aspect of our lives, take action, observe the results, and reflect back to alter the original plan. This behaviour, however, is habitual, completely subjective, and likely to be based on incomplete knowledge. He emphasizes that action research is conscious and leads to 'action based on understanding that results from the rational analysis of research quality information'.

The methodological variations give rise to a variety of types of action research, ranging from that based on positivist assumptions to that based on critical social science.

Types of action research

Action research theory has been within the positivist paradigm until recently (Usher and Bryant, 1989, p. 119). McCutcheon and Jung (1990, p. 146) state that positivist action research is characterized by an inclination to generalize results from the specific to the wider context, and to focus on ends and conclusions rather than processes. Kincheloe (1991, p. 19) terms this the 'technocratic co-option of action research'. Additionally, positivist research does little in sharing control of what research questions should be asked. The researcher determines the research questions, which may or may not be relevant to the needs of others involved.

The type of action research of interest here is 'emancipatory' or 'participatory', and is based on the socially critical paradigm. Tesch (1990, p. 49) declares:

> Emancipatory action research is a form of self-reflective inquiry undertaken by participants in social situations in order to improve the rationality and justice of their own practices, their understanding of these practices, and the situations in which the practices are carried out. As such, it is juxtaposed to 'technical action research' whose aim is efficient and effective practice judged by reference to criteria which may not themselves be analysed in the course of the action research process.

As discussed in Chapter 3, the critical paradigm has an over-arching objective of challenging and transforming the dominant social paradigm, whereas the positivist and interpretivist paradigms merely reinforce it. The critical paradigm is transformative in that it questions the hidden assumptions that underlie research and usually reinforce the *status quo*. Tripp (1990, p. 161) believes that as emancipatory action research is participatory, it is the most effective form of critical research, because it offers the opportunity to combine critical intellectual discourse with practical action.

A grassroots view of emancipatory action research:

> stresses respect for and reliance upon the needs and expertise of practitioners and citizens involved in issues, sites, or problems under study, and involves them in the direction of the entire endeavour from start to finish ... Through participation, local informants, citizens, and activists can increase the researcher's knowledge base directly and consciously. They can also learn new skills in gathering and analysing information, thus laying bare the workings of the social system of which they are a part and improving their strategic decision-making. Such participation in knowledge creation often is consciousness raising and empowering.
>
> (Chesler, 1991, p. 760)

The usefulness of emancipatory action research by geographical educators and researchers as a process which can empower citizens to take social action for a 'better' environment cannot be overstated. Additionally, it can be a professional development medium for educators, enabling them to undergo a 'critical analysis of theories, practices and settings' (Robottom, 1987, p. 108).

This dual potential has led to some individuals giving emancipatory action research an almost god-like status, claiming it as the cure for all our social problems. It has a lot to offer in a transformative and professional development role, and the discussion to date has been very much in favour of socially critical research. However, the limitations of this research methodology in regard to critical reflection should be examined. To employ a research paradigm effectively, it is important for geographical researchers to be aware of, and adjust for, its limitations.

The emancipatory potential of critical reflection

It has been argued that the critical paradigm seeks transformation through the process of critical reflection. The ability of this reflection process to initiate transformative change must be questioned. Usher and Bryant (1989, p. 132) declare:

> Critical social science is promissory, but unrealistic. It cannot justify the potential risks of abandoning one's interests in advance. Also there still remains a 'reflection problem', in that the power of interests is such that Habermas overestimates the power of reflection, so that it is extremely doubtful if reflection can reveal interests in an interest-free way. There are several aspects to the 'reflection/interests problem':
>
> 1. It is not in the interests of stabilized behaviour to be continually asking questions about the status of validity claims – one has to exercise trust even while recognising that what one is trusting may very well be a distortion.
> 2. It is not practically possible to establish the conditions for continuous reflection, and action research cannot do this.
> 3. It presupposes the artificial conditions for an unburdened self-conscious behaviour yet ... 'even when these conditions are fulfilled, one still has to take into account the pressure of time, the necessity of having to decide, the limited capacity to take up or alter topics of communication, and the fatigue of those participating in the dialogue'.

Even if the reflection problem discussed above is not relevant in a particular situation, then problems concerning the ability of critical reflection to transform behaviour remain. Kemmis (1991, p. 63) states that it is naïve to believe that coming to consciousness of one's values and how these dictate behaviour will necessarily lead to behavioural change. Individuals are restricted in their work and life circumstances and self-reflection will not inevitably overcome these surrounding structures (Cohen and Manion, 1989, p. 230). In other words, geographical educators and researchers are subject to structural constraints which can impede their capacity to work for social change, particularly in the classroom.

Usher and Bryant (1989, pp. 139–40) state that the above criticisms can be met to some extent by action research:

> 'being strategic' in action – that is, of informed, committed doing, which recognises the limits of its own situatedness and has an understanding of what is prudent in given circumstances. This 'being prudent' in action research therefore requires the acceptance of 'real' limits which cannot be simply thought away or reflexively dissolved. The idea is that one theorizes and takes action to identify and reach a limit situation; once one arrives at the limits, the situation is effectively changed, and the change opens up new possibilities for action that could not be conceived before the earlier action was taken.

Therefore, if action research defines achievable limits and works within them, the results could open up new possibilities for change. The gradual implementation suggested in this strategy has appeal. Veno and Thomas (1992, pp. 21–3) state that the major cause of stress in change is its perceived rate. If it happens too fast, it will be resisted. So action research may lead to significant changes in the medium to long term if the process planned is gradual.

Emancipatory action research has problems, and is not the sole avenue to social and environmental justice. However, a research paradigm which questions ideologies and seeks to be transformative is more likely to help initiate change for the general common good of individuals in society and the environment than those paradigms where underlying ideologies remain hidden and unquestioned.

Validation of emancipatory action research data

Despite these advantages, socially critical geographical researchers still need to reduce systematic bias in the data. In other words, critical research requires validation within its specific context, so that the researcher does not misconstrue the evidence due to personal bias. Without validation, the research process ceases and subjective pondering begins. In the critical paradigm there are four major means to validate the research:

1. triangulation;
2. face validity;
3. construct validity;
4. catalytic validity.

Triangulation

Exclusive reliance upon one method of collection and/or source of data may lead to bias in a study. This problem can be overcome by triangulation, which is the use of two or more methods and/or sources of data collection to establish the researchers' observations and findings. Lather (1986, p. 67) suggests:

> *Triangulation*, expanded beyond the psychometric definition of multiple measures to include multiple *data sources, methods*, and *theoretical schemes*, is critical in establishing data trustworthiness. It is essential that the research design seek counterpatterns as well as convergences if data are to be credible.

In particular, every research method has its peculiar strengths and limitations, and these can bias the research findings. Triangulation using different research methods can help minimize bias.

Face validity

This involves the research participants reviewing the findings and giving their reactions to the researcher. If this does not happen, the credibility of the data is suspect.

Construct validity

Construct validity exists when the experiences of the people involved in the research validate or extend the theory. Therefore, emancipatory action research must be continually grounded and enriched in the experiences of people's daily lives. Lather (1986, p. 67) states:

> A *systematized reflexivity*, which gives some indication of how *a priori* theory has been changed by the logic of the data, becomes essential in establishing construct validity in ways that will contribute to the growth of illuminating and change-enhancing social theory.

Catalytic validity

Critical research has catalytic validity if the research process results in the participants changing behaviours. Catalytic validity is vital to the emancipatory effectiveness of an action research project. Fien (1992, p. 176) suggests catalytic validity pertains 'to the extent to which the processes of face validity and participant reflection are capable of helping participants to understand themselves and their situation in order to transform it in ways of their choosing'.

Problematic issues

The management of an emancipatory action research project can present dilemmas for the geographical researcher. In particular, issues of incompatibility between expert and practical knowledge, and the role of the researcher, are important.

Expert and practical knowledge

Action research often brings together a mixture of people with different orientations to knowledge. A researcher is interested in theoretical or expert knowledge, which seeks consistent logic within and between various theories, while a practitioner or community member is concerned with practical knowledge, which will get things done. Practical knowledge does not necessarily require logic, and expert knowledge does not have to be practical. Cohen and Manion (1989, p. 229) state that expert and practical knowledge 'are so different and so often mutually exclusive that attempts to link them into a single process are likely to produce internal conflict and the subordination of one element to another'.

Usher and Bryant (1989, p. 122) state that this dichotomy and the resulting conflict of interests are one of the major problems with action research. This conflict can affect the researcher's actions and authority.

The role of the researcher

The disharmony between expert and practical knowledge is described at its worst by Kemmis (1991, p. 59):

> social science researchers had maintained a separation between research and action, and that this separation could be explained on the grounds that it was in the interests of an establishment of social science researchers to maintain forms of research which addressed their own problems even if they did not link so directly to problems of action.

Even if we dismiss the fact that geographical researchers can have hidden agendas, due to values and constraints imposed by the norms of the positivist scientific community, the role a researcher takes in an action research project can be in itself problematic. Critical geographic researchers with the best of intentions can unwittingly contribute to the *status quo*.

Chesler (1991, p. 763), Kincheloe (1991, p. 23) and McTaggart (1991, p. 170) state that emancipatory action research is a group process. McTaggart (1991, p. 170) points out that, in action research groups, people typically have differences in power, vocabulary, influence and status. The very fact that the researcher has knowledge of and skills in action research immediately causes a power imbalance. If the process is to be emancipatory, these differences have to be dealt with to ensure no one in the group is disempowered by them. An effective way of doing this is by facilitative and democratic leadership (Nichols and Jenkinson, 1991, pp. 10–11). Therefore, action researchers may have to separate themselves from the other participants and take on the group facilitation role whether they like it or not.

However, Smith *et al.* (1990, p. 229) suggest there can be problems in the facilitative approach, as it is often seen as the researcher guiding participants towards enlightenment. They claim this situation has the participants as sources of information rather than empowered and equal collaborators. In contrast, Tripp (1990, p. 165) states:

> the quality of relationships between participants [is] more important to outcomes than formal procedures ... a formal aspect of collaborative research such as the mission statement will have less of an effect on the outcomes of the research than the relationships between the participants, the participants and their practice, or the participants and the institution.

Tripp warns that the role of facilitator ultimately decides whether the action research process is to be emancipatory, as facilitation is 'an issue about the kind of relationship in terms of power and autonomy that exists between the practitioner and the facilitator' (p. 164). Thus, this role of the geographical researcher is an important aspect of the emancipatory action research process. This issue will be elaborated further in the first example of an action research project.

The remainder of this chapter provides three such examples. The first gives a detailed discussion of an action research that I was involved in, and the other two are brief descriptions of other action research studies.

EXAMPLES OF ACTION RESEARCH PROJECTS

A support group for activists

Description of the study

Critical educators stress the importance of educating people in skills and knowledge to take the action necessary for meaningful social change. They argue that, unless people can analyse the fundamental causes of and propose feasible solutions to environmental and social problems, meaningful social change will not occur. However, they generally overlook the fact that social change is a slow and long-term process which has its share of let-downs and frustrations. Consequently, it is crucial that educators educate people not only in skills and knowledge but so that their social action activities become sustainable.

Hillcoat (1992) examined the issue of sustaining social action in an activist support group. This group of four females and two males was formed by some of the participants in a *re-earthing workshop*. Four of the six people had extensive experience of social action, while the other two were intending to become social activists.

Data collection

Three forms of data collection were used: the researcher's diary, written comments by group members at the end of each meeting, and interviews with each group member.

My diary, which constituted the case record for this study, was based on group meetings and had the following major components:

- Meeting One;
- Meeting Two;
- Meeting Three – cancelled;
- Meeting Three.

Each of these major components, except 'Meeting Three – cancelled', was organized around four themes: description of the meeting, reflections on issues for the researcher, reflections on the group process, and reflections on the action research process.

The method for observing each meeting varied. The first meeting was informal: we shared dinner and discussed what was happening in our lives since the re-earthing workshop. Immediately following this meeting, I wrote detailed notes about what had transpired. I taped the second meeting, with the other group members' permission. This was felt necessary as I was facilitating a very involved meeting in terms of both process and content. I wrote detailed notes immediately after the meeting and then elaborated on these using the tape. No taperecording was used for some of the group activities as they were experiential in nature and the use of a taperecorder was deemed obtrusive. Immediately afterwards, I wrote a detailed account of those aspects of the meeting.

The other people in the group were initially excluded from deciding how to report their experiences of it. I had dictated to the group in the first meeting how the reflecting was to be done. As a result of this hierarchical process, no comments were made by members about their experiences in the first meeting. The form of data collection did not suit their busy lifestyles. In the second meeting, the group said that they wished to collect data by writing reflections at the end of each meeting.

A schedule of open-ended questions based on the main themes of this study was prepared. A probe interview technique was used, where I asked questions to elaborate a response to a particular theme. This technique allowed not only some interview questions in common to all members of the support group, but also the flexibility to pursue promising lines. Thus, the schedule of questions was not followed in a rigid order, as the group members were allowed to pursue their thoughts throughout the interview with minimal prompting from me. During the interviews, I disclosed my feelings and experiences in order to establish a trusting and safe atmosphere for the particular member being interviewed. Each member was interviewed separately in a location of his or her choosing.

Validation of the data

The data were *triangulated* in a number of ways:

- The three methods of data collection – researcher's diary, member's written comments, and interviews – were compared. The triangulation of my diary and the written comments was particularly valuable, as I obtained confirmation or otherwise of my observations of the mood and satisfaction of members in regard to the group process.
- The reflective process undertaken in the diary developed some central themes. Member feedback in the interviews gave insight into whether these were group issues in general or of importance only to me, due to my unique position in the group.
- Members' written comments and interview data were compared for any inconsistencies in their views.

Face validity allowed the other people involved in the research to review the research findings. A letter to participants on my perceptions of the functioning of the group was to have been presented to group members after a few meetings, with their reaction to this as a component of the face validation process. However, there were unforeseen problems with having meetings, so that only three were held in the research time frame. As a result, it was decided to establish face validity during the interviews by my elaborating viewpoints and observations, and seeking responses from the support group members.

Systematic reflection, which involved relating the experiences of both the researcher and other group members within support group meetings to the theory concerning group process, provided *construct validity*. In addition, concepts such as 'burnout' and 'power' were used consistently throughout this study. These terms were validated by discussing aspects of support group functioning with individuals experienced in group processes. Construct validity was also provided using the interviews to ground the experiences of the group members in their daily lives.

Catalytic validity was not established in the study. The time constraints and difficulty with arranging meetings limited the capacity of face validation and participant reflection for helping group members 'understand themselves and their situation in order to transform it in ways of their choosing' (Fien, 1992, p. 176). However, during the interviews the beginnings of catalytic validity were observed. Over a considerable period of time since the research concluded, it has become apparent that the critically reflective research process has impacted upon the participants' lives, particularly in the area of behaviours to help sustain social action activities.

Some issues for the researcher

My control of the research process was a major issue. I felt very strongly in agreement with one of the major principles of emancipatory action research – group members contributing equally to the decision-making process – but the idea of giving up complete power was frightening, as I had a specific research agenda. However, this agenda was in tension with my desire for a democratic group process to decide its ultimate direction:

> I find the notion of letting the group decide the nature of the group's focus and hence, by default, the research focus a bit worrying. I am used to having complete control of my research and this is a very different experience. I suppose I am quite excited because it will give the research a rich quality and bring up all sorts of interesting things that would not normally occur in the usual research monoculture. Also the participatory nature of the experience will be satisfying for me as it will be alive and in no way boring. I just hope that letting the group into the research process will not cause it to go off the rails at some point during the process.
>
> (Diary, 1.4.3, pp. 16–17)

As the research progressed, I finally became used to the notion of letting the group take control of the process. However, I still felt uneasy and uncomfortable in my role.

Another issue arose which was difficult for me as a socially critical researcher: what was my role in the group? I had begun to move away from that of authoritarian researcher, but I could not determine just how active my role should be. I had to decide either to take a facilitative role or to be 'just' another group member.

My knowledge about group processes indicated to me the importance of the group establishing its purposes and foci. It was clear I was the person in the group to do something about this, as I had the group process skills and research that the others did not. I clearly had an advantage in terms of power and influence. Thus, I had to approach the situation carefully and sensitively, as in my role as facilitator it was still quite possible (and easy) to abuse power. I had grave doubts about my role as facilitator and wondered if I, in some way, was using this role to maintain power over the research process. My diary (2.11, p. 36) illustrates this:

> The really big issue for me this week has been my role of leader/facilitator in the meeting. I started to get doubts about whether I was using leadership/facilitation as a front to keep control of the group and ultimately the research process. Once again the negativity of leadership issue for me!!! There has to be some structure and guidance for the meeting to achieve as much as it did. If I didn't lead and facilitate the discussion could the group still be in a very nebulous state about what it is to do?

Discussing this issue with people very experienced in group work and reading 'The tyranny of structurelessness' (Joreen, 1972) brought me to realize that my role as facilitator was necessary so that the group could begin to clarify its purposes and how to go about them. Additionally, it assisted the progression of the action research process. Nevertheless, I was still wary of unintended consequences of my power position.

Thus, through this reflective process, it became clear to me that as an action researcher I could not be just another group member, since I had knowledge of both group and action research processes. This set me apart from the group. Recognition of this power advantage was important so that I could consciously attempt to mediate possible misuses of it. Paradoxically, this recognition simultaneously put me in the position where I could have exploited my power consciously to my own advantage for the purposes of my research.

With hearing-impaired students

Dianne Lostroh conducted an environmental education research project with people who were hearing-impaired. Her concern was that hearing-impaired students have had little exposure to formal environmental education and that little research had been conducted concerning how environmental education could best be implemented for such a group. Key aspects of her study were that:

> This research study will focus on environmental education for the hearing impaired, particularly taking into account the problems associated with low self-concept experienced by these people. Social integration of hearing and hearing-impaired communities will be discussed.
> (Lostroh, 1992, p. 1)

At the conclusion of the study, Lostroh noted that the participatory action research approach assisted the hearing-impaired students to gain knowledge and feel good about themselves. She recommended that action research as a learning strategy should be incorporated in teacher training programmes for intending educators of the hearing-impaired.

The ENSI action research projects

Posch (1993) discusses the Environment and Schools Initiatives (ENSI) Project, involving schoolchildren in environmental issues at the three levels of:

- personal experience and emotional commitment;
- interdisciplinary learning and research (the generation of 'local knowledge');
- socially important action (Posch, 1993, p. 448).

This approach lends itself to action research and through the ENSI a number of such projects have been set up.

One action project involved the study of a conflict between a teacher and some students. As the project progressed, the teacher gave the students increasing power to decide the pace of and methods for learning. This produced a lot of fascinating interactions between teacher and pupils, and among the pupils themselves (Schlinder, 1993).

The teacher appeared to learn a lot from the critically reflective process, and Schlinder (1993, p. 457) states:

> One outcome was an involuntary caution in the use of words in his interactions with the students and a more intense respect for them as young personalities. Another was a reconstruction of his strategic approach to the design of project work.

CONCLUSION

Emancipatory action research offers geographical educators and researchers the means to bring about social change at the local level by involving the relevant people in the research process. Research becomes a means by which questions important to communities, etc., can be asked, and those involved in the research can be empowered.

However, there can be problems concerning the emancipatory potential of critical reflection, the compatability of expert and practical knowledge, and the role of the researcher in setting the research agenda. The action researcher must openly acknowledge his or her power advantage due to knowledge of the research process. Additionally, it is important that the action researcher is well versed in good group process and meeting facilitation skills.

REFERENCES

Chesler, M. (1991) 'Participatory action research with self help groups: an alternative paradigm for inquiry and action'. *American Journal of Community Psychology*, **19**(5), 757–68.

Cohen, L. and Manion, L. (1989) *Research Methods in Education*. 3rd edn. London: Routledge.

Fien, J. (1992) 'Education for the environment'. Unpublished PhD Thesis, University of Queensland.

Hillcoat, J. (1992) 'Beyond the Cartesian worldview: towards an environmental education for sustainable social action'. Master of Environmental Education Dissertation, Griffith University.

Joreen (1972) 'The tyranny of structurelessness'. *The Second Wave*, **2**(1).

Kemmis, S. (1991) 'Emancipatory action research and postmodernisms'. *Curriculum Perspectives*, **11**(4), 59–65.

Kemmis, S. and McTaggart, R. (1988) *The Action Research Planner*. 3rd edn. Victoria, Australia: Deakin University Press.

Kincheloe, J.L. (1991) *Teachers as Researchers: Qualitative Inquiry as a Path to Empowerment*. Lewes: Falmer.

Lather, P. (1986) 'Issues of validity in openly ideological research: between a rock and a soft place'. *Interchange*, **17**(4), 63–84.

Lostroh, D. (1992) 'Environmental education as a tool for promoting the integration of hearing and hearing-impaired communities, and for enhancing self-concept in the hearing impaired'. Master of Environmental Education Dissertation, Griffith University.

McCutcheon, G. and Jung, B. (1990) 'Alternative perspectives on action research'. *Theory into Practice*, **XXIX**(3), 144–51.

McTaggart, R. (1991) 'Principles for participatory action research'. *Adult Education Quarterley*, **41**(3), 168–87.

Nichols, K. and Jenkinson, J. (1991) *Leading a Support Group*. Melbourne: Chapman and Hall.

Posch, P. (1993) 'I: Action research in environmental education'. *Educational Action Research*, **1**(3), 447–55.

Robottom, I. (1987) 'Towards inquiry-based professional development in environmental education'. In I. Robottom (ed.) *Environmental Education: Practice and Possibility*. Deakin University: Deakin University Press.

Schlinder, G. (1993) 'II: The conflict'. *Educational Action Research*, **1**(3), 457–68.

Smith, B., Connole, H., Speedy, S. and Wiseman, R. (1990) *Issues and Methods in Research Study Guide*. Adelaide: South Australian College of Education.

Tesch, R. (1990) *Qualitative Research: Analysis Types and Software Tools*. Lewes: Falmer.

Tripp, D.H. (1990) 'Socially critical action research'. *Theory into Practice*, **XXIX**(3), 158–66.

Usher, R. and Bryant, I. (1989) *Adult Education as Theory, Practice and Research. The Captive Triangle*. London: Routledge.

Veno, A. and Thomas, D. (1992) 'The process of social change'. In D. Thomas and A. Veno (eds) *Psychology and Social Change*. Palmerston North, NZ: Dunmore.

Chapter 13

Discourse Analysis: A Method for Deconstruction

Sharon Bennett

Many of the data collected and presented by geographers are in the form of language. Furthermore, language is used to summarize and interpret geographical data, be they statistical, graphic, cartographic or verbal. The way in which these data are interpreted, the selection of vocabulary and grammar with which they are presented, and the 'knowledge' conveyed by those words will, to varying degrees, reflect or support particular ideologies.

Yet the study of language, especially as a medium of ideology, has largely been ignored by geographers (Henley, 1989, p. 162). The highly specialized vocabulary of linguistic theory has perhaps served as a barrier to language analysis in geography and geographical education research. Indeed, emancipatory text analysis has lain outside the major methodologies that form the framework of research in all the social sciences. This chapter focuses on research through deconstruction, currently gaining academic acceptance largely through the work of methodologists such as Kress and Hodge (1979), Fairclough (1989, 1992) and Lather (1992). The significance of textbooks in geography teaching and the nature and purposes of discourse analysis are explained. The chapter then focuses on the work of Gilbert (1989b) and Fairclough (1992), whose explanations of their methods are both easily accessible and adaptable to the needs of geographical educators. The examples provided are drawn from research on school geography textbooks. However, the methods are equally relevant for research in other school subjects.

DECONSTRUCTION: AN ALTERNATIVE METHODOLOGY

Deconstruction is essentially a critical, emancipatory methodology. The qualitative research is framed by the premise that the forces creating and supporting power structures, including those of class, gender and culture, may be revealed by pointing to contradictions within texts. Deconstructionists seek to expose 'the logic of a text's language as opposed to the logic of its author's claims' (Jefferson and Robey, 1982, p. 110). Fairclough (1989, p. 85) notes that 'texts do not typically sprout ideology'. Rather, ideology is most effective when it is least visible. Discourse, the active process by which language discretely achieves ideological ends, allows ideology to function coercively or consensually to gain the acceptance of less powerful members of society (Fairclough, 1989, p. 33). The role of deconstruction is to identify the nature of discourse, and the depictions of reality and the bias it conveys, to produce an ideological critique.

Deconstruction, text and power

Most modern linguists and analysts of discourse agree that text, and therefore textbooks, potentially contain multiple meaning. School textbooks do not simply convey the meaning intended by the author; rather, their meaning is subject to many possible modifications before and during the transfer of the content to the student. For example, textbooks are edited according to and constrained by the influences of market requirements identified by publishers (Apple, 1986). Teachers play a significant mediatory role in conveying textbook knowledge: they interpret, define, emphasize, de-emphasize and elaborate on textbook material. Students bring to texts their own body of knowledge and beliefs, which are modulated by their gender, class, culture and previous experiences. The context of textbook use, including regular examinations, influences what is regarded by students as the 'correct' interpretations of texts (Luke *et al.*, 1989, pp. 252–4). These factors notwithstanding the power of textbooks in the classroom, and consequently of the ideologies they contain, makes a considerable contribution to the formal education of students. Their *potential* meaning or meanings, produced either overtly or covertly, are thus of the highest significance.

Lather (1992) stresses the relationship between text and power. In particular, she highlights narrative authority, the almost subconscious legitimacy readers assign to texts and their authors. This general attitude is, in part, perpetuated by the teacher, a person whose status as 'learned' is reinforced by his or her profession, referring the students to textbooks and basing classroom activities on them. Geography textbooks, among others, attempt to explain social experiences, and consequently convey assumptions about political and social theory (Gilbert, 1984, p. 8). The 'biblical' status of the textbook in the classroom in explaining the way in which the world works may have a powerful impact on student knowledge. The potential effects of the textbooks' power are notable in particular when their content does not include the voices of workers, women, minority groups and others who are powerless (Apple and Christian-Smith, 1991, p. 6). Freedom from the influences of narrative authority, the factors which legitimate textbook knowledge, is a prominent concern for many geographical educators and an essential facet of deconstruction.

DISCOURSE ANALYSIS: A METHOD OF DECONSTRUCTION

Linguists and other language theorists have developed various methods for analysing texts, with the aim of fully understanding how authors and language transmit messages to the reader. Gilbert notes that, historically, the view that language was 'transparent' dominated language theory. Language existed merely as a medium of thought, thus 'well-intended or careful scholarship would reveal the true nature of reality through agreement on definition of terms, and agreement on how they would be operationalized' (Gilbert, 1989a, p. 151). In contrast, language is coming to be recognized as a 'concrete element of culture rather than a communication medium' (Gilbert, 1989a, p. 151). This section explains the nature of discourse and its links to meaning and power. Techniques for analysing discourse are described.

The nature of discourse

Throughout this century, the many branches and philosophies of the fields of linguistics, literary criticism and content or discourse analysis have tackled language and texts, with the aim of drawing definitive rules for the determination of meaning, enabling language to be used as an indicator of culture and ideology. For example, structuralists following Ferdinand de Saussure based their research on the notion that the meaning of words is determined by convention, rule or agreement among their users (Fiske, 1982, p. 56). They failed to study the social motivation of words (or signs), or the lexical choice (for example, using the word 'terrorist' rather than 'freedom fighter'). Instead, many modern language theorists believe that meaning is better understood in terms of *discourse*. Discourse is a relatively modern concept, not becoming prominent until the 1960s (MacDonnell, 1986, p. 11). MacDonnell writes that discourse is the social aspect of language:

> A 'discourse', as a particular area of language use, may be identified by the institutions to which it relates and by the position from which it comes and which it marks out for the speaker. That position does not exist by itself, however. Indeed, it may be understood by the position through its relation to another, ultimately opposing discourse.
>
> (MacDonnell, 1986, pp. 2–3)

Thus, a discourse centres on certain objects and concepts at the expense of others. Discourse also exists in relation to other opposing *discourses*, because the relationship is not necessarily a binary one. A Marxist discourse, for example, is not simply Marxist because it conveys a different message to one which is not Marxist. A Marxist discourse will convey differing positions when compared with a multiplicity of other discourses, including, perhaps, ones which might be labelled 'Marxist'.

MacDonnell highlights the role of the speaker's or author's 'position' in the production of discourse. The ideological position of the author may also be referred to by the simpler terms of 'bias' or 'perspective'. It is influenced by political, cultural, economic, gender and other social factors. The social group or groups to which an author belongs may influence the lexical choices made, the status accorded to agents within the text and the tone generated by the text. No author is an isolated generator of meaning. Rather, authors are generators of meaning which are constantly influenced by their ideological position.

The influences of the ideology of an author on text are only one aspect of discourse. Texts convey meaning; they potentially affect the knowledge base, opinions and beliefs of the reader or listener. These constructive effects of language allow text to act effectively as a mode for political or ideological practice (Fairclough, 1992, p. 67). Discourse, then, is more than simply a textual feature. It is an active process that is shaped and constrained by social structures in the broadest sense. It achieves ideological ends through text and spoken language. Fairclough expands this notion to identify three constructive effects of discourse, based on the ideas of Michael Foucault. First, discourse constructs social identities and subject positions – notions of personal 'self'. Secondly, it constructs social relationships – the symbolic representation of society contained in textbooks may legitimize the dominant status of particular individuals or groups within society. Finally, discourse constructs systems of knowledge and belief, or ideology. For example, in education, discourse can affect the way in which a student views himself or herself, that self in relation to others (such as neighbours, the government, people of developing nations), and his or her political, spiritual or other beliefs. Thus the discourse generated through texts can act as a means of social control or social transformation, by limiting or informing the reader's world view.

The constructive effects of discourse can be transformative, reproductive or both. Consequently, discourse can be linked to both overt and covert practices in educational institutions. The oppositional and selective nature of discourse may serve to limit or direct the development of the 'world view' of the individual, and thus has been linked to cultural production by Giroux (1989, p. 136). However, language and discourse are also a 'central force in the struggle for voice' (Giroux, 1989, p. 135), a means by which cultural and ideological processes can be examined, contested and transformed for positive social (political and environmental) change. Discourse analysis can provide the means for the critical examination of text, allowing the subtle processes of discourse to be highlighted and challenged by the researcher.

Discourse analysis

The development of the notion of discourse had a profound impact on the ways in which sociolinguists and other analysts studied text. MacDonnell writes that 'since 1968, the questioning of the relation between power and the discourses of knowledge [has] taken several forms, following along no single line' (1986, p. 15). She discusses the significance of Althusser's work during that decade in showing how both ideologies and discourses are maintained, and the effects of these discourses. In questioning the ideologies of State apparatuses, Althusser argued that the ruling ideology secures the 'reproduction of capital relations through instituting social division', such as class (MacDonnell, 1986, p. 27).

During the same period, Michel Pecheux was drawing on similar Marxist theories about discourse and linguistics. Pecheux believed that linguistic mechanisms form a backdrop to philosophical reflection. While he acknowledged that 'the system of language is indeed the same for the materialist and the idealist, the revolutionary and the reactionary', he identified the fact that individuals will use varying discourse, and that language is the common basis for differentiated discursive processes (Pecheux, 1975, p. 58). Like Saussure, Pecheux defined language as 'relatively autonomous', but contrasted this with discursive processes, stating that 'every discursive process is inscribed in an ideological class relationship' (p. 59). He further distinguished between this *discursivity* and Saussure's *parole* – personal forms of language that are an individual activity and, therefore, not amenable to semiotic study (Fairclough, 1992, p. 63). Thus, the discourse of language is not a personal effect of language. Therefore, it can be studied as an element of text. Although the language of authors may be shared, the meanings of the words used will change according to the ideological positions of those authors.

In expanding and modifying these ideas, Foucault identified the concept of 'inter-discourse'. No text exists in isolation; rather, texts draw upon and transform other contemporary and historically prior texts. In recognizing the phenomena of inter-discourse, Foucault suggested that meaning can be either transformed or reproduced as the signs denoting or connoting it are used in texts over time.

During the 1970s, critical linguistics was developed by a group at the University of East Anglia. Their work constituted an attempt to blend linguistic theory with the theories of the role of language in political and ideological processes, and involved the analysis of complete texts. The basis of the method is grammar. Emphasis is placed on the way in which words are transformed. For example, transformation may be achieved by 'nominalization'– the conversion of a clause into a nominal, or noun. A simple example of this process is:

(1) 'X criticised Y a lot' to (2) 'there was much criticism'.

(Fairclough, 1992, p. 27)

The identity of the agent, the source of the 'criticism', is deleted by changing the structure of the sentence.

Another key concept is 'passivization'. For example:

(1) 'police shot demonstrators' to (2) 'demonstrators were shot'.

(Fairclough, 1992, p. 27)

As in nominalization, the role and power of agency are obscured: the police, who are deemed more powerful than the demonstrators in the first statement, are hidden in the second. The involvement of the police in the action might be assumed by readers of the second statement. However, the writer has placed less emphasis on their role. Critical linguistics draws attention to ways in which grammatical choice may serve particular ideological interests through such analysis, highlighting a careful or unconscious manipulation of language which may not be readily recognized by the participants in the discourse.

Critical linguistics is a form of critical analysis that aims not only to describe discourse practices but, unlike non-critical approaches, to show how discourse is shaped by power and ideology. Thus, critical linguistics continues the trend set by Pecheux, Foucault and others, and demonstrates the constructive effects of discourse on social identities, relations between them, and ideologies.

The central notions of critical linguistics have been further developed and practised in recent years, with a particular emphasis on the ways in which these methods can be used in education research and in the classroom. The critical analysis of textbooks and the promotion of strategies to achieve this may be an empowering activity for both teachers and students. Thus discourse analysis can play a significant role in the development of a critical pedagogy.

Gilbert's works, including *The Impotent Image* (1984), represent a positive step in this respect, demonstrating analyses of the language and ideologies of geography textbooks for geography teachers. Similarly, Fairclough's *Language and Power* (1989) provides a model for discourse analysis which is intended to accommodate researchers with only a modest background in linguistic theory. The techniques offered by both Fairclough and Gilbert may assist geographical and environmental educators not only to identify the ideologies embodied in texts, but to develop some critical reading skills in their students. The next section outlines two sets of methods which can facilitate discourse analysis in geographical education research.

DISCOURSE ANALYSIS IN GEOGRAPHICAL EDUCATION RESEARCH

This section will highlight two similar discourse analysis techniques, those of Gilbert (1989b) and Fairclough (1989), which might meet the demands of geographical educators. The case study that follows draws on the key questions of Gilbert and Fairclough throughout the analysis process.

Gilbert (1989b) suggests that the structure of an image – that is, the representations of a theory or ideology – is constructed by the presentation of data and generalizations in texts (p. 65). Gilbert proposes five general questions which can help in the identification of these images. They are:

1. What topics, propositions or broad concepts provide the organising of the discourse?
2. How do concepts, terms, metaphors, jargon and other stylistic devices elaborate the structure of the discourse?
3. What are the underlying problems which have generated this discourse? How has the discourse articulated these problems? From whose perspective?
4. What theories provide the descriptions and explanations thought relevant? What relationships, causes and consequences are proposed? On what premises is the account based and what assumptions are made in the course of the explanation?
5. What perspectives, questions and theories are not developed?

(Gilbert, 1989b, p. 65)

Fairclough (1989) describes a methods of discourse analysis which occurs in three phases: description, interpretation and explanation. The description of the formal properties of the text (such as vocabulary) and interpretation occur together, while the explanation reveals the broader conclusions about the function of discourse in the text (p. 26). The selection of text or textual elements is at the discretion of the analyst. A set of ten guide questions is provided by Fairclough to assist in the description and interpretation of the text. These are:

A. VOCABULARY
   1. What *experiential* values do the words have?
      What classification schemes are drawn on?
      Are there words which are ideologically contested?
      Is there *rewording* or *overwording*?
      What ideologically significant meaning relations ... are there between words?
   2. What *relational* values do the words have?
      Are there euphemistic expressions?
      Are there markedly formal or informal words?
   3. What *expressive* values do the words have?
   4. What metaphors are used?

B. GRAMMAR
   5. What experiential values do grammatical features have?
      What types of *process* and *participant* dominate?
      Are processes what they seem?
      Are *nominalisations* used?
      Are the sentences active or passive?
      Are the sentences positive or negative?
   6. What relational values do grammar features have?
      What *modes* ... are used?
      Are there important features of *relational modality*?
      Are the pronouns 'we' and 'you' used, and if so, how?

7. What expressive values do grammatical features have?
8. How are (simple) sentences linked together?
    Are logical connectors used? ...

C. TEXTUAL STRUCTURES
9. What interactional conventions are used?
    Are there ways in which one participant controls the turn of others?
10. What larger-scale structures does the text have?

(Fairclough, 1989, pp. 110–11)

Relatively simple schemata such as those outlined by Gilbert (1989b) and Fairclough (1989) provide opportunities for geographical educators to analyse the texts in their own fields, and understand the way in which discourse constrains or liberates the messages of the text.

DISCOURSE ANALYSIS IN THE WORK OF GEOGRAPHICAL EDUCATORS: A CASE STUDY

Discourse analysis can assist geographical educators to evaluate the ideologies and discourse of textbooks and other resources. An example of such research is Bennett (1993). This study explored the extent to which the texts of the Geography 16–19 Project promote its environmental education goals, the degree to which they empower readers and the type of future environment promoted by the texts. The study is one of the first research projects to use the methods outlined by Fairclough and others to analyse an education project in this way.

Although the method of discourse analysis used was based upon the questions posed by Fairclough (1989), the structure applied to the method was discretionary, as some questions were not appropriate for all of the texts. Thus the questions merely guided the analysis. The selected sections of text were read in turn, and the various guide questions posed. The significant samples of text were then recorded. Words and phrases were grouped according to common themes, and analysed to determine both explicit and implicit meanings. Alternative text was occasionally posed to emphasize the lexical choice the author had made. The study was limited to only one interpretation or reading.

One of the texts studied by Bennett was *Manufacturing Industry and the Environment* (Chaffey, 1987). The book presents a case study of the impact of manufacturing on the city of Liege. An analysis of the introductory paragraph to the text demonstrates several of the methods proposed by Fairclough (1989), and illustrates the ways in which conclusions may be drawn. The key words and phrases analysed have been printed in italics for ease of recognition.

The paragraph reads:

> In this unit *you* are going to examine the impact of industry on the environment. Although industry can bring positive benefits to a region, environmental costs can be high. In particular, industries which developed in the nineteenth century may have *an effect* on the surrounding area *considerably greater than the newer, perhaps more environmentally conscious industries of the latter part of the twentieth century*.

(Chaffey, 1987, p. 4)

An initial reading of this passage might suggest that the textbook is presenting a geographical case study of the Liege industries within the framework of environmental awareness. A closer reading of the text suggests otherwise.

The use of the word '*you*' in the opening sentence positions the reader to follow the instructions given later in the text. The sentence does not imply that the reader may choose to do this; the statement is presented as fact. Thus the sentence positions the reader as an obedient follower of the author's instructions.

Industries of the nineteenth century are said to have had '*an effect*' on the city of Liege, rather than 'many effects'. The phrase can therefore be assumed to be highly euphemistic. Furthermore, this '*effect*' was '*considerably greater*' than those generated by modern industries, which are '*perhaps more environmentally conscious*'. The author, in effect, uses the fact that Liege still bears the visible and maybe invisible scars of the Industrial Revolution as a point of comparison for modern industry. The positive tone and content of the statement, while identifying the fact that some industries have reduced their impact on the physical environment in recent decades, fail to encourage readers to judge modern impacts by modern standards and values. Instead, nineteenth-century industry is the only benchmark provided for the evaluation of the effects of modern industry.

Economic and social issues are also discussed in this text. The effects of changing economic situations on the poorer people of Liege are explained thus:

> As the older industries become less competitive, partly because of the old buildings and equipment and their location in the cramped, poorly serviced valley, *so mergers and closures* are *forced upon them*. Inevitably, this leads to *a loss of jobs, the need to find new employment opportunities* and to *retrain a labour force* in newer, more relevant skills. *New jobs are needed with financial help to generate those coming from central and local government and the European Community.*
>
> (Chaffey, 1987, p. 4)

People are not specifically mentioned in this paragraph. There is a distinct sense of inevitability or lack of control for people, generated by the way in which the agents are disguised by the vocabulary and the use of passive voice. '*Mergers and closures*' are described as being '*forced upon*' less competitive industries, because of aged facilities, rather than the decisions of people. People are described only as being a '*labour force*', and are readily comparable to the buildings or the machinery, which need updating. The final sentence of the paragraph does not easily make sense. The author's recognition that '*financial help*' is needed points to some of the failures in the economic and industrial systems in the area. However, he does not elaborate or explore the consequences of his assertion.

Discourse analysis may also be used to study the ideologies upon which student activities are based. For example, Exercise 10 in each of the Geography 16–19 Project textbooks is designed by the Project team as a 'prediction' activity, as a conclusion to the inquiry-cased learning procedure. More specific inquiry questions that fall under this heading are:

> What might be the consequences of location change and environmental change? What influence will these have on the lives of people? What might be alternative ways of organising space and managing the environment?
>
> (Naish *et al.*, 1987, p. 57)

The Project team intended that these questions would 'lead towards an understanding of specific guiding concepts: environmental impact, social impact, spatial justice and social justice' (Naish *et al.*, 1987, p. 57).

Exercise 10, as it appears in *Manufacturing Industry and the Environment*, does not necessarily incorporate the key questions cited above:

> *Exercise 10* is essentially predictive. Liege has much to offer twentieth-century Europe, and students are asked to *examine its potential*. Some of the more modern developments are illustrated, and students are asked to comment on their *success* ... The science-based industries in the Sart Tilman industrial science *park* are an example of the newer, footloose industries that Liege *has to attract* ... *As a summary of the whole unit, students are asked to contribute to a new brochure aimed at attracting industry and business to Liege in the closing years of the twentieth century*. This calls for a range of writing and communication skills, and the development of a *persuasive style of writing*.
>
> (Chaffey, 1987, p. iii)

The author's final activity is extremely biased in relation to the type of future that will be best for Liege and its environment. The students do not have the option of exploring any alternatives other than drawing more industries into the city and its surrounds. The '*potential*' of the city is restricted by the author to its potential as a site for the industries that Liege '*has to attract*'. In analysing modern developments students are asked to comment on their '*success*', but not on their failures, or ways of improving the sites in the future. The word '*park*' is used euphemistically to describe an industrial estate. Finally, the students are required to write a positive, '*persuasive*' brochure aimed at attracting more business and industries. Despite the narrow approach of the activity, it is intended as '*a summary of the whole unit*.

Several conclusions might be drawn about the discourse in the paragraphs cited in this section. First, the terms used to indicate the position and status of the reader are less than egalitarian. The reader appears to be given no choices by the author as to completing tasks, ways of approaching problems and forming opinions. This restrains the reader to a position of uncritical obedience, and it is therefore undemocratic. Secondly, this text largely does not challenge environmental issues, even though the project of which it is a product claims to do so. Thus, readers may mistakenly believe that they are involved in environmental problem solving, when in fact their learning merely supports the dominant social paradigm, perpetuating the social and environmental problems of Liege. Thirdly, the text unquestioningly supports the myth that modern technology has little detrimental effect on the natural environment – that modern industry is *clean*.

A complete analysis of the text and of the Geography 16–19 Project texts as a set could illuminate some of the inconsistent messages students and teachers may receive from the work. Such research might then serve as the basis for many different projects, such as a review of the textbooks by the Project team, and the development of activities for geography textbook authors to make themselves more aware of the power of discourse.

The critical analysis of textbooks in the classroom may be an emancipatory activity for students, by highlighting the ways in which 'common-sense' statements can disguise values that serve existing inequitable power relations, including those among people and between people and the environment. Thus, the development of an action research by teachers to improve the critical literacy of their students is another useful activity which could result from this work.

CONCLUSION

Discourse analysis offers geographical educators the means to analyse pedagogy critically and to contribute to the emancipatory learning of students, through a focus on the communication between the participants in the learning. Deconstruction points to the ways in which communication can convey 'common-sense' messages that create or support significant power structures within our society. It reveals the contradictions within text, allowing the bias towards particular ideologies to be exposed. The contribution that discourse analysis may make to geographical education research is enhanced by the way in which the method acknowledges that teaching strategies, as well as content, have political implications. They convey to the students an understanding of the nature of themselves, what types of social relationship should be accepted in society, and what ways to view the world are appropriate in their society. The analysis of discourse, using the techniques displayed in the case study or others currently being developed, may strengthen general awareness of the power of text to reinforce or modify student attitudes and knowledge. Thus, discourse analysis is a research method which may prove to be an effective tool of social or environmental change, in particular in the field of education.

REFERENCES

Apple, M. (1986) *Teachers and Text: A Political Economy of Class and Gender Relations*. New York: Routledge.
Apple, M. and Christian-Smith, L. (eds) (1991) *The Politics of the Textbook*. New York: Routledge.
Bennett, S. (1993) 'The role of geography textbooks in education for the environment: a discourse analysis of Geography 16–19 Project texts'. Unpublished thesis for Master of Environmental Education, Faculty of Environmental Science, Griffith University, Brisbane.
Chaffey, J. (1987) *Manufacturing Industry and the Environment*. Harlow: Longman.
Fairclough, N. (1989) *Language and Power*. Harlow: Longman.
Fairclough, N. (1992) *Discourse and Social Change*. Cambridge: Polity.
Fiske, J. (1982) *An Introduction to Communication Studies*. London: Methuen.
Gilbert, R. (1984) *The Impotent Image: Reflections of Ideology in the Secondary School Curriculum*. Lewes: Falmer.
Gilbert, R. (1989a) 'Language and ideology in geography teaching'. In F. Slater (ed.) *Language and Learning in the Teaching of Geography*. London: Routledge.
Gilbert, R. (1989b) 'Text analysis and ideology critique in curricular content'. In A. Luke, S. de Castell and C. Luke (eds) *Language, Authority and Criticism*. Lewes: Falmer.
Giroux, H. (1989) *Schooling for Democracy: Critical Pedagogy for a Modern Age*. London: Routledge.
Henley, R. (1989) 'The ideology of geographical language'. In F. Slater (ed.) *Language and Learning in the Teaching of Geography*. London: Routledge.
Jefferson, A. and Robey, D. (1982) *Modern Literary Theory*. London: Batsford Academic and Educational.
Kress, G. and Hodge, R. (1979) *Language as Ideology*. London: Routledge and Kegan Paul.
Lather, P. (1992) 'Critical frames in education research: feminist and post-structuralist perspectives'. *Theory into Practice*, **31** (2).
Luke, C., de Castell, S. and Luke, A. (eds) (1989) *Language, Authority and Criticism*. Lewes: Falmer.
MacDonnell, D. (1986) *Theories of Discourse: An Introduction*. Oxford: Blackwell.
Naish, M., Rawling, E. and Hart, C. (1987) *The Contribution of a Curriculum Project to 16–19 Education*. Harlow: Longman.
Pecheux, M. (1975) *Language, Thematics and Ideology: Stating the Obvious*. Trans. H. Nagpal, 1982. London: Macmillan.

Chapter 14

Textbook Research in Geographical and Environmental Education

David R. Wright

Textbook research is a recognized field of study, with its own international journal, *Internationale Schulbuchforschung*, published in Brunswick by the Georg Eckert Textbook Research Institute. The journal is not easy to find outside Germany, but it is held in some major university libraries. UNESCO backing for this venture has been important, particularly in the early years of this field of research, which were dominated by the traumas of war in Europe during both the world wars and their aftermath. There was a feeling that incorrect textbook messages could have led to hatred of other peoples and nations, and ultimately to two devastating wars. Hence, there was a concern for factual accuracy.

Textbook research does not need to be boring. The fact that the findings of such research often are so can lead to two opposite reactions: *either* avoid it like the plague *or* try some yourself and do better. There is vast scope for genuinely original work. Some of it will lead to findings that can be significant, interesting, and useful to others as well.

It will be apparent that the wide variety of approaches outlined means that parts of this chapter could be considered objectivist/technical; other parts subjectivist/interpretive; and yet others as critical/emancipatory. But all the approaches are united in basing research on real objective data – the words and images of real textbooks.

OBJECTIVE APPROACHES

Textual analysis

A concern for accuracy has continued to dominate much textbook research. Many international gatherings have been held, and participants have compared the treatment of each other's countries in each other's textbooks.

The international conference reports tend to be full of such statements as: 'The population of Amsterdam was not over one million, but 718,000.' This is a case of not seeing the wood for the trees: the correction may be strictly true, yet the original statement is actually more meaningful. Children think of a city as the whole built-up area, not just the area within some administrative boundary used for census purposes. The textbook author, aware of the needs and understanding of children, may be much wiser than the researcher realizes. This suggests a more fruitful research topic: how do textbook authors simplify without distortion, and clarify without misleading the readers?

Another, more productive, approach would be to start with a hypothesis – such as 'Textbooks ignore Indonesia' or 'Images of the Netherlands are too selective' – seek evidence, and then evaluate that. Yet another approach is to go deeper into a single book, challenging assumptions and suggesting alternatives. It is, of course, much more satisfying to undertake the study oneself than to have a study undertaken on one's own writings. This type of study is particularly rewarding if the source of the book is itself suspect. For example, for many years a book was available free from the American embassy, for schools in the United Kingdom, entitled *The USA: Its Geography and Growth*. Teachers accepted the gift readily (doubtless free books from less 'acceptable' countries were treated with more suspicion). Analysis of the book raised more and more questions, eventually leading to an article with the significant title 'Whose outline of American geography?' (Wright, 1986a). Here is an example (p. 45) of the contents:

> What is missing?
> Above all, the problems are missing. There is virtually nothing about pollution. Urban problems are non-existent! Unemployment is unheard of. Racial issues are a thing of the past.
> The problem for teachers is that these absences are not immediately obvious. The book is divided into regions and so the themes tackled in the book as a whole are difficult to identify. The lack of an index makes this analysis even more difficult.

The danger of subjectivity is, of course, very great: is this research, or is it merely exchanging the textbook author's prejudices for another set? This is where 'hard' evidence is needed.

Several attempts have been made to quantify the analysis. A group of British geography teachers drew up a very helpful list of questions to ask about specific textbooks (CWDE, 1979). But once the questions are answered in numerical terms, we are liable to get complex nonsense. The nonsense seems to have a veneer of objectivity, and hence looks 'true', and this merely compounds the problem. It is so easy to believe data that look convincing (see CWDE, 1979, pp. 12–19).

Another interesting approach, developed by Hicks (1979), was to plot textbooks on a graph with two variables and hence four quartiles. Again, the researcher's subjectivity may be concealed beneath the veneer of an apparently objective structure, but it is certainly an approach on which to build.

Also, one needs to take account of 'readability'. Thousands of teacher-hours have been devoted to counting syllables and counting words in sentences – an adult version of children's 'busywork'. Using a square-root formula makes it look learned. If you believe that a word like 'aeroplane' really is three times more complex for a child than words like 'through', 'trough' and 'though', then go ahead with this kind of research! To me, it seems not just a futile waste of time, but also simply wrong – to borrow an expression from computer studies, a case of GIGO: garbage in, garbage out. However, before we dismiss attempts to calculate readability, one positive statement is in order. You may not know that the 'Fog Index' used in readability studies does not refer to a learned researcher called Fog but is instead a mnemonic for 'frequency of gobbledygook'. How

Table 14.1 *Picture Analysis: Books on Africa*

Author	Coysh and Tomlinson	Honeybone and Roberson	Jackson and Penn	Dempster	Beddis	Hickman	Wicks	Poxon	Rice	Fyson	Clare	Philips
Date (and Edition)	1951 (1966)	1958	1959 (1967)	1967	1968	1973	1973	1974	1975	1975	1977	1977
Est. Age Group	14–16	12–13	11–14	11–14	12–13	14–16	14–16	12–14	12–13	13–16	13–16	12–16
No. of pages[1]	98	93	46	18	38	116	130	27	16	44	24	46
Animal farming — T[5]		•••	•	•	•	•	•	•	•	••	•	••
Animal farming — W							•			•		
Animal farming — U										•		
Arable farming (inc. tree crops) — T	•	•	••	••	••	•	•	•••	••••••	•	•	••••
Arable farming — W		••••		•	••	••	•••	•••••	••	•		•••
Arable farming — U		•••••••	••	•	••	x	••••x	•••••x	•••••	•x		••x
Fishing — T							••			•		
Fishing — W							•					
Fishing — U												
Mining — T				•	•	••	•	•••				•
Mining — W		•					••					•
Mining — U			•									
Industry (inc. crafts and power) — T		••										
Industry — W	•••	•••••	•	•	••	••	••••	••••	••	••••	••	••
Industry — U			•					•		x		
Transport — T		•	••	••	••	••	•	•••	••	•	••	•
Transport — W		•••••	•••••		•••	•••••	•	•••••	•	•••	•	•••••
Transport — U					•							
Other 'tertiary' activity[2,3] — T				••••	•	••	••••••			•		•
Other 'tertiary' activity — W				••		••	••••	•		••	•	•
Other 'tertiary' activity — U												
Buildings and settlements[3] — T		•••••••	••••••	••••	••	••	••••••	•••	••	•••	••	••••
Buildings and settlements — W	•	••••	••••	••	••	••••	••••	••••••		••••••••	••••••	•••••••
Buildings and settlements — U						•				•••		

Table 14.1 (*cont.*)

		A	B	C	D	E	F	G	H	J
People[3]	T	••••	•	••	••••••	••	•••	••••	•••••••	•
	W	•	•	•	•	••	•••••••	•••••••	•••••	•
	U	••	•	••	•••	•••	•	•	••	•
Animals[3,4]		•••	••	••	•••				•	
Scenery[3]		••• •••••	••••••• •	•••	••••••	••••••••	••••••	•	••••••	

Notes
1. No. of pages: tropical Africa only; Egypt, Mediterranean coastlands and South Africa are excluded.
2. Includes shops, markets, trading, services and professions.
3. Excludes pictures included in any previous section.
4. Includes wild animals, birds and insects, but *not* animals included in 'Animal farming'.
5. Character: T = traditional; W = Western; U = Undefined, *or* both traditional and western.
× A picture of 'intermediate technology'.

References
A. Coysh and M. Tomlinson, *The Southern Continents*. University Tutorial Press, London, 1951ff.
R. Honeybone and B.S. Roberson, *The Southern Continents*. Heinemann, London, 1958.
N. Jackson and P. Penn, *Groundwork Geographies: The Southern Continents*. George Philip, London, 1959ff.
P. Dempster, *Britain and Southern Lands*. Ward Lock Educational, London, 1967.
R.A. Beddis, *New Secondary Geographies Book 2: Africa, Latin America and Lands of the S.W. Pacific*. University of London Press, London, 1968.
G.M. Hickman, *The New Africa*. University of London Press, London, 1973.
G.R.E. Wicks, *Africa*. Pergamon, Oxford, 1973.
J. and E. Poxon, *Africa and the Middle East*. Wheaton, Exeter, 1974.
W.F. Rice, *Patterns in Geography Book 2*. Longman, London, 1975.
N.L. Fyson, *Resources for World Geography: Africa*. Nelson, London, 1975.
R. Clare, *The New Africa*. Macdonald, London, 1977.
H. and J. Philips, *Progress and Change in West Africa*. Longman, London, 1977.

Source: Wright, 1979, p. 207. Reproduced with permission of The Geographical Association.

sad that this wonderful phrase has itself been buried beneath an avalanche of yet more gobbledygook!

Analysis of maps and diagrams in textbooks

This topic should be ideal for geographers. There is ample scope for research here. In children's atlases, for example, what are the implications of the choices made for the scale of area maps? Am I guilty of pro-Anglophone prejudice by mapping New Zealand (population 3,500,000) at a scale of 1:7,500,000, while Indonesia (population 184,000,000) is only at 1:25,000,000? In terms of areal scale, this is ten times smaller (Wright and Wright, 1994). Do other authors, or, more likely, their publishers, make similar decisions? Are there any reasons for this?

What causes confusion for children in studying textbook diagrams? For example, do children fail to distinguish between the representation of land and sea? Such failure is quite understandable in some cases: brown was used in one popular British textbook for colouring the sea instead of (more conventionally) the high land. Similarly, do children grasp when a diagram is a cross-section rather than a map?

How do colour-blind children cope with textbooks where the colours are used to distinguish land use categories? Do other children find full-colour diagrams much clearer than monochrome ones?

All these and other questions about whether the maps and diagrams really enhance or confuse geography teaching are legitimate areas for research.

Analysis of visual resources

This topic has considerable scope for research. Studying visual resources is an enjoyable exercise: many of us first became geographers because of a fascination with photographs of faraway places. We can continue to enjoy this activity and find some significant information. The research activity can be justified by the simple fact that pictures and photographs make a much stronger impact on pupils than text does.

What major images are emphasized? It is worthwhile to start with a hypothesis, or even with a feeling that 'balance' would be helpful. For example, in one investigation (Wright, 1979) it seemed to me that a wholly 'traditional' or a wholly 'westernized' view of tropical Africa would be inappropriate: some attention to 'both Africas' was needed. This early study, the findings of which are shown in Table 14.1, is now of historical interest, and a study of a new generation of textbooks using the same criteria would make an interesting comparison.

Another study (Wright, 1988, 1989) was undertaken at the invitation of Australian geographers, and the key question was: what images of Australia are found in UK textbooks? Again, the photographs made the strongest impression on children (Table 14.2). The findings were surprising (Wright, 1989). The table was not printed at the time because of space constraints, so it is printed here for the first time. The text discussed the significance of the findings.

Purists can challenge the accuracy of the findings, the small size of the sample and the deductions made from the data. They would be right in principle, but, in practice, a

Table 14.2 *Photographs of Australia in UK geography textbooks*

Textbooks	Natural scenery	Agriculture	Outback farming	Mining	Power/ dams industry	City centres	Suburbs	Small towns	Aborigines	Whites at leisure	Total photographs
1937:1948 G. for T.	3	3	3	1	0	2	0	0	1	0	13
1958 H and R	7	12	5	2	4	4	0	1	1	1	37
1968 Beddis	4	6	5	2	4	2	0	3	1	1	28
1975 Rice	2	13	15	4	9	1	0	3	0	0	47
1982 Beddis	2	0	0	0	1	3	1	0	2	1	10

Note
The figures should be treated with some caution as some photos fit several categories. The table should be studied for the broad trends only.

References
Beddis, R. (1968) *New Secondary Geographies Book 2: Africa, Asia, and the Lands of the South-West Pacific*, University of London Press, London.
Beddis, R. (1982) *A Sense of Place Book 2: The Changing World*, Oxford University Press, Oxford.
Geography for Today, Book 2: The Southern Continents, Longman, London 1937; 1948; 1960.
Honeybone, R.C. and Roberson, B.S. (1958) *Geography for Schools Book 2: The Southern Continents*, Heinemann, London.
Rice, W. (1975) *Patterns in Geography 2: Australia, W. and S. Africa, and the Middle East*, Longman, London.

Source: Wright, 1989.

study of this type both raises awareness and challenges assumptions. It may even lead to improvements in teaching and learning about Australia. For example, until this study was undertaken, the absence of suburbia, the major settlement style in Australia, had not been commented on. And for those who are planning a major research study, it is perhaps comforting to know that a modest textbook research exercise of this type was good enough to be considered for publication on both sides of the world!

Research into change and continuity over time

'Pure' historical research into textbooks is beyond the scope of this chapter, but a 'past-into-present' study makes for fascinating research and can yield some surprising findings. It is possible to focus on an area or a theme. Access to old textbooks can be a problem, but it is not insuperable. In the UK there are textbook collections in some universities, such as Cambridge, Liverpool, London and Sheffield, and many individual schools have kept copies of textbooks used for years.

The most significant findings I have obtained concern the topic of race. As a geographer, I started with relatively recent textbooks and traced their themes back into history, rather than using the historian's approach of starting in the past. In one study (Wright, 1986b, pp. 227–8) when analysing two books published in the 1970s, I recorded:

> My first hypothesis was that the original material might be from the inter-war period. *Gill's Oxford and Cambridge Geography*, completely revised and edited by L. Dudley Stamp in 1933, did indeed contain the same phrases: 'Indo-European (Caucasian or Aryan) race; fair skins; silky hair. Negro race: black woolly hair; flat noses; thick lips. American Indian Race: coarse black hair; sharp intelligent features'. But, despite Stamp's reputation of being one of the greatest geographers of all time, his 'complete revision' was markedly less than thorough in this instance. Forty years earlier, in the 1893 edition of *Gill's Imperial Geography*, exactly the same phrases are present. Could it be pure Darwinism, I wondered?
>
> To my amazement, I then found exactly the same phrases in Rev. J. Goldsmith's *Grammar of Geography* (1827): 'the jet black negroes and other Africans of various shades of black, having woolly hair, thick lips, flat noses, prominent chins and downy skins'. These phrases are thus over 150 years old, and predate by more than a generation Darwin's *Origin of Species*. The phrases in an elementary book, designed for rote-learning by young pupils, have apparently been copied and recopied over the years until they now appear in new books for senior pupils of high intelligence.

SUBJECTIVE APPROACHES

Pupil response

This is the simplest suggestion in this chapter: yet, perhaps, it is the most radical. It is based on the premise that we should listen to pupils and students; we should reflect on what they say.

I am always impressed by the perceptiveness of children if they are invited to say or write what they like and what they do not like about textbooks. The freshness of their comments and the unconventional originality of their turns of phrase is a welcome breath of fresh air in the aridity of much 'textbook research'. Here are some examples (Wright, 1987, p. 137) of comments made by 12–13-year-olds about a large variety of geography textbooks in use in the UK:

Favourable
I like the pictures of this book because they have full variety.
The photos are in motion, not just posing.
I can understand all of what the words mean. I can't find one fault with this book.
Lots of colourful pictures, and good colourful diagrams.
The writing and words explain things easily.
Not too many hard words
Very interesting.

Critical
It's too complicated.
It's too plain and boring, and doesn't give you anything to have any excitement and adventure in.
It's not easy to follow.
Not much life in it at all.
Boring – boring again – just boring.
Some pictures seem too far away.

Objectivists would want to develop methods for testing for validity, but emancipatory researchers would find the data significant in themselves.

Work in Australia on student evaluation of textbooks produced many insights and led to these ten conclusions (Wright, 1990, pp. 452–4):

1.   Firstly, 'finding out about the textbook' could be tackled.
2.   The great majority of pupils do not find black-and-white photographs stimulating ...
3.   The strong criticisms, by every age-group, that the books are too long and too heavy ...
4.   Motivation is a key factor for pupils.
5.   Not a single pupil, of any age, expressed any praise or criticism of the values, attitudes and bias of any of the textbooks, whether implicit or explicit ... If we could encourage pupils to be critical evaluators, rather than receivers of views and information, they [would] be much better prepared for the outside world.
6.   One outcome of asking pupils to respond to textbooks is that teachers will come to know and understand their pupils better.
7.   Another valuable outcome of this activity can be the new ideas for classroom work which it stimulates.
8.   Publishers should consider setting up an 'Authors-into-schools' scheme ...
9.   Pupil reviews of textbooks would be an interesting and innovative feature in subject teachers' journals.
10. The main conclusion ... is that we should invite pupils to react to, and to respond to, books, and we should listen to and reflect on their responses.

Interviews with authors

There is a great contrast between the high-profile world of novelists (champagne, the Booker Prize, TV appearances, newspaper features) and the world of the textbook author. A textbook author may well sell millions of books – far more than some prize-winning novelists – and remain largely unknown and unnoticed; just a surname on the spine of a book.

These authors have a huge influence, yet few of them have been interviewed in any depth. For example, Rex Beddis was the author of major textbook series in England and Wales in the 1960s and 1980s, and director of the Schools Council Geography for the Young School Leaver Project in the 1970s. He died at a relatively early age and there is no published interview with him.

The case study approach to research (see Chapter 11) is well suited to the study of authors. Extracts from a published interview (Young, 1977) with E.W. Young, who wrote innovative geography textbook series which sold several million copies from 1949 until the 1970s, illustrate the technique:

Interviewer: You were the first person to design the page as you wrote the text, weren't you?
Author: You've put your finger on the most important thing. I decided to think of myself as 'selling' Geography – using some of the techniques of the copy-writer who designs adverts, to catch the eye and get the message across. Although it seems very ordinary nowadays, having pictures and questions integrated with the text, and varied page-openings designed individually to catch the eye, so that the child has some flash of interest on turning over the page – these are the things I was aiming at ...
   I feel that Geography teachers have a great social responsibility, and that Geography teaching should have a moral, perhaps even a spiritual, motivation ... And I hope that I can help young people derive some interest and pleasure and satisfaction from the diversity of humanity and the Creation as a whole, and develop a feeling of inter-dependence of the human species – of One World, which was a prevalent idea in the post-war years and is now a common-sense necessity of world survival ...

> Another important thing, to my mind, is to write for girls as much as for boys. In fact I originally wrote for my three young daughters! A lot of the keen young textbook-writers of today – they're nearly all men – seem to overlook the fact that 50% of their clientèle are female, and are not on the whole deeply stirred by mathematical abstractions.

It is fascinating to see that half a century ago Young had adopted the strategies that are now familiar to key personnel in marketing departments. Furthermore, he was into moral, gender and conservation issues before any of them were fashionable in school geography in Britain. It is easy to assume that everything was boring and irrelevant in geography until a few years ago: this interview contradicts this assumption. But this is only one example, and there are dozens of other authors whom it would be interesting to interview now and whose opinions and insights could be analysed later.

How do teachers use textbooks?

This topic is very important and well worth researching. Lidstone (1990) undertook a doctoral study in this field, and it was clear that the data are hard to gather and clear conclusions difficult to establish.

Teachers' opinions of textbooks might be a more productive research topic – though the battered feelings of many teachers in England and Wales at present might yield responses that they feel they should give rather than their actual feelings.

Anti-textbook sentiments are a puzzling and continuing feature of many British conferences and conversations – yet this is a confused area. The multicoloured textbook may be condemned as 'boring' by a geography teacher who readily inflicts monochrome, teacher-prepared worksheets on his or her pupils. It is a topic that cries out for research, and pupils' opinions would enhance any investigation in this field.

CRITICAL OR EMANCIPATORY APPROACHES

Studying textbook treatment of controversial issues

Of all the sections in this chapter, this is arguably the most important. The researcher identifies a controversial issue which greatly interests him or her. The textbooks provide the data for analysis. So there is a clear *purpose* to the study, and strong motivation for the researcher.

I have had a number of graduate students who have produced very worthwhile studies on such themes. Many remain unpublished, such as one by a student of Polish descent of the treatment of Poland in UK textbooks, and another on the Catholic/Protestant issue in Northern Ireland. Atkinson (1992) wrote a valuable study of the role of women in the Third World, which was based on some existing work (Wright, 1985). The same techniques produced an up-to-date study that was relevant to the National Curriculum in England and Wales. It was a picture-based study based on the premise that pictures make the strongest impact on children.

Environmental issues are a stimulating focus. Thrush and Wright, in an unpublished study of nuclear power in UK textbooks, analysed textbooks from the 1970s and 1980s. The conclusion was fascinating: most textbooks from the 1970s are unduly uncritical and positive towards nuclear power; most textbooks from the 1980s are very negative towards it. Only a few gave fair treatment to both 'sides' of the argument. Our findings included the following:

> The question of bias can be related to the age of the book. In the 1960s and 1970s nuclear power was the latest technology and very much promoted by the government. Consequently, one might expect textbooks, published at this time, to show a pro-nuclear bias ...
>
> One can see that all the books with a pro-nuclear bias were published in the late 1970s and all the books with an anti-nuclear bias were published in the mid to late 1980s.
>
> As long as a teacher is aware of the biases that may be found in these textbooks, then there should be no difficulty in using them in the classroom. The problem with many of these textbooks, however, is that the bias is subtle, unlike information from Greenpeace or BNFL (British Nuclear Fuels Limited), and therefore goes unnoticed.

Similar studies could be undertaken on many other controversial geographical and environmental issues: the field is wide open for established and new researchers.

Cross-disciplinary comparison

There is much concern about the overlap between science and geography in British school curricula, and this is a fertile area for textbook research. How do scientists tackle the teaching of, for example, plate tectonics, volcanoes, limestone, power and energy? A comparative study is likely to be revealing – perhaps based on the hypothesis that specialists in both subjects can learn from each other.

A study of modern religious education textbooks is likely to reveal much more common ground with geography than many teachers of the latter might expect. How are the same moral issues tackled in geography and religious education? Once again, teachers of both subjects have much to learn from each other. Perhaps such studies would help to emancipate geography specialists from some of their shackles?

But what do the pupils *do*?

A study of suggested pupil activities in textbooks is likely to be an informative activity. Some of the research questions include: do some textbooks still ask children to copy and regurgitate – even if it is disguised? Do others only suggest vague discussion? What are the successful forms of pupil activity, and how are they expressed?

This topic is at the heart of classroom activity in geography and yet it is surprisingly neglected in textbook research.

CONCLUSION

There is plenty of opportunity for worthwhile textbook research in geographical and environmental education, and even more opportunities for using textbooks as firm evidence in other types of research. This chapter has indicated the wide range of questions to be asked and the variety of methods available to be employed. Textbooks are a rich source of data for experienced and less experienced researchers.

REFERENCES

Atkinson, J. (1992) 'How do geography textbooks portray women of developing countries?' *Teaching Geography* 17(4), 179–80.

CWDE (1979) *The Changing World in Geography*. London: Centre for World Development Education.

Hicks, D. (1979) 'Bias in Geography Textbooks.' Working Paper No. 1. London: Centre for Multicultural Education, University of London Institute of Education.

Lidstone, J. (1990) 'Researching the use of textbooks in geography classrooms.' *Internationale Schulbuchforshung*, 12, 427–44.

Wright, D.R. (1979) 'Visual images in geography texts: the case of Africa.' *Geography*, 64, 205–10.

Wright, D.R. (1985) 'Are geography textbooks sexist?' *Teaching Geography*, 10, 81–5.

Wright, D.R. (1986a) 'Whose outline of American geography? An exercise in textbook research.' *The Social Studies (USA)*, 77, 44–7.

Wright, D.R. (1986b) 'Racism in school textbooks.' In D. Punter (ed.) *Introduction to Contemporary Cultural Studies*. London: Longman.

Wright, D.R. (1987) 'A pupil's perspective on textbooks.' *Internationale Schulbuchforshung*, 9, 137–42.

Wright, D.R. (1988) '200 years of teaching about Australia.' *Times Educational Supplement*, 1 April.

Wright, D.R. (1989) 'Images of Australia in UK textbooks.' *Geographical Education (Australia)*, 6(1), 43–5.

Wright, D.R. (1990) 'The role of pupils in textbook evaluation.' *Internationale Schulbuchforshung*, 12, 445–54.

Wright, D.R. and Wright, J.A. (1994) *Philip's Children's Atlas*. 6th edn. London: George Philip.

Young, E.W. (1977) 'A walking-stick, not a crutch.' *Teaching Geography*, 2, 173–5.

Chapter 15

'Audience-centred' Teaching and Children's Writing in Geography

Graham Butt

'Audience-centred' teaching attempts to involve children in talking to, and writing for, audiences different from the ones they would usually encounter in the geography classroom. In effect children are encouraged to produce work within geography lessons that communicates with an identified audience other than that of the 'teacher as assessor'. Research evidence suggests that as children gradually become more aware of the forms of communication that are most appropriate to use with these different audiences, they become more involved in the whole learning process.

The links between language and learning, together with the role played by language in the development of a child's thought processes, are well documented and researched (Piaget, 1959; Vygotsky, 1962; McNeill, 1966; Chomsky, 1968, etc.). However, more contemporary work in this field, stimulated in the 1970s partly by the report of the Bullock Committee (DES, 1975), now attracts little attention in geography education research. The 'Language Across the Curriculum' groups which were formed in the 1970s certainly answered many questions about how children used language in the classroom, but many of the issues they raised were never fully explored within geography. The impetus for investigation into these questions, which were often concerned with the process of using language to develop conceptual understanding, has unfortunately almost disappeared. The only recent exceptions are the work of the National Oracy Project (Wilding, 1989a, 1989b) and the publication *Talking About Geography* (Carter, 1991). Research into the whole issue of 'talking and writing to learn' in geography has therefore largely become marginalized.

Little has changed recently concerning the ways in which teacher talk dominates classroom practice (Barnes, 1976). This is one of the reasons why children visualize teachers as 'assessors' rather than as 'facilitators' of learning. The role of the teacher can even be described as that of a language 'gatekeeper', closely determining the form and function of the language used by children and often restricting its range of applications. Neglecting to introduce a variety of activities which elicit different forms of language from children, such as decision-making and reasoning activities, has a limiting effect on the role that language can play in helping to broaden conceptual development. In emphasizing narrow purposes of control, discipline and assessment, the language of the classroom often fails to fulfil its potential as an effective vehicle for children's learning.

For many geography teachers, the distinction between using language solely for communication purposes and recognizing its role in the whole process of learning remains poorly defined. The literature available to help explore this functional difference, often with special reference to geography, has fortunately become more comprehensive of late (see Gilbert, 1984, 1989; Henley, 1989; Hull, 1985; Roberts, 1986; Slater, 1989).

WHAT ROLES CAN AUDIENCES PLAY IN CHILDREN'S LEARNING?

The 'role of audience' in talking and writing has been mentioned by a number of researchers and writers (Martin *et al.*, 1976; Williams, 1981; Slater, 1983; Carter, 1991), but few have extended their ideas into empirical research. In the late 1970s, the London Writing Research Team attempted to engage children in writing for 'audiences outside the classroom', for they believed that changing the audience that children wrote for (or talked to) helped to stimulate both thought and understanding. The amount of fully documented work in this field is small, partly because collecting and interpreting evidence are both complicated and problematic. Isolating the specific learning activities associated with audience-related work from the other learning processes within the classroom is not easy. Despite these research difficulties, the importance of audience-centred writing has often been reaffirmed; for example, the Cox Report (DES, 1989, Section 17.15) states that children's writing should be 'appropriate for the purpose, audience and subject matter' and should be read by a variety of real audiences.

The variety of potential audiences has been considered by both Britton *et al.* (1975) and Slater (1983). These can be listed as follows:

- pupil to self;
- pupil to trusted adult;
- pupil to teacher, as partner in a dialogue;
- pupil to teacher, as examiner or assessor;
- pupil to pupil, or peer group.

Carter (1991) extends the list further, often centring the audience on the teacher (although note the strategy of minimal intervention: see Figure 15.1).

Children given the task of writing for, or talking to, different audiences have a greater responsibility to direct their own learning, and must contextualize their language to the particular situation they are placed in. Often the writing tasks given to children fail to fulfil this purpose and therefore do not extend the knowledge and understanding of the child. Undemanding and repetitive comprehension-style exercises in geography do little to advance real learning. Audience-centred writing ensures that children have to think for themselves rather than merely feed back the information previously given to them by the teacher or text.

Children have to be given flexibility to explore the language they can use. This may require teachers to 'relax' their enthusiasm for dominant interventions during child-centred learning; a difficulty perhaps when one is aware of the need to maintain control and management of the group. A learning atmosphere of freedom and experimentation

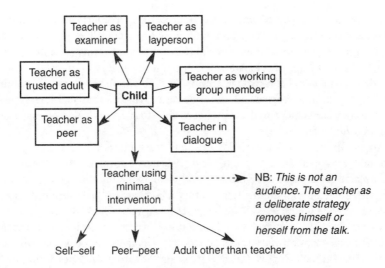

Figure 15.1 *Talk for Learning: an audience model for classroom practice.*
Source: Carter 1991, p. 7.

has to be established, where children are trusted to direct their own learning within the structure of the lesson imposed by the teacher. Children also need to be aware that their initial contributions in language work will be welcomed, for these will often be tentative, unsure and poorly formed, representing the first stages of thinking and learning.

New forms of writing and talking will only be forthcoming if children believe that adults are genuinely interested in the work they are producing. This may require the teacher to adopt the role of a 'mentor' rather than an 'assessor' in the classroom.

APPROACHES TO AUDIENCES

The importance of considering the audience that children write for can be witnessed when one reflects upon the amount of inert or inept writing produced in schools. The natural process of internalizing the sense of audience, a process learned through speech, is prevented by the regular testing or reproductive writing children are asked to produce at the expense of other forms of writing.

The function and sense of audience are therefore important. Carter (1991, p. 9) implies that it is often hard for teachers to create real audiences for children to write for, and that during lessons 'opportunities suddenly present themselves' for audience-centred work in an erratic way. This is certainly often the case, although audiences can be identified and engineered by the teacher to a far greater extent than Carter suggests. These audiences are not only those of 'teacher as layperson' or 'teacher as trusted adult', but also what might be referred to as 'teacher as audience suggester' or perhaps 'teacher as catalyst'.

Selected audiences should help children to develop writing in geography that is more original and reveals greater individuality of expression. Writing then becomes creative rather than transactional and, if developed correctly, audience-centred writing can represent a key to promoting learning.

Consideration of the types of language children most regularly use in the classroom, and their impact on learning and understanding, is important. The work of Britton *et al.* (1975) and Barnes (1976), who describe linguistic forms in terms of expressive, transactional and poetic language, provides a starting point for analysis.

Briefly, the transactional form of writing is the one which teachers most regularly ask pupils to engage in. It is formal in its style and is often used to classify and record information into a convenient and easily accessible form. This tends to mask the child's own values, attitudes and beliefs.

Poetic, expressive (or as Slater, 1989, prefers, 'exploratory') language is less clearly structured and less goal-oriented. The less restrictive form of this language perhaps allows for greater conceptual development and enables the child to give broader scope to his or her affective development. Exploratory language is, however, only infrequently used in geography teaching. As Rosen (quoted in the Bullock Report, 1975, p. 190, para. 12.6) states: 'The demand for transactional writing in schools is ceaseless, but expressive language with all its vitality and richness is the only possible soil from which it can grow.' The Bullock Report (DES, 1975) also illustrates the point that children are often required 'to report conclusions in writing . . . but not to produce the kind of writing that most effectively helps them *arrive at* these conclusions' (p. 190, para. 12.6).

The Language Across the Curriculum groups encouraged teachers to let their pupils experiment with writing in the poetic and expressive forms. The audience-centred teaching approach provides a suitable vehicle for this. The need for a greater awareness of audience is taken up by Johnston (1987) who recognizes that much of the writing produced in the classroom is of questionable educational value because of the '. . . failure of teachers to emphasize the process of writing about "something" for "someone".'

Thus 'talking and writing to learn' is recognized as being important in the educational process. The role that this plays in trying out new ideas and encouraging first-draft thinking has been noted. The notion that student dialogue is often more educational than teacher monologue is also clear.

THE FUNCTION OF GENRE THEORY IN AUDIENCE-CENTRED TEACHING

Current thinking with regard to the role and form of language used in learning has advanced beyond earlier descriptions of 'transactional', 'expressive' and 'poetic' language into theories related to 'genre'. Use of the term 'genre' in everyday life has increased over the last ten years, and it is now frequently applied in a variety of contexts. Broadly speaking, 'genre' refers to 'a kind or a type' (Andrews, 1992), and in this sense it has been applied to paintings, literature, films, non-literary texts and speech. Narrower definitions of its meaning, primarily for use in educational contexts, have been created by various 'genre theorists' working in the field of English language education.

Genre theory has been debated primarily in the Journal of the Australian Association of Teachers of English (Rosen, 1988) although its impact has now extended beyond this forum. The basic theory, although not 'highly unified' (Kress, 1989), relates to the styles of writing, textual form and origins of the writing process. This is naturally often closely linked to the audience that the writer is addressing.

The language genres that surround us in everyday life have a great diversity, ranging from weather reports, letters to editors, and job applications to lab reports, jokes, sermons, etc. In the classroom, genres can help both teachers and pupils make distinctions between different types of language situation. They have a role in shaping, clarifying and giving a functional purpose to discourse and text. Genres also have a particular social context and meaning (Kress, 1989), which may be appropriate to either large, small, select or specialized audiences. The key idea is that writing styles are mostly a product of the social context in which they are produced and therefore reveal more than a mere set of words on a page. According to Kress and Knapp (1992), children will not develop different forms of language if they do not have access to various genres, or get to use them regularly. Children therefore need to be made aware of the range of genres that regularly occur in social situations, and should become empowered to understand and use them for different audiences. These genres can be taught, for they have become 'conventionalized' and are recognizable as specific language forms.

The functional element of genres is important, because, as Poynton (1985, p. 9) states, they may best be understood as 'structured or staged ways of getting things done by means of language in a particular culture'. This definition of their function is broadly supported by the work of Kress (1989) and Christie and Rothery (1989).

Thus genres have a fundamental role in language use, because they are closely linked to the audience one is communicating with and the ways in which information is received and understood by that audience. When teachers give children a writing task, they must therefore be fully aware of its implied purpose and function, and the audience for which it is being prepared. When reading or writing a text, one must always consider *who produced it? For whom was it produced? In what context and under what constraints . . .*' (Kress and Knapp, 1992, p. 8). If the genre the teacher expects from the child is one that the child has little or no experience of, then the writing task will most probably not be completed satisfactorily. It may therefore be appropriate to teach children about genres, social contexts and audiences before writing tasks are undertaken.

Genre theorists such as Christie, Martin and Rothery believe that any study of writing is incomplete without an awareness of its origins of 'social place and power'. This they believe to be as important as studying what the text actually 'says':

> without the capacity to handle the written genres in which information is processed and understood in the contemporary world, people will be truly left out, unable to participate in a world of increasingly sophisticated information, construction and exchange.
>
> (Christie and Rothery, 1989, p. 3)

The difficulty that this presents is contained in the assumption that when children write for different audiences they can automatically 'release' the necessary language resources needed to complete their task successfully. It may be argued that if children have a real motivation to write, they will extend their mastery of language resources to cope with the demands made upon them. However, it is clear that we are all limited in our concept development by the range of words available to us; if the necessary words are not at our disposal, the creation of new learning becomes problematic. Major difficulties occur because it is impossible just to 'give' children words to help them complete their learning tasks.

Genres can only be explored if children are placed in realistic situations. These, as Rosen (1988) explains, must take the children beyond rather sterile tasks such as being presented with a letter to a newspaper about an issue, and seeing whether they can write one like it. Because of this Rosen (1988), Stratta and Dixon (1992) and others are critical of the application of genre theory and its power to develop children's learning and linguistic ability. Unlike Christie, Martin and Rothery, they feel that genre theory may have more limited applications in the classroom.

For the purposes of the research undertaken here, the audiences that children addressed were classified as either 'known and restricted' (usually the teacher) or 'unknown and unrestricted' (for example, other adults, unknown peers or younger audiences). Teachers do not generally create the opportunities for children to talk to, or write for, a wide range of audiences during their lessons; therefore establishing these audiences became a major focus for the research work.

CLASSROOM RESEARCH INTO AUDIENCE-CENTRED TEACHING

The overall aim of the research was to explore whether audience-centred writing had an impact on learning geography. This aim was extended into a series of key questions, which drew upon an understanding of audience-related work and genre theory. The questions then acted as a guide for the research methodology that was developed:

1. Can empirical evidence be collected to illustrate the effects of using audience-centred writing tasks to improve children's learning of geography?
2. Does changing the audience that children write for (or talk to) alter their processes of thought, learning and understanding?
3. Can specific audience-related learning be isolated from other learning processes in the classroom?
4. How easy is it for children to change from writing for 'known and restricted' audiences, such as the teacher as assessor, to those that are 'unknown and unrestricted'?
5. Can audience-centred materials be produced to promote effective geographical education?

From these questions a working hypothesis was constructed:

> That by introducing a wide variety of audiences into their work children will improve their writing, talking and learning in geography.

The adoption of a rigid theoretical and methodological approach to classroom research was discounted from the start. This was to ensure that the research was responsive to the types of data collected and that new research questions could be accommodated during the course of the work. No single approach was obvious as being the most appropriate to use, or indeed appeared reliable enough to answer all the questions posed.

In a consideration of the continuum that exists between broadly 'quantitative' and 'qualitative' research methods it was apparent that the latter would probably present more opportunities for collecting data. Qualitative research often creates insight (rather than striving for narrow statistical certainties) and as such holistic, subjective and impressionistic methods of research have a degree of attractiveness. Overconcentration on the directly measurable can ignore useful qualitative data and result in a reductionist view of classroom events (see Delamont, 1984).

The research methodology adopted might be described as being focused on action research and case studies of lessons taught in three Birmingham comprehensive schools (Butt, 1991, 1993). The data collected was in the form of written work produced by the children, but this was also supplemented by observation of the learning activities and by a questionnaire survey. This meant that the major research was qualitative, but that certain quantitative methods were also used if they appeared to be appropriate to a particular research question. Findings were regularly fed back to the schools concerned, although the observations and comments made by the schools did not warrant major changes in the research methodology. Access to different groups of children was negotiated at the start of the study.

A total of 14 audience-centred lessons were taught in the Spring and Summer terms of 1991 just prior to the implementation of Key Stage 3 of the geography National Curriculum. Pupils from years 7, 8 and 9 (11 to 14-year-olds) were chosen for the research because of the greater timetable flexibility within these year groups, although subsequently some research was also carried out with a year 10 group as well.

The audiences that pupils had to write to, or for, included an aid agency, a wood gatherer, shanty town dweller, hospital consultant, industrialist, government housing department, television audience, and a Member of Parliament.

Each of the research lessons began with an explanation of the aims of the lesson and exercises to establish the basic knowledge and understanding of geographical content to be covered. This might occupy one third of the lesson time, with the remaining two-thirds dedicated to active, pupil centred work on an audience-related theme. Resources used were varied, ranging from pictures, photographs, cartoons and texts, to personal narratives and video. Pupils were organized to work individually, in pairs or in groups according to the nature of the writing they were to undertake for a particular audience.

An audience-centred research lesson

By considering the teaching methods and materials used in one lesson, the ways in which the research was conducted can be illustrated. The stimulus material here was a photograph of a woman from a developing country carrying a very large stack of firewood that she had just gathered (Fien and Gerber, 1986, pp. 189–90).

After the children had looked briefly at the photograph in pairs or threes they were given a worksheet to direct their audience-centred work (see over page).

Once the children had completed their discussion and writing, each piece of their work was collected and analysed with regard to its 'level of geographical attainment' and 'sense of audience'. In defining the 'sense of audience' and 'levels of geographical attainment' a series of extracts and guidelines was devised (see Appendix).

It was hoped that a relationship could be established between work that revealed both a high level of geographical attainment and a similarly advanced sense of audience, although it was realized that establishing a causal link might be difficult. A simple matrix (Table 15.1) was constructed for each of the audience-centred lessons taught. The 'x' in the matrix here stands for the number of pupils perceived to be in the category stated.

Look at the photograph: the burden of firewood collection

With a partner, or in groups of three, discuss what you think the picture shows.

Try to make up some questions about the photo to explore together. Discuss these questions and then record what ideas you have come up with.

Here are some questions that you might ask:

'Where do you think the picture is taken?'
'What is the person in the photo doing?'
'Where do you think she is going?'
'What type of life does she lead?'
'How old is she?' etc.

Ask and answer any questions that come to mind.

After you have 'brainstormed' all you can about the photo in your group, write down a conversation between yourself and the woman shown there. Imagine that you have just discovered this woman carrying her wood (how you happened to be here at the time I'll leave up to you!) and ask her some questions. What is she going to reply?

If it helps try this out in discussion first and then write it down!

Table 15.1 *Matrix of achievement in audience-centred lessons*

Level of geographical attainment	Sense of audience		
	Poor	Average	Advanced
Low	x	x	x
Medium	x	x	x
High	x	x	x

In total, some 241 pieces of written work were collected and about half of these (118 pieces) were analysed. The reason for not closely analysing all of the work was that some of it was collected from 'trial' lessons, where teaching materials needed subsequent reorientation to make them more appropriate, and some was incomplete. In addition, sixty-three questionnaire responses were taken from two of the classes involved in the research. Accumulated totals across the different schools and the different learning activities set gave an overview as shown in Table 15.2.

The evaluation of data produced from this small-scale research project was obviously tentative and partial, but there are clear indications from the evidence collected that changing the audience that children write for has some effect on the learning process they experience. Table 15.2, however, fails to distinguish between the lessons where the audience-centred activities had a broadly positive effect on student learning, and those

Table 15.2 *Overview of achievement in audience-centred lessons*

	Sense of audience			
Level of geographical attainment	Poor	Average	Advanced	Total
Low	16	13	15	44
Medium	7	17	29	53
High	2	3	16	21
Total	25	33	60	118

where misconceptions and problems occurred in the learning of geography. In addition, the fact that research/teacher was unknown to the groups may have skewed the reactions of certain children to the tasks they were presented with.

The range of 'secondary' effects that audience-centred writing tasks create is of interest, as these appear to be mostly beneficial to the whole process of learning. One regularly noted facet was the increase in work-related discussion throughout the lesson. This signified a genuine desire by children to inquire not only about the form and technicalities of written presentation, but about the geography as well. Initially, much of this questioning was directed at the teacher to discover (or reconfirm) the 'rules of presentation' required. This served the purpose of giving children reassurance in their new tasks. The next stage, once the children had established that the format for writing was flexible and negotiable, was for the teacher to be used as a kind of 'geographical consultant' to supply needed information.

In achieving the 'correct' genre on which to base their response, pupils often found themselves placed in the initiating role of asking questions. This was particularly apparent when they wrote in the form of a dialogue. The structure of the dialogue was often based on a question-and-answer format, though, which usually gave this genre a formal, interrogative air rather than that of a genuinely balanced, two-sided discussion.

The questions that pupils found themselves asking regularly extended their thinking into the affective domain of 'values and attitudes' in geography. Responding to an audience in an appropriate genre required the children to appreciate their audience's perceived point of view, beliefs and feelings. Certain exercises naturally elicited these types of response better than others and led more effectively to advanced and empathetic audience-centred writing. Here the assumptions made by children about people revealed their own stages of affective development. Unfortunately this sometimes masked the level of geographical learning achieved by becoming the major focus for the children's writing.

FINDINGS AND IMPLICATIONS

For audience-centred work to succeed, it became clear that certain learning conditions needed to exist.

First, the teacher had to be trusted. It was apparent that boys did not perform as well on the writing tasks, partly because they may have felt that a supportive and trusting element was somehow lacking in the teacher/researcher they were writing for. They tended either not to risk advanced audience-centred writing, or to revert to transactional or 'humorous' styles. The whole issue of trust became an intriguing one, for within the space of a lesson or two some children were keen to reveal thoughts, feelings, values and attitudes openly, whereas others did not want to make the effort or take the risk. Some were obviously confused by being asked to write in a style not normally associated with geography lessons, while others found confidence in the fact that there were going to be few 'right answers' to the tasks.

Secondly, the teacher had to ensure that children kept themselves focused on the audience-centred nature of their writing. Even though pupils were encouraged to write for an audience other than the 'teacher as assessor', many still saw this as being the 'real' audience. The work that children produced would often refer briefly to the audience specified in the exercise, but would in fact be dominated by transactional forms of writing. It proved extremely difficult to break down the conditioning of writing in a transactional style for an 'assessor' – a situation established through years of schooling.

Thirdly, the teacher had to be aware of the stages through which audience-centred writing helped children develop their understanding of geography. There was some evidence that the writing that children undertook represented a transitional stage in their learning, where they were beginning to explore their own knowledge and understanding more closely. Here language and genre may have been used as tools to help conceptual development.

Lastly, the realistic, but misguided, fear that no real geography was being learnt had to be countered. There is some evidence that geographical attainment can be masked by an overzealous adoption of an audience, although there is no reason to believe that this restricts the child's geographical understanding any more than simple transactional writing does.

The factor of pupil enjoyment of lessons is important, as most pupils (95 per cent) stated in the questionnaire survey that they enjoyed 'all' or 'most' of the lessons, understood the content (86 per cent), had learnt 'a lot' (57 per cent) and were well supported in their learning (81 per cent). The link between enjoyment of lessons and learning is well established.

With older children it became noticeable that they were capable of quite advanced audience-centred writing, although they often did not adopt this style because they believed a more transactional form was really required. The division between those children that successfully utilized an audience-centred style and those that did not was more marked in the older age range.

DOES AUDIENCE-CENTRED TEACHING IMPROVE CHILDREN'S WRITING IN GEOGRAPHY?

In conclusion, the major question of whether audience-centred writing truly advanced the learning of geography is difficult to answer. For those pupils willing to experiment and adopt new styles of learning, the evidence is that their learning of geography also improved. These children enjoyed the variation and challenge, and benefited accordingly. For others, the work encouraged experimentation with a genre without necessarily advancing geographical learning. It became an opportunity to talk with a neighbour, a chance to engage in some comedy writing, or an excuse to dole out more of the transactional forms of writing they usually engaged in. The reasons behind this are various, partly one suspects related to conditioning and motivation.

In general, then the characteristic effects of adopting audience-centred approaches appear to be:

1. an increase in work-related discussion between pupils, and between pupil and teacher;
2. an increase in the number of questions asked by pupils, often extending their thinking into both geographical concepts and the realms of values and attitudes;
3. an appreciation of the audience's perceived viewpoints and values. This was necessary to create plausible pieces of writing, although sometimes, in an attempt to produce empathetic writing, the pupils' sense of audience rather masked the levels of geographical attainment;
4. clarification of personal values and attitudes.

The preconditions for successfully introducing an audience-centred approach appear to be that:

5. a sense of trust and purpose needs to be established before good audience-centred writing will appear. Boys did not reveal this sense of trust as readily as girls;
6. removing the idea of the 'teacher as assessor' in pupils' minds is important, but also extremely difficult;
7. audience-centred writing should be integrated into schemes of work, but not overused;
8. audiences should be realistic and plausible;
9. if levels of pupil involvement, discussion and inquiry are allowed to rise through audience-centred work, geographical attainment may also rise.

This concurs with Slater's findings that children may not initially be said to be 'learning geography' more fully, but that they are certainly 'learning through geography'. The distinction is important, for the latter is often an effective vehicle for achieving the former.

APPENDIX

The following are extract exemplars of the different senses of audiences and levels of geographical attainment (from pupil's work on 'The burden of firewood collection').

Poor sense of audience:
'I was walking through the desert longing for a drink because I was so thirsty when I came across a woman carrying firewood on her back. She looked tired. I thought I was really tired but she looked really pale. I stopped and asked her where she was going. She told me she was going to a little hut.'

Average sense of audience:
'Hello, I'm Celia and she's Helen.'
'Oh, hello. My name is Suzanne.'
'Do you want us to help you?'
'Oh, no thanks. I've got it all strapped on well, but thank you for asking.'
'We thought we'd better ask because it seems a bit heavy.'
'Well, it's not too bad. I have to do this every day though and it's not very comfortable because the sharp bits stick into my back.'

Advanced sense of audience:
I was driving through the desert in Africa. I saw a woman walking down a small path. She had a large bundle of sticks on her back. I stepped down from the jeep; and said:
'Hello, what's your name?'
'My name is Winnie.'
'Is that wood you're carrying very heavy? It looks as though it is more than you can manage!'
'Yes, it is heavy but I'm used to the weight.'
'Do you have to carry it far?'
'Only until I get home, which is about 5 miles away now.'
'Would you like me to carry the wood for a while in my jeep? You look very tired!'
'Yes, that would be very helpful, thank you. I have to collect as much wood as I can because there may not be as much left tomorrow. Wood seems to be running out fast around here. It is very hard work.'
'Is this one of the jobs you do every day?'

Low geographical attainment:
Simple comments pertaining to geography. Only a basic understanding of geographical concepts and principles covered.
Little notion of interrelationships of people with their environments.
Little appreciation of the role of geography in addressing issues.
Few, if any, solutions offered to geographical problems stated. No mention of alternative solutions. Little appreciation of consequences of actions.
Use of geographical terms limited, inappropriate or incorrect.
Role of values misunderstood.

Medium geographical attainment:
Detailed comments pertaining to geography. Understanding of a number of geographical concepts and principles covered.
Some notion of the interrelationships of people with their environments.
Some appreciation of the role of geography in addressing issues.
Solutions offered to geographical problems stated. Some mention of alternative solutions. An appreciation of consequences of actions revealed.
Use of geographical terms usually appropriate and correct.
Role of values largely understood.

High geographical attainment:
Detailed and accurate comments pertaining to geography.
Understanding of geographical concepts and principles covered.
Clear notion of the interrelationship of people with their environment.
Appreciation of the role of geography in addressing issues.
Appropriate solutions offered to geographical problems stated. Mention of appropriate alternative solutions. A clear appreciation of consequences of actions revealed. Use of geographical terms appropriate and correct.
Role of values understood.

REFERENCES

Andrews, R. (1992) 'Editorial'. *English in Education*, **26**(2), 1–3.
Barnes, D. (1976) *From Communication to Curriculum*. Harmondsworth: Penguin.
Barnes, D., Britton, J. and Rosen, H. (1971) *Language, the Learner and the School*. Harmondsworth: Penguin.
Britton, J., Burgess, T., Martin, N., McLeod, A. and Rosen, H. (1975) *The Development of Writing Abilities (11–18)*. London: Macmillan.
Butt, G. (1991) 'An investigation into the effects of audience centred teaching on children's writing in geography.' Unpublished MA dissertation. University of London Institute of Education.

Butt, G. (1993) 'The effects of "audience centred" teaching on children's writing in geography.' *International Research in Geographical and Environmental Education*, 2(1), 11–24.

Carter, R. (ed.) (1991) *Talking about Geography*. Sheffield: Geographical Association.

Christie, F. and Rothery, J. (1989) 'Genres and writing: a response to Michael Rosen.' *English in Australia*, 90, 3–4.

Chomsky, N. (1968) *Language and Mind*. New York: Harcourt, Brace, Jovanovich.

Delamont, S. (ed.) (1984) *Readings on Interaction in the Classroom*. London: Methuen.

DES (1975) *A Language for Life: The Bullock Report*. London: HMSO.

DES (1989) *The Cox Report*. London: HMSO.

Fien, J. and Gerber, R. (eds) (1986) *Teaching Geography for a Better World*. Brisbane: AGTA/Jacaranda Press.

Gilbert, R. (1984) *The Impotent Image*. Lewes: Falmer.

Gilbert, R. (1989) 'Language and ideology in geography teaching.' In F.A. Slater (ed.) *Language and Learning in the Teaching of Geography*. London: Routledge.

Henley, R. (1989) 'The ideology of geography language.' In F.A. Slater (ed.) *Language and Learning in the Teaching of Geography*. London: Routledge.

Hull, R. (1985) *The Language Gap*. London: Methuen.

Johnston, B. (1987) *Assessing English*. Milton Keynes: Open University Press.

Kress, G.R. (1989) 'Texture and meaning.' In R. Andrews (ed.) *Narrative and Argument*. Milton Keynes: Open University Press.

Kress, G.R. and Knapp, P. (1992) 'Genre in a social theory of language.' *English in Education*, 26, 4–15.

McNeill, E. (1966) *The Concept of Human Development*. London: Wadsworth.

Martin, N., D'Arcy, P., Newton, B. and Parker, R. (1976) *Writing and Learning Across the Curriculum*. London: Ward Lock.

Piaget, J. (1959) *Language and Thought of the Child*. London: Routledge.

Poynton, C. (1985) *Language and Gender: Making the Difference*. Victoria: Deakin University Press.

Roberts, M. (1986) 'Talking, reading and writing.' In D. Boardman (ed.) *Handbook for Geography Teachers*. Sheffield: Geographical Association.

Rosen, M. (1988) 'Will genre theory change the world?' *English in Australia*, 88, 18–23.

Slater, F.A. (1983) *Learning Through Geography*. London: Heinemann.

Slater, F.A. (1989) *Language and Learning in the Teaching of Geography*. London: Routledge.

Stratta, L. and Dixon, J. (1992) 'The National Curriculum in English: does genre theory have anything to offer?' *English in Education*, 26(2), 16–27.

Vygotsky, L.S. (1962). *Thought and Language*. Cambridge MA: MIT Press.

Wilding, S. (1989a) *A Shift from Monocultured to Polycultured Approaches in Geography*. Occasional Paper No. 3. Staffordshire Oracy Project. Stafford: National Oracy Project.

Wilding, S. (1989b) 'Geoging along.' *Staffordshire Oracy Project*. Stafford: National Oracy Project.

Williams, M. (ed.) (1981) *Language, Teaching and Learning Geography*. London: Ward Lock.

Chapter 16

Matching Practice and Vision: Evaluating Global Education

Miriam Moscovitch Steiner

This chapter describes some recent research to evaluate how effectively active learning methodologies help children understand the issues, develop the skills and explore the attitudes central to global education. It will provide a background about world studies in Britain, discuss the interrelationship between research *questions* and research *methodologies*, and share the processes and results of the research. The terms 'world studies' and 'global education' are used interchangeably throughout.

WORLD STUDIES: A BRIEF OUTLINE

'World studies' is a short-hand term. It describes the need for a multicultural and global dimension to the curriculum, and ways to achieve this: 'World studies aims to develop the knowledge, attitudes and skills which young people need in order to practise social and environmental responsibility in a multicultural society and an interdependent world' (Hicks and Steiner, 1989, Preface). It is grounded in a radical and critical analysis of society and economics, which is essentially transformational rather than reforming (Richardson, 1990, pp. 42–3; see Tables 16.1 and 16.2 on pp. 210–11). The pedagogical principles underpinning global education classroom methodologies and activities derive from Paulo Freire (1976) and from the field of humanistic psychology, as exemplified in the work of Carl Rogers (Rogers, 1969, 1983).

The particular programme which underlay the research described in this chapter is World Studies 8–13. The Project's handbook (Fisher and Hicks, 1985) sets out a series of learning objectives based on a framework of core concepts, attitudes, skills and knowledge (see Figures 16.1 and 16.2). These objectives draw together the *values* of a radical political perspective; the *procedural principles* of liberal education (for example, the Humanities Curriculum Project and the Place, Time and Society Schools Council Project (History, Geography and Social Science 8–13) of the 1970s); the *critical analysis* of the then (early 1980s) emerging view of environmental education as education for sustainability; and the *global focus* of development education and peace education.

Pike (1990) provides a fuller account of the evolution of world studies in the UK. (A chronological history of world studies/global education is found in Appendix 1.) He points out that the parallel American movement was influenced by the dynamics of the cold war and tended to focus on knowledge-based 'area studies' to promote international understanding. Two other developments in American educational thought and practice were more significant for British world studies. One was the *Taba Program in Social Science* (Ellis and Durkin, 1972; Taba, 1982), which linked a closely structured instructional framework to a holistic model (intellectual, social and affective) of children's development. The other was the cluster of handbooks and manuals promoting conflict resolution and peace education (such as Prutzman *et al.*, 1978).

In World Studies 8–13, issues of social and economic justice, sustainability and global interdependence are introduced to children at appropriate levels of description and conceptualization. The arguments of writers such as Huckle (1983, 1988), Hicks, D. (1988) and Fien (1992) about the role of geographical and environmental education as a transformative agency, the application of a holistic systems model to explain global interdependence (Pike and Selby, 1988), and the perceptions about the structural violence of patriarchy and the need for new paradigms and perspectives for the future (Hicks and Steiner, 1989) are not spelled out in the classroom for activities for 8–13-year-olds. They are, however, clearly argued in the chapters for teachers in the texts which formed the basis of the research described here, and in many excellent development education and global education resources for primary education (e.g. Whitaker, 1984; Fisher and Hicks, 1985; Hicks and Steiner, 1989; McFarlane, 1986, 1991).

World studies and controversial issues

World studies is not tied to particular subjects or disciplines (although it has been shown to support the current emphasis on subjects in the English and Welsh National Curricula: Steiner, 1993). The holistic framework is naturally grounded in a conceptual approach to learning:

> pupils were able to explore quite complex ideas because teachers had recognised the impossibility of defining today exactly what knowledge will be essential for the 1990s and beyond. As a result they had adopted a conceptual approach to learning, helping children to understand and use some of the key concepts relating to world society and world studies. To do this involved the children in a continual process of thinking about both their own experience and that of others.
>
> (Fisher and Hicks, 1985, p. 14)

Research in the UK during the late 1970s and early 1980s demonstrated that children in pre-adolescent middle years are potentially more tolerant and open-minded about difference than they are later (Carnie, 1972, p. 9).

Piaget's view (1926), suggesting that young children are incapable of abstract and logical thought, may in the past have discouraged teachers of younger children from using an issues-based inquiry approach. Recent research has shown that children are much more capable of making distinctions, of reasoning and of articulating opposing viewpoints (Short, 1988), and my own experience in classrooms supports this. It seems unquestionable that either the television images and reportage children experience at a very early age have accelerated their development beyond the levels Piaget described, or that his original observations were insufficiently wide.

While world studies is not tied to specific subjects (such as geography), it is not content-free. Global education has been characterized by some critics as being 'process-rich but content-poor'. This is a misunderstanding of its framework, although the manner in which individual teachers choose to use any curricular programme is beyond the control of its developers. Both *World Studies 8–13: A Teacher's Handbook* (Fisher and Hicks, 1985) and *Making Global Connections* (Hicks and Steiner, 1989) explicitly link participatory activities to topics that illuminate key concepts such as *justice, interdependence*, *power* and *change*. Specific global issues (such as unequal trade and development, sex-role stereotyping, aboriginal perspectives, consumption and environment) form the content for many discussion-based activities.

It is because controversial themes such as these form the substance of world studies that its approach to learning is so clearly linked to the traditions of democratic procedural values.

World studies and active learning

The global education view of the curriculum supports a cross-curricular approach, and its classroom principles promote learner autonomy and empowerment. On the one hand, a critical, self-actualizing pedagogy, building the habits of critical reflection and democratic discussion, is clearly implied in any programme grounded in social justice. Creating democratic people for life in just communities should take place in environments where learner autonomy, openness, co-operation and civility are prized above deference and unquestioning conformity:

> Democracy is best learned in a democratic setting where participation is encouraged, where views can be expressed openly and discussed, where there is freedom of expression for pupils and teachers and where there is fairness and justice. An appropriate climate is, therefore, an essential complement to reflective learning about human rights.
>
> (Council of Europe, 1985, Appendix 4.1)

Humanistic psychology also argues that the more the learning experience engages a range of senses, feelings and critical faculties; and the more interactive the relationship between teacher and learner, between learner and subject matter, the deeper and more enduring the learning (Hicks and Steiner, 1989). Starting from this premise, one could expect to see a cluster of learning outcomes ranging from deeper understanding of facts and principles, through greater self-esteem and self-confidence, increased motivation, more understanding and tolerance of peers and others, to a greater commitment to the procedural values of democracy and the skills to practise them.

Student-centred learning (Brandes and Ginnis, 1986) is about an attitude to the relative power positions of teacher and learner: it does not rule out instructor-led teaching. *Active learning* is logically applicable to a diverse range of learning activities, ranging from individual or group problem solving (with or without computers), small-group discussion (with or without critical examination of 'evidence'), and affective experience through role-play and simulation.

The essence of active learning is defined by phrases such as 'learning by experience', 'learning by doing' or 'through action', 'through talk', 'decision making', and 'co-operative and collaborative groupwork':

My view is that active learning, in essence, can be described as the use of learning activities where pupils are given a marked degree of ownership and control over the learning activities used, where the learning experience is open-ended rather than tightly predetermined, and where the pupil is able to actively participate and shape the learning experience.

(Kyriacou, 1992, pp. 310–11)

A large body of research supports both the social and cognitive gains children can make through participating in structured collaborative and co-operative activities (e.g. Johnson and Johnson, 1975; Biott, 1984; Slavin, 1989; Bennett and Dunne, 1992; Galton and Williamson, 1992).

RESEARCHING WORLD STUDIES AND ACTIVE LEARNING

After over a decade of global education work in primary education throughout the UK, and with the advent of the changing National Curriculum, it seemed pertinent to go beyond the generalizations that had sustained this approach and to find out what was going on in the field. What impact, if any, did teachers using this approach perceive it had had on children's development and understanding? The National Curriculum was generating a renewed debate about how children best learn and about the content of the curriculum. The developmental touchstone was the set of twenty-five learning objectives described in the *World Studies 8–13 Teacher's Handbook* (Fisher and Hicks, 1985), which have been accepted as a representative statement of the cognitive and social aspects of global education (see Figures 16.1 and 16.2).

I wanted to find out whether the kinds of discussion-based, experiential and co-operative groupwork activity described in the *World Studies 8–13 Handbook* (Fisher and Hicks, 1985), *Making Global Connections* (Hicks and Steiner, 1989), *Global Teacher, Global Learner* (Pike and Selby, 1988) or the many other publications in this field actually do contribute to the process of children becoming more able to express thoughts and feelings in a constructive way, to listen to and respect others' opinions, to work collaboratively and so forth. Do these kinds of activity help them understand very basic concepts, like change, justice and interdependence? Will children demonstrate greater tolerance and understanding of difference – different places and ways of life – and greater *in*tolerance of racism, sexism and all kinds of discrimination? The research task was to find out whether, and where, any of these developments had occurred.

Evaluation as engagement: ethical and methodological issues

Evaluation is the process of marshalling information and arguments which enable interested individuals and groups to participate in the critical debate about a specific programme.

(Kemmis, 1986, p. 118)

The time (1990–92) for this was ripe. The 1988 Education Reform Act had led to profound structural changes in education in England, Northern Ireland and Wales. By 1990, the National Curriculum (Mark I) was already causing sleepless nights to teachers throughout the land. There was also a growing concern about how to promote children's moral, spiritual and cultural development. The constrained curriculum and pressure on teachers to work in new ways had created a challenge for less formal approaches to teaching and learning. If teachers believed that world studies classroom methodologies were a valid 'instrument' to enhance knowledge and understanding of the world, learning and communication skills, and social development, global education could have solid grounding in the emerging educational context.

How would teachers already familiar with world studies be reacting? Anecdotal evidence indicated that even some long-experienced 'global educators' were feeling the need to change to more formal methods. With a growing emphasis on assessment and testing, many teachers were looking for more child-centred ways to assess children's performance and development.

The 'evaluand' would be the set of *methodologies* described in the resources that support world studies, not the *performance* of either individual teachers or children. There was a host of 'clients' with an interest in reviewing their investment in the work, including:

- charitable funders of World Studies 8–13 and of other similar projects in development education (one large funder had withdrawn from funding the public education sector about this time, because its trustees concluded there were insufficient 'results' in the form of changed social attitudes or behaviour);
- local education authority (LEA) advisers, inspectors and education committees who had committed time and money to in-service and dissemination programmes for world studies (over 50 LEAs throughout England);
- teachers who had invested time, effort and commitment;
- individuals in the development education centres (DECs) throughout Britain who work with this programme and other similar philosophies and resources.

The World Studies Trust obtained funding from a group of development education charities for an evaluation project which I was asked to direct. In the jargon of this enterprise, I was both a 'client' for this evaluation and a 'stakeholder' in its success: as a former classroom teacher, in-service provider and co-author of a World Studies 8–13 text, I had participated in its construction and evolving practice. Would (and should) the fact that I was clearly an advocate rule me out as its evaluator?

I believed that it was both practically, theoretically and ethically possible to construct an evaluation programme that would provide opportunities for practitioners to feed back their views and judgements on the basis of their own beliefs, experiences and practices. I shared the view held by Parlett, *inter alia*, that:

> the respect for different outlooks is based on the conviction that those in, say, an educational programme (the different teachers, the outside supervisors or advisers, the students) have not only insights that are worth knowing about but also have a right to be heard. Each participant in an enterprise is a theory-builder, explainer, advocate, observer, rapporteur, informant: each has a unique perspective, vantage point and 'stance'.
>
> (Parlett, 1981, p. 224)

A growing body of argument and research supports the proposition than neither research nor evaluation is value-free, and that the researcher/evaluator is not, and cannot and should not claim to be, a 'neutral outsider', other than in Parlett's (1981, p. 224) sense of '... not endorsing any one viewpoint, outlook or set of beliefs to the exclusion of others'. This evaluation started from the premise that it could be ethically undertaken by a researcher committed to the project under review and that a body of methodologies existed which would enable the process to be accurate, valid and consistent with its own value position. Qualitative research is itself an ethical endeavour – ethical in its purposes and its processes. It would therefore draw from an illuminative/qualitative/naturalistic/ constructivist model, which is also congruent with a feminist perspective (e.g. Kirkup, 1986; Harding, 1986; Guba and Lincoln, 1989).

The constructivist approach sets itself in opposition to the positivist on ontological and epistemological grounds, arguing essentially for the contextual (cultural, social, political, geographical, professional, genderized, etc.) specificities of experience and the impossibility of universal 'laws'. Feminism, in its widest sense, provides added moral, as well as epistemological, weight for acknowledging the value of the individual stance. It critiques '... a positivistic epistemology which separates the body from the mind, which extracts feeling and emotion from the material ...' (Blackmore, 1989, p. 119).

Feminist theorists argue that women's experiences are qualitatively different from men's, providing women with perspectives and understandings that are both unique in individual terms yet similar within our gender set. We reconstruct our actions and explain them to ourselves in the light of theories based on male norms. Furthermore, because of a sense of disconnection from a male-defined 'reality', women often feel deprived of an authentic voice to share any understanding of our experiences with others (Calloway, 1981; Gilligan, 1982; Belenky *et al.*, 1986). As so many primary teachers are women, it seems vital to embed this understanding in classroom research.

Thus the methodological stance of constructivism would also provide a framework to hear these voices; for women (and men) teachers to 'tell their stories'. Other research into how teachers construct personal and professional meanings for and out of their experience underpins this methodology, and also confirms that most teachers engage in teaching on the basis of strong value positions, both moral and social (Nias, 1989).

These paradigms, in which the social, political, value-oriented and relative nature of inquiry is made explicit and in which the research tools maximize opportunities for individual narrative, are evidently congruent with a global education framework:

> Paradigms are called worldviews not only because they premise an undergirding set of beliefs about the nature of the world and how to inquire into it, but also because they have profound implications for how we construe our political affairs, how we adjudge activity to be moral or ethical, and how we provide for justice in social relations. They represent more than a philosophical backdrop – the scenery – against which resonant inquiry methodologies – the scenario – can be constructed and tested. They are ultimately the touchstones of our lives.
>
> (Guba and Lincoln, 1989, p. 117)

Furthermore, I would argue that these are the only appropriate methodologies for inquiries set in the contexts where value issues are overtly on the agenda – including geographical and environmental education – as well as the more obvious members of the 'social curriculum' (Dufour, 1990): 'The truths to be told about educational programmes are social truths. They are negotiated among those who claim to know it and those who want to know better' (Kemmis, 1986, p. 119). In this paradigm, such 'truths' are not necessarily linked to measurable phenomena, although it can be appropriate to use a multifaceted research model in which quantitative methods are employed. The philosophical baseline must be to reject the premise that what cannot be measured cannot be real or knowable or true. If you can measure it, does that make it 'true'; and if you cannot, is it not?

Starting from this perspective poses interesting questions in respect of formulating 'performance indicators' in global education. You can find out whether children know what the words 'co-operation' and 'justice' mean; you cannot give a mark out of ten for how co-operatively or justly they behave. You can test whether they know facts about both their own and other countries and cultures; you cannot grade their sense of interdependence or lack of prejudices. However, this does not mean that it is either inappropriate or impossible to attempt to see whether these kinds of skill or attitude are growing. What you are looking for and how you define development are the key questions. I have explored the question 'Are "performance indicators" and attainment targets the most appropriate concepts in such contexts?' elsewhere (Steiner, 1993).

> At root here is a fundamental dilemma. Those personal qualities that we hold dear – resilience and courage in the face of stress, a sense of craft in our work, a commitment to justice and caring in our personal relationships, a dedication to advancing the public good in our communal life – are exceedingly difficult to assess. And so unfortunately, we are apt to measure what we can, and eventually come to value what is measured over what is left unmeasured. The shift is subtle, and occurs gradually. It first invades our language and then slowly begins to dominate our thinking. It is all around us, and we too are part of it. In neither academic nor popular discourse about schools does one find nowadays much reference to the important human qualities listed above. The language of academic achievement tests has become the primary rhetoric of schooling.
>
> (Committee of the National Academy of Education, 1991, p. 22)

Framing the inquiry

The key question was how a 'globally educated' young person might be recognized. Some key possibilities presented themselves.

- What would she or he say or do (or not say and not do)?
- How might she or he behave in school? Would there be evidence of more co-operation in the classroom and more peaceful playgrounds?
- Would she or he more clearly and confidently express opinions based on fact?
- Would there be evidence of wider social behaviour, such as clearly being more environmentally responsible, taking up issues of discrimination?

The inquiry had two components:

1. Finding out what people who have used this approach (teachers, advisory teachers, DEC workers) thought about World Studies 8–13. What were their views about its goals and its claims about children and learning?
2. Setting up a programme in which teachers would observe and report back on a group of children taking part in activities based on global education – process *and* content.

Asking the users

I set out to discover the opinions of people who had been involved with world studies as theorists and as users. I wanted to find out what their definitions of 'success' were: what did they think a 'world studies' child would look like? I felt that using a variety of methods to collect these data would provide depth, vigour and comparability. This was done through:

- direct interviews with people throughout England, known to me either through their writing or through the networks within world studies: theorists, headteachers, advisers, inspectors, teachers, lecturers and workers in the development education community (eighty-six people);
- written personal statements from people in the categories above whom I was unable to meet (twenty-three letters);
- a structured, 'closed' questionnaire sent to teachers who had previously taken part in LEA-wide initiatives: Bury, Trafford and South Tyneside (forty-four respondents). This asked for a rating on a five-point Likert scale of the themes and resources associated with world studies. Space was also provided for written comment and feedback about use of the project in the respondent's school;
- an open-ended questionnaire sent to teachers participating in the classroom research exercise (forty respondents: see Appendix 2);
- speaking with classes I had taught in several Manchester primary schools.

The responses

In this way almost two hundred people shared their opinions about whether world studies processes 'work'; about how they believed it had (or had not) contributed to children's development and understanding. Three categories of response emerged. The 109 people who wrote to me voluntarily or took part in an interview can be described as *advocates*, *enthusiasts* or *sympathizers*. *Advocates* are generally people professionally involved in fields like development education. Their working lives are concerned with the promotion of the global dimension. *Enthusiasts* are teachers or advisory teachers who have attended in-service courses or conferences and whose practice in the classroom has been significantly affected. Their accounts focused essentially on personal practice and convictions. The *sympathizers* are predominantly headteachers and LEA advisers and inspectors (some of whom are also enthusiasts). They described the impact of world studies with the overview of a whole school or LEA.

This last group generally lauded the effect both on children's learning and behaviour, and on the overall atmosphere in a school. Their analysis of how teachers translate world studies into their practice was that teachers are enthusiastic about the focused affirmation, co-operation and self-esteem work. Those who feel interest or conviction about the wider 'issues' will take these on too. They were divided in their predictions about the impact of the National Curriculum: optimists seeing opportunities and, indeed, insisting upon them; pessimists fearing a narrowing down, with an escalating emphasis on teaching to tests. The advocates and enthusiasts were essentially all optimists!

A picture emerged about how the different elements of the '8–13' model were actually used in the classroom. Most teachers concentrated on the self-esteem building, interpersonal and co-operative elements of the world studies approach. In terms of work engaging with 'global' issues, the environment, local or 'rainforest', was a common theme, as well as activities that question stereotypes such as racism or sexism. Structural issues, such as those to do with the injustice inherent in the current systems of the global economy, or, conversely, deliberately highlighting the positive cultural and social attainments and self-sufficiency of southern societies in order to counter the media-projected images of dependence, received far less attention. As in all summaries of such surveys, there are significant variations at both ends of the scale. While such 'global issues' may be a lower priority for most primary teachers, it appears from their responses that those who do take it on do so with commitment, vigour and balance (Steiner, 1992).

'Performance indicators' in global education? Establishing a framework

As discussed earlier, it seemed clear from the outset that any 'performance indicators' could not be about measurable phenomena. This is reinforced by the fact that the active learning methodologies in question are, by their nature and design, open-ended. Their aim is to foster critical thinking and self-awareness, not to inculcate specific, measurable opinions.

World studies is not a formal knowledge curriculum, such as can be found in some states in the US that have Model Learner Outcomes for International Education (e.g. Minnesota Department of Education: Wangen *et al.*, 1991). One American approach has been to develop test formats which measure how much information about global issues children have learned and whether attitudes have been affected (e.g. Torney-Purta, 1986). The British position has been that increased knowledge, which is an essential part of global education, is achieved through the way teachers interpret and augment the given content of whatever curriculum they are teaching. Previously this was left to individual teachers and schools; the common framework of the new National Curriculum offers exciting scope for wider learning about the world.

The map by which the children's development would be charted was the twenty-five learning objectives published in the *World Studies 8–13 Handbook* (Fisher and Hicks, 1985, pp. 25 and 30; see below). Did they use these specific skills more, less or about the same? Did they show that they grasped these concepts well, somewhat or not at all?

Unless assessment of the children's development is based exclusively on right-or-wrong factual tests, the teacher's professional judgement will always be the means through which outsiders come to know an individual child's performance and potential. What did teachers have in mind when they used these ideas and associated resources? The teacher is the prism through which the original 'pure' concept is filtered. What were her or his intentions and hoped-for outcomes in the children's learning, understanding and behaviour?

The evidence of interviews, questionnaires and letters shows what advocates, enthusiasts and sympathizers believed about the effectiveness of active learning. There is wide agreement in the fields of educational evaluation and values education about the inherent difficulties in establishing valid and consistent performance indicators in fields akin to world studies (Black and Dockerell, 1980; Price, 1984; Dorion, 1990). If they were presented with tasks with a global education focus, would teachers assess children's reactions in similar and consistent ways? Having identified possible performance indicators, how could a teacher systematically look for evidence?

There were a number of possible options:

- construct from scratch or use already-tested attitudinal measurements instruments, administered before and after a fixed piece of work about other cultures or countries;

Knowledge

Ourselves and others

Pupils should know about their own society and culture and their place in it. They should also know about certain societies and cultures other than their own, including minority cultures within their own society. They should understand the nature of interdependence, and the economic and cultural influence – both helpful and harmful – of other people on their own way of life.

Rich and poor

Pupils should know about major inequalities of wealth and power in the world, both between and within other countries and in their own. They should understand why such inequalities persist and about efforts being made to reduce them.

Peace and conflict

Pupils should know about the main conflicts currently in the news and in the recent past, and about attempts to resolve such conflicts. They should also know about the ways of resolving conflicts in everyday life.

Our environment

Pupils should know about the basic geography, history and ecology of the earth. They should understand the interdependence of people and planet and should know about measures being taken to protect the environment both locally and globally.

The world tomorrow

Pupils should know how to investigate and reflect on a variety of possible futures: personal, local, national and for the world as a whole. They should also be aware of ways in which they may act to influence the future.

Attitudes

Human dignity

Pupils should have a sense of their own worth as individuals, and that of others, and of the worth of their own particular social, cultural and family background.

Curiosity

Pupils should be interested to find out more about issues related to living in a multicultural society and an interdependent world.

Appreciation of other cultures

Pupils should be ready to find aspects of other cultures of value to themselves and to learn from them.

Empathy

Pupils should be willing to imagine the feelings and viewpoints of other people, particularly people in cultures and situations different from their own.

Justice and fairness

Pupils should value genuinely democratic principles and processes at local, national and international levels and be ready to work for a more just world.

Skills

Enquiry

Pupils should be able to find out and record information about world issues from a variety of sources, including printed and audio-visual, and through interviews with people.

Communication skills

Pupils should be able to describe and explain their ideas about the world in a variety of ways: in writing, in discussion and in various art forms; and with a variety of other people, including members of other groups and cultures.

Grasping concepts

Pupils should be able to understand certain basic concepts relating to world society, to use these concepts to make generalisations and to support and test these.

Critical thinking

Pupils should be able to approach issues with an open and critical mind and to change their ideas as they learn more.

Political skills

Pupils should be developing the ability to influence decision-making at local, national and international levels.

- work alongside a small sample of committed and uncommitted teachers to observe and record children's behaviour;
- design an exercise that teachers, whether experienced or inexperienced in world studies, could use independently.

Surveying attitudes did not seem right on a number of grounds. It was only one part of the story. Considerable research into children's attitudes about other groups, based on word association and similar exercises, already exists (Price, 1984; Jungkunz, 1987; Thomas and Chapman, 1991), though I have long shared reservations about these techniques with others (e.g. UNESCO, 1965). These reservations include the following:

- Explicitly articulating negative views about any group can be dangerous in case these are reinforced or legitimized (for example, 'Circle the word that best describes your opinion: Russians are honest, lazy, dangerous, jolly ...' etc.).
- Most attitudinal instruments are closed – that is, they offer a limited range of answers – making them at worst unreliable and at best trivial. One cannot know whether the child is trying to guess a 'right' answer or expressing genuine convictions.
- Even with more open-ended formats, children may decide they know or can guess the 'proper' answer and put down what they think the teacher wants to hear.
- Children in different schools and in the same classroom will be starting from different knowledge bases. This can influence both the *kinds* of attitude expressed (from deriving from 'informed opinion' at one end of the scale to being totally new territory for the child at the other) and their *authenticity* (deep or superficial conviction). This weakens any comparability.

Concepts for use in world studies

Causes and consequences

Our actions and also events in the wider world have different sorts of causes. Similarly, actions and decisions, whether ours, other people's or those of governments or big business, have different sorts of consequences, often unintended or unforeseen. Understanding causes and consequences can give us more control over our own lives and also make events in the wider world more comprehensible.

Communication

People exchange information, views and feelings in a variety of different ways and languages, both with and without words. Clear communication is essential if we are to understand the motives and actions of others and if we are to be understood by others. The mass media are primary communicators of information about the wider world and, inevitably, of bias and distortion also.

Conflict

We live in a world of conflict. Human beings continually disagree with each other, and often fight with each other. This happens in our own society, in other societies and between our society and others. Conflicts can be analysed and resolved in a variety of ways. Understanding how conflicts occur can make it easier to resolve them constructively.

Co-operation

Individuals, groups and countries often work together, or at least wish to appear to be doing so, in order to tackle common problems. Co-operation enables tasks to be performed which would not otherwise be possible. It is essential if conflicts are to be resolved peacefully. Co-operation can be as stimulating and rewarding as many forms of competition, requiring as it does a high level of communication and sensitivity to others.

Distribution of power

People and groups are able to influence what happens in the world. In most groups, countries, and in the world as a whole, power and wealth are distributed unequally. This affects people's life chances, their freedom and welfare. An awareness of this inequality raises important questions about fairness and justice.

Fairness

Fairness involves respecting the rights of other people and seeking solutions to conflict which take into account the interests of all parties. Some laws are an attempt to institutionalise fairness at national and international levels. For the world to be a fairer place, priority needs to be placed on the fulfilment of essential human needs through patterns of living which are equitable and in harmony with the planet.

Interdependence

People depend on each other in a variety of ways, ranging from caring and emotional support to the exchange of goods and services. This interdependence pervades every aspect of life, at individual, group and international level. It can have both positive and negative effects. The most urgent problems facing humankind need to be tackled at the global level and across national boundaries, as well as at the local level.

Similarities and differences

There are many different ways of doing things and not all human beings do the same as we do. But everyone has a similar nature deep down, the same physical needs and similar wishes and hopes, for example for friendship, love, happiness, enjoyment. It is important to find out about and understand both the differences between people, and those things which we all have in common.

Social change

Change is a constant feature of world society. It is brought about by people, whether deliberately or by accident. The best place to begin changing things for the better is where each individual happens to be, each with their own background, needs and aspirations. In order to do this people need to be free to take maximum control over their own lives.

Values and beliefs

People have different views about what is important. Ways of live, behaviour and traditions vary. Our values and beliefs, our sex, social and cultural background, affect the way we perceive people and events, and the way other people see us. Finding out about the values and beliefs of other people can help us to understand them, and ourselves, better.

● The same applies to reading levels. Too simple a task cannot elicit a subtle response; a too complex one will be unequal.

Thus I decided on the third option: a task in which teachers on their own would observe children using active learning methodologies at two different periods in the school year, describing and evaluating their behaviours:

> It is well known that almost any course works well in the classroom if it is taught by its inventors or by a few of their highly trained converts ... To get a valid test of feasibility you must turn over the programme to teachers who are a fair sample of the people who would be teaching it if it were adopted on the scale for which it was intended.
>
> (Moise, 1968, p. 20)

Classroom-based research also offered an opportunity both to compare how teachers in different parts of England approach global education and to see whether there are any differences in the way they might interpret World Studies 8–13, development education and global education. Insights into this might emerge through the volunteers/recruits.

Preparing the ground

This exercise had three components:

1. to design a research package that could be used by a wide range of teachers in a variety of schools;
2. to prepare a bank of commonly agreed outcomes, at different levels, for the '8–13' framework of objectives;
3. to identify volunteer teachers, representing a spectrum of experience, from as diverse and geographically wide an area as possible.

The literature of evaluation (e.g. Parlett, 1981; Kemmis, 1986; Guba and Lincoln, 1989) emphasizes the importance of consultation in the design and process of evaluation. Thus I set up a consultation day, at which a group of teachers, LEA advisers, inspectors and workers in development education from around the UK met and drew up representative outcomes (what a child might say or do) to show some grasp of the world studies object-ives. They also suggested some core activities from the large repertoire of global education that could be widely adapted across the curriculum, and advice on appropriate ways for teachers to record their observations (Steiner, 1993, pp. 32–3, 56–9).

Following this consultation, I designed a classroom investigation in which teachers would set up an active learning exercise, observe a small group (eight children), record their reactions and behaviour, relate these to a common set of criteria drawn from global education, and send me the results. This was to be done twice: early in the autumn term (1991) and repeated towards the end of the spring term (1992). A compact booklet described the organization of the research exercise, explained the three core activities, and suggested suitable content and resources for global education within the context of the National Curriculum (in its summer 1991 form). It also provided several formats for lesson plans, individual and group observation schedules, and lesson evaluation by both teacher and children. There were forms to record basic data about the school and children. An open-ended questionnaire, 'World studies: experiences, views and visions', enabled me to be in touch with the participants' views about teach-ing and learning in its widest sense, as well as their criteria for success in terms of world studies (see Appendix 2).

The format was open-ended throughout, other than the requests for background in-formation. The world studies principle of valuing the individual and individual expression was placed at the heart of the exercise. All the teachers' response sheets and the activities the children used invited people to state their ideas, beliefs and values. The children were asked for feedback, using both an evaluation sheet with a four-point positive–negative rating of several components of the group activity, and written opin-ions (which they used to pleasing effect).

I identified potential participants by writing to LEA advisers, inspectors and develop-ment education workers I knew throughout England in July 1991. Clearly it was essential that anyone taking part shared a common broad understanding of, and commit-ment to, the core practices and values entailed in global education. My contacts looked to their own constituencies and passed on the names of teachers who, in their judge-ment, had this background and who had agreed to take part. The final group ranged geographically from South Tyneside to Bournemouth, with solid representation from the North West and Midlands.

The teacher/researchers

What might be the characteristics of teachers who are drawn to and use a world studies approach whose values system and pedagogy have been described above? Those who 'sign on' implicitly and explicitly accept a set of beliefs/values about human beings (they are essentially good, improvable and autonomous), about education (it is fundamentally an instrument for personal development and social justice), and about social and economic systems (they are, currently, unjustly constituted and deforming).

Within the overall framework, they may range in their positions from 'conforming' to

Table 16.1 Attitudes to the Status Quo: Stances Amongst the Power-less

FOUR COMPONENTS OF POLITICAL OUTLOOK

	FOUR TYPES OF RESPONSE TOWARDS THE POLITICAL STATUS QUO			
	(1) CONFORMING	(2) REFORMING	(3) DEFORMING	(4) TRANSFORMING
(1) DESCRIBING What is the problem?	EITHER – 'There is no problem': OR – 'Survival, how to get through one day at a time ...'	'We're not clever enough, not good enough ... and certain individual oppressors are to blame ...'	'The oppressor is the problem ...'	'Unequal benefits and losses, therefore, injustice ...'
(2) DIAGNOSING What is the cause of the problem?	'There is no cause, things just happen, it's luck, chance, the stars, the gods ...'	'The attitudes and abilities of certain individuals ...'	'Oppressors never give up power of their own free will ...'	'The whole network of structures and attitudes which we inherit from the past'
(3) ACTING What should be done?	'Nothing can be done, just hope for a miracle or saviour, a change in your luck ...'	'Improve ourselves, take pride in ourselves, remove certain individuals ...'	'Disengage from, resist, struggle against, eventually destroy, the oppressor ...'	'Both structural and personal change — towards ever greater equality of work, power, wealth, esteem ...'
(4) WANTING What is the aim?	'Paradise — an end to all our troubles and anxieties, an end to conflict ...'	'Make the system work well – harmony, tolerance, equality of opportunity ...'	'It is not profitable to speculate about utopia — first destroy the oppressive present ...'	'Never-ending self-critical development towards new power relations and new people ...'

Source: Richardson, 1990, published by Trentham Books. Reprinted by permission of the publisher.

Table 16.2 Attitudes to the Status Quo: Stances Amongst the Power-ful

FOUR COMPONENTS OF POLITICAL OUTLOOK	FOUR TYPES OF RESPONSE TOWARDS THE POLITICAL STATUS QUO			
	(1) CONFORMING	(2) REFORMING	(3) DEFORMING	(4) TRANSFORMING
(1) DESCRIBING What is the problem?	EITHER — 'There is no problem (all's well with the world)': OR — 'Survival is the problem — trouble-makers. enemies of the state...'	'If people are poor, that is mainly their own fault ... but certain individuals in power need to change as well ...'	'The oppressor is the problem'	'Unequal benefits and losses, therefore, injustice ...'
(2) DIAGNOSING What is the cause of the problem?	'Problems are caused by *evil* — evil people, evil power, plotting revolution, plotting world domination...'	'The attitudes and abilities of certain individuals ...'	'Oppressors were created by history ...'	'The whole network of structures and attitudes which we inherit from the past ...'
(3) ACTING What should be done?	'Evil should at least be resisted and contained ... preferably should be stamped out...'	'Give people more skills and will to achieve ... promote greater responsibility amongst leaders ...'	'Sabotage the system from inside .... *or* disengage from it altogether...'	'Both structural and personal change — towards ever greater equality of work, power, wealth, esteem ...'
(4) WANTING What is the aim?	'Security, order — an absence of threat, anxiety, conflict ...'	'Make the present system work well — harmony, tolerance, equality, of opportunity...'	'It is not profitable to speculate about utopia — first destroy the oppressive present...'	'Never-ending, self-critical development towards new power relations and new people ...'

Source: Richardson, 1990, published by Trentham Books. Reprinted by permission of the publisher.

'transforming' (see Tables 16.1 and 16.2 on pp. 210–11). I would argue that teachers of geography and environmental education fall within the same spectrum, and this has implications for the teaching methods they adopt and the values they disseminate. This example (Richardson, 1990, pp. 42–3), touches on fundamental views about children, difference and education. The teachers taking part in the world studies research were predominantly in the 'reforming' zone.

The nature of this exercise, seeking breadth and variety rather than a tight, in-depth focus, meant that the inquiry rested on a loose set of common, core elements. These formed a strong foundation for comparability:

1.   All the teachers were self-elected, that is, they agreed to take part voluntarily and without any payment for their help.
2.   They all shared a basic understanding of, and adherence to, the processes and principles of global education. Even though their degree of experience and levels of commitment varied, their personal profiles showed that they all agreed on basic principles and practices.
3.   They all used the same reporting sheets from the research guidelines. The material provided forms the basis for a common understanding of:

      (a)   the World Studies 8–13 objectives;
      (b)   the model of groupwork;
      (c)   the nature of the potential learning and behavioural outcomes.

      A common framework was provided, and the goals and methodologies of world studies were made explicit.
4.   It seems appropriate to assume a common professional understanding of what constitutes 'development' in principle as well as what this means for specific children. This is embedded in the professional understanding of what it means to be a teacher.

Some unavoidable questions

Most of the teachers involved never met me or each other. A number of them were supported by LEA multicultural advisers or local DEC staff; others worked entirely on their own. No attempt was made to find out what kind of teaching and learning went on between the two observations, and therefore I have no sense of comparability. Did child X in classroom Y have the same opportunity to experience the kinds of learning situation, and to use resources that both inform and support learning in these areas, that child W in classroom Q had?

For reasons to do with the timescale of the project, this part of the inquiry covered two and a half terms. The children were thus seen in brief snapshots. How long might it take to see full-scale development in terms of being 'globally educated' – that is, active, participating, concerned citizens? As a headteacher in an inner-city primary school commented in a project interview (1992):

> In education there are few times one can say *that* input produced *that* output, but over a period of four or five years I am sure that the ethos, the personality, the character of the school reflected by the children has changed, in the way we wanted it to change ... We are very proud of the children, the product at the end of the day, because they are, on the

whole, confident, articulate, pleasant, well-adjusted children who in school work well together with other children, with adults and with strangers who come into the school. We have children who are aware of issues that arise from the work we intended to aim at in terms of cooperation, understanding of other cultures, sensitivity towards other people's feelings, fairness and justice. It's particularly noticeable that our Year 6 children are able to articulate some quite abstract concepts and I think that's quite a significant achievement. I don't think they would be doing that unless they had been through four years of world studies, to whatever degree.

None the less, the affinity and similarities between the teachers' responses, wherever their schools, convince me that I can draw from their returns the kinds of conclusions presented below. This is based in part on the very anonymity of the exercise: these teachers spent hours on organizing lessons, writing notes about the children and filling in some rather detailed forms for the sake of the research and not the researcher. The staying rate was excellent. There was an undeniable sense in which it could be said that these teachers, ranging from South Shields to Crawley, share a very similar 'vision' (and I use that term deliberately) of what teaching, learning and global education are all about.

A thumbnail sketch of the inquiry

It was made very clear that the aim of the exercise was to evaluate the methodologies, and was not about assessing children. The research question was: are these approaches effective in helping children develop cognitively, socially, and in skills and understanding?

The teachers watched and listened to small groups of children, aged between 6 and 13, over two and a half terms (Table 16.3). The majority were in the 7–11 age bracket. The children were involved in activities which gave them scope to talk, listen, make decisions, consider some wider issues and work co-operatively. The topics they discussed included the environment, views about other countries, gender roles, how their classrooms and playgrounds were organized, and their hopes for the future. The teachers planned lessons within the framework of the National Curriculum, recorded what the children did and said, and assessed whether each child was growing in awareness, co-operation and communication. The structure of the activities was fixed; it was up to each teacher to supply the global dimension through the content. Virtually all of them did so.

Table 16.3 *Number of children and schools involved*

	Evidence from both terms	Autumn term 1991	Spring term 1992	Total number
schools	21	31	24[*]	34
classes	27	47	30[**]	45
children	216	336	240	300

Notes:
[*] Three new schools joined
[**] One school providing five classes dropped out

OBSERVATIONS AND CONCLUSIONS

The following summary of observations is based on the analysis of the teachers' questionnaires, field notes and assessments of children's behaviours.

Teachers' choices and children's learning

Teachers appear to transform curriculum programmes into something they are comfortable with, adapting them to their own professional needs, and professional and personal values. They generally pick and choose among the themes identified with World Studies 8–13. On the whole they tend to favour the affective measures, which focus specifically on communication and co-operation skills and on self-esteem. They may address global themes – such as the environment, equal opportunities in the students' lives and in the UK, life in the developing countries – if they are personally interested in these issues. Having good, convenient resources, such as photopacks, is also a powerful encouragement to do world studies work.

The children really enjoyed working in this active, open-ended way. Moreover, the teachers who took part in interviews, questionnaires and the classroom exercise generally agreed that these approaches *do* develop communication and co-operation skills. A large number also felt that the children's thinking skills were extended.

Children's awareness and understanding of global issues can be enhanced through this approach if teachers provide opportunities and use resources that address global issues. Children's ideas and attitudes are powerfully influenced by experience outside the school – by the significant adults in their lives, by the media, by the interchange of opinions within their peer group – and many have ideas and attitudes which are, in a general sense, 'negative'. They believe that life in the South is unattractive, poverty- and disease-ridden; people from other countries have strange customs; a person's gender determines what is 'appropriate' behaviour for him or her. Difference is generally construed as 'worse than'. However, children can and do become more open-minded and prepared to question these assumptions in the context of discussion activities when they can examine evidence that challenges them. Discussion activities that encourage children to engage with evidence and decision-making can contribute to greater flexibility and tentativeness – the ability to question assumptions and accept uncertainty. They also contribute to tolerance.

Children gain confidence and communication skills through addressing issues and sharing opinions in small groups. Structured active learning exercises help them make gains in individual oracy skills (such as expressing thoughts and feelings, listening) and cognitive processes (such as forming and testing hypotheses, presenting arguments, analysing ideas). These activities also lead to gains in working effectively and co-operatively with others.

Development of a more positive self-concept through these methodologies appears to be more age-related. Children in the 6–14 age range enjoy participating in discussion activities which have a clear structure and direction and for which they can see a purpose. They are aware of the various skills they are using in these activities, and even quite young children are able to perceive and articulate the more implicit characteristics of these discussion activities, such as the importance of attending to what others think.

Up to 70 per cent of the children investigated believe that they are 'learning' through these activities.

Children can develop the skills, knowledge and understanding described in the World Studies 8–13 objectives if they are given opportunities to consider appropriate and relevant information and engage in active learning activities. They can also be working towards and developing the specific learning objectives within the National Curriculum at the same time.

World studies and the whole school

The support of the headteacher and a sympathetic attitude in the school contribute importantly to a teacher's involvement in world studies work. They are not determining factors, however: there are committed headteachers with uninterested staff and enthusiastic teachers with neutral or negative headteachers and colleagues.

The majority of teachers in the classroom project and also of the others contacted believed that a whole-school approach would have a more significant impact on children's overall development (conceptually, socially, and in skills and knowledge). A whole-school approach is characterized as one where the general atmosphere is caring, where the individual (child and adult) is both valued and respected, and where exploration of issues through discussion and exchange of ideas is encouraged and supported.

General conclusions and reflections on the classroom investigation

There is no irrefutable evidence that working in collaborative groups, participatory exercises, and discussing in an open-ended way global issues, such as the environment, development, injustices and human rights, make young people any more likely to take part in social action outside the school than any other style of education. It is also clear from this investigation, as from so much that has preceded it (e.g. UNESCO, 1965; Jungkunz, 1987; Mares and Harris, 1987), that no one is yet able to prove that specific techniques or curricular input can be used to form attitudes.

None the less, the evidence of this research points to positive gains in understanding and skills, and to children showing a greater openness to considering a range of perspectives. The classroom investigation, the interviews, the written testimonies and questionnaires all suggest that when children work in small groups, discussing an issue and sharing opinions, they gain confidence and skill in communicating. Both the conclusions of the many people who shared their experiences with me, and the classroom study, testify that you can see a positive change in the overall atmosphere of the classroom and school. It is widely accepted that schools shape attitudes and convey messages that influence behaviour. These can be benign, such as working mutually in a community of shared tasks, or disabling, making children feel limited and alienated by narrow views of gender, class and ethnic origin. This hidden curriculum can contribute to children gaining and growing less than they deserve to, and it clearly has an impact on their actions, particularly as they internalize some notion of what is thought to be 'appropriate' to their gender, class or race.

However, while there is evidence that the school environment and relationships between the children and adults help children to gain a more positive self-image based on their uniqueness as individuals, there is no proof that any specific teaching style or type of activity makes them any more likely to choose one course of action or life outside the school gates than any other.

In the end, this is a relief. While I and others believe it is essential for education to promote a global perspective based on social and environmental responsibility, other less constructive or positive perspectives are also competing for young people's minds. Schools and teachers do matter, but they are only part of the sea of noise bombarding the young. Teachers concerned to help children grow into the kinds of adult who will be committed to creating a more socially and environmentally just world will have to continue developing the appropriate skills and communicating the relevant information, without any guarantees. As one 10-year-old in an inner city school commented: 'World studies teaches you that you should think what you want to think, not what other people want you to think.'

APPENDIX 1: DEVELOPMENT OF WORLD STUDIES AND GLOBAL EDUCATION IN BRITAIN

1970s:
● World Studies Project set up in London:
  - focus on secondary education;
  - seminal texts: Richardson, 1976; Richardson *et al.*, 1979.

1980s:
● World Studies 8–13 Project (Lancaster):
  - seminal texts: Fisher and Hicks, 1985 (over 20,000 copies sold); Hicks and Steiner, 1989.
● Centre for Global Education (York):
  - seminal texts: Greig *et al.*, 1987; Pike and Selby, 1988;
● Establishment of national network of DECs and range of publications.

1990s:
● World Studies Project (Manchester):
  - research and focus on teacher education (initial and in-service);
  - seminal text: Steiner, 1993.

APPENDIX 2: WORLD STUDIES: EXPERIENCES, VIEWS AND VISIONS

The following questionnaire was originally reproduced on two sides to allow more space for responses:

1. Experiences

I have been a teacher for   years. I have worked in this school for   years.
This class is new to me/I'm familiar with these children.
In general, this school is/is not supportive of a world studies approach.
I am coming fresh to/have come experience of/am very familiar with an activity and issue based way of working.

2. Views and visions

To me, the purposes of education are:
I would describe my teaching style as:
I think children learn best when:
In my judgement, world studies/global education is about:
I find world studies/global education sympathetic because:

I'd know that world studies was successful in the school when I'd see or hear
   (a) in the classroom:
   (b) in the playground:
   (c) when my colleagues also:
   (d) when the headteacher:
   (e) when the children, wherever they were:

Things going on in the world which depress or worry me are:
Things going on in the world which excite me are:
I think I'm an optimistic/pessimistic person.

REFERENCES

Belenky, M., Clinchy, B.M., Goldberger, N.R. and Tarule, J.M. (1986) *Women's Ways of Knowing: The Development of Self, Voice and Mind*. New York: Basic Books.

Bennett, N. and Dunne, E. (1992) *Managing Classroom Groups*. Hemel Hempstead: Simon and Schuster.

Biott, C. (1984) *Getting On Without Teacher: Primary School Pupils in Cooperative Groups*. Collaborative Research Paper 1. Sunderland: Sunderland Polytechnic Centre for Education Research and Development.

Black, H.D. and Dockrell, W.B. (1980) 'Assessment in the affective domain: do we, can we, should we?' *British Educational Research Journal*, 6(2), 197–208.

Blackmore, J. (1989). In J. Smyth (ed.) *Critical Perspectives in Educational Leadership*. Lewes: Falmer.

Brandes, D. and Ginnis, P. (1986) *A Guide to Student-Centred Learning*. Oxford: Blackwell.

Calloway, H. (1981) 'Women's perspectives: research as revision.' In P. Reason and J. Rowan (eds) *Human Inquiry: A Sourcebook of New Paradigm Research*. Chichester: Wiley.

Carnie, J.M. (1972) 'Children's attitudes to other nationalities.' In N. Graves (ed.) *New Movements in the Study and Teaching of Geography*. Temple Smith.

Committee on the National Academy of Education (1991) Commentary on the *Nation's Report Card: Improving the Assessment of Student Achievement*. Report of a study group of the National Academy of Education. In *Education Counts: An Indicator System to Monitor the*

Nation's Educational Health. Washington, DC: National Center for Education Statistics.

Council of Europe (1985) *Teaching and Learning About Human Rights in Schools*. Brussels: Council of Europe.

Dorion, C. (1990) 'Environmental education in the primary school curriculum: an investigation into teachers' perceptions and practice in Herts., Berks., and Avon.' PhD dissertation, University of Reading.

Dufour, B. (ed.) (1990) *The New Social Curriculum: A Guide to Cross-curricular Issues*. Cambridge: Cambridge University Press.

Ellis, K. and Durkin, M.C. (1972) *The Taba Program in Social Science*. Menlo Park, CA: Addison-Wesley.

Fien, J. (1992) *Overcoming the Fear of Indoctrination in Environmental Education*. Perth: Australian Association for Environmental Education Conference.

Fisher, S. and Hicks, D. (1985) *World Studies 8-13: A Teacher's Handbook*. Edinburgh: Oliver and Boyd.

Freire, P. (1976) *Education: The Practice of Freedom*. London: Writers' and Readers' Publishing Cooperative.

Galton, M. and Williamson, J. (1992) *Groupwork in the Primary Classroom*. London: Routledge.

Gilligan, C. (1982) *In a Different Voice*. London: Harvard University Press.

Greig, S., Pike, G. and Selby, D. (1987) *Earthrights*. London: WWF/Kogan Page.

Guba, E. and Lincoln, Y. (1989) *Fourth Generation Evaluation*. Newbury Park, CA: Sage.

Harding, S. (ed.) (1986) *Feminism and Methodology*. Milton Keynes: Open University Press and Bloomington, IN: Indiana University Press.

Hicks, D. (1988) 'Teaching geography for a better world.' In J. Fien and R. Gerber (eds) *Teaching Geography for a Better World*. Edinburgh: Oliver and Boyd.

Hicks, D. and Steiner, M. (1989) *Making Global Connections: A World Studies Workbook*. Edinburgh and New York: Oliver and Boyd.

Huckle, J. (1983) *Geographical Education: Reflection and Action*. Oxford: Oxford University Press.

Huckle, J. (1988) 'Geography and World Citizenship.' In J. Fien and R. Gerber (eds) *Teaching Geography for a Better World*. Edinburgh: Oliver and Boyd.

Johnson, D.W. and Johnson, R.T. (1975) *Learning Together and Alone: Cooperation, Competition and Individualisation*. Englewood Cliffs, NJ: Prentice-Hall.

Jungkunz, T. (1987) *How School Children View Third World Countries: A Preliminary Investigation into Research Methodologies*. Oxford: Oxford Development Education Unit.

Kemmis, S. (1986) 'Seven principles for programme evaluation in curriculum development and innovation.' In E. House (ed.) *New Directions in Educational Evaluation*. London: Falmer.

Kirkup, J. (1986) 'The feminist evaluator.' In E. House (ed.) *New Directions in Educational Evaluation*. London: Falmer.

Kyriacou, C. (1992) 'Active learning in secondary school mathematics.' *British Educational Research Journal*, **18**(3).

McFarlane, C. (1986) *'Hidden Messages?' Activities for Exploring Bias*. Birmingham: Development Education Centre.

McFarlane, C. (1991) *Themework: A Global Perspective in the Primary Curriculum in the 90s*. Birmingham: Development Education Centre.

Mares, C. and Harris, R. (1987) *School Links International: Interim Report on the Evaluation of Pupils' Attitudes*. Schools Research Project, Brighton Polytechnic. Brighton: Avon County Council and the Tidy Britain Group.

Moise, E. (1968) 'The New Mathematics Program.' In S. Boocock and E.O. Schild (eds) *Simulation Games in Learning*. London: Sage.

Nias, J. (1989) *Primary Teachers Talking: A Study of Teaching as Work*. London: Routledge.

Parlett, M. (1981) 'Illuminative Evaluation.' In P. Reason and J. Rowan (eds) *Human Inquiry: A Sourcebook of New Paradigm Research*. Chichester: Wiley.

Piaget, J. (1926) *The Language and Thought of the Child*. London: Routledge & Kegan Paul.

Piaget, J. (1977) *The Moral Judgement of the Child*. London: Penguin.

Pike, G. (1990) 'Global education: learning in a world of change.' In B. Dufour (ed.) *The New Social Curriculum: A Guide to Cross-curricular Issues*. Cambridge: Cambridge University Press.

Pike, G. and Selby, D. (1988) *Global Teacher, Global Learner*. London: Hodder and Stoughton.

Price, G. (1984) 'Classroom techniques for demonstrating and assessing change in pupils' attitudes and values; with special reference to development education.' Unpublished Diploma in Curriculum Development, Oxford Polytechnic.

Prutzman, P., Burger, M., Bodenhamer, G. and Stern, L. (1978) *Friendly Classroom for a Small Planet*. Santa Cruz: New Society Publishers.

Richardson, R. (1976) *Learning for Change*. London: World Studies Project.

Richardson, R. (1990) *Daring to be a Teacher*. Stoke-on-Trent: Trentham.

Richardson, R., Flood, M. and Fisher, S. (1979) *Debate and Decision: Schools in a World of Change*. London: World Studies Project.

Rogers, C. (1969) *Freedom to Learn*. Columbus: Merrill.

Rogers, C. (1983) *Freedom to Learn for the 1980s*. Columbus: Merrill.

Short, J. (1988) 'Children's grasp of controversial issues.' In B. Carrington and B. Troyna (eds) *Children and Controversial Issues*. London: Falmer.

Slavin, R.E. (1989) *School and Classroom Organisation*. Hillsdale, NJ: Erlbaum.

Steiner, M. (1992) *World Studies 8–13: Evaluating Active Learning*. Manchester: Metropolitan University Manchester.

Steiner, M. (1993) *Learning from Experience: World Studies in the Primary Curriculum*. Stoke-on-Trent: Trentham.

Taba, H. (1982) *Curriculum Development, Theory and Practice*. New York: Harcourt, Brace and World.

Thomas, O.G. and Chapman, J. (1991) *14 Year Olds' Images of 'Third World' Countries: A Comparison of Two Research Methodologies*. Oxford: Oxford Development Education Unit.

Torney-Purta, J. (ed.) (1986) *Evaluating Global Education: Sample Instruments for Assessing Programs, Materials and Learning*. New York: Global Perspectives in Education.

Torney-Purta, J. (1989) 'Issues of evaluation.' In D. Hicks and M. Steiner (eds) *Making Global Connections: A World Studies Workbook*. Edinburgh: Oliver and Boyd.

UNESCO (1965) *International Understanding at School: Report on Associated Schools Project in Education for International Understanding and Cooperation*. Paris: UNESCO.

Wangen, R. and Mammenga, G. (1991) *Model Learner Outcomes for International Education*. St Paul, MN: Minnesota Department of Education.

Whitaker, P. (1984) 'The learning process.' *World Studies Journal*, 5(2).

Chapter 17

Policy-making in Geographical and Environmental Education: The Research Context

Nicholas H. Foskett

Undertaking and interpreting research in geographical and environmental education necessitates some understanding of the context of the subject of the research. No educational process is context-free in its existence, for it takes place in its own distinctive framework – a complex environment that has many dimensions. The individual geography lesson, for example, is shaped in no small way by both the location in which it is taught and the perspectives of the teacher working with a particular class. Some of these dimensions might be seen to reflect the operational environment of teaching, such as pupil numbers, the availability of resources, or the size and disposition of the teaching rooms used. Others are part of the philosophical environment, for they represent the interpretation of alternative perspectives on the nature and purpose of geographical and environmental education, or of education and training as a broad concept, often in the context of different ideological frameworks. These two dimensions are clearly entwined, and the relative importance and influence of each will vary from case to case. Much of the more influential research literature in recent years explores the role of these factors as individual influences; for example, the role of phenomenology (McEwen, 1986), the influence of the development of the concept of geography as a school subject (Goodson, 1983), or the role of ideology (Slater, 1992). Each of these elements, however, is only one component of a broader policy framework within which every aspect of education operates, and it is the significance of understanding policy-making and policy processes that is the focus of this chapter.

POLICY AND RESEARCH

The translation of philosophical perspectives into practical proposals is the essence of policy development, and Kogan has described policy as 'the authoritative allocation of values statements of prescriptive intent' (Kogan, 1975, p. 55). This has two implications for educational research. First, policy is an imposed element of the environment of education at any level. Understanding educational processes, therefore, requires an understanding of the nature of policy, the processes of its generation, and the process and outcomes of its implementation. Secondly, with its basis in value systems, which in turn may reflect particular ideological stances, policy is an inevitable focus of potential conflict in educational organizations. Ozga (1987) introduced the concept of 'policy sociology' to encompass a focus on the sociological dimensions of policy development and interpretation, and this field has generated a significant research literature, notably that of Ball (e.g. 1987, 1990). Few geographical and environmental studies have focused primarily on the policy process, yet it would seem inappropriate to consider any study to be complete without some reference to the policy framework within which the activities at the focus of the research actually operate. Researchers need to include key questions in their research strategies relating to policy; for example, 'What is the policy framework within which the research subject is operating?', 'What policy processes are at work?', or 'What responses to policy have shaped the practice being observed?'

The link between research and policy is not, of course, one-way. Finch has emphasized that the tradition within educational research has been to focus on the study of the operation of existing policies and to 'document and analyze the impact of ... policies upon their target populations' (Finch, 1985, p. 111). This sees the researcher in passive mode, describing and commenting on policy impacts but not seeking to influence policy. Finch advocates a more proactive perspective, however, which involves 'identifying "policy makers" as a key audience which researchers have to address' (Finch, 1985, p. 111).

This may be overt in that the focus of research may be to inform specific dimensions of the policy process with 'studies which aspire to feed directly into the policy-making process, usually with a view to producing some kind of policy change' (Finch, 1985, p. 111) – what Finch describes as an 'advocacy stance' (p. 122). Alternatively, it may be less directed, in simply ensuring that policy-makers have access to the knowledge, understanding and ideas that research has generated. In the latter case, the purpose is to ensure that researchers and their research evidence have a high profile in the decision-making process, through what Janowitz has described as an 'enlightenment model' which seeks to 'help society clarify or alter its social and political goals and objectives' (Janowitz, 1970, p. 251). Questions of importance to researchers in geographical and environmental education for the future might well include 'How far has our research influenced national education policy?' and 'How far should we be seeking to use our understanding from research to advocate specific policy directions?'. We are clearly found wanting in answer to both at present.

POLICY DEVELOPMENT AND POLICY PROCESSES

Understanding the role of policy requires an understanding of policy processes, both in development and in implementation. The making and interpretation of policy occurs at a large number of different levels, of which some lie within the educational arena and some beyond or above it. Lawton (1989) has identified five levels of responsibility for the implementation of the National Curriculum in the education system of England and Wales, and it is reasonable to extend this analysis to a more general model of policy development.

The lowest level is seen as that of the *individual teacher*, who has responsibility for lesson planning on a day-to-day basis and may have some degree of control in the generation of schemes of work. The teacher operates within the framework of policy and practice of those with responsibility at *departmental* level, whose management role includes the planning of syllabuses and programmes and the co-ordination of resources to implement them through the work of individual teachers. This, however, is conducted within whole-school policy relating to the whole curriculum, developed at *institutional* level. At higher levels, regional and national responsibilities may be identified. In many countries education is managed at the *regional* level by education authorities or school boards, and they in turn are responsible to authorities at *national* level. For education, these may include government education departments, but also national bodies charged with broad educational policy and practice responsibilities (for example, the School Curriculum and Assessment Authority in England), or with specific academic or sectoral interests (for example, the Joint Committee on Geographic Education in the USA). This may be seen as a hierarchy of policy-making and interpretation. Policy is made at each of these levels, but in each case it is constrained or at least influenced by that made at higher levels. Policy implementation is essentially a top-down process, although the degree of influence of lower levels in the hierarchy in the formulation and development of policy will always be important – either because that influence has been significant or, perhaps more frequently, because it has not!

The policy framework now stretches beyond the national level, however. The development of policy by government is only in part dictated by domestic objectives, and governments operate as members of international groupings both formal and informal. In the United Kingdom, government policy is in part influenced by decision-making at the level of the European Union and by policies agreed by all members of the Union. In addition, the government's participation in wider international forums and its voluntary agreement and role as signatory to international treaties and protocols provides a framework within which domestic policy will operate and be developed.

Similarly, the educational community is international in nature, and policy development is in part informed if not driven by the development of practice and the outcome of research in other countries. The International Geographical Union (IGU) and UNESCO as organizations, and journals such as *IRGEE* (*International Research in Geographical and Environmental Education*) act as the co-ordinators, leaders and communication vehicles of this international exchange (Wise, 1992).

However, insights into the process of policy formation are not yet well developed. Howell and Brown (1983, p. 14) suggest that 'policy initiatives are the product of interaction between political controllers and professionals providers', yet indicate that 'the policy making processes themselves still have something of the black box about them' (p. 5). In Lawton's hierarchical model, for example, the role of each level is as both professional provider *and* political controller dependent upon context, and understanding the upward and downward processes is complex. Bush (1986) has provided useful summaries of alternative interpretational frameworks for such processes, and it would seem essential in any geographical or environmental education research to develop some understanding of the role of political, collegial and bureaucratic organizational structures.

Understanding the structural characteristics of policy development and implementation can only be one part of any effective analysis. There is a need also to understand the processes of policy implementation in the micro-political arena that is the school and its management activities. The way in which policy generated from higher centres is implemented in schools has been an active area of research (e.g. Ball, 1987, 1990; Alford and Friedland, 1988; Dale, 1989; Gleeson, 1989; Bowe *et al.*, 1992). These studies analyse the process in two different frameworks, the linear (e.g. Dale, 1989) and the heuristic (e.g. Bowe *et al.*, 1992).

The linear models see the policy process as a simple route between policy generation and policy implementation, where policy 'gets done to people by a chain of implementors whose roles are clearly defined' (Bowe *et al.*, 1992, p. 7). Bowe *et al.* contend that such a model of linear policy implementation is not a true reflection of reality, that there is not 'an unequivocal governmental position which will filter down through the quasi-state bodies and into the schools' (Bowe *et al.*, 1992, p. 10). They suggest that there are many intervening opportunities for the interpretation of meaning between the development of educational policy and its implementation, and that policy should be seen as:

- a discourse, with a range of interpretations of policy documents in terms of possible implementation mechanisms and routes, the constraints within the document, the contradictions within it, and clear gaps, omissions or spaces;
- an 'operational statement of values' (Bowe *et al.*, 1992, p. 13);
- an area to be contested by those implementing policy, who must resolve inherent conflicts between current practice, their interpretation of policy and their own and their school's values.

The heuristic model of the policy process arises from this critique. Bowe *et al.* (1992) suggest that policy emerges from three contexts, each of which is a dynamic 'arena of action'. The 'context of influence' is the arena of public policy debate in and around the political parties and government, together with representative groups and national bodies. The 'context of policy text production' represents the formal articulation of policy through a range of media, but usually through text. The third context is the 'context of practice', where:

> policy is not simply received and implemented [but] is subject to interpretation and is then 're-created' ... Practitioners do not confront policy texts as naive readers, they come with histories, with experience, with values and purposes of their own, they have vested interests in the meaning of policy.
>
> (Bowe *et al.*, 1992, p. 22)

The commencement of policy implementation is, therefore, a point of departure for micro-political conflict within the school. 'Active processes of accommodation and mediation' (Ball and Bowe, 1991, p. 23) characterize the interaction between managers in schools and the policy documents they receive, and also between individuals and groups of staff within the broad school community. Ball (1987, p. 263) has indicated that, for externally initiated changes, 'their acceptance and their implementation become the site as well as the stake of internal dispute.' This idea clearly supports the views of Moran (1989), who argues that the creation of legislation and policy at government level should not necessarily be seen by those working in schools as the inevitable precursor of their professional role. He asserts that 'the local outcome of a distant intent is conditioned more by local circumstance than by remote control' and that 'a potentially hostile measure can be redirected into a productive outcome' (Moran, 1989, p. 87).

It is reasonable to conclude from this analysis that predicting the form of policy interpretation is very difficult, with a wide range of possible outcomes and effects. In particular, it means that we should not expect to find a simple pattern of responses within schools to a national view of geographical or environmental education. Rather we should expect to find different interpretations of these developments reflecting the internal and external environments in which schools operate. Equally, we must recognize that a diversity of response does not indicate a lack of policy direction but may be simply the product of a range of interpretations. Saunders (1985) has identified the fact that in the context of the Technical and Vocational Education Initiative (TVEI) programme in the United Kingdom, schools responded in one of three ways:

1. adaptive extension, where the concept or policy is taken strongly into the culture of the school with a vision that reflects clearly the original policy intent;
2. accommodation, where the policy is interpreted and adjusted to fit the existing *modus operandi*;
3. containment, where the policy is absorbed by the existing school pattern.

The precise nature of this response will depend on the outcome of the micro-political contests that follow its entrance into policy dialogue in the school. A challenging focus of research into curriculum change in geography and environmental education might be a consideration of this model in a range of subject-specific contexts.

POLICY PROCESSES AND RESEARCH IN GEOGRAPHICAL AND ENVIRONMENTAL EDUCATION

The issue of policy formation and interpretation may be exemplified in the context of geographical and environmental education by considering two specific examples drawn from England and Wales: the implementation of the geography National Curriculum, and the development of environmental education policy.

Implementation of the geography National Curriculum

The development and implementation of the National Curriculum in England and Wales have been the focus of substantial research both in general terms (e.g. Bowe *et al.*, 1992) and with specific reference to geography. While much of this research has focused on practical implementation issues (e.g. Butt, 1992), a focus on policy issues may be identified in the work of a number of writers, including Roberts (1991), Bailey (1992), Rawling (1992), Graves (1993) and Lambert (1994). The development of policy as expressed in the geography Statutory Orders (Department of Education and Science, 1991) at national level has been a significant area of comment.

Bailey (1992) has explored the political influence of, *inter alia*, the Geographical Association in ensuring the presence of geography in the National Curriculum, while Rawling (1992) considered the policy development surrounding the development of the geography curriculum itself. Rawling emphasized the influence of perceptions of geography by government in structuring the discussions leading to the geography orders, because of the 'deficit view of geographical education [that] prevailed in Whitehall' (Rawling, 1992, p. 299), and the broader perception in government that 'the theorists had had their day, geography was not the property of school teachers and educationalists' (p. 299). Rawling suggests that:

place was clearly a key issue. Newspaper articles during 1988 reported the results of an International Gallup Survey ... drawing attention to the apparent appalling ignorance displayed by the British public about 'where places are' and 'what they are like'. Much of the blame had been laid at the door of school geography and it was clear that the politicians saw a major role for the subject in addressing this issue.

(Rawling, 1992, p. 299)

Lambert (1994) adds to this insight a view on the importance of the broader policy-forming debates about education in England and Wales that influenced all National Curriculum developments, including debates across a number of polarities, 'given dramatic relief in recent years in the so-called "standards debate" ... subject vs child, high culture vs low culture, instruction vs enquiry, traditionalist vs progressive and knowledge vs process' (Lambert, 1994, p. 70).

The complexity of the development of policy challenges perceptive insight through research. Direct observation of the process is difficult, and official documentary evidence may be either absent or incapable of revealing the subtleties of the interplay of people, ideas and ideologies. Even the players themselves may not be truly aware of the factors influencing their own role in the process, let alone that of others, a view confirmed by Rawling (1992) and Bennetts (1994). Polarized views that characterize the process of policy developments as 'conspiracy' or 'cock-up' hide an analytical mine-field, which Bennetts has interpreted in the following kindly way:

It seems to me that the government has not worked out a satisfactory relationship between itself, local communities and schools; it holds too much of the power and at times that tempts Ministers and their political advisers to interfere in the details of the curriculum rather than restrict themselves to broader matters of policy. There is little escape from polit-ical ideology if it is aggressively pursued from the Centre.

(Bennetts, 1994, p. 6)

Reflecting on the interpretation of policy is perhaps somewhat more straightforward, if not necessarily more prominent in the research literature. Lambert broadly supports the views of Bowe *et al.* (1992) in indicating the range of possible interpretations of policy as indicated in the National Curriculum, since 'no-one can fail to accept the potential of the Order to be read in a thousand different ways' (Lambert, 1994, p. 66). However, he also suggests that this potential for a wide range of policy interpretation is not necessarily being fulfilled, with a surprising conformity of interpretation between teachers. Lambert questions whether this is 'a retreat from critical reflection and a raised propensity to seek refuge in following what are imagined to be the rules' (Lambert, 1994, p. 66). There remains much scope for research into alternative inter-pretations of the National Curriculum at the stage of implementation.

Development of environmental education policy

Policy development in the field of environmental education has a more overt basis at national and international level than does geographical education, and its international dimension is particularly important. Few subject areas in the schools' curriculum have as high an international profile as those relating to the environment. It is a field which stimulates interest and strong emotional reaction in all sectors of society: in business, in government, in education, in pressure groups and in individuals. High levels of environmental awareness have stimulated international discussion and action with a high profile, which feeds through into policy-making at all levels. As a result, at national level many countries have clearly defined policies for environmental education, while at institutional or individual level the influence of environmental awareness among pupils and parents is substantial in the formation of policy. Environmental issues themselves often require solutions at a transnational or global level, too, involving collaboration between states. Collaboration in policy terms at this level is, therefore, essential, and the development of environmental policy has frequently contained or been paralleled by the development of environmental education policy (Convey, 1994).

The international policy process may be traced back to the Stockholm Conference on the Human Environment in 1972, which spawned a sequence of events resulting in the Belgrade Charter (1975) and the UNESCO/UNEP First Conference on Environmental Education at Tbilisi in 1977 (Tilbury, 1994). The declaration from this conference in turn provided the fundamental principles for the education content of Agenda 21, the broad policy statement emanating from the United Nations Conference on Environment and Development held in Rio de Janeiro in 1992 (the 'Rio Summit'), which includes an emphasis on:

- reorientating education towards sustainable development
- increasing public awareness about the nature of the environment and their role in relation to environmental processes and change
- promoting training that has a greater awareness of environment and development as a key principle.

(UNESCO, 1992, p. 21)

As one of the 132 signatories to the UNCED declaration at Rio, the UK is committed to supporting the policy ideals of Agenda 21. In addition, the European context adds a further influence on policy at the national level. The Council of Europe, essentially an educational and cultural organization representing all European nations, has developed its own recommendations on environmental education, which emphasize the key role of geography in its delivery in schools (Council of Europe, 1988). The European Union, too, has environmental policies, expressed through its five Action Programmes on the Environment since 1972, which have consistently referred to the need for education as a vehicle for improving environmental performance, albeit through the mechanisms of industrial training and education rather than within schools.

A clear consequence of such international concern for environmental matters has been the development of what Tilbury (1994, p. 13) describes as 'an internationally defined environmental education'. She expresses the primary goal of this consensus in the following way:

Environmental education should aim to contribute to environmental improvement by developing citizens who are aware of environmental problems and are concerned about the environment and have the skills, knowledge, attitudes and commitment to work individually and collectively towards the solution of existing and the prevention of future problems.

(Tilbury, 1994, p. 15)

This approach to environmental education is further expressed in terms of a number of characteristics, which she suggests include an emphasis on interdisciplinarity and the need to provide environmental education at all levels of education.

The transfer of such policies into environmental education at the national level may be illustrated by the case of England and Wales. Here the establishment of the National

Curriculum saw the development of environmental education as a broad cross-curricular theme (National Curriculum Council, 1990), but with significant elements of knowledge, skills and understanding delivered through the traditional vehicles of geography and science. Huckle (1994) reflects upon the policy framework of environmental education in the National Curriculum and offers both positive and negative interpretations of its position. While suggesting that environmental education is perhaps more firmly established in the curriculum than at any time in the past, he concludes that:

> most environmental education will continue to be delivered through Geography and Science [rather than as a cross-curricular theme] ... for most schools and teachers ... will understandably concentrate on the subjects on which pupils are to be tested and in which they are examined and appraised.
>
> (Huckle, 1994, p. 103)

The demise of environmental education as a cross-curricular theme may be a consequence of this development, therefore, highlighting a tension between the policies of different groups. Furthermore, in an important reflection on the link between ideology and policy, Huckle is critical of the emphasis in the curriculum, emanating from government hierarchies, on environmental technocentrism rather than ecocentrism (O'Riordan, 1989) as a philosophy underpinning the curriculum.

It is of interest to compare the developments in England with those in Holland (Van der Schee, 1994), where curriculum policy also dictates the centrality of traditional subjects such as geography and biology and 'areas such as environmental education, peace education and third world education which are not embedded in existing subjects are doomed to suffer' (Van der Schee, 1994, p. 113). Research focused on a comparison of environmental education in a range of national and policy environments is a field yet to be explored. It may offer useful insights into policy sociology in the context of environmental education.

CONCLUSION

This chapter has sought to demonstrate a number of key issues. First, the study of policy and the framework it provides for the practice of education are an important context for most educational research. Education operates in the political arena, and may be interpreted as a political process itself, so to consider any aspect of education as if the policy processes were absent is to miss an important dimension of the study.

Secondly, the policy framework for geographical and environmental education operates at all scales from global to the individual classroom. Understanding the way in which national, school and individual teacher activities in the field are shaped by international perceptions and policy is particularly important in geographical and environmental education research. The concept of 'Think global, act local' might be applied to research planning as well as to environmental responsibility!

Thirdly, it is clear that the policy dimension has not been prominent in geographical and environmental education research. The examples considered briefly here show that reflection on the role of policy has been tentative at best. Research into practice tends to focus on the tangible and the concrete rather than the philosophical, and this may reflect the emphasis in the geographical tradition and the environmental science tradition (from which most researchers in this field of *education* have originated) on the empirical and the positivist approaches. Perhaps it also reflects the struggle of geography and environmental science/studies for recognition as an academic and school subject, as described by Goodson (1983), which may have deterred researchers from considering too far the influence of factors beyond the subject's own boundaries. This chapter has presented some perspectives from policy sociology that might act as a focus for a research thrust considering the policy implications of developments in geographical and environmental education.

Finally, I have considered the view that there is a role for the use of educational research outcomes in influencing policy development. If we have a genuine concern for the role of geographical and environmental education, we should regard it as a duty to seek to heighten the professional side of the politician–professional dialogue that Howell and Brown (1983) have identified as a key component of policy development. Our own future as researchers may depend on our ability to be proactive in policy development at all levels, for we operate in an essentially political environment.

REFERENCES

Alford, R. and Friedland, R. (1988) *Powers of Theory: Capitalism, the State and Democracy*. Cambridge: Cambridge University Press.

Bailey, P. (1992) *Securing the Place of Geography in the National Curriculum of English and Welsh Schools: A Study in the Politics and Practicalities of Curriculum Reform*. Sheffield: Geographical Association.

Ball, S.J. (1987) *The Micro-Politics of the School*. London: Methuen.

Ball, S.J. (1990) *Politics and Policy Making in Education*. London: Routledge.

Ball, S.J. and Bowe, M. (1991) 'The micropolitics of radical change: budgets, management and control in British schools.' In J. Blase (ed.) *The Politics of Life in Schools: Power, Conflict and Cooperation*. London: Sage.

Bennetts, T. (1994) 'Reflections on the development of geography in the National Curriculum.' In R. Walford, and P. Machon (eds) *Challenging Times: Implementing the National Curriculum in Geography*. Cambridge: Cambridge Publishing Services.

Bowe, R., Ball, S.J. and Gold, A. (1992) *Reforming Education and Changing Schools: Case Studies in Policy Sociology*. London: Routledge.

Bush, T. (1986) *Theories of Educational Management*. London: Harper and Row.

Butt, G. (1992) 'Geography.' in P. Ribbins (ed.) *Delivering the National Curriculum*. Harlow: Longman.

Convey, A. (1994) 'Environmental education: international approaches and policies.' *International Research in Geographical and Environmental Education*, 2, 92–6.

Council of Europe (1988) 'Resolution of the Council and Ministers of Education Meeting with the Council, Environmental Education.' No. 88/C177/03.

Dale, R. (1989) *The State and Education Policy*. Milton Keynes: Open University Press.

Department of Education and Science (1991) *Geography in the National Curriculum (England)*. London: HMSO.

Finch, J. (1985) 'Social policy and education: problems and possibilities of using qualitative research.' In R.G. Burgess (ed.) *Issues in Educational Research: Qualitative Methods*. Lewes: Falmer.

Gleeson, D. (1989) *The Paradox of Training: Making Progress out of Crisis*. Milton Keynes: Open University Press.

Goodson, I. (1983) *School Subjects and Curriculum Change*. London: Croom Helm.

Graves, N. (1993) 'The genesis of the geography curriculum in the English and Welsh National Curriculum.' In H. Haubrich (ed.) *Liber Amicorum: Gunther Niemz*. Berlin: IGU.

Howell, D.A. and Brown, R. (1983) *Educational Policy: An Analysis*. London: Heinemann.

Huckle, J. (1994) 'Environmental education and the National Curriculum in England and Wales.' *International Research in Geographical and Environmental Education*, 2, 101–4.

Janowitz, M. (1970) *Political Conflict*. Chicago, IL: Quadrangle.

Kogan, M. (1975) *Educational Policy Making*. London: Allen and Unwin.

Lambert, D. (1994) 'The National Curriculum: What shall we do with it?' *Geography*, **79**, 65–76.

Lawton, D. (1989) *Education, Culture and the National Curriculum*. London: Hodder and Stoughton.

McEwen, N. (1986) 'Phenomenology and the curriculum: the case of secondary school geography.' In P.H. Taylor (ed.) *Recent Developments in Curriculum Studies*. London: NFER-Nelson.

Moran, M. (1989) 'Schools and public relations.' In J. Sayer and V. Williams (eds) *Schools and External Relations: Managing the New Partnerships*. London: Cassell.

National Curriculum Council (1990) *Curriculum Guidance 7: Environmental Education*. London: NCC.

O'Riordan, T. (1989) 'The challenge for environmentalism.' In R. Peet and N. Thrift (eds) *New Models in Geography. Vol. 1*. London: Unwin-Hyman.

Ozga, J. (1987) 'Studying educational policy through the lives of policy makers; an attempt to close the macro–micro gap.' In S. Walker and L. Barton (eds) *Changing Policies, Changing Teachers*. Milton Keynes: Open University Press.

Rawling, E. (1992) 'The making of a national geography curriculum.' *Geography*, **77**, 292–309.

Roberts, M. (1991) 'On the eve of the geography National Curriculum: implications for secondary schools.' *Geography*, **76**, 331–42.

Saunders, M. (1985) *Emerging Issues for TVEI Implementation*. Lancaster: University of Lancaster.

Slater, F. (1992) '... to travel with a different view.' In M. Naish (ed.) *Geography and Education: National and International Perspectives*. London: University of London Institute of Education.

Tilbury, D. (1994) 'The international development of environmental education: a basis for a teacher education model?' *Environmental Education and Information*, **13**, 1–20.

UNESCO (1992) 'UNCED: The Earth Summit.' *Connect*, **17**, 1–5.

Van der Schee, J. (1994) 'Geography teaching and environmental education: a Dutch perspective.' *International Research in Geographical and Environmental Education*, **2**, 113–15.

Wise, M.J. (1992) 'International geography: the IGU Commission on Education.' In M. Naish (ed.) *Geography and Education: National and International Perspectives*. London: University of London Institute of Education.

Chapter 18

Understanding and Improving School Geography: The Training of Beginning Teachers

David Lambert

This chapter is concerned with two related areas of research interest. Each is a vast field in its own right, but the aim is not to review their territories as distinct and separate entities. Rather, it is to explore the interface between the two, namely the way in which the developing models of *teacher education and training* in England have potential in supporting the wider project of *school improvement*. I am writing from the perspective of a trainer of secondary school geography teachers, but I suspect the discussion has relevance beyond geography education. However, for the purpose of this chapter it is beginning teachers[1] of geography, and specifically their work with experienced colleagues in school geography departments in England, that provide the main context.

The discussion which follows is not based on empirical research, being more interpretive and conceptual in nature, but it does draw directly from the evolving new patterns of postgraduate initial training in England and one course in particular, the Postgraduate Certificate in Education (PGCE) at the University of London Institute of Education (ULIE). Recent government reforms of initial training (DfE, 1992; CATE, 1992), put simply, are designed to reduce the dominance enjoyed traditionally by the university departments of education. Although there is a sense in which this was merely to formalize an evolutionary track in teacher education which can be traced back many years and which has come from within the teacher education community itself (e.g. Graves, 1985), it has nevertheless had a radical and destabilizing effect. All providers of PGCE courses for secondary school specialists have had to move swiftly to arrange partnership structures to 'enable' (Alexander, 1990, p. 60) the delivery of a competency-driven curriculum. Partnerships have had to become quasi-contractual, with substantial financial resources (currently, approximately one third of the *per capita* fee income) following the student teachers into their placement schools (SHA, 1993). The chronic underfunding of the PGCE, hidden in the past by informal *ad hoc* arrangements with schools based on goodwill, has suddenly become all too clear. It is in this context that the government has actively encouraged wholly 'school-centered initial teacher training' (SCITT), in which schools, or small groups of schools, may receive the whole part of a significantly higher *per capita* fee and are not required to consort with higher education (HE) institutions in any way. As student teachers entering SCITT are likely to receive a generous government bursary as well, it is difficult to escape the conclusion that, for whatever reason, government policy in England and Wales is to marginalize or eradicate completely the HE component in the preparation of postgraduate teachers (e.g. Bolton, 1994).

Such an outcome is supported by very few in the teaching profession; after all, on purely pragmatic grounds, most schoolteachers see their main priority as teaching children not training teachers. And yet this is not to abrogate all responsibility for preparing the next generation of teachers, most schools being happy with the idea of some form of partnership with HE (e.g. Iven, 1993). It is the *nature* of the partnership, therefore, how it can be interpreted and conceptualized in order to strengthen and, ultimately, preserve it, that forms my major point of interest. Later I will outline some possibilities for empirical research studies which may in turn serve a useful purpose in the evaluation and support of developments suggested in the main body of this chapter.

THE CONTEXT OF CHANGE

Changes in initial teacher education in England and Wales are taking place against a backdrop of even more far-reaching reform affecting the state schools. Local management, open enrolment, published league tables of examination results and truancy rates, opting out, inspections every four years: such reforms have been rapid and have changed the climate or culture of school communities. The competitive environment has forced a more urgent look at the nature and meaning of school improvement (e.g. Fullan, 1991; Hammersmith and Fulham, 1993; Louis and Miles, 1990). As individual teachers come to terms with other elements of these systemic reforms, such as appraisal or performance-related pay, the National Curriculum – the single biggest component of the 1988 Educational Reform Act (ERA), itself sold to the public by the then Secretary of State Kenneth Baker as the means to 'lever up standards' – has been seen as something serving the needs of the administration more than educational aims. The National Curriculum was hasty and ill-conceived, being saved from shambolic collapse only by the appointment in England of an adviser and in Wales of a committee to consult with educationists and serving teachers in order to review, simplify and rationalize the whole apparatus (Dearing, 1993, 1994; Curriculum Council for Wales, 1993).

The recommendations of the Dearing Review have been accepted by the DfE and have received widespread support from parents and teachers as well as administrators. The impact of the National Curriculum to date has been dramatic and itself forms a long research agenda (e.g. McNamara, 1990). Much of this agenda has, as McNamara suggests, what we might refer to as 'action' connotations. The content of lessons, the strategies employed by teachers, the use of learning resources (including textbooks); these issues embody questions which have practical possibilities and may help feed teachers' action research questions, such as 'How can I do this better?' or 'What happens when I do that?' These are also questions which are in the forefront of the minds of beginning teachers.

In this way, then, we have a potentially intriguing research interface. To be sure, it has always been present, because 'partnership has been on the agenda a long time' (Alexander, 1990, p. 59), and institutions have been mindful of the benefits which ought to accrue from partnership work: 'improved initial teacher training for students can go hand in hand with authentic professional development for teachers and contribute to schools' programmes of curriculum review and classroom evaluation' (Everton, 1991, p. 1). But what has given it fresh appeal is the energy released by various changes and reforms experienced in their different ways by the schools and HE institutions. We now have postgraduate beginning teachers entering schools for a greater proportion of their training than previous generations of PGCE students, and partnerships committed in varying degrees to the notion that such recruits into teaching should not simply be recipients of more practice; in other words, resisting the felt pressure to return teacher education and training to a restricted and simple version of 'apprenticeship'. The question arises, then: what should student teachers be doing if not in the role of apprentice learner?

At the same time, we have secondary schools and school geography departments coping with unprecedented change, feeling accountable for every action and under pressure. Curriculum design is a major concern with teachers trying to attend to urgent questions, such as how to 'deliver' the mandatory content, or somewhat less immediate ones, such as how to incorporate information technology. It is perhaps not surprising that teachers around the country have tended to rely on rapidly published 'formula' textbooks which claim to do the delivery job (e.g. Waugh and Bushell, 1991). The arrival of the student teacher on this scene could be seen as the last straw. Or could it be something else? Could the beginning teacher, who straddles the HE–schools interface, become the catalyst in taking forward specific aspects of curriculum development?

To reiterate, it seems that there could be a considerable convergence of interest between those who work in schools, the needs of beginning teachers, and those in HE who now work in redefined 'partnership' settings.

THE TEACHER AS RESEARCHER

I wish to argue that the point on this interface, where, so to speak, the rubber hits the road is in research activity. Fien (1992) has written persuasively about the way school geography can be linked with HE through a symbiotic action research methodology, and makes the point that, 'There can be no curriculum development without teacher development. [This assumption] provides the key to strengthening the links between research and training' Fien, 1992, p. 273). The thrust of Fien's argument, which takes forward earlier conceptions of the 'teacher-researcher' (Stenhouse, 1975), is for experienced teachers of geography to engage in 'critical action research' in collaboration with HE (and probably under the guise of award-bearing courses such as Masters degrees). Such research would be interpretive, highly embedded in the particular and thus very practical.

We may correctly conclude, therefore, that Fien's picture of continuous teacher development also contains a key to school improvements. As he goes on to say, 'university research workers need to question their motives in wanting to undertake educational research and respond to the voices of their teacher colleagues as much as, if not more than, they do to each other' (Fien, 1992, p. 273). What is of special interest is how this sort of thinking impinges on the induction of new teachers with a research *disposition* to their education and training. Realizing this has implications for all who work with beginning teachers, and moves us perhaps closer to bridging the gap between school and HE cultures of training at what Alexander (1990) calls the 'action' level, as opposed to the bureaucratic or 'enabling' one.

It is worth re-emphasizing that, although the precise context of a beginning teacher's inquiry-based learning (its embeddedness) may be a particular school geography department, it is not the only dimension of his or her education and training. The assumption that runs through this chapter is that, to understand and improve school geography in the 1990s and beyond, we need to concentrate first and foremost on how best to prepare the people who are going to teach it. The ULIE version of PGCE Partnership in Training (ULIE, 1994) attempts to do this through its identification of three interrelated, indeed interlocked, foci:

1.   the teacher as competent practitioner;
2.   the teacher as reflective professional;
3.   the teacher as researcher.

These recurring themes run through the whole course, providing the three principal course components (professional studies, practical teaching and curriculum studies), coherence and a distinctive texture. There is significance in maintaining distinctions between these themes for, as I show later, we do not seek simply to integrate the roles of teacher and researcher. As Hammersley has argued persuasively, 'while teaching does involve processes of reflective inquiry, these often, and rightly, take a different form from conventional educational research' (Hammersley, 1993, p. 441).

The concept of embeddedness (Donaldson, 1978, 1992) describes the power of placing learning within the known and familiar context of 'real life', and it is this that can explain simply the attraction of 'teaching practice' to beginning teachers, and the value they attach to it. But as student teachers they need to be taken beyond immediate situational exigencies, to be encouraged and provided with the tools to develop in personal terms to become what we have called the 'reflective professional' (ULIE, 1994). Slater (1994) lucidly describes a form of reflexivity which can bring together the 'knowledge' and 'feeling experience' (after Reid, 1986) aspects of learning in the context of children's education through geography. The critical reflection which I have in mind for adult learner teachers is not far removed from this idea, and centres on the question of how to construct a meaningful intellectual framework for a course which is (correctly) based upon experience and values-learning by doing.

The PGCE can do this, I believe, through the explicit recognition of the beginning teacher's postgraduate status. I shall go on to show the 'teacher as researcher' (ULIE, 1994) as a key with the potential to realize the goal of the 'reflective professional'. Before pursuing this, however, we must first return to a brief examination of the other part of my chapter title: understanding school geography.

UNDERSTANDING SCHOOL GEOGRAPHY IN ENGLAND AND WALES SINCE ERA

It has been argued that the 1988 ERA represented a clear break with the past in a number of ways (e.g. Bennetts, 1994; Dowgill and Lambert, 1992). School geography in England and Wales has benefited from – or has been burdened with, depending on your point of view – the National Curriculum, which became law in 1991. The geography curriculum has been controversial and has had signal impact on school geography (e.g. Lambert, 1994; Rawling, 1992). The full story of its technical and philosophical impact on what may be termed 'teacher work' is complex, but, in essence, it is somewhat as follows.

The ambitious assessment framework (TGAT, 1988; Lawton, 1992), based upon a ten-level scale of attainment, was designed to show criteria-referenced progress for all children in compulsory (state-funded) schooling for each National Curriculum subject. In the case of geography, progress levels were described in predominantly content, or knowledge, terms (Bennetts, 1994), which led to a number of problems for teachers. This was not least because of the predictable proliferation of criteria purporting to describe progress in such a manner. Furthermore, teachers were confused about how isolated bits of *content* could become agreed assessment criteria for *levels* of attainment. In the early years of implementation, geography teachers were in danger of having to work with an unwieldy curriculum and assessment structure which had spurious validity. The Dearing Review was formulated, and offered timely simplification and clarification (Dearing, 1993, 1994). In the consultation proposals for geography, the ten-level scale of attainment has been retained, though each level is no longer described by atomistic 'Statements of Attainment'; instead, more rounded, less content-specific 'Level Descriptions' have been written. Attempts to introduce external standardized tests for geography were also put off for the foreseeable future. Such changes amounted to a radical shift in the arrangements for geography only three years after the original Order passed through Parliament in 1991 (DES, 1991).

Thus, these have been difficult years for teachers, and an immense amount of energy has been expended in attempting to put into place what teachers have perceived to be the requirements. A raft of publications, both from official sources (e.g. NCC, 1991; SEAC, 1991, 1993) and from other sources like the Geographical Association (e.g. Bailey, 1992; Balderstone and Lambert, 1992; Fry and Schofield, 1993), is testament to this, and these stand as interesting historical documents. Superficially, much has been gained from these years. Few school departments are without documentation to support their Key Stage 3 (11–14-year-olds) scheme of work, and many have assessment policies and lively internal meetings in order to operate them. A massive publishing effort accompanied the launch of the National Curriculum, with virtually all the major educational publishing houses offering lavishly illustrated, full-colour series of texts. Geography in school has raised its profile generally, some schools increasing the amount of curriculum time devoted to it, others unscrambling certain timetables of convenience in which it was swallowed in an undifferentiated, humanities-flavoured blancmange. The National Curriculum even managed to raise the spectre of teacher shortages, as head-teachers moved to fill vacancies with specialist geographers rather than generalists.

However, there is another interpretation of these years. A clue to this is to be found in the textbook phenomenon whereby one series – the first to emerge which claimed complete 'coverage' of the National Curriculum specifications – seems almost to have swept the board, with the books, according to the advertisments present in a surprising 50 per cent of secondary schools nationally (Waugh and Bushell, 1991). It appears that the books were seen to 'do the job' at a time when teachers felt vulnerable. The question this raises concerns how teachers have interpreted *their* job – particularly in the context of the school text market being awash with choice and quality, as any visitor to the publishers' exhibition at the annual Geographical Association conference will testify.

Similar concerns were raised by some small-scale research (Daugherty and Lambert, 1994) conducted between 1992 and 1993 which examined how teachers had interpreted the National Curriculum assessment arrangements and specifically their so-called teacher assessment responsibilities. (This included all the day-to-day assessment of pupils which teachers make, using both formal and informal methods, to judge pupils' progress.) The majority of teachers were found to be sceptical over some of the rhetoric which accompanied the introduction of the National Curriculum, but, nevertheless were seemingly swept along in the bureaucracy of its apparatus, feeling acutely the needs of the administration and, in some cases, subjugating educational perspectives and responses. The authors acknowledged the possibilty of this being a temporary phenomenon, but nevertheless expressed the need for teachers to reassert a broader, more autonomous vision of their work than that which the data suggested had been taken up – at least by some. As Daugherty had stated in an earlier paper, 'We are not in the position of mere functionaries waiting for a new curriculum and assessment system to be imposed upon us ... we are the experts and can influence the way the new system evolves' (Daugherty, 1990, pp. 299–300). In the early years of the National Curriculum at least, few teachers felt in a position to agree with this sentiment.

If this was true of experienced colleagues, then what might we infer about the state of mind of new entrants to the profession? It would be interesting to examine, possibly through analysis of the nature and contents of tutors' observation notes on student teachers over recent years, whether a similar effect can be described in post-National Curriculum beginning teachers. Are they more constrained in their interpretation of 'teacher-work'? Are lessons seen as episodes in the delivery of someone else's curriculum (using a textbook as the sole resource) or are they (still?) the responsibility of teachers to design and justify in terms of aims, objectives and the 'elements of learning' (e.g. Hacking, 1992; Walford and Machon, 1994, pp. 13–50)?

My argument, then, is that the National Curriculum has brought into focus some questions concerning the very nature of what it is to be a geography teacher. Before 1988, such issues certainly existed, but were part of an ill-defined agenda which allowed a take-it-or-leave-it attitude to innovation and development on the one hand, and overindulgence, even self-indulgence, on the other. The argument has been put that it was this state of affairs which led to the easy lampooning by political critics of a number of curriculum developments, such as 'world studies', and left teachers with an undeniably difficult task in accounting for themselves (e.g. Walford, 1992, pp. 90–1). The low-level, corrosive feeling that something was wrong with education, and perhaps geography education in particular, was impossible to counter with success. It was this, the argument goes, which led directly to a heavily prescriptive national curriculum and perhaps the resulting reaction of teachers to the accompanying accountability pressures.

In the period post-1988, we now have a number of fixed points. For example, the question 'What should I teach?' is, to some extent, answered. Also, in the consolidation phase of the National Curriculum, it is becoming increasingly clear that so-called teacher assessment is primarily formative, and practices and procedures need to be appropriate for this purpose. This is helpful to teachers, to beginning teachers and to those involved in teacher training. A common language and a common list of practical concerns are comforting, though possibly also beguiling, as Edwards has pointed out:

> The predictability and control that the doctrine of technical rationality seemingly offers provides comforting reassurance to educational practitioners faced with constant uncertainty.

This need for certainty and control is, however, a major inhibitor of educational change. Thus, Ladner (1984) is right in arguing that in education there is a need to restore *ambiguity* to its proper place.

(Edwards, 1992, p. 465)

The crucial point, then, is not to focus on the questions which are answered in some way by the National Curriculum, but to identify those issues left untouched. For although it is helpful to know *what* to teach, effective teachers know that a number of key questions remain: how do I teach this material? What are the pitfalls with those methods? How do I cater for differing 'abilities' in the same classroom? How do I acquire up-to-date materials? How do I translate this material into a learning resource for 12-year-olds? Of course this is just the start, as such questions concern only individual lessons; another list can readily be compiled to look at planning priorities on a broader scale – that of a sequence of lessons or, ultimately, a scheme of work for the whole year. And, if we venture into the field of teacher assessment, it is clear from the research quoted earlier (Daugherty and Lambert, 1994) that there is no consensus in the responses to the questions it raises: what it is, when to do it, how to do it, how often to do it, how to use it, and so on. And yet, like the National Curriculum itself, teachers know they do have to do it.

These sorts of question lie at the heart of school improvement. Those who see geography as a medium for education must accept that teaching is a responsibility-bearing transaction, which may involve propositional, performative and even dispositional dimensions. If, as a basic premise, we can accept that, 'Education is a social product, in which a person's capacities for realistic and effective intervention in the world are developed' (Kleinig, 1982), then we can perhaps readily agree that largely bureaucratic solutions to curriculum development or raising pupils' achievements (such as the National Curriculum appears to be), are unlikely to satisfy the longer-term aspirations of teachers or pupils. In place of the administrative 'crackdown', which risks turning a teacher into a form of administrator or manager, there needs to be a re-creation of attitudes and approaches more resonant with the features of a 'learning' culture, which, for example, Barth (1990) writes about in the context of schools 'improving from within'. It is something like this that HE, in a redefined and willing training partnership, can help to support and nurture. The relationships in the partnership must be symbiotic and need to be built on trust. Part and parcel of this is that the work of the partnership is rigorous and challenging, and it is to this I now turn.

WAYS OF WORKING WITH THEORY AND PRACTICE

As is the case with any educational and training programme, the PGCE course possesses a distinctive pace and rhythm. This is manifest in the provision, as an entitlement, of particular kinds of experience for beginning teachers, which can precipitate active engagement with a range of theoretical and practical issues. As Slater and Rask put it:

Experience needs to be seen as an antecedent to the two concepts – theory and practice – and, as such, experiencing plays a crucial role in our attempts to get to grips with the problem of merging theory and practice. Experience makes practice and practicing gives us experience to think about, to reflect on and to begin to either theorise for ourselves or match our experience and practice with the theories of another.

(Slater and Rask, 1983, p. 183)

Experience is best understood in the widest possible sense as 'human experience, what we acquire as we attempt to do things, partly succeeding and partly failing' (Maxwell, 1992, p. 60). As such it is both a process and an achievement. In terms of teaching, experience is in general both what is (being) learned about how to do relevant and appropriate things of value as a result of actions, policies, methodological principles and programmes being implemented, and also that in terms of which those same actions, and the policies and aims that they embody, are to be judged (Maxwell, 1992, pp. 58–60). In other words, educators committed to life-long learning are also committed to the belief that genuine learning occurs when people reflect on their experience and test their understanding. Furthermore, this reflection involves both drawing upon previous experience – including possibly an already 'established role and expertise in life' (Finnegan, 1992, p. 19) – and listening and attending carefully to what we are told, and evaluating it according to the best workings of our minds and senses.

There is a link between this view and Schon's widely accepted notion of 'reflection in action', which occurs through the arrangement (by the 'coach') of the 'right set of experiences' (Schon, 1987, p. 93). What we are attempting at ULIE is a more explicit and more tangible reworking of this idea in order to strengthen it, for it sometimes has the appearance of no more than a slogan, lacking 'sufficient conceptual elaboration and programmatic strengths' (Liston and Zeichner, 1987, p. 27). We are doing this through the involvement of beginning teachers in 'research and development projects' (Lambert and Totterdell, 1993).

Observers have noted that, 'In essence these are small scale research enquiries undertaken in cooperation with the staff of the placement school or college' (Grace, 1993, p. 5). They have been welcomed as representing a significant innovation at the beginning of a process of professional formation and development for beginning teachers (Grace, 1993, p. 6), and possibly provide a unique basis for achieving a balanced integration between education scholarship and practical applications in specific school settings.

Their basis is to overcome the dualism apparently inherent in the concepts of 'theory' and 'practice'. The ULIE initial training course takes the alternative view that, 'Intelligent practice is not a step-child of theory. On the contrary, theorising is one practice amongst others and is itself intelligently or stupidly conducted' (Ryle, 1966, p. 27). To put this differently, beginning teachers are encouraged to dig as deeply as possible into specified practical questions and to understand that *to do so* they must ask theoretical questions. At the same time, tutors, teachers and beginning teachers can observe that the more they delve into the academic the more they will inevitably move into the practical side of things. Theory and practice, then, are not oppositional, in that *theorizing* at its best is not distant and removed; it is attentive to what obtains in a way that clarifies.

Beginning teachers are guaranteed a range of experiences, of which some are designed to develop primarily their capacities as 'competent practitioners' (ULIE, 1994), and others emphasize the complementary foci of the 'reflective professional' and 'teacher as researcher'. The intention is that beginning teachers see that the three foci are not exclusive of each other. 'Theorizing', as I have described it, is formalized somewhat in the research and development projects, and the role of the HE tutor is crucial and quite distinctive in this regard (being rather like that of the research supervisor); but it happens within the particularity of the placement school(s). It is intended to complement, not undermine, the mission of the school (or department within the school). As such, it provides essential 'practice'.

It is clear that there is much that could be explored in detail, not least the nature of the relationship that exists between the 'student' teacher and the school; what kinds of question is the student teacher-as-researcher permitted to ask, for example? There is not the space here to pursue this satisfactorily, and indeed this is itself the subject of further inquiry as the new partnership gains experience. Suffice it to say that it is exactly this prospect – that of inviting disciplined and sensitive challenge from new entrants to the profession – which implies some kind of dialogue, in which the school or subject department in a school has to account for its way of doing things, that we hope will attract schools into the partnership. It has long been accepted that 'students' bring a lot to the department and school: the implications of what I am arguing here is that, properly guided and resourced, the beginning teacher can bring a lot more than a set of interesting worksheets, up-to-date material or the odd simulation game, important though these things are. He or she can focus thinking on precisely framed issues or concerns, and arguably there is no aspect of geography education more suitable for this scrutiny than the National Curriculum – both in its detail and in terms of the bigger picture, as I outlined earlier in this chapter – and no department which would not benefit from this kind of activity.

To elucidate further, the main emphasis in this account has been on 'research', but the 'development' aspect of the work also carries significance. It brings to the surface a distinction recently articulated by Barnett, 'that between learning conceived as an individual enterprise and learning conceived as a social activity' (Barnett, 1992, pp. 74–5). He continues:

> Appropriateness, effectiveness, soundness, and worthwhileness of one's learning can only be judged by others. Questions, therefore, need to be asked of any learning process: to what extent is it under the control of the learners? What opportunities are there for the learners to learn from each other?
>
> (Barnett, 1992, p. 75)

Beginning teachers must subject their own work to scrutiny. Some form of presentation must be made to the school subject department in an appropriate form, which probably requires a reworking of 'findings' from the formal written 'assignment' to something more suitable for oral presentation and discussion. As Ryle put it:

> In the special business of teaching, we are much more concerned with people's competences than with their cognitive repertoires ... we are interested ... in their capacities to find out truths from themselves and their ability to organise and exploit them, when discovered.
>
> (Ryle, 1966, pp. 28–9).

The dialogue which all this implies is exciting and challenging for both experienced colleagues and beginners, though probably for different reasons. I have not listed examples of research and development projects, for potential studies are not difficult to identify. They fall into two broad groups. First are those of a more general pedagogical flavour (but which nevertheless require distinctive subject-based definition), such as developing strategies for differentiation, teacher assessment or effectiveness with early-stage bilingual children. Secondly, there are those specifically 'geographical' concerns, such as how to introduce and teach distant and unfamiliar places, the graphicacy skills base of Year 7 children or the acquisition of particular concepts in, say, physical geography. Particularly interesting areas to develop with beginning teachers – ones which can have tangible impact – are researching and developing the use of information technology in geography teaching (in the placement school) or the range of data children are exposed to, and the images they assimilate, regarding people and places.

CONCLUSION

I have attempted to relate the needs of beginning teachers and a professionally based view of school improvement under a system of school-oriented teacher training which preserves, indeed develops, an HE dimension and perspective. What I have described is largely in operation, though it remains to be seen whether it is too fanciful to imagine this continuing to develop in the future. The experience of the ULIE partnership is that, other things being equal, a large enough number of schools are coming forward to be willing 'partners' on the basis outlined here. Such is the under-resourcing of the whole enterprise, however, that it is impossible to be optimistic about the future of the PGCE. It is currently in a deeply unstable condition.

Teachers will always wish to be trained, and few schools are in a position to take on the task alone. It could be that out of the ashes of the PGCE, if it comes to that, will rise a new definition of the HE role in initial training; one which is overtly more research-based, with beginning teachers following a mix of both taught and research-based modules of a higher degree. There may be indications already of moves to 'inflate' teacher qualifications through the use of portfolios to gain MA credits. Such developments may be welcome in themselves, but far more important in my mind is the need to pursue the notion of bringing together tutors, teachers and beginning teachers in the creative tension that the PGCE research and development framework can deliver.

What I am arguing for is a balance of attitude and approach in schools to the tasks that fall to them, in particular in interpreting and implementing the National Curriculum. I am urging an understanding of school geography as a precursor to improving it, and essential to this is an acknowledgement of a constructionist perspective. This is far-reaching, as Edwards has observed:

> School and their communities have to be understood for what they invariably are: sites of value pluralism and potential conflict where power is unevenly distributed, not sites of consensual harmony secured through democratic means. The pursuit of consensus as a democratic ideal has to be seen as practically problematic, if not logically contradictory, in situations characterised by plurality of values. In such circumstances procedures which legitimate only one version of 'the truth', however representative, are inherently undemocratic and, in relation to the curriculum, anti-educational.
>
> (Edwards, 1992, p. 467)

Not for the first time in this chapter, this signals some substantial issues which will need to be faced under the 'critically reflective' paradigm of initial teacher education and training being proposed here. During the previous period, when constructionist approaches had the upper hand in educational thinking, such crucial issues, including the very nature of successful learning communities, were dodged at great cost.

This chapter, then, has been exploratory, even tentative, for there is much work to be done at the research interface I have identified. But the potential to engage initial training with the larger project of school improvement is compelling. Is it convincing enough to safeguard the HE contribution to developing teachers and teaching in England under the recently (1994) formulated Teacher Training Agency.

NOTE

1. The term 'beginning teacher' has been adopted at the University of London Institute of Education to denote postgraduate student teachers. It is designed to signal to 'students' that partnership training involves them fully in school life and thus assumes certain professional obligations, duties and attitudes from the start of the course.

REFERENCES

Alexander, R. (1990) 'Partnership in initial training: confronting the issues.' In M. Booth, V. Furlong and M. Wilkin (eds) *Partnership in Initial Training*. London: Cassell.

Bailey, P. (1992) *Securing the Place of Geography in the National Curriculum of English and Welsh Schools: A Study in the Politics and Practicalities of Curriculum Reform*. Sheffield: Geographical Association.

Balderstone, D. and Lambert D. (1992) *Assessment Matters*. Sheffield: Geographical Association.

Barnett, R. (1992) 'The learning society?' *Reflections on Higher Education*, 4, 70–5.

Barth, R. (1990) *Improving Schools from Within*. San Fransisco: Jossey-Bass.

Bennetts, T. (1994) 'Reflections on the development of geography in the National Curriculum.' In R. Walford and P. Machon (eds) *Challenging Times: Implementing the National Curriculum in Geography*. Cambridge: Cambridge Publishing Services.

Bolton, E. (1994) 'One last push.' *Guardian Education*, 17 May.

CATE (1992) *A Note of Guidance*. London: Council for the Accreditation of Teacher Education.

Curriculum Council for Wales (1993) *The National Curriculum and Assessment Framework in Wales: The Final Report from CCW to the Secretary of State for Wales*. Cardiff: Curriculum Council for Wales.

Daugherty, R. (1990) 'Assessment in the geography curriculum.' *Geography*, 75 (4), 289–301.

Daugherty, R. and Lambert, D. (1994) 'Teacher assessment and geography in the National Curriculum.' *Geography*, 79 (4), 339–49.

Dearing, R. (1993) *The National Curriculum and its Assessment: Interim Report*. London: NCC/SEAC.

Dearing, R. (1994) *The National Curriculum and its Assessment: Final Report*. London: School Curriculum and Assessment Authority (SCAA).

DES (1991) *Geography in the National Curriculum (England)*. London: HMSO.

DfE (1992) *Initial Teacher Training (Secondary Phase). Circular 9/92. London: Department for Education*.

Donaldson, M. (1978) *Children's Minds*. London: Fontana.

Donaldson, M. (1992) *Human Minds: An Exploration*. Harmondsworth: Penguin.

Dowgill, P. and Lambert, D. (1992) 'Cultural literacy and school geography.' *Geography*, 77 (2) 143–52.

Edwards, G. (1992) 'A strategy for the curriculum.' *Journal of Curriculum Studies*, 24 (5), 463–8.

Everton, T. (1991) *Partnership Newsletter*, 1. University of Leicester School of Education.

Fien, J. (1992) 'What kind of research for what kind of teaching? Towards research in geographical education as a critical social science.' In D. Hill (ed.) *International Perspectives on Geographical Education*. Boulder, CO: Center for Geographical Education, University of Colorado.

Finnegan, R. (1992) 'Recovering the "academic community": what do we mean?' *Reflections on Higher Education*, 4, 7–23.

Fullan, M. (1991) *The New Meaning of Educational Change*. London: Cassell.

Fry, P. and Schofield, A. (1993) *Geography at Key Stage 3: Teachers' Experience of National Curriculum Geography in Year 7*. Sheffield: Geographical Association.

Grace, G. (1993) *London Institute of Education PGCE: Visiting Examiners' Reports for 1992/1993*. Durham: University of Durham.

Graves, N. (1985) *Teacher Education in Adversity*. London: University of London Institute of Education.

Hacking, E. (1992) *Geography into Practice*. Harlow: Longman.

Hammersley, M. (1993) 'On the teacher as researcher.' *Educational Action Research*, **1** (3) 425–45.

Hammersmith and Fulham (1993) 'Schools make a difference project.' Project leaflet.

Iven, H. (1993) 'Teachers should be trained in partnership.' *Teaching Today*. Spring, p. 1.

Kleinig, J. (1982) *Philosophical Issues in Education*. London: Croom Helm.

Ladner, B. (1984) 'Introduction: the humanities and the schools.' In B. Ladner (ed.) *The Humanities in Precollegiate Education*. 83rd Yearbook, Pt 2, of the National Society for the Study of Education. Chicago: NSSE.

Lambert, D. (1994) 'The National Curriculum: what shall we do with it?' *Geography*, **79** (1), 65–76.

Lambert, D. and Totterdell, M. (1993) *Professional Studies and the Post-graduate Beginning Teacher*. Occasional Papers in Teacher Education and Training No. 3. London: University of London Institute of Education.

Lawton, D. (1992) 'Whatever happened to the TGAT Report?' In C. Gipps (ed.) *Developing Assessment for the National Curriculum*. London: Kogan Page.

Liston, D.P. and Zeichner, K.M. (1987) 'Reflective teacher education and moral deliberation.' *Journal of Teacher Education*, November/December, **38** (6), 2–8.

Louis, K. and Miles, M. (1990) *Improving the Urban High School*. London: Cassell.

McNamara, D. (1990) 'The National Curriculum: an agenda for research.' *British Educational Research Journal*, **16** (3), 225–35.

Maxwell, N. (1992) 'What the task of creating civilisation has to learn from the success of modern science: towards a new Enlightenment.' *Reflections on Higher Education*, **4**, 47–69.

NCC (1991) *Geography in the National Curriculum: Non-statutory Guidance*. York: National Curriculum Council.

Rawling, E. (1992) 'The making of a national curriculum.' *Geography*, **77** (4), 192–309.

Reid, L.A. (1986) *Ways of Understanding Education*. London: Heinemann.

Ryle, G. (1966) *The Concept of Mind*. Harmondsworth: Penguin.

Schon, D.A. (1987) *Educating the Reflective Practitioner*. San Francisco: Jossey-Bass.

SEAC (1991) *Teacher Assessment at Key Stage 3 (Geography)*. London: School Examinations and Assessment Council.

SHA (1993) 'Teacher training: further advice'. Secondary Heads Association Information Sheet. October.

SEAC (1993) *Pupils Work Assessed*. London: School Examinations and Assessment Council.

Slater, F. (1994) 'Education through geography: knowledge, understanding, values and culture.' *Geography*, **79** (2), 147–63.

Slater, F. and Rask, R. (1983) 'Geography teacher education.' *European Journal of Teacher Education*, **6** (2), 183–9.

Stenhouse, L. (1975) *An Introduction to Curriculum Research and Development*. London: Heinemann.

TGAT (1988) *Task Group on Assessment and Testing: A Report*. London: DES.

ULIE (1994) *Partnership in Training: The Secondary PGCE Course*. London: University of London Institute of Education.

Walford, R. (1992) 'Creating a national curriculum: a view from the inside.' In D. Hill (ed.) *International Perspectives on Geographical Education*. Boulder, CO: Center for Geographical Education, University of Colorado.

Walford, R. and Machon, P. (eds) (1994) *Challenging Times: Implementing the National Curriculum in Geography*. Cambridge: Cambridge Publishing Services.

Waugh, D. and Bushell, T. (1991) *Key Geography: Foundations*. Cheltenham: Stanley Thornes.

Chapter 19

Assessment in Geographical Education: A Review of Research

Richard Daugherty

The assessment of students' learning in geography, especially in the context of external tests and examinations, has been a continuing focus of interest in geographical education. The very first issue of the Geographical Association's journal, *The Geographical Teacher*, published an article on 'Recent examination papers' (Wilkinson, 1901). Wilkinson, like many of those who have written subsequently about assessment and examinations, offered a review and critique of current practice. As systems of external examinations have evolved, the literature on the assessment of geographical learning has been punctuated by such reviews, often accompanied by a commentary bemoaning the constraining influence of examinations on teaching, learning and the curriculum.

However, as with so much else in geographical education, the professional discourse about assessment has only infrequently been informed by research studies seeking to gather evidence from empirical investigation. In the established traditions of educational assessment, many of those studies have dealt with the analysis of candidate performance, with test validity and with the techniques employed in test design. Only in the past two decades has there been a broadening of the scope of research, with studies which have explored the use of criterion-referenced assessment, the ways in which assessment practice impacts upon students' learning, and the role of assessment in state-defined geography curricula.

In the longer perspective of a century of change, geography assessment has mirrored trends in the aims and content of the geography curriculum. Daugherty (1990) reviewed in broad terms how assessment practice has reflected the curriculum, while Underwood's (1983) study revealed more of the detail of the changing context and cognitive demands of geography examinations over almost a century. For most of that period, practice in testing and examinations drew on the dominant psychometric tradition in educational assessment in attempting to measure learning outcomes. However, since the late 1960s, the flowering of curriculum development in geographical education has stimulated a search for assessment techniques and processes which would better serve the aims and objectives of the new curricula. Among curriculum developers, there has been a concerted move to break 'the vicious circle of curriculum under-development' (Tolley and Reynolds, 1977), with external examinations being seen as an obstacle to those learning outcomes which conventional examining methods were incapable of measuring. At the same time, assessment has moved up the agenda of geography educators and, within less than a decade from the mid-1960s, an area of interest which had seldom merited more than a few pages in handbooks on geography teaching had become the subject of widespread debate (e.g. Biddle, 1968; Kurfman 1970) and was well served by authoritative guides for practitioners (Senathirajah and Weiss, 1971; Marsden, 1976).

The research methods employed to investigate practice have developed in response to that broader agenda. The quantitative analyses of candidate performance which characterized the pre-1970 era have been augmented, though only to a limited extent, by qualitative methods, including the use of open-ended questionnaires, interviews and observation techniques. The growing recognition of assessment as a process rather than an event and as integral to learning rather than a separate operation has prompted researchers to look for a methodology which is appropriate to that changed focus of attention.

PERFORMANCE OF CANDIDATES IN EXAMINATIONS

A few published studies have applied the established techniques of analysing candidate performance in the context of geography examinations. For the most part they are of historical interest only, but they do reveal something of the preoccupations and the methods of both the examinations being studied and the researchers undertaking the studies. A 'Statistical analysis of a geography examination' (the 1919 Central Welsh Board's senior-stage paper) led Whitehouse (1920) to a discussion both of candidate performance and of the questions set. Thirty years later, Daniels (1954) analysed the marks awarded on three parallel General Certificate of Education (GCE) Ordinary-level papers – essay questions, objective questions, data interpretation – to determine the contribution each paper made to the overall grade awarded and to explore correlations with teacher estimates. A further thirty years on, Webb (1986) was able to make use of computer analysis to study the contribution of factors such as family background and study habits to an explanation of the performance of candidates in the 1982 University of Cambridge GCE Advanced-level geography examination. Over the period separating Webb's work from that of Whitehouse, the research methods had moved on from means and percentages to factor analysis, while the research agenda had shifted from patterns of marks awarded in examinations to the background influences which might help explain the variability of performance.

In other respects, the research agenda has changed less. As early as 1933, Jones was publishing the findings of a study of the 'Differences in the geographical work of boys and girls'. It is, however, disappointing that such work stands in isolation rather than as the first step in a developing tradition of research of this nature. The potential for gender bias in the conduct of tests and examinations has never been higher on the wider educational agenda than it was during the 1980s (e.g. Goldstein's summary of the research evidence in Department of Education and Science/Welsh Office, 1988) but, though the debate is still very much alive (Larsen, 1989), there is little evidence of that concern finding expression in empirical research in the field of geographical education. One recent study in Finland (Rikkinen and Houtsonen, 1992) revealed that boys were still rather more successful than girls at answering geography questions but that the gap had narrowed during the 1980s, a trend explained in part by reference to changes in the curriculum. Further studies of this kind could help in interpreting continuing gender differences in examination performance, and the data are in many cases already available; the organizations responsible for administering examinations in the UK routinely monitor differences in the performance of male and female candidates.

More generally, the relative invisibility of the evidence obtained by examining bodies is to be regretted, since studies undertaken by them in recent years have explored some fundamental issues in geography examinations. Massey (1983) analysed the patterns of performance of candidates across each component in one '16+' geography examination in an attempt to answer the question: 'What knowledge and skills in geography can one expect of candidates awarded a given GCE or CSE [Certificate of Secondary Education] grade?' As Massey himself concluded, the absence of a clear profile of performance characteristics for all the candidates awarded any one grade cast serious doubt on the feasibility of the proposed move to criteria grading in the new General Certificate of Secondary Education (GCSE) examinations in England and Wales and the revised Standard-grade examinations in Scotland. As so often with research evidence, Massey's conclusions did little to temper the enthusiasm of policy-makers for the idea which he had shown to be so problematic (Secondary Examinations Council, 1985).

In another published study which has much to offer geography educators, the staff of a different examining body, the Welsh Joint Education Committee (WJEC), turned their attention to the well-recognized problem of setting examinations in ways which differentiate effectively across a wide range of attainment levels. Davies and Davies (1991, p. 1) analysed 'the factors which influence differentiation in the terminal examinations of the WJEC's 'Avery Hill' and 'Mainstream' geography examinations'. Drawing on their research evidence, they proposed a model for achieving better differentiation in geography examinations. In a further study, extending the scope of the work to include differentiation in coursework and involving a team of teacher/researchers, Davies (1991) looked at how teachers attempted to provide for differentiation in the classroom.

What Davies's work does is to expose the examining process to more fundamental questioning as to its procedures, the assumptions it makes and the impact it has on teaching and learning. Though the procedures used by examining bodies may often seem to be a set feature of the educational landscape, they are of course in principle as appropriate a focus for research as is what goes into the process – the test items – or what comes out – the candidates' performance characteristics. There is an as yet largely untapped potential for research which uses qualitative methodology to look at how assessment decisions are made, whether during a course by teachers or at the end of a course by those responsible for marking and grading examination papers. Daugherty (1985) undertook one such study of '16+' geography examinations, revealing through participant observation of question-setting, marking and awarding meetings something of the decision-making which examiners normally engage in behind closed doors.

TEST DESIGN, VALIDITY AND RELIABILITY

More traditional research methodologies have been used to scrutinize not the process of making assessment decisions but the form of the tests and the responses of candidates which will be the basis for eventual judgements about their attainments.

The development of taxonomies of educational objectives during the 1960s and the search, referred to above, for assessment techniques which could measure attainment in geography across the full range of those objectives led geography educators to explore issues both of test design and of assessment methods (e.g. Cox, 1968, on the use of objectives in designing tests and Styles, 1973, for a discussion of the measurement of affective objectives). Those advocating the greater use of objective tests in school geography (e.g. Monk, 1971; Hones, 1973) were optimistic about the potential of that technique for reducing the perceived mismatch between learning objectives and the techniques in use for measuring learning outcomes. Wiegand (1982) administered such a test to a sample of secondary-school students in London, obtaining evidence about the use of objective questions to measure (in Bloom's terms) knowledge, comprehension, application and analysis. He concluded that an objective test as a component in the examining of geography at 16+ was both feasible and desirable.

The way in which the mix of assessment techniques deployed in a test or examination can affect validity or reliability has in fact rarely been a subject for empirical study in geographical education. Biddle's (1973) article on 'the quest for reliability in marking responses to essay questions in geography' gives an account of practice in one examination, but there has been little research on techniques of assessment beyond that undertaken by examining bodies in routinely monitoring their own examinations.

More recent work includes Stimpson's (1992) study of the use of a taxonomy of structured learning outcomes in the design of graded tests in geography, leading him to conclude that a theoretical model of levels of understanding can be a useful tool in the devising of geography test items. In general, however, the central issue of test validity – an assessment is pointless if it is not valid – has received surprisingly little attention from researchers in geographical education.

What remains in the area of test design are studies within which geography has been one of the subjects under scrutiny. For example, Taylor and Nuttall (1974) studied the work of 220 candidates taking a CSE examination with a view to understanding the way in which question choice might affect a candidate's grading. Having given the candidates more time to answer questions they had not opted for originally, Taylor and Nuttall concluded that 'the geography study showed that candidates were often able to do rather better on questions which they had not chosen' (p. 146), to the extent that a quarter of them could have achieved a higher grade if they had been graded on the answers in which they had performed best.

The comparability of grading standards across several examining bodies (with their own syllabuses and schemes of assessment, but making awards of grades in a national examination system) has been a longstanding issue for assessment research (e.g. Willmott, 1977). One approach adopted was to devise a reference test with a view to obtaining a separate, independent assessment of the attainment objectives measured by the examinations being compared. Hoste's (1972) reference test for geography (discussed in Hall, 1976, p. 71) exposes some of the pitfalls of this approach, but in doing so it also, interestingly, reveals what the teachers questioned by Hoste would see as an appropriate balance of geographical objectives to be tested – the underexplored issue of what constitutes a valid test of geographical attainment. More recent comparability studies have tended to rely on a cross-moderation methodology, in which examiners rate the work of candidates from examining bodies other than their own. The latest of these (Northern Examinations and Assessment Board, 1994) offers some useful insights into the differences in practice across the six GCSE examining groups in England, Wales and Northern Ireland, but also emphasizes the difficulty of making any objective comparison of syllabuses and assessment schemes which differ quite markedly.

NEW DIRECTIONS IN ASSESSMENT AND IN RESEARCH METHODS

While the world of external examinations has continued on a steady path of evolution in its structures and procedures, the wider issues of assessment as an aid to learning and as a day-to-day part of the work of the teacher came to the fore during the 1980s. Increasing emphasis has been placed on maximizing the validity of assessments in the context of a broadly defined curriculum, and the practice of formal assessment has also moved out of the examination room and into the classroom.

Two themes recur in the assessment debates which have been associated with changing practice in curriculum and in pedagogy. First, the choice of criterion-referencing as the frame of reference, for formative as well as summative assessments, has influenced practice both in the classroom and in externally controlled systems of assessment. Secondly, the way in which those external systems interact with classroom practice has been a continuing issue, taking forward the 1970s debate about using assessment as a positive influence for supporting the individual student's learning and for stimulating curriculum change. Such themes require the use by researchers of methods more varied than those appropriate to more narrowly focused studies of test design and of candidate performance.

A major project exploring the application of criterion-referenced assessment to the routine assessment of students' learning was undertaken by Black and Dockrell in Scotland. Their interest in using assessment diagnostically led them to construct a curriculum and assessment scheme which sought to place assessment firmly in the role of learning support (see Black and Dockrell, 1980, for guidance on this approach to geography assessment). The same authors subsequently published a research report outlining the main findings of the research and development project, which covered work in several subjects (Black and Dockrell, 1984). While there were observable gains from the approach adopted, questions remained about the feasibility for day-to-day use in schools of a relatively elaborate scheme which encompassed the specifying of curriculum objectives, the choice of curriculum content and the design of criterion-referenced test items.

The use of criterion-referencing in public examinations has, however, continued to develop across the world in the 1980s and 1990s. Logie (1992) reported on the development of assessment using grade-related criteria in New Zealand, and argued that 'achievement based assessment' had an important place in the design of examinations at the level both of form 5 (School Certificate) and of form 7 (University Bursary). Equivalent developments are occurring in many national systems in the 1990s.

The adoption of a criterion-referencing frame for reporting has influenced practice across the full range of contexts in which attainment is measured and reported. In addition to the use of explicit criteria in classroom assessment and in public examinations, there has been a notable trend towards the use of profiles and records of achievement to give a broader picture of what students have achieved than is typically provided by norm-referenced grades. Competency-based assessment in vocational educational is another application of the principle that prior definition of objectives, measurement of performance in relation to those objectives, and reporting of specific learning outcomes can make assessments both more transparent and more useful. There is fertile ground here for research into how geographical attainment is defined, measured and reported.

The second theme referred to above – that of how external assessment systems interact with classroom practice – has inevitably been a matter of interest to those who have seen the design of a unified curriculum and assessment scheme, linked to external examinations, as a vehicle for curriculum change. All the main curriculum development projects of the 1970s and 1980s in England and Wales – Geography 14–18, Geography for the Young School Leaver (GYSL)/Avery Hill, Geography 16–19 – ensured that the work of students following courses based on their curriculum schemes could be certificated through public examinations. Research into the work of those projects has therefore focused in part on the role of assessment in curriculum change. Boardman (1988), for example, used a variety of methods, including participant observation and case studies, to investigate the implementation and dissemination of the GYSL Project. One section of his report deals with 'the link with examinations'; it points both to the crucial role of public examinations in legitimizing the Project's approach to the geography curriculum, and to the way in which the Project helped to establish the assessment of work done by pupils during the course as a significant element in the process leading to certification.

More broadly, and across all subjects examined in England, Wales and Northern Ireland, the GCSE examination, aimed primarily at 14–16-year-olds and introduced in the 1986–88 examination cycle, offers a prime example of assessment-led curriculum change. Daugherty *et al.* (1991) used several methods – questionnaires to all secondary schools in Wales plus structured interviews and classroom observation in fifteen case study schools – to investigate the impact of the new examination on the teaching of three subjects, including geography, in Wales. The findings range across matters such as teaching styles, differentiation strategies and in-service training, and reveal how teachers were responding to England and Wales's first truly national examination system and its distinctive curriculum philosophy. More specifically, the research shows something of how teachers were interpreting the syllabus requirement to set and mark coursework, which had, with the advent of GCSE, become an integral feature of all geography examinations at this level.

NATIONAL AND INTERNATIONAL ASSESSMENT SYSTEMS

One notable feature of the changing picture in geography assessment has been the increasing attention given to assessment arrangements, other than examinations geared to certification and selection, which operate across whole educational systems, whether at the nation-state level or at that of states within a federal system of government. There is potential here for studies which cut across state boundaries and either attempt to measure the attainments of geography students in different countries, or employ the methodology of comparative education, in investigating the differing ways in which educational systems are attempting to define and measure geographical attainment.

The 'InterGeo' initiative (Niemz and Stoltman, 1992) is of the former type and is self-evidently at an early stage in its development. However, the evidence of student attainment obtained to date is sufficiently robust for it to be analysed and form the basis of tentative conclusions. Looking ahead to InterGeo III, Lambert and Purnell (1994) argue for an international item bank consisting of tasks and strategies which target aspects of the International Charter on Geographical Education (International Geographical Union, 1992). Though the methods used in making international comparisons have been more fully developed in other subjects, such as mathematics, and any conclusions reached are typically surrounded by numerous caveats, there remains considerable potential here for the development of appropriate assessment instruments and for research into the performance of students taking InterGeo tests.

But, however much progress is made in international assessments, what is already with us in many of the educational systems across the world is a trend towards regular assessment of attainment and its inevitable accompaniment, the attempt to describe the attainments which are to be assessed. There is great scope here too for research at two levels.

The definitions of attainment and the methods being used for measuring attainment are, in themselves, a worthy focus for study. One such example is the National Assessment of Educational Progress Geography Consensus Project in the USA (National Assessment Governing Board, 1994), while in England (Department of Education and Science, 1991) and Wales (Welsh Office, 1991) the geography National Curriculum has been central to all curriculum and assessment debates in the 1990s. There is much to be learned from comparative study of the systems now being put in place in many countries across the world (Daugherty, 1992).

Beyond the official definitions of attainment and the required procedures for assessment are the essentially educational questions as to how teachers and students are responding to the new requirements. In England and Wales, researchers such as Roberts (1991) have investigated many aspects of national curriculum implementation, including assessment, in schools in the South Yorkshire area. Others (Lambert and Daugherty, 1994) have used questionnaire and interview methods to examine how teachers were interpreting, and reacting to, the specific requirements for day-to-day 'teacher assessment' of pupils' work. In a further analysis, drawing on the same body of data from teachers in South Wales and the London area, Daugherty and Lambert (1994) raise issues about the process of curriculum and assessment change, pointing out that the way teachers perceive their assessment role is closely tied up with their views on the character and purpose of geography as a medium for education.

CONCLUSION

In a world of state-wide geography curricula and their associated assessment systems, the old research priorities of analyses of test items and of candidate performance must remain on the research agenda. There is an important role for investigations of the validity and reliability of tests and of the characteristics of candidate performance on those tests. But assessment research can no longer be a small and largely separate backwater in the wider stream of research into geographical education. Tolley and Reynolds (1977) argued the essential interdependence of curriculum and assessment, a lesson which seems not always to have been learned in the design of the state-wide systems of the 1990s. If the way in which curriculum, assessment and pedagogy interact is a central issue for those engaged in planning for geographical education, then the research agenda must be as much about how assessment arrangements interact with curriculum and pedagogy as about the assessment process itself.

REFERENCES

Biddle, D. (ed.) (1968) *Readings in Geographical Education. Vol. I.* Sydney: Whitcombe and Tombs.

Biddle, D. (1973) 'The quest for reliability in marking responses to essay questions in geography.' In D. Biddle and C.E. Deer (eds) *Readings in Geographical Education. Vol. II.* Sydney: Whitcombe and Tombs.

Black, H.D. and Dockrell, W.B. (1980) *Diagnostic Assessment in Geography.* Edinburgh: Scottish Council for Research in Education.

Black, H.D. and Dockrell, W.B. (1984) *Criterion-Referenced Assessment in the Classroom.* Edinburgh: Scottish Council for Research in Education.

Boardman, D. (1988) *The Impact of a Curriculum Project: Geography for the Young School Leaver.* Birmingham: University of Birmingham.

Cox, B. (1968) 'Test items in geography for a taxonomy of educational objectives.' In D. Biddle (ed.) *Readings in Geographical Education. Vol. I.* Sydney: Whitcombe and Tombs.

Daniels, J.C. (1954) 'Testing geography at the Ordinary level of the General Certificate of Education.' *British Journal of Educational Psychology*, **24**, 180–9.

Daugherty, R. (1985) *Examining Geography at 16+: A Study of Decision-making in Two Geography Examinations.* London: Secondary Examinations Council.

Daugherty, R. (1990) 'Assessment in the geography curriculum.' *Geography*, **75** (4) 289–301.

Daugherty, R. (1992) 'The role of assessment in geographical education: a framework for comparative analysis.' In D. Hill (ed.) *International Perspectives in Geographical Education.* Boulder, CO: Center for Geographic Education.

Daugherty, R. and Lambert, D. (1994) 'Teacher assessment and geography in the national curriculum.' *Geography*, **79** (4), 339–49.

Daugherty, R., Thomas, B., Jones, G.E. and Davies, S. (1991) *GCSE in Wales.* Cardiff: Welsh Office Education Department.

Davies, P. (1991) *Differentiation in the Classroom and in the Examination Room: Achieving the Impossible?.* Cardiff: Welsh Joint Education Committee.

Davies, P. and Davies, B. (1991) *Differentiation in Examinations.* Cardiff: Welsh Joint Education Committee.

Department of Education and Science (1991) *Geography in the National Curriculum.* London: HMSO.

Department of Education and Science/ Welsh Office (1988) *National Curriculum Assessment and Testing: A Report.* London and Cardiff: HMSO.

Hall, D. (1976) *Geography and the Geography Teacher.* London: George Allen and Unwin.

Hones, G. (1973) 'Objective testing in geography.' *Geography*, **58** (1), 29–37.

Hoste, R. (1972) *Educational Test Bulletin No. 3.* Slough: NFER.

International Geographical Union (1992) *International Charter on Geographical Education.* Freiburg: IGU Commission on Geographical Education.

Jones, W. (1933) 'Differences in the geographical work of boys and girls.' *Geography*, **18** (1), 37–54.

Kurfman, D. (ed.) (1970) *Evaluation in Geographic Education.* Belmont, CA: Fearon.

Lambert, D. and Daugherty, R. (1993) 'Teacher assessment in Key Stage 3.' *Teaching Geography*, **18** (3), 113–15.

Lambert, D. and Purnell, K.N. (1994) 'International testing in geography: comparing students' achievements within and between countries.' *Assessment in Education*, **1** (2), 167–79.

Larsen, B. (1989) 'Gender bias and the GCSE.' *Contemporary Issues in Geography and Education*, **3** (1), 80–4.

Logie, M.J. (1992) 'Achievement based assessment in New Zealand.' In D. Hill (ed.) *Interdependence in Geographic Education.* Boulder, CO: Center for Geographic Education.

Marsden, W. (1976) *Evaluating the Geography Curriculum*. Edinburgh: Oliver and Boyd.

Massey, A.J. (1983) 'Grades and performance in 16+ geography.' *CORE*, **7** (1), F8, C5.

Monk, J. (1971) 'Preparing tests to measure course objectives.' *Journal of Geography*, **70** 157–62.

National Assessment Governing Board (1994) *Geography Framework for the 1994 National Assessment of Educational Progress*. Washington, DC: NAGP.

Niemz, G. and Stoltman, J.P. (1992) 'The field trials report on InterGeo II.' In D. Hill (ed.) *Interdependence in Geographic Education*. Boulder, CO: Center for Geographic Education.

Northern Examinations and Assessment Board (1994) *A Comparability Study in GCSE Geography*. Manchester: NEAB.

Rikkinen, H. and Houtsonen, L. (1992) 'Achievement differences in Finnish boys and girls in school geography.' In D. Hill (ed.) *Interdependence in Geographic Education*. Boulder, CO: Center for Geographic Education.

Roberts, M. (1991) 'On the eve of the geography National Curriculum: the implications for secondary schools.' *Geography*, **76** (4), 331–42.

Secondary Examinations Council (1985) *Report of Working Party: Geography Draft Grade Criteria*. London: Secondary Examinations Council.

Senathirajah, N. and Weiss, J. (1971) *Evaluation in Geography*. Toronto: Ontario Institute for Studies in Education.

Stimpson, P. (1992) 'Assessment in geography and the SOLO taxonomy.' In D. Hill (ed.) *Interdependence in Geographic Education*. Boulder, CO: Center for Geographic Education.

Styles, E. (1973) 'Measurement of affective educational objectives in geography.' In D. Biddle and C.E. Deer (eds) *Readings in Geographical Education. Vol. II*. Sydney: Whitcombe and Tombs.

Taylor, E.G. and Nuttall, D. (1974) 'Question choice in examinations: an experiment in geography and science.' *Educational Research*, **16**, 143–50.

Tolley, H. and Reynolds, J. (1977) *Geography 14 to 18: A Handbook for School-based Curriculum Development*. Basingstoke: Macmillan Education.

Underwood, B.L. (1983) 'An analysis and interpretation of the changing structure, content and cognitive demand of selected geography examinations in geography at sixteen and eighteen plus, from 1882 to 1980.' Unpublished PhD thesis, University of London Institute of Education.

Webb, G. (1986) 'Factors affecting achievement in the University of Cambridge GCE A level geography examination.' *Educational Research*, **28** (2), 123–38.

Welsh Office (1991) *Geography in the National Curriculum (Wales)*. Cardiff: Welsh Office.

Whitehouse, W.E. (1920) 'Statistical analysis of a geography examination.' *The Scottish Geographical Magazine*. **36**, 21–9.

Wiegand, P. (1982) 'Objective testing in geography at 16+.' *Geography*, **67** (4), 332–6.

Wilkinson, F.J. (1901) 'Recent examination papers.' *The Geographical Teacher*, **1** (1), 39–44.

Willmott, A.S. (1977) *CSE and GCE Grading Standards: The 1973 Comparability Study*. London: Macmillan.

Chapter 20

Raising Attainment in Geography: Prospects and Problems

David Leat

The history of the National Curriculum Geography Orders in England and Wales[1] provides a depressing commentary on the status of educational research, especially in relation to curriculum development. Rawling (1992) provides a telling account of the political constraints that operated inside the Geography Working Group, set up by the Department of Education and Science (DES) and the Welsh Office, which placed much emphasis on the mastery of knowledge by pupils. She writes of the Interim Report (DES and Welsh Office, 1989) 'with many paragraphs drawing attention to pupils' lack of place knowledge and the inadequacy of thematic-based courses (e.g. see para 2.14) (Rawling, 1992, p. 229). She further quotes the Secretary of State for Education calling, in the House of Commons, for young people to learn about places and where they are and not just vague concepts and attitudes. As recorded in the government prescribed Orders, the Statements of Attainment (SoAs) constitute a deficit model of the curriculum by stating precisely what pupils need to know.

While some members of the working group and many correspondents in the consultation process made cogent arguments for alternative ways of framing the document, the political view prevailed. The imperative was that, 'Children don't seem to know where places are, what they are like, or why they are as they are – so they had better be taught.' There was no irrefutable case that could be made against this deficit model; there was no weight of evidence that could persuade doubting minds that this was the wrong construction.[2] Research into geographical education or attainment had not generated a compelling alternative.

Sadly, therefore, geography teachers had to proceed with a model that looked doomed from the start, particularly because the assessment framework appeared totally impractical. So the profession beavered away, producing schemes of work, manufacturing elaborate assessment frameworks and consuming literally millions of teacher-hours, only for the inevitable climbdown to occur. In January 1995, after much consultation, new orders were distributed to schools removing some, if not all, of the absurdities of the original orders.[2]

However, before too much blame is attached to educational researchers, it must be said that where strong evidence did exist to guide the construction of the assessment framework, most notably in science, it did not significantly influence the curriculum orders.

THE PIAGET STUMBLING BLOCK

It is extraordinary just how tarnished the words 'theory' and 'research' are in education. Medical charities attract millions with the promise that the money will improve the treatment of ailing bodies, but there is virtually no public perception that educational research can improve the learning of disadvantaged minds. Theory has, in certain circles, become almost a term of abuse or ridicule. Politicians are inclined to use it to vilify certain styles of teaching associated with 1960s' progressivism. A false dichotomy is presented in some educational debates between a theoretical stance which is rubbished and a practical approach which is lauded. Practical is good and theoretical is bad.

This trend is perhaps encapsulated by the current status of the work of Piaget among teachers. Those trained in the 1960s and 1970s seem to shiver at the mention of the name. They can recount lecture courses which detailed Piagetian experiments and theory, but they cannot trace any practical application of this knowledge to their classroom teaching. Thus, the name 'Piaget' has become a trigger to switch off and discount the possible relevance of educational research. This is not a fair judgement of the value of Piaget's work, more a reflection of the failings of initial teacher-training courses. Teacher education institutions, reacting to the charge of being too theoretical, have tended to remove or reduce inputs about learning theory. There is a strong irony in the fact that one of the major milestones of twentieth-century educational research has helped create a barrier to the assimilation of research findings into the practice of teaching.

Piaget's work does have important implications for teaching, although it is more recent work which has made these implications most tangible. Piaget proposed that children do not think in the same way as adults; rather, they go through a series of neuro-physiological stages of mental development – sensorimotor, pre-operational, concrete operational and formal operational (see Beard, 1969, for further detail). Some cognitive scientists would prefer to argue that there are trends rather than stages in the development of individual minds. Flavell (1985) suggests that perhaps the most important difference distinguishable in young minds is that they know less and therefore their concepts are less elaborated and powerful. None the less, whether it is attributable to stages or trends, it is widely accepted that there are differences in the cognitive attributes of children at different ages, and these differences are a powerful organizing framework for considering the purpose of teaching.

Shayer (1991) calculated which stages of Piagetian development were a necessary condition for attaining levels in the (then) seventeen science Attainment Targets (ATs). He concludes that, on average, concrete operational thinking will not get a pupil past Level 4 and that formal operational thinking is required for Level 5 and upwards. This information is given further significance by results from the Concepts in Secondary Science and Mathematics Programme (Shayer *et al.*, 1976), which showed that only about 15 per cent of British 14-year-olds were operating at this cognitive level. No such calculation has been done for geography, but even without it the implication is clear. A pupil's level of cognitive development places an absolute ceiling on his or her academic achievement as measured by the National Curriculum levels or public examinations, because, unless he or she employs formal operational thinking, the higher levels are out of reach.

It is as well to remember that, despite the low standing of theory as a concept, we all operate as teachers from a basis of personal theory (e.g. Calderhead, 1987). This personal theory may or may not bear much resemblance to more formal theory, but it will inevitably influence the image we have of what constitutes good teaching and suitable learning activities. It is important, therefore, that we operate from good theory, although the judgement of what constitutes good is, of course, problematic.

THE LIMITS OF CONCRETE THINKING

This is not an appropriate place to rehearse descriptions of Piagetian stages, but it may be helpful to give some indication of the significance of formal operational thinking to geographical attainment. One characteristic of concrete thinking is that conversations or stories are reported in detail as blow-by-blow accounts, whereas formal operations are characterized by the ability to analyse speech and reduce it to principles, ideas and generalizations. As Shayer (1972, p. 342) comments, 'Matters of ethics become discussible on the more complex plane of the reconciliation of interests and responsibilities of people.' In any controversial issue, one principle, rule or moral stance is the yardstick to measure and judge, ruling out compromise, modification and accommodation of alternative views. There is a rigidity that denies the consideration of an alternative point of view. Having recently studied the work of a Year 7 (11–12 years of age) class on the removal of hedgerows, I was struck by the starkness of their views – this was a black-and-white issue. The common view was that it was bad for farmers to remove hedgerows because it affected wildlife, therefore it was unreasonable for farmers to do this. There was little room for compromise in their plans for the farm that they were studying.

Formal operational thinking allows the world to be considered more flexibly, because situations can be formulated and represented in some symbolic form. For some years, as a schoolteacher, this meant nothing to me; I did not understand its significance. However, my second teaching post was in a field-study centre, where a popular activity with Year 7 classes was measuring aspects of rivers. Over time, it became clear that relatively few pupils could grasp the idea that a shallow, fast stretch of river had the same amount of water flowing through it per second as a slow, deep stretch just downstream. Some would latch on to the speed and others on to the depth to conclude that one or the other had more water. Life became very confused if the width varied also. I began to appreciate that the majority could not accommodate more than two variables in their thinking at once: either depth and discharge or speed and discharge. This is one of the strongest distinguishing features of concrete thinking – an inability to manipulate more than one variable mentally. However, with experience, I found that I could explain the concept of discharge fairly successfully to most by resorting to variously shaped cardboard boxes and describing discharge as a box of water that goes by you in a second, if you are on the bank. On reflection, I realize that this concrete demonstration had reduced the number of variables.

Typically, concrete thinkers cannot hypothesize. This is rooted in their difficulty in 'playing with' variables. This clearly makes any task requiring a plan or solution problematic. While concrete thinkers will be able to produce a plan, it will tend to lack a considered justification. When I taught near Reading, we took our Year 11 (15–16-year-old) pupils to do an environmental assessment of a stretch of the Kennet Valley, which suffered a range of pressures common in urban fringe areas. Following the fieldwork, the pupils had to produce a plan to deal with the pressures. The less successful pupils produced neat plans, but the explanations betrayed not only the sense of a black-and-white world but also an inability to predict the problems that their plans would create. They were unable to rehearse mentally the interplay of factors such as landscape, land use, conflict, access and environmental quality.

A last illustration of the limits of concrete thinking relates to explanation. Concrete thinkers are characterized by not asking why things happen and certainly not checking the validity and plausibility of explanations. They concentrate on what happens. Again, this is a function of their difficulty in handling variables. In some recent work with Year 9 pupils (13–14 years old) on the Los Angeles riots, with a teacher colleague, the difficulty of explanation became very clear. The causes of the riots were the beating of Rodney King, the subsequent acquittal of his assailants and the public reaction to these events – that is, what happened. The pupils could explain the deeper causes of the riots only if this could be achieved through text comprehension. In other words they scanned text for the words 'the causes were ...'. Isolating a variable such as poverty and tracing its effects through to the riots was an uphill task that needed a lot of scaffolding.

IMPLICATIONS FOR NATIONAL CURRICULUM GEOGRAPHY

Piaget's work has been subject to a great deal of criticism and revision in the last twenty years. There has been much adverse discussion of his experiments, particularly in the way that the tasks were explained and framed for the children (e.g. Bryant, 1974; Donaldson, 1978). It has been argued that concrete and formal operational thinking are not necessarily constant states, and, indeed, pupils can vary between the two depending on the domain, subject or subject matter. However, Piaget's stages are still generally accepted as a reasonable description of cognitive development.

As Key Stage 3 (age 11–14) is the time when many pupils are moving towards the boundary of concrete and formal operational thinking, it is an appropriate section of the National Curriculum to consider. Before the Dearing-proposed revisions in 1994, there were for geography 114 SoAs spread over Levels 3 to 7. Of these, twenty-five SoAs included the word 'explain' and at least another 7 implied it; twelve included the word 'analyse', and seven included 'evaluate'. Furthermore, a large proportion of SoAs directly demanded an understanding of relationships between one variable or set of variables and another variable or set of variables; thirty-one were very explicitly about relationships and a further twenty-three involved cause or effect (which are essentially about relationships between variables, either over time or in space). A few examples of statements (NCC, 1991) will serve to illustrate these points:

> AT4 L5b analyse the factors that influence the location and growth of individual settlements, and identify the effects of such growth
> AT3 L6f describe characteristics of one type of vegetation and relate those characteristics to environmental conditions and processes, including climate and human actions
> AT5 L7a analyse the effects of technological developments on the exploitation of natural resources and the management of environments.

These statements contain multiple factors and demand an understanding of how they interrelate. They also require explanation, prediction, analysis, synthesis and evaluation, all processes that require the manipulation of sets of variables, which is just what concrete thinkers cannot do. The majority of Key Stage 3 (Ks) pupils are concrete thinkers, at least most of the time, so one can argue that if statements are interpreted literally, then most are beyond the target pupils.

Although the revisions are widely welcomed the new orders have not removed this fundamental issue. The level 5 description contains the following (Schools Curriculum and Assessment Authority, 1995):

> They (pupils) describe how ... processes can lead to similarities and differences between places ... They offer explanations for ways in which human activities affect the environment.

At level 6 it is expected that:

> They describe ways in which processes operating at different scales create geographical patterns and lead to changes in places. They describe and offer explanations for different approaches to managing environments and appreciate their different approaches have different effects on people and places.

These descriptions require the use of the schemata of formal operational thinking.

The National Curriculum emerged out of a concern to raise standards, and better teaching or, more accurately, better instruction and clearer targets were to be the means to achieve this. The argument presented here offers another view, namely that better attainment is dependent on teaching pupils to think, or, to be more accurate, to develop their capacity to think.

THE EVIDENCE FROM SCIENCE AND MATHEMATICS

There is now very promising evidence from science education to suggest that attainment can be raised by focusing on meaningful learning and teaching thinking.

The Cognitive Acceleration in Science Education (CASE) Project was developed at King's College, London, by Shayer and Adey. The CASE activities were developed following a study of research into cognitive acceleration (Adey and Shayer, 1994). It is classified as an infusion approach to teaching thinking, because it seeks to achieve this through the medium of teaching a curriculum subject. This contrasts with direct or bolt-on approaches, such as de Bono's (1986) CoRT (Cognitive Research Trust) programme.

The CASE Project research phase involved schools in a cross-section of local education authorities. The procedure was to teach a two-year course, either in Years 7 and 8 or 8 and 9, using CASE materials, which included a problem-solving activity at least once a fortnight. In all schools, control classes were established.

The course team identified central concepts in science, in order that they would be explicitly taught for; for example, variables, relationships, probability and the use of abstract models to explain and predict. There are strong echoes here of some of the central concepts in geography. The authors would describe themselves as post-Piagetians, and they make clear reference to the influence of both Piaget and Vygotsky in their work. So, for example, they start most units with concrete activities, and they explicitly aim to accelerate students from the concrete to the formal operational thinking stage and thereby raise attainment. The activities were built around three important concepts derived from cognitive psychology: *cognitive conflict, metacognition* and *bridging*.

Cognitive conflict is a term used to describe the dissonance that occurs when a child is presented with a situation which challenges his or her existing conceptual framework or understanding. The constructivist view of learning describes how the learner's existing knowledge resides in a series of schemata, which may be viewed as packages of information about related objects, actions or feelings. It is conceived that there are components within each schema and that there are relationships both within and between schemata. If new information is presented which conflicts with the existing schema, it may be rejected because no links can be made with the information already possessed. If the new information accords with the existing information, adjustment and growth can take place in the structure of the schema, altering the understanding of already encoded information, but this may be a slow process (for further detail see Driver *et al.*, 1985, 1993). For the dissonance to take effect, the learner needs to be prepared carefully, so that the new experience is not only a shock but also connects with existing understanding. The carefully prepared shock is vital in the accelerated development of important concepts. In the Children's Learning in Science Project (e.g. Driver, 1989), this concept has been used as the root approach in getting pupils to expose their existing conceptualizations and then to test them in experiments.

The issue here is that lessons must be demanding but accessible. There is evidence from both Britain and the USA that what happens in many classrooms is routine 'busywork', and that in many instances teachers avoid setting difficult and demanding tasks because it can make classroom management more difficult (Carter and Doyle, 1987). Reports from Her Majesty's Inspectors (HMI) frequently point to lack of challenge being a significant problem in many lessons in English and Welsh schools. This may be exacerbated in many instances by pupils' low self-esteem and a culture of low expectation. Trainee teachers at Newcastle University often complain that pupils will automatically say, 'I can't do it', when faced by a task that requires some thought.

One of the most pertinent illustrations from geography classrooms of what cognitive conflict may look like is provided by the inquiry process. At the beginning of this, one can encourage pupils to identify their existing understandings and attitudes. By judicious presentation of material through the rest of the process, one can lead pupils to question their baseline knowledge. In the case of hedgerow removal mentioned earlier, it is possible to start the unit by asking the question, 'Who is the best farmer?' and using data on costs, output and income to lead pupils to a conclusion that the best farmer is the one who makes the most profit. By following this with photographs and maps which compare the wildlife and landscape on intensive farms with unimproved farms, the pupils are forced to reconsider their earlier understanding of good farming, and they develop more extensive schemata, and with them understanding, relating to farming.

Metacognition is a term first coined by Flavell (1977), and at its simplest means to be aware of one's own thinking. In time, the term has come to take on an extended meaning with increased use. It also carries an implication that, through thinking about thinking, the individual can begin to make conscious choices about the strategies that he or she employs in tackling a problem. Metacognition is a common feature of thinking skills courses (Perkins and Salomon, 1989).

Mathematical education has developed a particular interest in metacognition, through the effort to shift the understanding of mathematics from being a body of knowledge to be learned and towards being an active process of inquiry and generalization (Mason, 1988). In teaching pupils to be expert modellers, it is proposed that they need to develop 'inner speech' in which they are able to discuss and argue with themselves (Schoenfeld, 1987). Inner speech is a representation of metacognition and avoids the pitfall of reducing thinking to a checklist of strategies. Metacognition offers the prospect in maths of teaching pupils to model rather than a model.

Turning to *bridging*: it has long been the cherished ambition of educators to bring pupils to the point where they are able to tackle unfamiliar problems. This is deemed to be increasingly important in an era of rapid technological and economic change. People will rarely do the same jobs throughout their working lives and they will need to be able to transfer skills and knowledge from one context to another. In the CASE project, therefore, a conscious effort was made at the end of lessons to help pupils to recognize other contexts to which the concept or reasoning pattern could be applied, to increase the chances of transfer. The teacher sought to identify similar contexts in science, in other subjects and even in everyday life. In a recent teaching episode with an ex-PGCE student and his Year 7 class, who were investigating the closure of a village shop, the central concepts of the lesson were cause and effect. At the end of the lesson, therefore, the pupils were asked to list all the topics in humanities during the year in which they had studied causes and effects. They did this readily and seemed to register that any issue or event in humanities would have causes and effects. Although this was not explored, it is not a huge leap to consider that, with reinforcement, they could begin to use these concepts as a broad framework for approaching any issue.

Tanner and Jones (1993), reporting on a project to investigate the development of metacognitive skills in Welsh mathematics students, discerned a difference in the debrief questioning skills of some teachers. Some tended to ask questions which were specific to the task, leaving the pupil to generalize and make links. Others asked more general questions which encouraged pupils to transform their experience into internal processes for self-regulation. They reported that in the latter case the pupils were more able to assimilate the processes into their conceptual schema.

I would add to this important list a fourth principle that is implicit in the CASE project, but is worth stating because it may be more readily identifiable for geography teachers – namely the value of groupwork and talk. This is not the place to discuss the importance of language in geography teaching (e.g. Williams, 1981; Slater, 1989). Suffice it to say that the development of higher-level thinking is inextricably bound up with language. Bruner (1985) regarded groupwork as a form of scaffolding which allows the successful completion by groups of tasks that are too difficult for some individuals in the group. This, of course, can be a very important approach to differentiation. These suggestions have been further elaborated and evidenced in mathematics and science (Forman and Cazdan, 1985; Wheatley, 1991).

It is pertinent here to refer to the work of Vygotsky (1978). He saw cognitive development as a largely cultural phenomenon, passed on through mediation of the child's experience. The mediator was critical in helping the child learn from experience. Vygotsky developed the concept of the Zone of Proximal Development (ZPD), which he described as, 'the distance between the actual developmental level as determined by independent problem solving and the level of potential development as determined through problem solving under the guidance or in collaboration with more able peers'

(Vygotsky, 1978, p. 86). This definition encapsulates both the prospect of raising the cognitive performance of pupils, perhaps to formal operational thinking, and the importance of interaction between pupils. Put simply, it is the very process of talking that precipitates learning. The CASE authors do stress, however, the importance of the way in which teachers frame tasks that will be the basis of talk.

Parallel to the 'teaching thinking' movement there is also a growing interest in concept mapping, particularly in science, as a route to encouraging more meaningful learning. Concept mapping has its origins in Ausubel's (1963, 1968) assimilation theory, which proposed that what the learner already knows is the most important determinant of further learning. This is a constructivist viewpoint. Concept mapping was developed from this principle by Novak with colleagues at Cornell University (Novak and Gowin, 1984; Novak, 1990). Concept maps are drawn representations indicating the relationships between concepts. For any individual concept, the greater the number of links to other concepts the greater will be the elaboration and understanding of that concept. In science, three stages are usual in constructing the map:

1. the concepts pertaining to the topic are listed;
2. the concepts are arranged hierarchically, with arrows connecting them;
3. words or phrases are added to the lines to explain the nature of the relationship.

Some geographical topics are not as tidy as science, and in some instances factor maps might be more appropriate organizers. Thus in seeking to understand the demise of the British coal industry, factors such as mechanization, competition from other fuel sources, government policy, foreign competition, safety standards, the miners' unions and investment could be set out as a set of factors, the interplay between which could be explored on the map. However, the topic of glaciation would be amenable to a traditional concept-map approach.

The extent to which science educators have become interested in concept mapping may be judged by the fact that a whole special issue of the *Journal of Research in Science Teaching* was devoted to it in 1990. One article included in the issue listed one hundred references related to concept mapping (Al-Kunifed and Wandersee, 1990). The range of beneficial outcomes proposed for the use of concept mapping includes improved understanding of scientific topics (Gurley, 1982), more meaningful learning (Lehman *et al.*, 1985), reduced anxiety among students (Jegede *et al.*, 1990), and better subject knowledge and a changed view of the curriculum among teachers (Starr and Krajick, 1990). While concept mapping is a single tool with a strong pedigree, it also nests within the 'teaching thinking' universe, as successful concept mappers are also better problem solvers (Okebukola, 1992). This would imply that concept mapping is one way of developing metacognitive awareness.

IMPLICATIONS FOR TEACHING STYLE

The foregoing suggests that different teaching styles are required to implement these approaches to teaching thinking. This is not a simple matter of learning a few new skills, but raises a more fundamental question as to how a teacher conceives her or his subject and therefore how it should be taught. Tanner and Jones (1993) noted the contrast in approach between teachers who regarded mathematics as a static unified body of knowledge and those with a largely constructivist stance, who perceived the subject as actively built up by the pupil in the form of connected schemata. Novak (1990) reports a similar difficulty with science teachers who regard science as a large body of knowledge to be mastered. From my own experience, teachers who are introduced to teaching thinking through geography all have difficulty with the change in teaching demanded, and to some extent are reduced to the status of novices, a finding also reported by Rich (1993).

Debriefing at the end of lessons is one of the keys to metacognition. It is part of the CASE style of teaching to encourage pupils to talk openly about how they have tackled problems. A typical question in a whole class debrief might be, 'How did you do that?' or, 'Did you have a different approach?' Through this consideration of the lesson as a learning experience, it is hypothesized that pupils develop reasoning patterns. I recently taught a lesson to a group of Year 7 pupils in which groups of four pupils were given twenty-six separate pieces of information relating to possible causes and effects of the closure of a village shop. Many of these items were red herrings. The groups had first to establish which items were relevant and then build them into an explanation. This was the fourth of a series of problem-solving and decision-making activities. In the discussion at the end, some groups outlined how they had tackled the problem. In the written evaluations by the pupils, there were many comments to suggest that a level of metacognitive awareness was beginning to emerge; for example, 'I learnt how to decide what information to use and what information not to use' and, 'I learnt that it is important to consider everything before making conclusions and also to link clues together to make one reason covering everything.' These are emergent reasoning patterns which, given further reinforcement, could substantially alter cognitive functioning.

DOES COGNITIVE ACCELERATION WORK?

Until recently, the claims for thinking skills programmes were not well substantiated. Commonly, the programmes have not been evaluated systematically. In a review of the evaluation evidence centred on the most popular intervention programmes, Sternberg and Bhana (1986) concluded that the studies were seriously flawed because outcome measures were of a testimonial nature or so closely linked to the programmes that they were biased. Resnick (1987), in a summary of evaluation studies in America, reported findings of some improvement in reading comprehension, grade averages and improved problem solving in mathematics and science, but no evidence of transfer. It is against this background that the results of the CASE project can be seen (Adey and Shayer, 1994).

By 1989, CASE pupils had taken their General Certificate of Secondary Education (GCSEs), having been remixed with control pupils in GCSE classes using normal teaching approaches. Not only did CASE pupils achieve substantially higher grades in science but, more significantly, they achieved higher grades in English and mathematics as well. Thus, in 1989, 41.7 per cent (science), 49.1 per cent (mathematics) and 44.6 per cent (English) of CASE boys got grades C and above, while the figures for the non-CASE counterparts were 12.8 per cent, 16.4 per cent and 16.1 per cent. For 1990 girls (CASE figures first), the results were 50.0 per cent against 33.3 per cent in science, 55.16 per cent against 42.42 per cent in mathematics, and 85.18 per cent against 58.06 per cent in

English. It must be pointed out, however, that there was a reverse effect in lower grades, with CASE male pupils scoring a higher percentage of grade G in all three subjects. This transfer lends weight to the notion that reasoning patterns can be developed and applied to other subjects. Unfortunately, there are no results to indicate whether there was any effect on geography. These findings await replication, but there are some other promising signs.

St Mary's Roman Catholic Comprehensive School in Newcastle has been running a cognitive acceleration programme for more than five years, as a whole-school policy. This involves three 'teaching thinking' approaches. The lower band are given Instrumental Enrichment (IE) (Link, 1989), an intervention strategy developed by the Israeli psychologist Feuerstein, during Years 7–9. The rationale here is that these pupils have generally failed to develop the cognitive functions which are the necessary precursors of higher-level thinking, such as the abilities to perceive and compare. Without these functions, pupils tend to be impulsive when faced with problems. The upper band receives both Somerset Thinking Skills (Blagg *et al.*, 1988) and CASE teaching. If lower-band pupils make sufficient progress, they graduate to CASE lessons in Year 9. The year 1993 was crucial for the school, as the first cohort who had experienced the cognitive acceleration curriculum from Year 7 took their GCSEs. In recent years, the highest percentage of pupils getting five or more GCSEs at grades A–C had been 27 per cent. In 1993, this rose by approximately 10 per cent.

THE PROSPECTS FOR COGNITIVE ACCELERATION IN GEOGRAPHY

The argument presented in this chapter has run as follows: the National Curriculum was founded on the notion that it would improve attainment. How this was to be done has never been made clear, except that there would be clearer targets and, somehow, better teaching as a result of the competition induced by market forces unleashed by the publication of league tables of Standard Attainment Tasks.

Despite a history of a very uncertain relationship between educational research and curriculum planning and implementation, there is real evidence to suggest how raising attainment should be tackled. An analysis of pre-Dearing-review KS3 SoAs suggests that attainment in geography will be limited if pupils cannot engage in formal operational thinking. The great majority of statements required an understanding of interaction between a number of variables, through the need to understand cause and effect or to explain and analyse. The new level descriptions have not removed this barrier; higher cognitive demand is embedded in the higher levels. Those pupils limited to concrete thinking will not be able to achieve these. There is good evidence from the CASE project, in particular, that cognitive acceleration or teaching pupils to think can substantially improve GCSE results and, one would anticipate, National Curriculum attainment. How can geography reap the same benefits?

First, groups of teachers can make their own efforts to fuse the successful principles of CASE and IE with the methodology of geographical inquiry and problem solving, with an emphasis on issues. An example was given earlier of the inquiry approach to the issue of 'Who is the best farmer?' I am currently engaged in the production of KS3 'thinking' units, which are being developed and tried with the assistance of teachers in the Tyneside area. The results are highly encouraging, but it will take many years before hard evidence about their efficacy will be available.

The second approach affects teacher education. Teaching pupils to think does require a paradigm shift in thinking about teaching. Most prospective teachers have been heavily influenced in their conception of what teaching is by the way in which they have been taught; indeed, it could hardly be any different. For most students, however, this experience is still heavily laced with didactic, transmission styles. If the gains in achievement generated by the CASE project are to be transferred across the curriculum, then there needs to be developed in geography teachers a new repertoire of skills that can be labelled as intervention skills. This is not to say that instruction skills are unnecessary, but that alone they are not sufficient to repair the disadvantage of slow cognitive development. Just how this can be accomplished within the framework of the government reforms of teacher education remains to be seen.

NOTES

1. The National Curriculum for Geography came into force for 5–7-year-olds (Key Stage 1), 7–11-year-olds (Key Stage 2) and 11–14-year-olds (Key Stage 3) in September 1991. Key Stage 4 for 14–16-year-olds should have started in September 1994, by which time the General Certificate of Secondary Education (GCSE) courses would have been brought into line with National Curriculum requirements. This change has now been postponed until at least 1996. Each Key Stage had a compulsory content of material to be taught, the Programmes of Study. The assessment framework was provided by 5 Attainment Targets (ATs): Skills, Knowledge and Understanding of Places, Physical Geography, Human Geography and Environmental Geography. Each AT had ten levels, which described, supposedly, progressive levels of attainment in those areas. Most levels had several statements. Problematically, nearly all the statements contained command words such as 'describe', 'explain' and 'analyse', and a geographical knowledge component. The framework for the geography proposals was produced by a working group appointed by the Secretary of State for Education.
2. The new orders for geography acknowledge the many weaknesses of the original, notably the difficulty of assessing the Statements of Attainment. The new orders contain one Attainment Target with 8 level descriptions, which attempt to characterize a range of performance outcomes. Teachers would have to decide which descriptions best fitted each pupil. There have been some reductions in the content coverage required.

REFERENCES

Adey, P. and Shayer, M. (1994) *Really Raising Standards*. London: Routledge.

Al-Kunifed, A. and Wandersee, J.H. (1990) 'One hundred references related to concept mapping.' *Journal of Research in Science Teaching*, **27**, 1069–75.

Ausubel, D.P. (1963) *The Psychology of Meaningful Verbal Learning*. New York: Grune and Stratton.

Ausubel, D.P. (1968) *Educational Psychology: A Cognitive View*. New York: Holt, Rinehart and Winston.

Beard, R. (1969) *Piaget's Stages of Development*. London: Routledge and Kegan Paul.

Blagg, N., Ballinger, M. and Gardner, R. (1988) *Somerset Thinking Skills Course*. Oxford: Blackwell.

de Bono, E. (1986) *CoRT Thinking*. Oxford: Pergamon.

Bryant, P. (1974) *Perception and Understanding in Young Children*. London: Methuen.

Calderhead, J. (ed.) (1987) *Exploring Teachers' Thinking*. London: Cassell.

Carter, K. and Doyle, W. (1987) 'Teachers' knowledge structures and comprehension processes.' In J. Calderhead (ed.) *Exploring Teachers' Thinking*. London: Cassell.

DES and Welsh Office (1989) National Curriculum Geography Working Group Interim Report. London: DES and Welsh Office.

Donaldson, M. (1978) *Children's Minds*. Glasgow: Fontana.

Driver, R. (1989) 'Changing conceptions.' In P. Adey, J. Bliss, J. Head and M. Shayer (eds) *Adolescent Development and School Science*. London: Falmer.

Driver, R., Guesne, E. and Tiberghian, A. (1985) *Children's Ideas in Science*. Milton Keynes: Open University Press.

Driver, R., Squires A., Rushworth P. and Wood-Robinson, V. (1993) *Making Sense of Secondary Science*. London: Routledge.

Flavell, J. (1977) *Cognitive Development*. 1st edn. Englewood Cliffs, NJ: Prentice-Hall.

Flavell, J. (1985) *Cognitive Development*. 2nd edn. Englewood Cliffs, NJ: Prentice-Hall.

Forman, E.A. and Cazden, C.B. (1985) 'Exploring Vygotskyan perspectives in education: the cognitive value of peer interaction.' In J.V. Wertsch (ed.) *Culture, Communication and Cognition: Vygotskyan Perspectives*. Cambridge: Cambridge University Press.

Gurley, L.I. (1982) 'Use of Gowin's vee and concept mapping strategies to teach responsibility for learning in high school biological sciences.' Unpublished doctoral thesis, Cornell University, Ithaca, NY.

Jegede, O.J., Alaiyemola, F.F. and Okebukola, P.A.O. (1990) 'The effect of concept mapping on students' anxiety and achievement in biology.' *Journal of Research in Science Teaching*, 27 951–60.

Lehman, J.D., Carter, C. and Kahle, J.B. (1985) 'Concept mapping, vee mapping and achievement: results of a field study with black high school students.' *Journal of Research in Science Teaching*, 22, 663–73·

Link, F.R. (1989) 'Instrumental enrichment: a strategy for cognitive and academic improvement.' in F.R. Link (ed.) *Essays On The Intellect*. Alexandria, VA: Association for Supervision and Curriculum Development.

Mason, J. (1988) 'Modelling: what do we really want pupils to learn?' In D. Pimm (ed.) *Mathematics, Teachers and Children*. London: Hodder and Stoughton.

Novak, J.D. (1990) 'A useful tool for science education.' *Journal of Research in Science Teaching*, 27, 937–49.

Novak, J.D. and Gowin, D.B. (1984) *Learning How to Learn*. New York: Cambridge University Press.

Okebukola, P.A. (1992) 'Can good concept mappers be good problem solvers in science?' *Research in Science and Technological Education*, 10, 153–70.

Perkins, D.N. and Salomon, G. (1989) 'Are cognitive skills context bound?' *Educational Researchers*, 18, 16–25.

Rawling, E. (1992) 'The making of a national geography curriculum.' *Geography*, 77, 292–309.

Resnick, L.B. (1987) *Education and Learning to Think*. Washington, DC: National Academic Press.

Rich, Y. (1993) 'Stability and change in teacher expertise.' *Teacher and Teacher Education*, 9, 137–46.

Schoenfeld, A.H. (1987) 'What's all this fuss about metacognition?' In A.H. Schoenfeld (ed.), *Cognitive Science and Maths Education*. Hillsdale, NJ: Erlbaum.

Schools Curriculum and Assessment Authority (1995) *The National Curriculum Orders*. London: Schools Curriculum and Assessment Authority.

Shayer, M. (1972) 'Conceptual demands in the Nuffield O-level physics.' *School Science Review*, 54, 26–42.

Shayer, M. (1992) 'Improving standards and the National Curriculum.' *School Science Review*, 72, 17–29.

Shayer, M., Kuchemann D.E. and Wylam, H. (1976) 'The distribution of Piagetian stages of thinking in British middle and secondary school children.' *British Journal of Educational Psychology*, 46, 164–73.

Slater, F. (ed.) (1989) *Language and Learning in the Teaching of Geography*. London: Routledge.

Starr, M.L. & Krajcik, J.S. (1990) 'Concept maps as a heuristic for science curriculum development: Towards improvement in processes and product.' *Journal of Research in Science Teaching*, **27**, 987–1000.

Sternberg, R.J. & Bhana K. (1986) 'Synthesis of research on the effectiveness of intellectual skills programmes: Snake oil remedies or miracle cures?' *Educational Leadership*, **44**, 60–7.

Tanner, H. & Jones, S. (1993) Developing Metacognitive Skills in Secondary School Students. In *Proceedings of the Second International Colloquium on Education: British and American Perspectives*, Swansea: Department of Education, University College of Swansea.

Vygotsky, L. (1978) *Mind in Society*. Cambridge, MA: Harvard University Press.

Wheatley, G.H. (1991) 'Constructivist perspectives on science and mathematics learning.' *Science Education*, **75**, 9–12.

Williams, M. (ed.) (1981) *Language Teaching and Learning – Geography*. London: Ward Lock.

Chapter 21

Researching the History of Geographical Education

William E. Marsden

History is approached in different ways by different people for different purposes. One reason for looking back into history is that it may be seen as germane to discussion about some current activity or debate, whether social, political or, for that matter, academic. History is neglected by some academics, and arguably as much by educationists as by others. The sceptical might suggest that ignoring the historical context of a particular sphere of academic activity has the advantage of enabling more extravagant claims to be made for the innovatory quality of current scholarship. During the 1960s and 1970s, as social scientific paradigms were promoted in the attempt to make academic work in education more respectable, consideration of historical contexts became increasingly marginalized. This was the case also with official reports, those in the postwar period not matching, for example, the interwar Hadow (primary and secondary) and Spens reports, in their recognition of the need to provide a substantial historical background to the matters they were considering.

A prominent social scientist who sought to break this mould was Lawrence Stenhouse. He looked for a public scholarly tradition for educational research which allowed a critique of current understandings, encouraging workers to act and react creatively rather than imitatively, yet to draw more easily on common sense and experience. This he found in the historical research tradition:

> The teacher might draw on research founded in the historical method to understand his context, thereby helping him to plot better his own educational adventure. This is to ask history to provide an authenticated context against which to imagine the significance of hypothetical actions tried out in the imagination. Such contextual understanding should allow us to create better the story of our own acts.
>
> (Stenhouse, 1978, p. 30)

In methodological texts in particular subjects, some attempt was made to offer a historical background, in the case of geography by Graves (1975), Marsden (1976) and Williams (1976). By the late 1970s, there was also a more general developing international literature on the history of the curriculum (Marsden, 1978). But the number of authentic historians of the curriculum was small. History was being written by non-historians for non-historical purposes. Some of the work produced was patently unhistorical, drawing uncritically on the historical record merely to sharpen a particular contemporary axe: what Silver referred to as 'raiding the past' (1977, p. 17) without understanding it. Seriously overstretched parallels, randomly selected from a past deemed to be anachronistic and more primitive than the present, were used to 'libel by label' disapproved contemporary educational policies or activities.

One important thrust, for example, was to hypothesize that the curriculum was socially determined, and to look to history to 'prove' the hypothesis. It was of course not difficult to find pieces of evidence to support the theory, though there might have been even more to justify an alternative one. Much of this social scientific work was, in the event, deterministic; for example, stereotyping broad, undifferentiated nineteenth-century groups as oppressors and oppressed. Adherents of the social control thesis thus recycled the dichotomized early nineteenth-century view that there was an education for the poor and an education for the rich. What they often failed to press on to discover was that the intentions of the controlling groups were more impressive than the outcomes they actually achieved; omitting to recognize the differentiated and often subtle status gradations, diversity of values, and resistances that existed within the broad class groupings, which often allowed so-called oppressed groups to maintain and enhance their positions. In consequence, social stereotypes emerged from the dubious historical scholarship which had swooped down on second- and even third-hand sources of reference, telescoping the arguments from the original to proclaim what were in the last analysis unhelpful generalizations.

THE NEED FOR HISTORICAL RESEARCH IN CURRICULUM STUDY

The past is a rich store of knowledge and experience, of course. The history of geographical education is a fascinating study in its own right. It can be argued that it is under-researched quantitatively, and under-critically researched qualitatively. The history of subject areas is a little like the history of schools: the story that is told is often of great names and heroic deeds. There can be no denying the quality and influence of the contributions to geographical education of Mackinder and Fairgrieve, for example. Their place in the hall of fame is secure. But how little of the writing about them has at the same time exposed their unacceptable faces: the unblushing imperialism and even explicit racism of their views, and the impact this had on their work (Marsden, 1990)? Similarly, how little attention has been addressed to the uses of geography and history for political ends (Marsden, 1989) or, for that matter, related cross-curricular activities (Marsden, 1993)?

In investigating the past, an authentic historical methodology is required. At its basic level, this means there must be a respect for evidence. Underpinning this is the need to unveil, collect and collate a massive amount of historical information, ensuring that the coverage is comprehensive, the chronology is correct, and the contemporary context understood, thus helping the acquisition of both a horizontal grasp of the interconnections in terms of a snapshot at a particular point in time, and longitudinal insights along the temporal axis which involve and probe continuity and change, cause and effect, and other key concepts. The historian in one sense is a conservationist, concerned for comprehensive, idiomatic and empathetic resource use. The data and the views of the participants must of course be placed in the context of their time. Thus it could be argued that Mackinder and Fairgrieve were creatures of their period, and that criticism of their values from a current standpoint is therefore illegitimate. Countering this is the fact that contemporaries of theirs were already contesting the imperialism and negative stereotyping of other peoples in concurrent methodological articles and texts, seeking to promote the values of international rather than national and imperial citizenship (Marsden, 1988, pp. 337–9)

The problem of overstretching the historical parallels in sharpening a contemporary axe can readily be illustrated from geographical education. The further we go back into the past, the more simplistic things are alleged to have been. An early criticism of the proposals of the National Curriculum Geography Working Group for example, was that the emphasis on place rather than on issues would drag us back into an era of 'capes and bays' geography. How much was known of what capes and bays geography truly embodied? What was the social context out of which it sprang? What content was included? With what teaching methods and styles was it associated? An undifferentiated grasp of what capes and bays was about was used to denigrate a contemporary proposal. A probing historical look would soon clarify that any overlap in thinking of the Geography Working Group and hard-core capes and bays teaching was minimal. The total of a hundred or so pieces of locational knowledge expected of children after six years of geographical work at Key Stages 1 and 2 would have been covered in the equivalent of little more than one chapter of a capes and bays text. The method of teaching would have been catechetical, whereby a standard question would be followed by a predetermined class response. Even though so mechanistic, there was at the same time much methodological discussion, highlighting different aspects of the capes and bays approach, and debating different ways of transmitting capes and bays knowledge. Each textbook claimed to be offering the one best system.

Neither was the 'capes and bays' period uniformly one of utilitarianism Alternative progressive ideas, derived from pioneers like Robert Owen and Richard Dawes in this country and, of course, Froebel abroad, advocated, among other things, work in the field. The *heimatskunde* or home studies tradition was well established by the second half of the nineteenth century. One of the first Her Majesty's Inspector's (HMIs) was dismissive of capes and bays geography, arguing that the subject acquired a value in education only when it lost the character of an accumulation of facts. The crucial starting point was to link content with the world of thought and action, making connections, first by promoting observational skills in the study of the home area (Moseley, 1845). Such preaching was apparently put into practice at Bruce Castle School, Tottenham, in 1837:

> As introductory to geography, we first take the topography of the place at which the instruction is given, together with that of the surrounding neighbourhood. We begin with the very room in which the class is taught ... the pupil is gradually rendered familiar with the conception of greater and greater magnitudes and distances, and with the habits of nations less and less intimately connected with our own.
>
> (Anon., 1837, p. 16)

There was a continuity of thinking from Moseley to other HMIs such as Matthew Arnold, and to a number of methodolgists, not least Sir Archibald Geikie, perhaps the first high-quality geographical educationist to promote continental ideas on home study. His major priority was to foster the enjoyment of children in physical geography and geology through active, research-type fieldwork, approaching these areas by way of the real world and not from second-hand verbal study. In his *The Teaching of Geography*, Geikie expressed his conviction that geography was 'a discipline of a high order in education', establishing bridges with history, literature and science, so long as it detached itself from its long-standing role of promoting the acquisition of locational knowledge by mere memory training (Geikie, 1887, p. 4): 'In dealing with the young we should try to feel ourselves young again, to see things as they are seen by young eyes, to realise the difficulties that lie in the way of children's appreciation of the world around them' (p. 7).

The history of geographical education also sheds light on an analogous present argument: the contention that the emphasis on place studies is leading us back, if not to the full horror of capes and bays, at least to the lesser peril of old-time regional geography. As we know, the emergence of regional geography, pioneered by Mackinder and systematized and implemented by Herbertson, offered an important new paradigm, designed in part to uplift the status of late nineteenth-century geography at secondary and tertiary levels. Instead of loose accumulations of facts, framed within thousands of political divisions and subdivisions, the facts and factors of geography would be connected through more probing studies of regions and sub-regions. But from the start, even Herbertson himself recognized that his regional frameworks would pose problems for younger children: 'the best logical order is not necessarily the best pedagogical order' (Herbertson, 1906, p. 281).

An element of this sophisticated new regional geography was present even in the syllabuses of elementary schools, as determined by the Educational Code of 1904, for example. This Code too has been referred back to in criticisms of the introduction of the current National Curriculum. The 1904 Code was similarly subject-based and the subject balance was not dissimilar from that of the today's National Curriculum. The Code equally ensured that geography was universally taught in elementary schools. A previous Board of Education Circular on 'the curriculum of the rural school' (1900) had stressed the importance of object lessons connected with the rural locality, of local mapping, school walks and their follow-up in the classroom. For urban schools, fieldwork was regarded as less suitable for many years. Even so, use of local parks for rural-type walks was a well-established activity in some elementary schools.

My father's experience of geography at the age of 6, according to the Log Book of his Southport school, included, *inter alia*, the use of learning geography; a plan of the classroom and position of other rooms; a plan of Southport; places of interest in the district (buildings, streets, parks, suburbs, villages near Southport, old Southport); then, in the third term, studies of child life in China, Japan, Russia, Holland, India and Arctic regions; finishing with work on the imports of the port of Liverpool from foreign lands. By contrast, my own experience in a similar church school some thirty or so years later, on the evidence of an old exercise book, was of an almost total neglect of any organized geographical input, confined as it was to odd stereotypical drawings of Red Indians or Eskimos. By this stage, about the beginning of World War II, there remained no compulsory 'broad and balanced' curriculum but rather a monotonous diet of religious instruction and the three Rs, designed to ensure a high level of success in the 11+ scholarship stakes. Thus the 1904 Code, the basis of a national curriculum at that time, does offer an interesting backcloth to the issues associated with the introduction of the present National Curriculum, but not a simple one. It suggests, if not a particularly progressive curriculum, at least one that was more balanced, less idiosyncratic and much less utilitarian than that which in many primary schools followed the abolition of the Code in the 1920s, when they were given more freedom of choice.

The complexity of the issues which we associate with curriculum development in geography today was matched in analogous situations in the past. Too much of the history of geographical education is, however, derived from a limited and predictable range of resources, such as material in subject journals like *The Geographical Teacher* and *Geography*. Paradoxically, some of the richest material on the development of geography teaching comes from a country we do not usually associate with giving much priority to its presence in the curriculum, namely the USA. This is not because geography was not taught, but because it was subsumed under a broader, social subjects umbrella.

American curriculum historians date the earliest promotion of formal curriculum theory and development to William Torrey Harris, superintendent of the St Louis school system during the 1870s (Cremin, 1971, p. 207). Equally sympathetic to such curriculum theory was the Herbartarian, Charles McMurry, Professor of Education at Chicago University. In his view, sustainable curriculum development involved addressing the nature of subjects as well as the nature of the child. In laying out a course of study in geography for the grades of the common school, McMurry, like Mackinder in Britain, saw geography as a critical bridging subject. The study of the earth was essentially scientific. The study of man was essentially historical. The study of the earth as the home of man was geographical:

> Every topic in geography has a double footing in natural science and history. This double or complex character is the distinguishing trait of a strictly geographical topic. The moment a topic becomes purely scientific or purely historical it loses its geographical character. Geography is the connecting bridge between the two great real studies, nature and man.
>
> (McMurry, 1899, pp. 124–5)

On this basis, the natural starting point for geography was the home area, explored by means of excursions, discussions about which offered a generous background for a movement outward from the locality to the United States and North America, and then the rest of the world: the classic concentric syllabus. Similarly, study was to be through detailed examination of places: what McMurry termed 'type-studies', which should be connected up with work in science and history, and linked with other topics. These were essentially what were later to be termed 'sample studies' or 'case studies', and today are referred to as locality studies.

By this stage there was an American geographical education journal, *The Journal of School Geography*, later to become *The Journal of Geography*. In the former, the geographer R.E. Dodge stressed the importance of using the 'pedagogical order', that is, of starting with the home area, moving out along the lines of least resistance to the causally related known, then unknown (Dodge, 1900). Like his counterpart in Britain, Sir Archibald Geikie, the famed physical geographer W.M. Davis urged the need for fieldwork in physical geography, which was to be based on observations that were 'logical, searching, critical' (Davis, 1902).

Perhaps of most interest to the educationist is the view of geography held by America's leading progressive educator, John Dewey. Geography he regarded as the unifying subject *par excellence*. It was, with history, the key information subject, but information was carefully defined in terms of means towards ends:

the difference between penetration of this information into living experience and its mere piling up in heaps depends on whether these studies are faithful to the interdependence of man and nature which affords these studies their justification ... Geography and history are the two great school resources for bringing about the enlargement of the significance of direct experience. Unless they are taught for external reasons or as mere modes of skill their chief educational value is that they provide the most direct and interesting roads out into the larger world of meaning.

(Dewey, 1916, pp. 210–13)

Through such approaches, geography enriched the imagination. Memorably, Dewey wrote of it as 'moving the mind from the monotony of the customary ... when the familiar fences that mark the limits of the village proprietors are signs that introduce an understanding of the boundaries of great nations, even fences are lighted with meaning' (p. 212).

This humanizing and integrating tradition was continued in the work of the American curriculum field in the interwar period and beyond, key figures such as Harold Rugg (1931, p. 269) and Ralph Tyler (1963) emphasizing the vital importance of incorporating into the curriculum specialist subject understandings, based on conceptual frameworks evolved from frontier thinkers. The influence of nearly half a century of curriculum development activity is evident in the thirty-second Yearbook of the National Society for the Study of Education on *The Teaching of Geography* (Marsden, 1992). A whole series of geographical educators tasted the fruits of this development, applying it, often somewhat mechanistically it has to be said, to the teaching of geography. But would we be justified in claiming we could in essence surpass Zoe Thralls's outline of the aims of geography of sixty years ago?

1. A knowledge of geographic facts, concepts, and relationships that will enable the individual to give more intelligent consideration to current problems – individual, community, national and international.
2. An understanding of how the varied problems of peoples are related to differences in natural environment; and, developed through this understanding, an interest in, and an open-minded attitude toward, the problems, achievements, and possible future developments of other peoples.
3. A growing power to sense and grasp the economic and cultural interdependence of regions and peoples.
4. A better understanding of the value of natural resources and the need for intelligent use of them.
5. The ability to make a worthwhile use of leisure time through the vitalisation of local field trips, of more distant travel, and of reading, because of an understanding of the interrelations between man's working, playing, living, and the elements of the natural environment.
6. The recognition and appreciation of the variety of human labor in the major types of regions throughout the world, arising from an understanding of man's adjustments to his natural environment.

(Thralls, 1933, pp. 202–3)

As with Dewey in the United States, so in England the Hadow Report of 1931 provided no authority for the later polarization between child-centredness and subject-centredness. As it stressed, work *in geography* in the primary school was to 'be thought of in terms of activity and experience rather than of knowledge to be acquired and facts to be stored' (Hadow Report, 1931, p. 171). It was, rather, progressive disciples of Dewey, Hadow and, later, Plowden who opened up ideological divides between topic and subject work in ways not authorized by the originators. A more careful exploration of what the pioneers actually said and did can give confidence to those who have never regarded their inquiry-based subject as being other than child-centred. At the same time, the historical record gives no reason to defend complacently the faded methodologies of the old regional geography as served up in many conventional grammar schools. These categorically cannot claim to be progressive.

AGENDA FOR HISTORIANS OF GEOGRAPHICAL EDUCATION

The implications of the discussion are therefore that historical knowledge and under-standing, and historical skills, properly applied, should tend towards more critical, sensitive, less polarized and, one would hope, more modest appraisals of present activ-ity, and more contextualized insights into current events. Much work has still to be done. Little of the ground has as yet been staked out, let alone colonized. Possibly there is more existing research on pressure groups for geographical education, and, as we have seen, on eminent geographers and geographical educationists, than on the detail of the development of particular aspects of the geographical curriculum and its methodo-logy. We sorely need the application of criteria which will ensure balance, objectivity and refined judgement, and which explore scrupulously and comprehensively a much wider range of resources than has been the case hitherto.

What is particularly required is a wider cultural sweep which, on the one hand, would seek to enshrine geography in the broader process of curriculum development and whole-curriculum planning and, on the other, would attempt to place national provision in the wider international context. In historical, as in other educational research, we have already implied that there is a 'structure of omission' (Marsden, 1991), which probably means that history continues to be used or misused to support or reaffirm a particular educational belief system, rather than dispassionately to illuminate and evalu-ate current practice. One test of suspect scholarship work is the nature of its citations: is attention paid to the deliberations of those on different ideological wavelengths, or is it largely confined to the writings of a network of fellow-travellers?

The agenda will be more satisfactorily dealt with if a more comprehensive acquisition of first-hand historical sources is achieved. Much research in the history of geographical education concentrates on a limited range of material, such as that found in readily accessible past geographical education journals, or textbooks, or the archives of subject associations, or, not least, the famous Keltie Report (Royal Geographical Society, 1886). Important though these are, consider also the following neglected sources, which often contain material specific to geographical education and, importantly, may help to link it with the broader educational and curriculum thinking of the time:

1. *Methodological texts*. Thus in Britain, Wyse (1836), Fearon (1876), Bain (1878), Combe (in Jolly, 1879), Symons (1879), Fitch (1884), Laurie (1888), Barnett (1897), Dexter and Garlick (1899, 1905) and Welton (1906) are all general methodological texts containing material pertaining to geographical education. More specific to geography teaching were the contributions of Meiklejohn (1869), William Hughes (1870) and particularly Sir Archibald Geikie (1887).
2. *Educational journals*. Throughout the nineteenth and twentieth centuries there were a large number of educational journals, which often included ideas and

information specific to particular subject areas. Thus in the nineteenth century, the *Educational Record, School Guardian* and *School Board Chronicle*, organs representing respectively the interests of the non-conformists, Anglicans and school-board supporters, often contain advice for teachers on how to teach geography, and reviews of and adverts for textbooks. Even more pertinent can be the journals for practising teachers, such as the *Practical Teacher, Schoolmaster, Girls' Mistress* and *Infant Mistress*.

3. *Official publications*. These include, particularly, the *Minutes* and *Reports of the Committee of Council of Education*, which contain HMI reports, in the pre-1862 period at least, very rich in comment and judgement on subject teaching in elementary schools all over the country. Useful material can also be found in the reports of the great commissions, such as, for example, the *Newcastle* and the *Cross Commissions*, which covered elementary education respectively in the late 1850s and mid-1880s. In addition there are the Codes, and the Circulars which even then poured out of the Education Department and later the Board of Education.

4. *School materials*. Here there are the log books for elementary schools which, in some cases, contain vivid first-hand material of relevance to geographical education, including timetable and syllabus breakdowns. For the secondary sector, contemporary school histories can also be revealing.

5. *Overseas materials*. Such derive not least from the USA, where, as has been suggested, the most rigorous and diverse curriculum-making movement yet seen in the English-speaking world addressed itself over the years to discussion of all the subjects of the curriculum, as well as to more general educational concerns.

CONCLUSION

Consideration of a range of materials that goes beyond the narrow subject archive is therefore of vital significance in the exploration of the wider connections and the hidden agendas. As already noted, the more limited approach through the discrete subject documentation can well circumscribe and decontextualize the range of explanation. If thus restricted, it is more likely to be of parochial interest than revealing to the outside world. Failure to appreciate the linkages contributes to the rivalry and misunderstanding that can subvert balanced curriculum development.

It is sometimes evident that particular individuals and endeavours have had more influence than others in affecting this development. It is interesting to speculate why, for example, despite some first-class work in proselytizing the case for geography in the curriculum, the American system, like others, came down on the side of social studies. It may be because of the greater power and influence of the professors of education rather than the professors of geography in the USA. The reverse happened in this country, particularly in the secondary schools, perhaps because the influential grammar-school and university sectors were more at ease with curricula that reflected fairly straightforwardly academic subject boundaries and were represented in geography in the long-standing and ultimately stifling devotion to the traditional regional paradigm (Biddle, 1980).

In England, for example, the influence of the geographical educationist James

Fairgrieve was crucially enhanced by earlier and concurrent efforts of that prestigious body the Royal Geographical Society (Marsden, 1986) and the subject association, the Geographical Association (at that time strongly supported by university professors and lecturers of geography), in successfully establishing the subject as a separate entity in the timetables of secondary schools. Geikie's resolution of child-centred and subject-centred principles foundered, in part because he, though a major establishment figure in the academic world on earth science in general, had offended the establishment at the Royal Geographical Society and in the universities by defending geography as a school subject, but not supporting it as an honours degree discipline. The fact that the Geikie synthesis was never transmitted effectively ultimately led to a growing polarization between the emerging grammar-school tradition, with its increasing devotion to a narrow, non-inquiry-centred view of geography, and the emerging progressivism of the 1930s and beyond in the primary sector, leading to a facile opposition of two traditions, and the belief that subjects *qua* subjects were hostile to the interests of children, a proposition dismissed as early as 1902 by Dewey as a 'radical fallacy' (Dewey, 1902, p. 30). The unravelling of the chronology and the contexts of this particular and subversive conflict, and no doubt many others like it, is one of the many exciting projects which await exploration by historians of geographical education.

REFERENCES

Anon. (1837) *Sketch of the System of Education, Moral and Intellectual, in Practice at Bruce Castle School, Tottenham*. London: Knight.

Bain, A. (1878) *Education as a Science*. London: Kegan Paul, Trench.

Barnett, P.A. (ed.) (1897) *Teaching and Organisation*. London: Longmans, Green.

Biddle, D.S. (1980) 'Paradigms and geography curricula in England and Wales, 1882–1972.' *Geographical Education* 3, 577–98.

Board of Education (1900) *The Curriculum of the Rural School*. Circular 435. London: HMSO.

Cremin, L.A. (1971) 'Curriculum-making in the United States.' *Teachers College Record*, **73**, 207–20.

Davis, W.M. (1902) 'Field work in physical geography.' In D.W. Johnson (ed.) (1954) *Geographical Essays by William Morris Davis*. New York: Dover.

Dewey, J. (1902) *The Child and the Curriculum*. Chicago, IL: Phoenix. University of Chicago Press reprint (n.d.).

Dewey, J. (1916) *Democracy and Education*. 1966 edn. New York: Free Press.

Dexter, T.F.G. and Garlick, A.H. (1899) *Object Lessons in Geography for Standard III*. London: Longmans, Green.

Dexter, T.F.G. and Garlick, A.H. (1905) *A Primer of School Method*. London: Longmans, Green.

Dodge, R.E. (1900) 'A school course in geography: IV. Home geography.' *Journal of School Geography*, **4**, 264–73.

Fearon, D.R. (1876) *School Inspection*. London: Macmillan.

Fitch, J.G. (1884) *Lectures on Teaching*. Cambridge: Cambridge University Press.

Geikie, A. (1887) *The Teaching of Geography*. London: Macmillan.

Graves, N.J. (1975) *Geography in Education*. London: Heinemann.

Hadow Report (1931) *Report of the Consultative Committee on the Primary School*. London: HMSO.

Herbertson, A.J. (1906) 'Recent regulations and syllabuses in geography affecting schools.' *Geographical Journal*, **27**, 279–88.

Hughes, W. (1870) *Geography: What It Is and How to Teach It*. London: Philip and Son.

Jolly, W. (1879) *Education: Its Principles and Practice as Developed by George Combe*. London: Macmillan.

Laurie, S.S. (1888) *Occasional Addresses on Educational Subjects*. Cambridge: Cambridge University Press.

McMurry, C.A. (1899) 'A course of study in geography for the grades of the common school.' *Supplement to the Fourth Yearbook of the National Herbart Society for 1898*.

Marsden, W.E. (1976) *Evaluating the Geography Curriculum*. Edinburgh: Oliver and Boyd.

Marsden, W.E. (1978) 'Historical approaches to curriculum study.' In W.E. Marsden (ed.) *Post-war Curriculum Development: An Historical Appraisal*. Leicester: History of Education Society.

Marsden, W.E. (1986) 'The Royal Geographical Society and geography in secondary education.' In M.H. Price (ed.) *The Development of the Secondary Curriculum*. London: Croom Helm.

Marsden, W.E. (1988) 'Continuity and change in geography textbooks: perspectives from the 1930s to the 1960s.' *Geography*, **73**, 327–43.

Marsden, W.E. (1989) '"All in a good cause": geography, history and the politicization of the curriculum in nineteenth and twentieth century England.' *Journal of Curriculum Studies*, **21**, 509–26.

Marsden, W.E. (1990) 'Rooting racism into the educational experience of childhood and youth in the nineteenth- and twentieth-centuries.' *History of Education*, **19**, 333–53.

Marsden, W.E. (1991) '"The structure of omission": British curriculum predicaments and false charts of American experience.' *Compare*, **21**, 5–25.

Marsden, W.E. (1992) 'The 32nd Yearbook of the National Society for the Study of Education on *The Teaching of Geography*: an external appraisal.' In A.D. Hill (ed.) *International Perspectives on Geographical Education*. Skokie, IL: Rand McNally.

Marsden, W.E. (1993) 'Recycling religious instruction? Historical perspectives on contemporary cross-curricular issues.' *History of Education*, **22**, 321–33.

Meiklejohn, J.M.D. (1869) *On the Best and Worst Methods of Teaching Geography*. London: Williams and Norgate.

Moseley, H. (1845) 'Report on the Midland District.' In (1846) *Minutes of the Committee of Council on Education, 1*. London: HMSO.

Royal Geographical Society (1886) *Report of the Proceedings of the Society in Reference to the Improvement of Geographical Education*. (The Keltie Report). London: John Murray.

Rugg, H. (1931) *Culture and Education in America*. New York. Harcourt, Brace.

Silver, H. (1977) 'Nothing but the past, or nothing but the present?' *Times Higher Educational Supplement*, 1 July.

Stenhouse, L. (1978) 'Case study and case records: towards a contemporary history of education.' *British Educational Research Journal*, **4**, 21–39.

Symons, J. (1879) *School Economy: A Practical Book on the Best Mode of Establishing and Teaching Schools*. London: Woburn Press. 1971 reprint.

Thralls, Z. (1933) 'Some general curricular principles and their applications.' In A.M. Whipple (ed.) *The 32nd Yearbook of the National Society for the Study of Education: The Teaching of Geography*. Chicago, IL: University of Chicago Press.

Tyler, R. (1963) 'Contribution.' In G.W. Sowards (ed.) *The Social Studies: Curriculum Proposals for the Future*. Papers presented at the 1963 Cubberley Conference, School of Education, Stanford University. Chicago: Scott, Foresman.

Welton, J. (1906) *Principles and Methods of Teaching*. London: University Tutorial Press.

Williams, M. (ed.) (1976) *Geography and the Integrated Curriculum*. London: Heinemann.

Wyse, T. (1836) *Education Reform: Or the Necessity of a National System of Education*. London.

Chapter 22

Partial Truths: Feminist Perspectives on Ends and Means

Janice Monk

Feminist researchers think of all knowledge as 'partial,' in both senses of the word, in that it has political implications and reflects the goals, values and experiences of the people who create it, rather than some objective, universalist reality. In the feminist case, the goals and values reflect commitments to gender equity and to giving visibility to the experiences and expressions of women and girls. It is a scholarship that seeks to contribute towards social change, challenging the gender inequities which are extensive around the globe as well as the mainstream research and teaching which have largely dealt with men's lives. In this chapter, I will identify important concepts in feminist geography, then discuss the methodologies it employs, drawing attention to current quandaries about their practice. I will illustrate my points with examples from geographical studies, including work in geographic and environmental education as much as possible. I should note, however, that feminist geographers' educational concerns have been directed towards critical assessments of existing educational materials and to prescriptive suggestions for curriculum change and pedagogical practices, rather than to other aspects of educational research and writing (LeVasseur, 1993). Further, in general, geographic and environmental educators have devoted more attention to creative tasks, such as developing curricula and materials, than to analytical research, so that we have limited notions of a research agenda (Downs, 1994); they have barely begun to attend to the implications of feminist scholarship for their research.[1] (These circumstances in themselves raise questions about what shapes the creation of knowledge.) In the concluding section, I will suggest ways of connecting feminism with research in geographic and environmental education. My chapter represents an exploration, rather than presentation of well-established practice. To set it in context, I will begin with some comments on the development of feminist geography over the last two decades.

SITUATING FEMINIST GEOGRAPHY

Feminist geography emerged in the 1970s in North America, Britain and the Netherlands as (chiefly women) geographers realized that the contemporary women's rights movement had implications for their own profession. They asked questions about the representation of women as geographers (Berman, 1977; McDowell, 1979; Momsen, 1980; Zelinsky, 1973a, 1973b), but soon extended their work to a critique of the masculine orientation of most geographic writing and teaching and to conducting new research on the lives of women and about gender relations between women and men (*Journal of Geography*, 1978; Monk and Hanson, 1982; Tivers, 1978; Women and Geography Study Group of the IBG, 1984; Zelinsky *et al.*, 1982). Most of this new research has been conducted by women.[2] With this history, feminist geography has played an important part in heightening disciplinary awareness that the creation of knowledge is closely tied to its cultural and political contexts and to the sociology of the profession. As feminist geography has become international in scope, distinctions in the topics addressed and approaches favoured can be seen across national boundaries, further demonstrating this point (Monk, 1994).

Within the discipline, feminist geography is now one of the established critical strands of thought and practice. From this perspective, it was preceded by Marxist-socialist scholarship but preceded postmodernism, while sharing some perspectives with both these schools. Early British feminist geography, for example, reflecting connections with socialist work, was especially concerned with questions of oppression and with the ways in which urban spatial structures reflected the priorities of industrial capitalism; yet it was distinctively feminist in examining how these spatial structures also depended on patriarchal social relations that legitimized the unpaid reproductive household work of women (MacKenzie and Rose, 1983; McDowell, 1983). A considerable amount of current feminist writing parallels postmodernists' focus on diversity, identity and cultural symbols while arguing for the instability of categories and 'truths' (see Chapter 23 in this book); yet feminists are uncomfortable with the relativism of the postmodernist position and argue that power differentials among groups must be addressed, affinities among groups sought, and efforts made to understand how space and place operate in the creation of differences, if research is to be of political value in promoting equity (Pratt and Hanson, 1994).

Over the course of its development, feminist geography has drawn significantly on interdisciplinary scholarship for its topics, theories, concepts and methods. As in other fields, identifying sexism in mainstream work was an important and enlightening project. It revealed that women's lives were generally not taken into account in posing research questions, developing theories and models, collecting data and reporting empirical findings. If women were dealt with, it was likely to be in very limited and stereotypical ways; for example, in discussions of fertility in population geography (Monk and Hanson, 1982). As feminists took up the task of representing women's lives, they focused on showing women as actors and explored the meanings women attached to their experiences, as well as demonstrating how larger social structures and the unequal power that characterized gender relations constrained women. They opened up new themes for inquiry, such as mothering, various kinds of unpaid work, the provision of services important to women (such as child care), domestic violence, relationships between language and power, and the histories and cultures of sexuality. They also revealed the inadequacy of standard data sources like censuses for documenting women's activities. Basic concepts, such as class (as it has been operationalized by stratifying men's occupations), were questioned for their utility in categorizing women. The critiques demonstrated that feminist research would need to go beyond adding information on women to existing frameworks and involve rethinking categories, models and methods. I will elaborate on some of the concepts and approaches that have been introduced to address these limitations later in this chapter.

Feminist scholarship is not unitary across cultures or within them, reflecting the diversity of its creators. To address what might seem like an infinite set of versions of 'truth' and to help us assess claims to knowledge, Haraway has introduced the idea of the 'situated' character of knowledges; she calls for authors to be explicit about their 'positionality' and to retain their commitment to social change by attempting to make visible the claims to knowledge of less powerful members of society (Haraway, 1988). Thus, in writing this chapter, I acknowledge that my goals include introducing feminist perspectives to wider audiences, and that my knowledge reflects my experience in geography within the United States; that my valuing of multiculturalism and cross-national dialogue leads me to include references to work by feminist geographers outside the dominant Anglophone communities of Britain and the United States; and that I see research in geographic and environmental education as encompassing questions about society outside the school and about schools as social institutions, as well as questions about formal instruction. That this view of research reflects my feminist understandings will become evident in the chapter.

Treatment of positionality in the interdisciplinary feminist literature and its salience for geographers has recently been discussed in some depth by McDowell (1992, 1993) and Pratt and Hanson (1994). Additionally, the complexities of and necessity for bringing together race/ethnicity (and, by extension, other contextually germane forms of social diversity) with gender in research and practice are increasingly being addressed as the challenges of working in multicultural societies are acknowledged. I will take up this theme in the section on methodology, but here wish to draw attention to two articles by 'minority' feminist geographers, Rickie Sanders (1990) and Audrey Kobayashi (1994), who emphasize the political aspects of knowledge creation (whose experiences do we take as the norm?) and the importance of relating scholarly work to life beyond the academy.

UNDERSTANDING GENDER

The concept of gender as an analytical category is central to feminist research. Masculine and feminine are understood as culturally created constructs that are related to biological sexual differences but not coterminous with them. What societies see as appropriate roles and activities for women and men differ from place to place and over time; although teaching (especially of younger children), for example, is identified primarily as a woman's profession today in most western societies, this has not always been the case, and patterns have varied spatially. Meusburger and Schmude (1991) have shown that strong rural–urban differences existed in the employment of women teachers throughout much of the twentieth century in Germany. Women were excluded from rural and small schools where teachers were expected to perform ancillary duties seen as masculine, such as community secretary, organist or head of the fire brigade; it was also claimed they could not handle several age groups in the one room. As small rural schools were consolidated, the percentage of female teachers increased. Women were also able to enter teaching at an earlier date in urban than in rural schools. At times of teacher shortage, regulations limiting women's participation in the profession (such as laws requiring women teachers to be celibate) were relaxed. This example not only shows that ideologies about gender influence employment opportunities, but also reveals than the state's construction of institutions (in this case, schools) is gendered. It helps us to counter the idea that differences between women and men are 'natural'.

We are socialized into gendered roles and behaviours from childhood. A few geographers have examined ways in which boys' and girls' out-of-school experiences are shaped by beliefs about gender with consequences for children's development of spatial competence and environmental knowledge. Hart (1979), working in a small community in the United States, showed that parents allowed their sons to range further from home than their daughters and excused boys more readily when they broke rules. Katz (1993) has drawn attention to the effects of parents' fears about their daughters' safety in large US cities on restricting girls' movement, even though data indicate that boys suffer more frequent physical and sexual abuse than girls in these settings. Her research in rural Sudan highlights the relevance of cultural values for opportunities to develop environmental knowledge. Pre-pubertal girls as well as boys had considerable freedom of spatial movement with settlement forms that fostered community surveillance of children (not only that by parents). Cultural values about sexuality restricted this freedom for girls when they reached puberty, however. Katz asks how the early opportunities might contribute to a knowledge formation that will be of value to women as their roles are changing under new pressures in global economy.

Geographers have devoted relatively little attention to studying how gendered ideologies influence the development of schooling in specific communities, but a project by a group of my students reveals how space and place come together in educational institutions so as to affect the reproduction of social positions. They examined the creation of two new high schools by the Tucson school district in the late 1950s, seeking to understand how class, ethnicity and gender distinctions might have been reinforced by the decisions of white middle- and upper-middle-class school-board members and the school superintendent about building design and curricular and extra curricular offerings. One school, Catalina, served middle-class neighbourhoods, the other, Pueblo, a working-class population with high proportions of Mexican American students. Architecturally, the design of Catalina was avant-garde, whereas Pueblo's was conventional. Overall, Catalina was larger, especially in spaces it devoted to 'public' uses. The auditorium at Pueblo was about 40 per cent of the size of Catalina's while the gym and locker rooms were less than 70 per cent of Catalina's, which were intended to accommodate championship games. Industrial arts and 'homemaking' classrooms occupied considerably more space at Pueblo than at Catalina. The insured value of the buildings and equipment markedly favoured Catalina. Students at Catalina had more choice of courses than those at Pueblo and the offerings revealed different expectations about the students' futures. More emphasis was given to preparation for higher education and cultural development at Catalina – foreign languages, physics, chemistry, speech and drama courses, for example, which were not offered at Pueblo, where industrial arts, homemaking and physical education occupied a larger place in the curriculum. The extracurricular activities are particularly telling in their reflection of a conjunction of values about gender and ethnicity. Girls at Catalina could join Future Nurses of America and Future Teachers of America (stereotypical but professional occupations for women), though these clubs did not exist at Pueblo. Catalina also focused on the 'feminine' role as decorative and supportive of males – cheerleading, pompon squads and beauty queens. In contrast, aspirations presented to Pueblo girls were for secretarial jobs (Future Business Leaders!) and homemaking. Peublo's Modeling Club aimed to teach girls good posture and grooming, not to generate 'beauty queens'.

This study also uses the concept of the gender division of labour, which occurs in paid employment, in work within the home, and in community activities. Documenting the nature of this division, its expression in different geographic contexts, and its implications for access to resources have been important themes of much feminist geography. Studies have investigated patterns at global (Momsen and Townsend, 1987), regional (e.g. McDowell and Massey, 1984) and intra-urban scales (e.g. Pratt and Hanson, 1994). In the process, they have shown how economic and social life (or productive and reproductive work) are closely intertwined, challenging disciplinary perspectives that have tended to study and teach these spheres separately. Employers have been shown to make locational decisions and use recruitment strategies that provide particular kinds of job for specific groups of women in particular places. Nelson (1986), for example, showed that Californian employers created low-wage office jobs in suburbs where they could recruit white, middle-class, married women rather than in other places where the labour pool included higher concentrations of female-headed households and minority women. Much previously unacknowledged labour by women has been documented, including the international incidence of the 'double day' and the exceptionally heavy work loads of Third World women. Variations have been identified across economic systems and seasonally (Mwaka, 1993; Oughton, 1993; Raghuram, 1993; Meertens, 1993), as well as the integration of women's informal work with national (Hays-Mitchell, 1993) and global (Sabaté *et al.*, 1991) economies, and the failure and negative effects of many development projects that have not taken women's work into account (e.g. Mackenzie, 1986). They show the importance of distinguishing among groups of women on the basis of local geography. Thus Ulluwishewa's (1993) research on Sri Lankan women's roles in traditional agricultural villages and in settlements within the Mahaweli water management project illustrates contrasting patterns in the two contexts in family structures, community relations, the extent of husbands' and children's participation in reproductive work, gender divisions of agricultural labour, women's access to income-generating opportunities, and their roles in decision-making about productive tasks and household expenditures.

Another important contribution of feminist research is the recognition that private spaces as well as public are important and that the two are connected. The work contrasts with much of geography, which focuses exclusively on the public world. Feminist geographers have opened up the scale of research to include the 'private', initially arguing that expansion was necessary because women's lives were associated with the interior spaces of the home, though as work progressed they have become more aware of the blurring of the boundaries and the interdependencies of the public and the private. Recent research on political struggles in Latin America, for example (Scarpaci and Frazier, 1993; Schirmer, 1993), identifies ways in which male state aggressors have entered private spaces to abduct state 'enemies', while women have drawn on the gender ideologies that support their private roles as mothers to enter public spaces to protest and give visibility to state violence. In a number of parts of the world women's concerns for private matters – the health of their families, household supplies of fuel, and the quality of water – have prompted them to enter the public sphere to protest against deteriorating and toxic environments and to initiate constructive environmental projects (Seager, 1993).

Although some of the studies I have cited do not bear directly on educational research, they are relevant for educators in that they expand our frameworks and heighten our critical consciousness about the content of curricula and materials. Drawing on such scholarship, geographers have published critiques of teaching materials for their representation of women and gender relations, revealing omissions and distortions, and suggesting potential revisions as well as pedagogical strategies for working with inadequate materials in the classroom (Larimore, 1978; Massey, 1986; Mayer, 1989; Monk, 1978, 1983; Wright, 1985). I will return to this theme in the next section of the chapter in my discussion of feminist methodologies.

DOING FEMINIST GEOGRAPHY

Feminist research does not apply a standard set of techniques so much as implement goals and conceptual understandings of the kind I have described above. It involves a critical perspective on society, reflection on the ends of one's project, and attention to gender as an analytical category. Nevertheless, feminist research employs some methodological approaches and techniques more extensively than others. Qualitative methods, especially the use of open-ended, in-depth interviews, have been especially important, both because of the desire to reveal hitherto neglected worlds and because of thinking that such methods are more respectful of the subjects of the research and permit representation of women's expressions and meanings. Analysis of 'texts' of all kinds is also important – for detecting sexist assumptions, for interpreting women's world views, and for exploring the symbolic dimensions of gendered responses to and constructions of place. I will return to these methods, but first will comment briefly on other approaches that have been used in feminist geography which have application for educational studies.

Recent work by Dutch feminist geographers (Droogleever Fortuijn, 1994; Karstens, 1994) and a student research exercise carried out at the Erasmus course held in Athens in April 1994 used systematic field observations of women's and men's behaviour in streets, squares, parks, and pubs on different days and at different hours to investigate how gender, age and ethnicity are implicated in use of public spaces and facilities. Katz's research on children's environmental knowledge combined observation of their everyday behaviour with interviews, 'ethnographic walks', experimental games and filming (Katz, 1989, 1991). Educational researchers have also used observations and videotaping in the classroom to observe how interactions between teachers and students are gendered, following their research with workshops designed to modify behaviour (Sadker and Sadker, 1990).

Quantitative analysis of primary data such as records of daily time use, travel diaries and some secondary source materials has also been useful to document the nature and extent of women's tasks (Wickramasinghe, 1993), and to reveal distinctions in women's and men's spatial behaviour which reflect their different roles and access to resources (e.g. Hanson and Johnston, 1985; McLafferty and Preston, 1991; Rosenbloom, 1993). Rosenbloom's work is interesting for researchers in geographic education, because it shows how parents' and children's daily movements (including travel to and from school) vary according to the age of children, the marital status of parents, and geographic context. Her findings have implications for children's spatial autonomy and for their differential access to after-school activities. Feminists have also used primary and secondary quantitative data to contextualize qualitative material (England, 1993).

It is in-depth interviewing which is most characteristic of feminist work, however, and which has recently generated considerable discussion for the challenges and dilemmas it poses. It has been an important mechanism in documenting activities unrecorded or under-recorded in official sources, as is well illustrated by Spanish research on women's work in agriculture, which has used both census data and in-depth interviews with women (Baylina *et al.*, 1991; García-Ramon *et al.*, 1990, 1991). It is also central in studies that seek to show how women see their own worlds; for example, in Christensen's (1993) research on women of different generations who have created home-based businesses and Fagnani's (1993) study of Parisian families' preferences for city or suburban residence. The quandaries arise with regard to questions of power and relationships in the research process. On the one hand, the in-depth interview has been considered to be a way of empowering the subject, respecting her dignity and presenting her world, rather than the preconstructed world of the researcher. Townsend explores these issues at length in discussing her research with Latin American women, in which she shifted from a socialist-feminist interest in women's daily work to concerns about domestic violence as she listened to women's life histories and presentation of their own problems (Townsend, 1994). On the other hand, feminists have recognized that issues of trust and confidence, selection of material for representation and publication, and use of material to advance the researcher's career but perhaps not to effect social change are not simple ones, ethically or methodologically. One of the most discussed issues is that of interviewing women who have less social power than or are of a different racial/ethnic group from the scholar. What are the implications of being an 'insider' or an 'outsider' to the group being interviewed (Dyck, 1993)? How does one deal with views with which one disagrees, such as expressions of racism (Gilbert, 1994)? Are there cases when research should be abandoned because of problems of trust or feelings of inappropriate voyeurism (England, 1994)? How should the feminist woman researcher behave when interviewing powerful men whose politics she does not share (McDowell, 1992b)? The issues of ends and means in the creation of 'truth' come together most critically in these discussions. Kobayashi (1994) argues that the responsibilities of study and representation ultimately lie not in some right or wrong answers to questions of means, but in those of ends, and one's personal history in crossing the boundaries between academy and community, research and action.

The reading of 'texts' to interpret values, assumptions, identities, symbolic meanings and power relations is also important in feminist work. The definition of 'text' is inclusive – from the built landscape to dress and presentation of the body, art, literature and other media to official documents, scholarly work and teaching materials. The study of Tucson schools that I discussed above formed its interpretations from close readings of the content and language of architectural plans, insurance documents, newspaper reports, school-board minutes and school magazines. Postmodern work invokes many types of 'text' – popular media, observation of dress and behavioural 'performances' as well as written texts – to yield meditations that may be 'non-linear, ambivalent, and multipositional' (Bell *et al.*, 1994), about the formation and expression of identity and resistance to dominant cultural values and practices.

My own reading of the representation of gender in an array of role-playing games designed to teach about locational and environmental conflicts is less complex than post-modern writing, but illustrates how we can decode the unspoken messages of educational materials (Monk, 1978). I analysed the number and content of roles assigned to males and females (and those of unspecified gender) as well as the language used to describe the actors. The results indicated a much greater number of male than female roles and that the male roles were both more specific and varied. Further, men were described in more active and potent terms – as 'youthful', 'competent', 'active', 'ambitious', 'responsible', 'confident', 'experienced' and so on – whereas women were described as 'not dynamic', 'works steadily and quietly', 'interested in short-term profits rather than long-term dreams', and 'goes along with the majority'. Donald Massey's (1986) similar reading of his own elementary-school geography text as it underwent revision by the publisher shows how such conservative visions are promoted in writing and illustrations.

CONNECTING ENDS AND MEANS: OPPORTUNITIES FOR FEMINIST RESEARCH IN GEOGRAPHIC AND ENVIRONMENTAL EDUCATION

As I have already noted, little feminist research has been done in geographic or environmental education. This does not mean that the question of gender (or rather of male/female differences) has been totally ignored. A considerable literature exists on differences in girls' and boys' spatial competencies and cartographic performance. Two excellent reviews of this work have been provided by Matthews (1992) and Self *et al.* (1992). They reveal one of the problems of positivist, experimental research that may not become clear except in such wide-ranging reviews – that is, that the research design, including the choice of tasks and instruments, has critical implications for the 'objective' findings, and the results across studies are often conflicting. In general, however, they reveal a deterioration in girls' scores and the greatest difference among girl and boys in spatial skills at puberty and adolescence, ages when they would be studying geography in secondary schools, when decisions regarding future careers are being shaped, and when girls' self-confidence appears to fall most substantially. Nevertheless, these studies have revealed some tasks on which girls perform as well as or better than boys, despite the more common finding of higher performance for boys. The literature, however, does not show evidence of projects designed to experiment with remediation or to examine the links between motivation, sense of competence and performance in geography. In other words, it is not directed towards the social-change goals of feminism, and it does not pay significant attention to the concept of gender as a cultural construct, tending instead simply to use sex as a variable.

The geographic literature also rarely addresses the interactions of gender with 'race', ethnicity, class or other aspects of social diversity. Studies from other fields suggest that these interactions are complex. Examinations of students' attitudes, achievements and aspirations, of parents' and teachers' expectations, and of interactions in the classroom show gender, 'race' and ethnicity to be associated with patterns of difference which shift in direction and intensity (e.g. MacCorquodale, 1982; Scott-Jones and Clark, 1986). A pilot study conducted recently for the National Council on Geographic Education's Task

Force on Underrepresented Groups in Geography[3] in a set of ethnically diverse class-rooms in Florida and Alabama revealed complex interactions among gender, ethnicity, grade level, attitudes and achievement in geography. Among these findings were that:

1. by Grade 9, minority boys were outperforming minority girls, though gender differences were not pronounced among white students;
2. that attitudinal differences were notable by school and grade level;
3. that among higher-achieving students, boys were more likely to describe the discip-line as 'fun', 'easy', 'cool', 'exciting' and 'interesting' and girls to see it as 'boring' and 'stupid';
4. that girls were more likely to describe geography by the content it covers than to identify with it affectively;
5. that boys had a wider range of ideas about careers associated with geography than girls did.

From a feminist perspective, these findings suggest the need, if girls' performance in geography is to be improved, to engage in research on their liking for geography and on the sense of the meaning it can have for their lives. It also implies that there is a need for action research that develops and evaluates projects directed towards affective goals.

These observations take me back to the theme of 'partial' truths and connecting the ends and means of research. I hope that my discussion of feminist research in geography in general has made it clear that such work incorporates a number of perspectives that would enrich research in geographic and environmental education, posing new chal-lenges and possibilities. First, it implies that we should adopt a critical perspective on research by asking whose world is being represented and what the implications of the project are for society. Does it reinforce the *status quo* or help us move towards a more equitable society? Second, it highlights the importance of seeing gender as socially and culturally constructed, and indicates that we should build that understanding into our research questions and designs, not simply add 'sex' as a variable. We need to explore how those social and cultural constructions arise, how they intersect with other sources of social difference, and what their long-term implications are. Third, we need to ask how our research questions would expand if we recognized social and cultural issues in education, rather than limiting our agenda to research on the classroom and the curric-ulum. Thus we would address questions about the school and schooling as social institutions that reflect and reproduce place-related ideologies and social patterns, and we would look at the gender socialization of teachers and students in relation to attitudes and behaviours that are germane for geographic and environmental learning, whether in the classroom or beyond it.

Methodologically, these suggestions will take us beyond the experimental, positivist mode that has characterized much research in geographic and environmental education. It will take us into new settings and prompt us to use open-ended, qualitative methods to explore the world views and experiences of girls and boys (and adult men and women) of diverse backgrounds, in order to widen and deepen our understanding of how these perspectives arise and how they constrain or enable people's experience of place and space. It may motivate us to undertake projects that involve action as well as research, both in school settings and beyond.

By way of example, I would like to conclude with a brief description of two projects carried out by Myrna Breitbart with children in Holyoke, Massachusetts. Many of the children are of Puerto Rican background. The school has experienced drastic budget cuts which have reduced the number of teachers (to the point where students have organized public protests) and the facilities are in poor repair. Dr Breitbart's first project, in collaboration with photographer Michael Jacobsen-Hardy and educator Gloria Caballer-Arce, involved the children in photography and in keeping journals about the kinds of place they would like to experience. The elementary-school children write that they would like peaceful places, places to ride bikes, places to be alone with friends. Middle-school boys and girls also express their desire for quiet places and security. When asked how they would like to change their communities, Bethzaida, a sixth-grade girl, wrote, 'I dream of a day when people will be able to walk the streets of Holyoke in safety.' Girls express their concerns in terms not only of fear but also of boredom. They describe how the lack of safe spaces confines their activities, and some look to the school to provide alternatives. Elizabeth, a middle-school girl, writes, 'I like it when it's June because the teachers have a field trip to Mount Tom or somewhere where it's safe for us.' The children's writings show them to be deeply affected by their environments, including the deteriorated condition of the school buildings, and the filthy and smelly bathrooms. For all ages, fixing up their school environment was a high priority.

This project did not end with the research. The team of scholars produced a museum exhibit and illustrated catalogue which brought the children's worlds to an array of Massachusetts communities to sensitize them to children's issues (Caballer-Arce and Breitbart, 1993). It also serves to reinforce Dr Breitbart's efforts to engage in action research with local children. In another project, she worked with children in a summer programme to help them reflect on places as they are and might be, and, with them, went through an extended process (including work with public authorities) of creating a significant community display of public art in the form of street banners (Breitbart, in press). The projects represent research efforts to understand the worlds of (largely Hispanic) girls and boys and their aspirations, to present these findings to scholarly audiences, to give the children a sense of their own worth and to develop their expressive capabilities, and to use their efforts to foster social awareness and change. Through their ends and means, such research creates feminists' 'partial' truths.

NOTES

1. For example, the *Journal of Environmental Education* contained no articles on gender themes between 1980 and 1994, and only one or two citations to works on gender were included in references to the articles it published.
2. This does not imply that feminist geography is not or cannot be written by men.
3. The results of this pilot research, conducted for the Task Force by Michal LeVasseur, have not been published. They are reported in a grant proposal recently submitted by the Task Force to the National Science Foundation (US), project directors Susan Hardwick and Rickie Sanders.

REFERENCES

Baylina, M., Canoves, G., García-Ramon, M.D. and Vilariño, M. (1991) 'La entrevista en profundidad como metodo de analisis en geografia rural: mujeres agricultoras y relaciones de genero en la costa gallega.' *VI Colloquia de Geografia Rural AGE Madrid*, 12–19.

Bell, D., Binnie, J., Cream, J. and Valentine, G. (1994) 'All hyped up and no place to go.' *Gender, Place and Culture*, **1**, 31–47.

Berman, M. (1977) 'Facts and attitudes on discrimination as perceived by AAG members.' *The Professional Geographer*, **29**, 70–6.

Breitbart, M.M. in press, '"Banners for the street": reclaiming space and designing change with urban youth.' *Journal of Planning Education and Research*.

Caballer-Arce, G. and Breitbart, M. (1993) *Facing Education/Enfrentando la Educacion*. Copyright, M. Jacobsen-Hardy, funded by the Massachusetts Foundation for the Humanities.

Christensen, K. (1993) 'Eliminating the journey to work: home-based work across the life course of women in the United States.' In C. Katz and J. Monk (eds) *Full Circles: Geographies of Women over the Life Course*. London: Routledge.

Downs, R.M. (1994) 'Being and becoming a geographer: an agenda for geography education.' *Annals of the Association of American Geographers*, **8**, 175–91.

Droogleever Fortuijn, J. (1994) 'Qualitative research methods – interviewing and observation in feminist geographical research.' In *Women in Public Space: Experiences from North and South*. Athens: Department of Urban and Regional Planning, National Technical University of Athens.

Dyck, I. (1993) 'Ethnography: a feminist method?' *The Canadian Geography*, **37**, 52–7.

England, K.V.L. (1993) 'Suburban pink collar ghettoes: the spatial entrapment of women?' *Annals of the Association of American Geographers*, **83**, 225–42.

England, K.V.L. (1994) 'Getting personal: reflexivity, positionality, and feminist research.' *The Professional Geographer*, **46**, 80–9.

Fagnani, J. (1993) 'Life course and space: dual careers and residential mobility, among upper-middle-class families in the Ile-de-France region.' In C. Katz and J. Monk (eds) *Full Circles: Geographies of Women over the Life Course*. London: Routledge.

García-Ramon, M.D., Solsona, M. and Valdovinos, N. (1990) 'The changing role of women in Spanish agriculture: analyses from the agricultural censuses.' *Journal of Women and Gender Studies*, **1**, 135–61.

García-Ramon, M.D., Cruz Villalon, J., Salamaña, I., Valdovinos, N. and Vilariño, M. (1991) 'Women and farm households: regional variations in gender roles and relations in Spain.' *Iberian Studies*, **20**, 81–112.

Gilbert, M. (1994) 'The politics of location: doing feminist research at home.' *The Professional Geographer*, **46**, 90–6.

Hanson, S. and Johnston, I. (1985) 'Gender differences in work trip lengths: explanations and implications.' *Urban Geography*, **6**, 193–219.

Haraway, D. (1988) 'Situated knowledges: the science question in feminism and the privilege of partial perspective.' *Feminist Studies*, **14**, 575–99.

Hart, R. (1979) *Children's Experience of Place*. New York: Irvington.

Hays-Mitchell, M. (1993) 'The ties that bind: informal and formal sector linkages in streetvending: the case of Peru's *ambulantes*.' *Environment and Planning A*, **25**, 1085–1102.

Journal of Geography (1978) **77** (5). Special issue on women in geographic curricula.

Karstens, L. (1994) 'Women in public space: the gender of the pub.' In *Women in Public Space: Experiences from North and South*. Athens: Department of Urban and Regional Planning, National Technical University of Athens.

Katz, C. (1989) 'Herders, gatherers, and foragers: the emerging botanies of children in rural Sudan.' *Children's Environments Quarterly*, **6** (1), 46–53.

Katz, C. (1991) 'Sow what you know: the struggle for social reproduction in rural Sudan.' *Annals of the Association of American Geographers*, **81**, 488–514.

Katz, C. (1993) 'Growing girls/closing circles: limits on the spaces of knowing in rural Sudan and U.S. cities.' in C. Katz and J. Monk (eds) *Full Circles: Geographies of Women over the Life Course*. London: Routledge.

Kobayashi, A. (1994) 'Coloring the field: gender, "race" and the politics of field work.' *The Professional Geographer*, **46**, 73–80.

Larimore, A.E. (1978) 'Humanizing the writing in cultural geography texts.' *Journal of Geography*, **77**, 180–3.

LeVasseur, M. (1993) *Finding a Way: Encouraging Underrepresented Groups in Geography – An Annotated Bibliography*. Indiana, PA: National Council for Geographic Education.

MacCorquodale, P. (1982) 'Interest in science courses and careers: a comparison of Mexican American and Anglo students.' In J. Martinez and D. Martinez (eds) *Aspects of American Hispanic and Indian Involvement in Biomedical Research*. Washington, DC: Society for the Advancement of Chicanos and Native Americans in Science.

McDowell, L. (1979) 'Women in British geography.' *Area*, **11**, 151-4.

McDowell, L. (1983) 'Towards an understanding of the gender division of urban space.' *Environment and Planning D: Society and Space*, **1**, 59-72.

McDowell, L. (1992a) 'Doing gender: feminism, feminists and research methods in human geography.' *Transactions of the Institute of British Geographers*, **17**, 399-416.

McDowell, L. (1992b) 'Valid games?' *The Professional Geographer*, **44**, 219-22.

McDowell, L. (1993) 'Space, place and gender relations. Part II. Identity, difference, feminist geometries and geographies.' *Progress in Human Geography*, **17**, 305-18.

McDowell, L. and Massey, D. (1984) 'A woman's place?' In D. Massey and J. Allen (eds) *Geography Matters*. Cambridge: Cambridge University Press.

MacKenzie, F. (1986) 'Local initiatives and national policy: gender and agricultural change in the Murang'a District, Kenya.' *Canadian Journal of African Studies*, **20**, 377-401.

MacKenzie, S. and Rose, D. (1983) 'Industrial change, the domestic economy and home life.' In J. Anderson, S. Duncan and R. Hudson (eds) *Redundant Spaces in Cities and Regions? Social Geography and Industrial Change*. London: Academic Press.

McLafferty, S. and Preston, V. (1991) 'Gender, race, and commuting distance among service sector workers.' *The Professional Geographer*, **43**, 1-15.

Massey, D. (1986) 'Inside a textbook.' *Journal of Geography*, **85**, 116-19.

Matthews, M.H. (1992) *Making Sense Out of Place: Children's Understanding of Large-scale Environments*. Hemel Hempstead/Savage, MD: Harvester Wheatsheaf/Barnes and Noble.

Mayer, T. (1989) 'Consensus and invisibility: the representation of women in human geography textbooks.' *The Professional Geographer*, **41**, 397-409.

Meertens, D. (1993) 'Women's roles in colonization: a Columbian case study.' In J.H. Momsen and V. Kinnaird (eds) *Different Places, Different Voices: Gender and Development in Africa, Asia and Latin America*. London: Routledge.

Meusburger, P. and Schmude, J. (1991) 'The relationship between community size, female employment rates, and educational level of the female labour force.' *Working Paper*, No. 12. International Geographical Union Study Group on Gender and Geography.

Momsen, J. (1980) 'Women in Canadian geography.' *Canadian Geographer*, **24**, 177-83.

Momsen, J. and Townsend, J. (eds) (1987) *Geography of Gender in the Third World*. London: Hutchinson Educational.

Monk, J. (1978) 'Women in geographic games.' *Journal of Geography*, **77**, 190-1.

Monk, J. (1983) 'Integrating women into the geography curriculum.' *Journal of Geography*, **82**, 271-3.

Monk, J. (1994) 'Place matters: comparative international perspectives on feminist geography.' *The Professional Geographer*, **46**, 277-88.

Monk, J. and Hanson S. (1982) 'On not excluding half of the human in human geography.' *Professional Geographer*, **34**, 11-23.

Mwaka, V.M. (1993) 'Agricultural production and women's time budgets in Uganda.' In J.H. Momsen and V. Kinnaird (eds) *Different Places, Different Voices: Gender and Development in Africa, Asia and Latin America*. London: Routledge.

Nelson, K. (1986) 'Female labor supply characteristics and the suburbanization of low-wage office work.' In M. Storper and A. Scott (eds) *Production, Space, Territory: The Geographical Anatomy of Industrial Capitalism*. London: George Allen and Unwin.

Oughton, E. (1993) 'Seasonality, wage labour and women's contribution to household income in western India.' In J. Momsen and V. Kinnaird (eds) *Different Places, Different Voices: Gender and Development in Africa, Asia and Latin America*. London: Routledge.

Pratt, G. and Hanson, S. (1994) 'Geography and the construction of difference.' *Gender, Place and Culture*, **1**, 5-29.

Raghuram, P. (1993) 'Invisible female agricultural labour in India.' In J.H. Momsen and V. Kinnaird (eds) *Different Places, Different Voices: Gender and Development in Africa, Asia and Latin America*. London: Routledge.

Rosenbloom, S. (1993) 'Women's travel patterns at various stages of their lives.' In C. Katz and J. Monk (eds) *Full Circles: Geographies of Women over the Life Course*. London: Routledge.

Sabaté, A., Martin-Caro Hernández, J.L., Martin Gil, F. and Rodríguez Moya, J. (1991) 'Economic restructuring and the gender divisions of labour: the clothing industry in the rural areas of the Autonomous Community of Madrid.' *Iberian Studies*, **20**, 135–54.

Sadker, M. and Sadker, D. (1990) 'Confronting sexism in the college classroom.' In S.L. Gabriel and I. Smithson (eds) *Gender in the Classroom: Power and Pedagogy*. Urbana and Chicago, IL: University of Illinois Press.

Sanders, R. (1990) 'Integrating race and ethnicity into gender studies.' *The Professional Geographer*, **42**, 228–31.

Scarpaci, J. and Frazier, L.J. (1993) 'State terror: ideology, protest, and the gendering of landscapes.' *Progress in Human Geography*, **17**, 1–21.

Schirmer, J. (1993) 'The seeking of truth and the gendering of consciousness: the Comadres of El Salvador and the CONAVIGUA widows of Guatemala.' In S.A. Radcliffe and S. Westwood (eds) *Viva: Women and Protest in Latin America*. London: Routledge.

Scott-Jones, D. and Clark, M.L. (1986) 'The school experience of Black girls: the interaction of gender, race, and socio-economic status.' *Phi Delta Kappan*, **67**, 520–6.

Seager, J. (1993) *Earth Follies: Coming to Feminist Terms with the Global Environmental Crisis*. New York: Routledge.

Self, C.M., Gopal, S., Golledge, R.G. and Fenstermaker, S. (1992) 'Gender-related differences in spatial abilities.' *Progress in Human Geography*, **16**, 315–42.

Tivers, J. (1978) 'How the other half lives.' *Area*, **10**, 302–6.

Townsend, J. (1994) *Women's Voices from the Rainforest*. London: Routledge.

Ulluwishewa, R. (1993) *Development Planning and Gender Inequality: A Case Study in the Mahaweli Development Project, Sri Lanka*. International Geographical Union Commission on Gender and Geography Working Paper No. 26.

Wickramasinghe, A. (1993) 'Women's role in rural Sri Lanka.' In J. Momsen and V. Kinnaird (eds) *Different Places, Different Voices: Gender and Development in Africa, Asia and Latin America*. London: Routledge.

Women and Geography Study Group of the IBG (1984) *Gender and Geography: An Introduction to Feminist Geography*. London: Hutchinson in association with the Explorations of Feminism Collective.

Wright, D.R. (1985) 'Are geography textbooks sexist?' *Teaching Geography*, **10** (2) 81–5.

Zelinsky, W. (1973a) 'The strange case of the missing female geographer.' *The Professional Geographer*, **25**, 101–6.

Zelinsky, W. (1973b) 'Women in geography: a brief factual account.' *The Professional Geographer*, **25**, 151–65.

Zelinsky, W., Monk, J. and Hanson, S. (1982) 'Women and geography: a review and prospectus.' *Progress in Human Geography*, **6**, 317–66.

Chapter 23

The Challenge of Postmodernism

John Bale

In this chapter, I seek to introduce the idea of postmodernism and speculate about its relevance to geographical education. I particularly want to utilize the notion of 'post-modernity' to explore the recent history of geographical education, to probe alternative forms of pedagogy and to present a personal 'reading' of the recent history and present condition of geography and environmental education in the British school curriculum. Implicit in my chapter are the implications for research in geographical education. Although most of my exemplars are taken from the British situation, I believe that my general thesis applies to the situation currently prevailing in many countries throughout the world.

A recent review of postmodernism started as follows:

> When I was sixteen I wanted a car desperately; it was all my male friends ever talked about. I felt excluded. I feel the same about postmodernism. At least having a car is useful ... I can find very little of any use in postmodernism and even *that* has been said before in a different form.
>
> (Skeggs, 1991, p. 255)

This sceptical view contrasts with one which asserts that 'to the extent that postmodernism challenges conventional assumptions about knowledge, morality, subjectivity, it raises fundamental questions about essential elements of modern educational thought' (Gilbert, 1992, p. 56). It has also been observed that postmodernism 'constitutes the most profound challenge to three hundred years of post-Enlightenment thinking' (Dear and Wassmandorf, 1993, p. 321).

Postmodernism as a subject of debate is currently *de rigueur* in higher education, and among the most celebrated contributions have been those of the geographers Edward Soja (1989) and David Harvey, the latter's highly readable *The Condition of Postmodernity* (1989) being widely cited within and outside geography and regarded by one educationist as one of the three best books on the subject 'for the uninitiated with plenty of time' (Skeggs, 1991, p. 266). Recent overviews of 'the history of geographical thought' provide the obligatory page or two on the subject, almost giving the impression that it is another bandwagon, one more in a long line of -isms, which geography is now embracing (Livingstone, 1992, pp. 343–4; Unwin, 1992, pp. 177–80). The diffusion of the debate on the relevance of postmodernism into school geography has been much less obvious. Indeed, it is hard to imagine a school geography department settling down to a meeting with 'the role of postmodernism in the curriculum' on the agenda. This is hardly surprising, given the geography teachers' myriad curricular concerns in recent decades. I would argue, nevertheless, that geography in schools – as elsewhere – exhibits a 'postmodern condition' and hence constitutes a valid subject for discussion among those involved in the geographical education of young people. If nothing else, a postmodern approach allows us to 'read' school geography in a new way.

POSTMODERNISM: WHAT IS IT?

The basic tenets of postmodernist and poststructuralist thinking have been neatly outlined in these words:

> Post-modernists reject the dominant idea of the past two centuries that asserts the possibility of: (a) understanding the world through a rationally-agreed theoretical approach; (b) of agreeing on a universal moral code; and (c) of human progress towards universally agreed goals. Post-modernism suggests that truths and meanings are relative to your standpoint – your 'place' – and that different individuals and groups will have competing, *but equally valid*, goals and interpretations of the world. Post-modernist and post-structuralist theorists attempt to 'deconstruct' dominant ideas and show both that they are less 'rational' than they appear – and that they are often based on unexamined and incorrect assumptions – and that they are the ideas of the powerful – that they exclude the experience and knowledge of subordinate groups.
>
> (Bowlby, 1992, p. 358)

Bowlby comes close to implying that 'postmodernism' is a new kind of 'grand theory' – something that would have to be rejected in view of the postmodern avoidance of 'meta-narratives' – and I should stress from the outset that 'postmodernism' is a term which refuses to be rigorously defined. Indeed, by being defined the concept comes close to being the very thing it tries to reject. Instead, it might best be viewed as a number of cultural tendencies which share some common characteristics. In particular, it can be viewed as 'a revolt against the too rigid conventions of existing method and language' (Dear, 1988, p. 265). Suffice it to say that it seems to imply that something really different is happening to the view of (and the way we view) the world. Postmodernism may be viewed as radical or conservative, utopian or dystopian; postmodernists themselves may affirm its potential or be sceptical about its claims. Whether we like it or not, however, postmodernism is a subject now being talked about in our subject – and in the broader arena of education.

Why should such interest have been shown in postmodern thinking? It has been suggested that 'modernity entered history as a progressive force promising to liberate humankind from ignorance and irrationality, but one can readily wonder whether that promise has been sustained' (Rosenau, 1992, p. 5). Witness, for example, Nazism, Auschwitz, genocide, global recessions, Hiroshima, Vietnam, Somalia, Bosnia, etc. Given the failure of the modern, therefore, the postmodern has to be viewed as a series of possible alternatives. But what has this idea got to do with geographical education in an age of state-prescribed curricula, as evidenced in the UK for example? I will suggest that it is of possible relevance in three main areas. I will consider:

1. the 'postmodern' or 'postmodernity' as an *object* to be studied (for example, post-modern landscapes or buildings);
2. 'postmodernism' as an *attitude* to or a *method* of studying, researching and teach-ing geography (for example, postmodern textbooks or postmodern classroom styles);
3. 'postmodernity' as a *period* within the evolution of our subject or an *epoch* marking a radical break with past trends in human affairs.

Each of these conceptualizations will be briefly considered in the following sections.

THE POSTMODERN IN GEOGRAPHY

A traditional view of geography, reflecting the ideographic approach to the subject, focused on *differences* between places. This philosophy was classically associated with regional geography in which the richness and variety of human–land relationships was stressed. Subsequently, geographers sought to identify, through the nomothetic approach, *similarities* between places as part of the tendency to construct models in geography, either as convenient generalizations of what actually exist or as prescriptions of what ought to exist, given certain norms and assumptions (Harvey, 1972). Such shifts in emphasis – but not revolutions, as I will argue later – are well known in many areas of school geography and can be evidenced by a cursory comparison of the content of school textbooks from the 1950s with that in those of the 1980s.

As an example of the postmodern as curriculum content, consider the case of urban geography. The term 'postmodern' is now widely applied to the city in at least two particular contexts:

1. that of its landscape (that is, its architecture);
2. in terms of its overall 'pattern' – or lack of it.

If we have 'postmodern' urban landscapes, when did the 'modern' ones come to an end? Many would argue that the modern city ended with the destruction of such build-ings as Ronan Point in London or the Pruitt-Igoe apartment blocks in St Louis. These structures, in the words of the modernist architect Le Corbusier, were 'machines for living in'; they typified the landscape of modernity – straight-edged, rational, anony-mous, international, predictable – and unlivable in. They were the architectural equivalent of the isotropic plane. Postmodern landscapes, on the other hand, include the architectures of the Las Vegas 'strip', Disneyworld, the Pompidou Centre, various kinds of vernacularization ('Prince Charles' styles), heritage, and ecological architecture. Postmodern places are 'surprising' and are often incongruously juxtaposed among and between quite different styles. But it is a world where the image is all-important, 'image' being a word widely used by postmodernists. The globe is seen as a 'world of simulations' (Baudrillard, 1989), while the future promises electronic landscapes and virtual reality. The changing landscape of London's docklands would also illustrate the postmodern landscape with its symbolic communities – but only symbolic ones in a world where 'image' is everything.

The overall form of the city can also be described as increasingly failing to conform to our classical models. Indeed, they often appear to be classical muddles – the complex (and seemingly quite chaotic) collision of *all manner of different objects* in the 'messy "collage" of contemporary people and places' (Cloke *et al.* 1991, p. 179) – the Los Angeles of Ridley Scott's *Blade Runner* or the London of Alan Ayckbourn's *Henceforward*. This is not the neat and tidy world of the planned city; it is a world of heterotopia – the opposite of the isotropic plane.

I think we need to consider two aspects of the above examples, ludicrously condensed as they are. First, does the postmodern condition of the urban landscape provide useful and enjoyable content for our syllabuses? If so what learning strategies might we employ? Consider, for example, the possibility of students' 'deconstructing' selected short 'clips' from the dystopian view of the city in the aforementioned *Blade Runner* or the more utopian view of Disney's EPCOT. Secondly, there is a need to *explain* the nature of the postmodern city; that is, is it really something different or is it simply a late stage of capitalism? If the latter is the case then the adjective 'post' might be better replaced by 'late'. This view would see much of the postmodern city as simply a superficial 'packaging' of architectural gimmicks.

Consider, as a second example, the case of world geography. The notion of time–space convergence is another theme reflecting the postmodern condition. Space has been replaced by time, according to some observers. An electronic age brings places closer together in a shrinking world, telecommunication overcoming the friction of distance. A result of such time–space compression is that a rich mixture of cultures pervades our day-to-day lives (look at the cultural composition of fast-food outlets, TV schedules and football teams, for example). These are the kinds of theme which I think progressive geographical educators ought to be addressing, seeking not only to describe such developments but also, with their students, to explore them for their many meanings.

POSTMODERN ATTITUDES TO LEARNING AND TEACHING

'Postmodernists in all disciplines reject conventional, academic styles of discourse; they prefer audacious and provocative forms of delivery, vital and intriguing elements of genre or style and presentation' (Rosenau, 1992, p. 7). According to Worth (1993, p. 5), postmodern pedagogy involves:

1. the opening up of discourse so that previously inadmissible questions and unheard voices can have access to it;
2. the erosion of the power/knowledge equation, hence giving a critically interactive role to students;
3. the provision for students to explore the mediations, interrelations, and interdependencies between a subject and its social and political context;
4. the rejection of the passive accumulation of 'knowledge' passed down by 'experts' and later regurgitated in examinations.

A cross-disciplinary approach would be favoured over the neat and tidy world of the 'school day' with its segmentation of time and space. An approach to geographical knowledge would include looking for 'meaning' in everyday things, viewing the landscape – indeed, the world – as a 'text' to be deconstructed, discovering the 'taken-for-granted' view as a myth. And crucially, as Gilbert (1992, p. 56) has pointed out, 'a feature of postmodernist styles is that they are archetypically the styles of the young – cinema, television, fashion, rock music, dance: cultural forms which are the expressive channels of a generation. Educators ignore this life world at their peril.'

Being suspicious of 'grand theory', a postmodern approach to teaching geography would value individuals' opinions and ideas, a less academic style allowing – indeed encouraging – the use of vernacular writing and talking styles, and a return to the personal pronoun 'I' in writing. Research would discourage 'the data-set, the passive voice, the Harvard reference system' (Gregory, 1994, p. 55). Such practices exhibit a 'hard scientific' style and give the impression of authority. In postmodern writing the author is no longer seen in a dominant power relationship to the reader, since a wide variety of 'readings' of any given 'text' are available. In a postmodern text, no *one* reading can therefore be defined as right or wrong, and the reader's role is one of 'producing' and 'constructing' alternatives to what is read. 'The text is written to be re-written' (Rosenau, 1992, p. xiv).

At a very basic level, such an approach could be illustrated in the geography curriculum by encouraging students to 'decode' such widespread icons as advertisements, landscape paintings, comics, news reports, films and school textbooks. Such approaches, borrowing ideas from media studies, is not as novel as might be first assumed. An example of such a Barthesian 'reading' of a 'text' was actually recommended in *Geography GCSE: A Guide for Teachers* (SEC, 1986, p. 39), where, in a table of suggested topics for coursework, is found 'the study of the landscape of an area seen through the work of artists, for example, Constable's Suffolk or Lowry's northern England'.

Attractive though these ideas may seem for teachers favouring an emancipatory form of education, certain problems, nevertheless, seem evident. Does such an approach, for example, open the door to an unbridled form of cultural relativism? Are the merits of any viewpoint or one 'reading' as valid as any other? How may writing be validated and assessed in such a situation? On the other hand, there may be ways in which such a postmodern approach can be utilized in order to legitimate children's vernacular knowledge.

Doll (1989) suggests three implications of postmodern thinking for curriculum development. These are that:

1. the curriculum should be less 'linear' and more like a 'matrix' – 'places where one begins are less important than how one explores the myriad connections, logical and personal, inherent in the matrix'. Flexibility and 'productive pathways' would take precedence over 'closure';
2. curriculum planning should be two-tier: the teacher would set general goals and other goals would emerge as teacher and pupil worked together;
3. the teacher and student should be seen as sharing the learning experience with each other; learning is viewed as a by-product of inquiry.

Some implications for research into environmental and geographical education emerge from the above discussion. Postmodern method is essentially 'a revolt against the rationality of modernism, a deliberate attack on the foundational character of most modernist thought'. Basically:

> the postmodern critique undermines the modern belief that theory can mirror reality and replaces it with a partly relativistic viewpoint that emphasizes the contingent, mediated nature of theory building. Metatheories and foundational thoughts are rejected in favor of microexplanations and undecidability. More than most, postmodernists learn to contextualize.
>
> (Dear and Wassmandorf, 1993, pp. 321-2)

In practical terms, this implies highly unconventional methods of inquiry and representation, most of which might well be unacceptable within the traditional frameworks of geographical and educational research. For example, if we accept that an accurate representation of the world is an impossible task, how do we begin to represent it? Does its chaos and disorder imply chaotic representations in text or forms of Joycean disorder in the style of Olsson (1980), who illustrates the inadequacy of language as a medium for representation by playing with it in order to make this very point? Or it is necessary to publish fieldwork results as a literal montage after the style of Quonian (1988), who records his landscape as a patchwork, a bricologe, of drawings accompanied by an illegible/incomprehensible text? It is the so-called crisis of representation which forms a central theme in postmodern thought; that is, the very possibility of representing something (such as a landscape) by another thing (such as words) without loss of content or meaning.

GEOGRAPHY AS A POSTMODERN SUBJECT

My third theme is that geography in mid-1990s' Britain is a paradigm for the postmodern school subject. Here I interpret the period since about 1969 as an epoch which has witnessed the emergence of a geographical education which is fundamentally different in form from that which preceded it. Note, however, the use of the word 'form' (as opposed to 'structure') in the previous sentence.

The National Curriculum for geography has been viewed as 'retro-geography' (Barratt, personal communication), a return to the 'bad old days' of regional geography and 'capes and bays'. It has also been viewed as 'the modernist legacy ... an attempt to impose structure on the actions of teachers and learners' (Lambert, personal communication). These are plausible readings of geography in the 1990s and would probably be widely endorsed by many teachers. I would adopt a different reading, however, and argue that events of the past decade, including the National Curriculum, simply reinforce the postmodern tendencies which have existed in geography since about the time Ronan Point collapsed. So when did 'modern' geography 'collapse'?

In my reading of the events in geographical education over the last quarter of a century, modern school geography in Britain can be said to have 'died' in 1968/69 with the publication of *New Ways in Geography* (Cole and Beynon, 1968), and shortly afterwards with that of the (arguably more influential) A-level text, *Settlement Patterns* (Everson and Fitzgerald, 1969). I believe that until then (and the remainder of this chapter stands or falls on this particular interpretation) a considerable degree of consensus existed in school geography with regard to its content and philosophy. It was dominated by regional geography and was philosophically idiographic. *New Ways* and *Settlement Patterns* changed that by presenting geography as spatial *science* – the search for order (in models), the use of statistical techniques and measurement, and the search for prediction. This was bolted on to, *and did not replace*, existing approaches to the subject. The (British) school geography curriculum, in my view, more than matches Harvey's description of the postmodern city; that is, one of 'fragmentation, collage, and eclecticism, all suffused with a sense of ephemerality and chaos' (Harvey, 1989, p. 98).

In terms of content, the 'new geography' may appear to be 'modern', but the disarray and disorder in the content of the ensuing geography curriculum seems undeniably 'postmodern' (the difference between modern content and postmodern curriculum reflecting the ambiguous character of modernity itself). This may require some elaboration. I am essentially taking the post-1968 geography curriculum as an 'object', in much the same way as Cloke *et al.* (1991) take the rock singer Prince as a postmodern 'object'. Like the geography curriculum, his repertoire is surprising, eclectic and unpredictable, taking in different styles and genres. This is not to say, however, that the industry of which he is part is anything but 'modern', with its rational and mass-produced forms of production. An analogy could also be drawn with architecture; postmodern buildings may be superficially, but not structurally (still being built of concrete and steel), different from what went before. This is essentially Harvey's (1989) view of the 'condition of postmodernity'. None of this denies that in music, architecture and the economy, superficial change has taken place.

In the case of education, the underlying structure is the state education system, the stage upon which the post-1969 geography curriculum emerged. The 'quantitative' movement was not, in my view, a revolution. Many teachers continued to teach regional geography, and the examination boards continued to cater to their needs. With the more conceptually based approaches, a veritable smorgasbord of adjectival geographies emerged; if it could be mapped it was geography, and GCSE and 'A-level' projects ventured into territory previously regarded as *terra incognita* (the geography of football grounds, for example). 'Incongruous juxtapositionings' of academic content were actually encouraged by examining boards and curriculum developers by allowing – indeed, insisting on – teachers' involvement in their own curriculum design and development, typified by the emergence of 'mode 3' CSE and its teacher-designed 'further curriculum units'. Some schools still used Young and Lowry; others used Beddis; there was even the emergence of a Marxist geographical education in the shape of the short-lived *Contemporary Issues in Geography and Education*. A 'green geography' arrived at about the same time as this 'red' variety. Books could be called *A Sense of Place* even though their titles belied their contents. Textbook publishers engaged in sales battles in which 'image' and packaging were all-important.

Such a *mélange* of approaches to the content of school geography was matched by the diffuse state of affairs pedagogically. Didactic modes of teaching were adopted next door to the work of teachers as facilitators who employed games and simulations. Chalk and talk and dictated notes co-existed happily with role-play and free drama. School geography became an enlarged mirror image of geography in higher education. As Soja (1989, p. 60) notes, modern geography has

> started to come apart at its seams, unravelling internally and in its old school ties with the other nineteenth-century disciplines that defined the modern academic division of labour. The grip of older categories, boundaries and separations is weakening. What was central is now being pushed to the margins, while the once tactful fringes boldly assert a new-found centrality. The shifting, almost kaleidoscopic, intellectual terrain has become extremely difficult to map for it no longer appears with its familiar, time-worn contours.

He goes on to state that 'this unsettled and unsettling geography is, I suggest, *part of the Postmodern condition ... with perils and possibilities*: filled with the simultaneous shock of the old and the new' (my italics). Likewise, it has been insisted that 'the presences and absences in the typical curriculum demonstrate that there has been no single canon of geographical thought. Instead there is merely a series of unresolved, even unacknowledged, conflicts that are kept from the classroom' (Dear and Wassmandorf, 1993, p. 323).

Such a 'postmodern' condition of both geography and education can be interpreted, of course, in various ways. It displays both utopian and dystopian characteristics; it can be viewed as affirmative postmodernism (Soja's 'possibilities'), for example, empowering teachers to do their own thing and legitimating children's own knowledge; or as sceptical postmodernism, that is, a world of intellectual and curricular chaos (Soja's 'perils').

As an example, consider the contents of *Geography in the National Curriculum (England)* (DES, 1991). Did it return us to a neat and tidy world of consensus geography, or is it an example of innovation without change, continuing the academic and disciplinary tendencies initiated by the emergence of Cole, Beynon, Everson and Fitzgerald? The initial National Curriculum cannot be said to have imposed any consistent view of geography. The regional attainment target was a mixture of capes and bays and 'knowledge' of regions, adopting an idiographic approach. I do not say this in any derogatory way, and I support a geography which recognizes the diversity of the human environment. The urban and economic attainment targets were broadly nomothetic, seeking generalizations and sticking to a 'model-based' approach. The curious 'environmental geography' claimed the 'green' ground and hence could have been labelled 'welfare' – even 'radical'. The entire document could be read as a strange mixture of geographical paradigms and an equally eclectic mix of educational philosophies – from utilitarian to reconstructionist (Soja's 'old' and 'new').

What is more, the wording of the statements of attainment were sufficiently (and deliberately?) broad (bland?) to allow teachers to interpret the numerous 'pupils-should-be-able-to-explain ...' statements in various ways. There appeared to be no prescription or suggestion that any particular approach should be used for such 'explanations'. Let me give one example, taken almost at random from the National Curriculum. It is AT4/5c, 'Pupils should be able to explain the reasons for the growth of economic activities in particular locations.' The examples given are those of out-of-town shopping and business districts or major industrial sites. The crucial words in the rubric are, of course, 'be able to explain'. These invite at least three readings:

1. Is there *an* explanation in the sense of there being an over-arching model of such locations?
2. Are there different possible explanations which might contribute to explanations of different locations?
3. Are there several possible explanations, each based on different philosophical/conceptual positions?

Such lack of precision in the wording of the statement of attainment provides the potential for personal knowledge, student-centredness, and the poststructuralist, practical and process/qualitative characteristics of the *postmodern* curriculum (Lambert, personal communication) to be employed. The fragmentation and eclecticism of the geography Order actually served to empower both teachers and students. For example, the major industrial site could be explained by (1) environmental determinism (flat, well-drained land); (2) economic determinism (Weber); (3) political determinism (Marx); and/or (4) 'structure-agency' (Gregory/Giddens). If teachers knew all four explanations, they could either provide them all or present students with the one they felt most approximated to the truth.

I therefore see the National Curriculum as a simple continuation of geography's postmodern trajectory, its break with consensus, its go-as-you-please ethos, launched in 1968 and successfully fuelled by the various curriculum developments since then. My visits to schools and my discussion with 'mentors' leads me to believe that the National Curriculum has not affected the kind of knowledge which was previously taught in any significant way, though it remains to be seen, of course, whether 'testing' will seriously constrain the content and approaches being used in British geography classrooms in the mid-1990s. The notion of the 'correct answer' is quite inconsistent with the structure and organization of the National Curriculum for geography. A modern reading of the Geography Order sees it as prescriptive and inhibiting. A postmodern reading of it is one of optimism. But 'tests' which constrain the freedom of thought of both teachers and students must be opposed. Geography in the mid-1990s can therefore be viewed as a paradigm for the postmodern 'subject', continuing, in Johnston's (1976) immortal phrase, 'branching towards anarchy'.

CONCLUSION

In this chapter I have introduced the notion of postmodernism in a context in which it has hitherto rarely been applied. Mass education, of which geographical education is a part, 'has been a modernist project par excellence with its stress on rationality, individual autonomy and the unified self, national histories (and geographies), hierarchical organisation, and progress' (Gilbert, 1992, p. 56). But this has been accompanied by the rejection of education by many children. A postmodern education may provide a solution to the problem of such rejection, if it can replace the elitist and authoritarian style of the modern.

I have suggested that in geography we can explore various postmodern *objects*, ranging from individual buildings to shopping malls, bringing the world of the student into the curriculum. I have also shown that there is a postmodern *approach* to teaching geography, one which encourages the deconstruction of existing texts, be they books, maps, diagrams or landscapes. I have further indicated that we live in a period of postmodernity, an *epoch* where anything goes in geographical education.

It is not possible in the space available here to develop the debate on whether postmodernism is a good or bad thing. If we go along this road we are, anyway, making postmodernism the very thing it claims not to be. Perhaps it is sufficient to say that postmodernism provides us with a new window on the world. With challenges to basic philosophical assumptions, and such outcomes as time–space compression, newer architectural styles and grassroots ecological movements, perhaps something new does seem to be happening.

REFERENCES

Baudrillard, J. (1989) *Simulations*. New York: Semiotext(e).
Bowlby, S. (1992) 'Feminist geography and the national curriculum.' *Geography*, 77 (4), 349–60.
Cloke, P., Philo, C. and Sadler, D. (1991) *Approaching Human Geography*. London: Chapman.
Cole, J. and Beynon, J. (1968) *New Ways in Geography*. Oxford: Blackwell.
Dear, M. (1988) 'The postmodern challenge: reconstructing human geography.' *Transactions of the Institute of British Geographers*, 13 (4), 252–74.

Dear, M. and Wassmandorf, G. (1993) 'Postmodern consequences.' *The Geographical Review*, **83** (3), 321–5.

DES (1991) *Geography in the National Curriculum (England)*. London: HMSO.

Doll, W. (1989) 'Foundations for a post-modern curriculum.' *Journal of Curriculum Studies*, **21** (3), 243–53.

Everson, J. and Fitzgerald, B. (1969) *Settlement Patterns*. London: Longman.

Gilbert, R. (1992) 'Citizenship, education and postmodernity.' *British Journal of Sociology of Education*, **13** (1), 51–67.

Gregory, D. (1994) *Geographical Imaginations*. Cambridge, MA: Blackwell.

Harvey, D. (1972) 'The role of theory.' In N. Graves (ed.) *New Movements in the Study and Teaching of Geography*. London: Temple Smith.

Harvey, D. (1989) *The Condition of Postmodernity*. Oxford: Blackwell.

Johnston, R. (1976) 'Anarchy, conspiracy and apathy: the three conditions of geography.' *Area*, **8** (1), 1–3.

Livingstone, D. (1992) *The Geographical Tradition*. Oxford: Blackwell.

Olsson, G. (1980) *Birds in Egg/Eggs in Bird*. London: Pion.

Quonian, S. (1988) 'A painter, geographer of Arizona.' *Society and Space*, **6**, 3–14.

Rosenau, P. (1992) *Post Modernism and the Social Sciences*. Princeton, NJ: Princeton University Press.

SEC (1986) *Geography GCSE: A Guide for Teachers*. Milton Keynes: SEC/Open University Press.

Skeggs, B. (1991) 'Postmodernism: what is all the fuss about?' *British Journal of Sociology of Education*, **12** (2), 255–67.

Soja, E. (1989) *Postmodern Geographies*. London: Verso.

Unwin, T. (1992) *The Place of Geography*. London: Longman.

Worth, F. (1993) 'Postmodern pedagogy in the multicultural classroom: for inappropriate teachers and imperfect students.' *Cultural Critique*, **25**, 5–32.

Chapter 24

Facilitating Research in Geographical and Environmental Education

Ashley Kent

Increasing numbers of teachers are nowadays engaging in educational research as a part of higher degree work. MA, MEd, MPhil and PhD qualifications have become an accepted route for professional development and advancement. Degrees in curriculum studies and educational management have, of late, proved particularly popular, but a number of others concern specific subject areas such as geography education.

In spite of these greater numbers, achievement of such qualifications is a considerable burden on teachers. Increasingly, as local education authority financial support has declined, teachers have had to pay their own fees, at the same time as finding that their profession has become ever more demanding, not least for middle managers who have been faced with greater administrative workloads. Successful completion of such degrees requires considerable commitment and efficient time management. This is the *raison d'être* of this chapter; that is, the identification of clear working principles to support teachers in conducting educational research. From now on, when the word 'student' is used it refers to teachers engaged in higher-degree research work.

The most common higher degree undertaken by teachers is at the MA/MEd level, and that is why this is the focus here. Since 1968, there has been an MA Geography in Education at the University of London Institute of Education. Established by Norman Graves, it continues to offer a unique qualification and professional development for geography teachers. For part-timers it is a two-year course, and nowadays requires a 25,000-word dissertation, two pieces of coursework and one examination paper. Most teachers take it part-time, but over the years full-timers, especially from overseas, have completed it within one year. The themes focused upon have varied with the concerns of different times, but most take on an action research approach; that is, the issues and concerns of teachers working in their own or similar establishments. The time available to complete such research is limited to a year, since it is usually in the second year that teachers focus on their dissertation research. This naturally restricts the scale of any such research, but none the less important insights are gained, often from case studies.

A flavour of the dissertation topics and approaches is given in the book by Graves *et al.* (1989). Interestingly, the demographic profile of students has changed over the last few years. Originally it was a course dominated by experienced teachers, often heads of department. Increasingly it tends now to be for the younger teacher recently having completed a degree and PGCE, who sees it as a way of furthering his or her professional development and a necessary qualification for advancement. Teachers consciously wish to complete the degree before they are engaged in burdensome head-of-department duties.

To write this chapter, I have relied on the experience and insights of my geography tutor colleagues, Norman Graves, David Lambert, Michael Naish and Frances Slater, who between them have supervised a considerable number of such MA-level research students. To frame our conversations, I put forward the headings listed below and these provide the structure for the rest of this chapter. I am most grateful to my colleagues for agreeing to be interviewed, thereby allowing me to communicate their often shared insights, which I feel are most valuable for tutors and tutees alike engaged in MA/MEd-level geography education research.

- Identifying an area of interest/finding a research question
- Choice of methodology and appropriate data collection techniques
- Literature search/reading around
- Time schedule/deadlines
- Starting to write/draft chapters
- Meetings/tutorials – role of the tutor
- Pitfalls/mistakes to avoid
- 'Doing it' successfully – tips/strategies.

A relatively recent development at the Institute of Education has been the provision of research training/techniques sessions for students up to PhD level. In this respect we in the UK have been well behind research training offered in the USA. In the MA Geography in Education course, in particular, there is now a 'Research and Research Methods' module over a ten-week period in the spring term, which addresses some of the methodological issues facing students and leans heavily on examples from dissertation research already completed. Panels of past students and homework tasks on earlier dissertations have been popular and are seen to be valuable.

A growing literature is now at the disposal of such researchers. These vary from the short, manageable and accessible, such as Bell (1987) and the Rediguide series from Nottingham University School of Education (now sadly out of print) to the more demanding and complex such as Burgess (1985, 1986), Cohen and Manion (1994) and Tesch (1990).

It is my intention that this brief chapter will offer practical guidelines and help to those tutors and tutees struggling with the challenge of conducting or supporting research into geography education. Clearly the scale and level of originality of an MPhil or PhD is greater, but all the working principles mentioned here are, it could be argued, just as appropriate for that level of research.

FINDING A FOCUS

Educational research has an unfortunate and somewhat misleading image, not least with teachers. It is felt to be something esoteric and 'out there', whereas in reality most MA-level research is highly focused, practical and based upon school realities. However, such research is a new way of working, and something of a culture shock, for those intimately involved in schools. It requires a critical, more distant look at the education system, and it is therefore helpful for a student to be well engaged on a higher degree course before making decisions about research focus. Lectures generate possible avenues for exploration, as do conversations with tutors and fellow students. These early experiences broaden a student's conceptual understanding of education and build confidence, which is vital. Indeed one colleague spoke of the necessity to get over the 'confidence hump', not least that the 'level' of writing will be seen to be of the requisite standard!

Most vital in determining a research focus is to identify a real interest, or a 'burning interest', as it was described to me. Very often that is likely to be concerned with students' professional lives and the problems and challenges associated with them. Tutors may in some cases feel the need to 'steer' this decision-making process heavily. For instance, they may well be aware of a current issue or concern that merits inquiry or on which previous research has been undertaken but further work is still needed. On the other hand, some students may not need or may even resent such a 'heavy steer'.

Particularly practical advice from my colleagues included the importance of not making a decision on focus too early, indeed considering at the start of the process a range of broad research avenues and keeping these going as long as necessary. Also important was to look at previous dissertations to get a 'feel' for style, organization, methodology and the like.

Similarly important is seen to be the opportunity of meeting with earlier researchers and discussing their approach and ways of coping. This can be immensely reassuring for students. Equally, fellow students and tutors are important sounding boards for research ideas, particularly when a brief written statement of a research focus can form the basis for discussion.

THE APPROACH TO TAKE

The choice of methodology and related data-collection techniques is an important one for any researcher. An unfortunate and inaccurate assumption made by many students is that the only approach possible is the 'hard', quantitative, scientific one. They are often pleasantly surprised that 'softer', more qualitative approaches have become both accepted and more common. The challenge for the latter, however, is the way of analysing the data collected. This is often not straightforward and needs to be the basis for tutorial discussions. Overall, as far as choice of methodology is concerned, the tutor's job is to widen the student's knowledge of possible approaches and methods of collecting data.

The choice of approach is made easier if a precise and focused research question is posed. Too many questions can be diverting and make the research unmanageable. Often students have over-ambitious research proposals, and these need considerable reduction through tutorial advice.

Pragmatism and manageability have to be the guiding principles in shaping the research design, since most researchers have little more than a year to complete such research part-time. As one colleague put it, 'You can't get perfection in data collection and it must be modest according to what can be achieved.' This practical reality determines the scale of survey or experiment, and a case study therefore has important advantages. Time available, the statistical and other expertise of the researcher, and access to resources at school will all determine the research approaches possible. Perhaps the most important advice of all is that the research focus comes first and will determine the methodology adopted.

Written guidance on research approaches and data-collection techniques exist in an expanding literature, but previous dissertations can be studied profitably for the methodological debates written in some of them. Research approaches are new concepts to students, which is why some sort of formal research training is needed. A particularly helpful model for structuring curriculum-oriented research used by two colleagues is Bastiani and Tolley (n.d.).

READING ROUND

Time is the greatest single bugbear for students engaged in geography education research, particularly for those who are fully employed elsewhere. Reading is a particular problem and some advocate attempting to ask for time from employers to undertake it. Most critical is the reading undertaken at the start of the research process, since that will strongly influence the form the research eventually takes. Here a tutor's role as guide is important; in addition, many of my colleagues advocate a computer search as the first step to take. Although there is the danger of throwing up too much literature, and a good deal of it inappropriately American, the choice of a few key words can generate vital early reading and influence thinking about research designs. Equally, the very act of devising the key-word search is an important element of the research process and a useful discipline to get students to focus on the essences of the work.

Apart from tutors' advice on reading, there is often a need to consult specialists. Those in curriculum studies, media studies and educational psychology are the colleagues most used by Institute of Education students. They can point out readings from quite different disciplines and perspectives.

When undertaking relevant reading, my colleagues suggest the 'bread and butter' skills of literature searching (in other words tracing back references, developing a systematic card index and writing everything down, including quotations) are vital if the writing stage is to go well.

So important is this reading-round stage of the research process, according to one colleague, that it can be the cause of borderline or failed dissertations. All the more reason therefore to build in reading time to the research schedule, remembering that books are rarely available in multiple copies nowadays in higher education, faced as it is by greater student numbers and pegged-back budgets. There is an important case here for ordering books and checking their availability ahead of time.

MAKING AND MEETING DEADLINES

Making out a firm time schedule and sticking to it as far as possible are advocated by all my colleagues. The schedule provides an important stimulus through an agreed set of time deadlines to make sure the work is completed. Working back in time from the bound and finished dissertation is one approach, and insisting on an early timetable as the basis for seminars is another. Some students need much less structure and 'heavy steering' and more encouragement than anything else. Given the time constraints on such research, the problem is that, as one colleague put it, 'Creativity doesn't work to time schedules.' One tutor's tactic is to organize tutorials only when the next phase of a schedule is completed and in particular a piece of writing has been produced. Seminars on a personal basis are profitably based on written work prepared for them. 'Keeping to deadlines is vital', argued one colleague, whereas another felt that it was those students who started to write early who tended to complete, and not to fail to finish the research.

STARTING TO WRITE

The act of beginning to write is clearly critical. Sometimes tutors ask for an early draft on the research topic and why it interests the student, so as to give an early indication of the level and style of writing. An outline of the research and a part of a chapter are regarded as important early objectives, since 'Writing at an early stage is absolutely crucial', as a colleague remarked. Students possibly find this first putting pen to paper the most demanding of all tasks. They lack confidence and struggle at first over the 'refining, recreating, revisiting' process. Usually students devise their own chapter headings, but in some cases tutors need to help by providing these.

Early, detailed constructive feedback on written work is much appreciated by students, although some expect every word to be read, sometimes more than once, which is often impossible. Others only proffer a selection of their work for tutors to comment upon. It is sensible for at least an early chapter to be looked at by a tutor to ensure that points are being communicated effectively. 'I haven't written anything like this since college' is a regularly heard remark and hides considerable anxiety – often unjustified.

MEETINGS

Regular meetings with a research supervisor are sources of encouragement and motivation and can also act as helpful deadlines. The personal relationship that often develops between tutor and tutee can be an important support for the student. If there is a mutual expectation for written work to form the basis of the meetings, and particularly if the work is submitted in advance of the meeting, then there is a clear stimulus for the student to produce work of quality, to be scrutinized and on time. 'To be critical yet supportive with this writing' was how one tutor put the tutor's role. Often the early meetings are organized and instigated by the tutor, and further dates are decided at those meetings. Equally, at each meeting the agenda for the next meeting needs to be discussed, and in particular the progress to be made by then. A letter is usually sent by a tutor to a student about whose progress little has been heard.

Interestingly, no formal training in the skills of tutoring are provided for tutors and most have to 'learn on the job', so to speak. Tutoring courses are run, however; for instance, by R.G. Burgess at Coventry.

Clearly, tutors see meetings as part supportive and part goading. As one tutor remarked, one 'needs to harass students a bit, particularly with part-timers, to produce something regardless of quality ... since there is a fear of putting pen to paper ... once that starts it tends to get easier.

PITFALLS

The overriding problems seem to be:

- over-ambitious research objectives;
- too many research questions;
- too much and diverse data;
- a lack of clarity in the statement of research question.

One tutor argued that students need to go through the painful and relatively lengthy business of devising a research methodology, since short cuts by the tutor can foreclose various options too quickly, so that the student fails to have a full grasp of the research exercise. This can be related to the small minority of students who are over-keen to finish it all too quickly, and thereby do not give sufficient reflection to the research and critical awareness to the proposals.

Overall anxiety can be a serious pitfall. It can cause students to worry about 'negative' results – research findings just as vital as those which confirm one's expectations! It can cause a felt need for constant reassurance and, from the tutor's perspective, near-harassment.

STRATEGIES

Most strategies have been encapsulated in the previous pages, but additional suggestions include the advice to be methodical throughout; for instance, systematically keeping records of the progress of the research and reading undertaken. Furthermore, students are advised to speak to tutors and to past and present students about their research. This can lead to helpful short cuts and the realization that one is not alone in facing the challenge. Such conversations offer considerable reassurance. Another specific suggestion is formally to set aside a time in the week for research and stick to it! However, probably the most recurring theme in my conversations with fellow tutors was the need for research to be, on the one hand, both tightly focused and circumscribed and, on the other hand, not over-ambitious.

REFERENCES

Bastiani, J. and Tolley, H. (n.d. but printed 1981/82) *Research into the Curriculum*. Rediguide 16. Nottingham: Nottingham University School of Education.

Bell, J. (1987) *Doing Your Research Project*. Milton Keynes: Open University Press.

Burgess, R.G. (1985) *Issues in Educational Research*. London: Falmer.

Burgess, R.G. (1986) *Strategies of Educational Research: Qualitative Methods*. London: Falmer.

Cohen, L. and Manion, L. (1994) *Research Methods in Education*. 4th edn. London: Croom Helm.

Graves, N.J., Kent, W.A., Lambert, D.M., Naish, M.C. and Slater, F.A. (1989) *Research in Geography Education MA Dissertations 1968-1988*. University of London Institute of Education.

Tesch, R. (1990) *Qualitative Research*. London: Falmer.

Index